HUME'S
MORAL AND POLITICAL
PHILOSOPHY

The Hafner Library of Classics

HUME'S MORAL AND POLITICAL PHILOSOPHY

Edited with an Introduction by

Henry D. Aiken

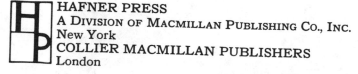

HAFNER PRESS
A DIVISION OF MACMILLAN PUBLISHING CO., INC.
New York
COLLIER MACMILLAN PUBLISHERS
London

Hafner Press
A Division of Macmillan Publishing Co., Inc.
866 Third Avenue, New York, N.Y. 10022

Collier Macmillan Canada, Ltd.

Printed in the United States of America

printing number

8   9   10

CONTENTS

I. A TREATISE OF HUMAN NATURE

SECTION

BOOK II: OF THE PASSIONS

BOOK III: OF MORALS

Part I: Of Virtue and Vice in General

Part II: Of Justice and Injustice

CONTENTS

Part III: Of the Other Virtues and Vices

II. AN ENQUIRY
CONCERNING THE PRINCIPLES OF MORALS

CONTENTS

III. ESSAYS, MORAL AND POLITICAL

INTRODUCTION

I

DAVID HUME'S CAREER was in most respects unusually fortunate. Rarely has there been a more admirable congruence of aspiration and achievement, of personal endowment and outward circumstance. Even occasional disappointments, such as his failure to secure a university professorship, usually served to preserve in him the unremitting independence of mind and breadth of interest which are among his most salient characteristics.

Hume's qualities both as a philosopher and as a man have not always been given their due. Among the orthodox and liberals alike, the detestation of his ideas spread also to his person. Thomas Jefferson, who with better understanding might have discovered in Hume much to admire, spoke of him contemptuously as "the great apostle of toryism . . . this degenerate son of science, this traitor to his fellow men." Others, less vehement, found him "curiously cool" and complacent, more eager to raise doubts concerning the ground of virtue than to sing its praises. Even his natural tendency toward corpulence, which gave rise to the tradition that he was a glutton, somehow seemed to typify the character of a man who was capable of minor vices, but otherwise deficient in the normal complement of human sentiments and passions. In short, there has been perpetuated among his detractors the legend of a person lacking in the high seriousness that ought to characterize a true philosopher: a precocious youth who failed to realize his full promise; a man who, having produced his one original work before the age of thirty, gradually lapsed into a rich, barren, and rather frivolous old age.

What shall be said of this representation of Hume? In the first place, I think we must say that there *was* a grain of truth in it, although not more. Hume was clearly not a person who felt violently about most things. He was, in a phrase which was used to describe his period but fits Hume much better, a man "more curious than devout." But precisely because of this, there appears throughout his work a remarkable capacity to distinguish between evidence and inclination. Few men, especially in moral philosophy, have projected their own predilections and preferences so little into their work.

If Hume's temperament did not incline him to splendid vices or heroic virtues, those who knew him best were all agreed that he was a person not only of rare charm and good humor but also of unusual benevolence and fortitude. Recent research tends increasingly to confirm the fact that *Le Bon David* belonged, to use his own phrase, to "the party of humanity."

It is likely that in the end the canny Scotch philosopher has appraised himself as shrewdly as, and certainly more delightfully than, anyone else is likely to do: "I am, or rather was," he wrote shortly before his death, "(for that is the style I must now use in speaking of myself, which emboldens me the more to speak my sentiments) — I was, I say, a man of mild dispositions, of command of temper, of an open, social, and cheerful humour, capable of attachment, but little susceptible of enmity, and of great moderation in all my passions. Even my love of literary fame, my ruling passion, never soured my temper, notwithstanding my frequent disappointments. My company was not unacceptable to the young and careless as well as to the studious and literary; and as I took a particular pleasure in the company of modest women, I had no reason to be displeased with the reception I met with from them. . . . I cannot say there is no vanity in making this funeral oration of myself, but I hope it is not a misplaced one; and this is a matter of fact which is easily cleared and ascertained."

Hume was born in Edinburgh, Scotland, on April 26, 1711. His father was a member of the landed gentry, but not well-to-do. Hence, as a younger son Hume was obliged to choose a career in which he could earn his living. Having "passed through the ordinary course of education with success" he therefore decided to enter into the law. But he soon acquired "an insurmountable aversion to everything but the pursuit of philosophy and general learning."

After giving up the study of law, he made "a feeble trial" at a merchant's career. But this, too, proved "unsuitable" to Hume's tastes and interests. He then went to France, at last determined to enter permanently upon the career of a man of letters.

The perils of such a choice must have seemed great indeed to his family and friends. His mother is reported to have said that "oor

Davie's a fine, good-natured crater, but uncommon wake-minded."
But Hume knew what he was about, and with a prudence as precocious
as his rapidly developing intellect, he laid "a plan of life" which from
thenceforth he steadily pursued. "I resolved to make a very rigid
frugality supply my deficiency of fortune, to maintain unimpaired
my independence, and to regard every object as contemptible except
the improvement of my talents in literature." Within three years of
his arrival in France, at the age of twenty-six, he had produced his
greatest work, the *Treatise of Human Nature*.

The extent of Hume's early achievement can only be measured
when we recall that the "ordinary course of education" to which he
was subjected was largely concerned with the learning of languages.
In philosophy he was almost wholly self-educated. Yet, in his mid-
twenties, he had already carried nearly a century of British philosophizing to its ultimate conclusion.

Even if he had written nothing else, it is safe to say that Hume's
place in the history of philosophy would still be securely within the
first rank. According to Hume himself, the *Treatise* "fell dead-born
from the press," and his chagrin was such that afterward he could
never regard his major work with anything but aversion. In a way
this was a pity, for his subsequent writing, although certainly impres-
sive, was on the whole sustained at a somewhat lower intellectual
level,[1] and written in a style more calculated to win immediate recog-
nition. His later style has been justly praised. It is remarkably clear,
although somewhat artificial and over-studded with elegant allusions
and quotations. At its best, as in certain parts of the *Enquiries*, there
is perhaps no finer philosophical prose in English. But it lacks a
certain sparkle and vivacity and that lovable candor which has
endeared the earlier *Treatise* to so many readers.

A volume of *Essays on Moral and Political Subjects* appeared in
1741, followed by a second edition, as well as by a second volume, in
the following year. In 1745 Hume had some hopes of being appointed
to a·professorship at the University of Edinburgh, but because of the
"popular clamour" against him, which he attributed to his "scep-

---

[1] A major exception to this is the *Dialogues on Natural Religion*, which, as a
noted contemporary philosopher has remarked, contains, along with Butler's
Analogy of Religion and the third part of Kant's *Critique of Pure Reason*, all that
the human mind is ever likely to know on the subject of philosophical theology.

ticism" and "heterodoxy," he failed to win the post. He then became tutor for a period to the Marquis of Annandale, a legally declared lunatic. Later he was secretary and judge-advocate to General St. Clair. These appointments were profitable to Hume, and the latter also gave him some opportunity for travel in France and Italy.

In 1748 and 1751, respectively, Hume published the *Enquiry Concerning the Human Understanding* and the *Enquiry Concerning the Principles of Morals.* The latter work he regarded as "incomparably [his] finest." These works provide, together with his *Dissertation on the Passions* — his most perfunctory performance — a less technical redaction of the main doctrines of the *Treatise.* Yet there are parts of both *Enquiries* which contain clearer and less equivocal statements of his position than are to be found in analogous portions of the *Treatise.* Here and there, also, as in the second appendix to the second *Enquiry*, there is a real advance in doctrine. It would be a mistake, however, to suppose that Hume's repudiation of the *Treatise* constitutes a rejection of its basic tenets. He himself seems to have acknowledged this: "The philosophical principles are the same in both, but I was carried away by the heat of youth to publish too precipitously."

In 1752, Hume was elected librarian of the Advocates' Library in Edinburgh. He retained this post for five years, during which he began work on his *History of England.* This work occupied him for nearly ten years. The *History* is no longer widely read, but it greatly added to Hume's fame and material prosperity during his lifetime, and was regarded as a standard work for many decades. It must be admitted, however, that Hume's *History* remained primarily political, both in its theme and in its moral — if it could be said to have one. It is rather disappointing that he who was a distinguished economist, and better qualified than any other historian of his time to grasp the intellectual movements of the periods with which he dealt, should have remained fundamentally without a positive conception of the dynamics of historical evolution, and without a clear grasp of the relation of the history of ideas to the march of social movements. As an historian Hume was, therefore, somewhat conventional and superficial. But only in this part of his work, if we also except his rather mediocre achievement as a literary critic and aesthetician, does Hume fall considerably below the highest rank.

By the age of fifty, Hume was "not only independent but opulent." Thenceforth his hope was to retire to his native Scotland and "never more set foot out of it." But in 1763, he went to France, and in 1765, he was appointed secretary to the British Embassy at Paris. His reception in Paris was extremely cordial. For a period he was, indeed, the philosophical idol of the French capital. But, while he enjoyed himself immensely, he was "determined to abandon the fine folks, before they abandon me."

When Hume returned to England, he brought with him Jean Jacques Rousseau, with whom he subsequently had a famous quarrel. Rousseau, who already had developed symptoms of persecution mania, conceived the fantastic notion that Hume was conspiring against him. Actually, Hume's motives toward Rousseau were wholly disinterested and benevolent.

In 1769, Hume settled again for the last time in Edinburgh. He occupied himself with polishing his *Dialogues on Natural Religion*, which were published posthumously, and enjoying the company of his friends. In 1775, he fell ill with the "disorder" from which he died in the following year. Throughout this period he remained in good and even serene spirits. There is a very moving letter from Adam Smith to William Strahan, describing the "behavior of our late excellent friend, Mr. Hume, during his last illness." There is also a hilarious account by Boswell of a visit during Hume's last days. Boswell successfully baited him into a discussion of the question of immortality, and was then appalled to discover one who could face the prospect of his own imminent annihilation with complete equanimity. Hume's death occurred on August 25, 1776.

II

We are accustomed to regard the centuries directly preceding the eighteenth as the epoch during which the mind of Europe was freed from the intellectual and spiritual bondage of the Middle Ages. This is to a large extent true in the case of the physical sciences and the philosophical speculation which took its cue from physics. But in the sphere of what Hume later called the "sciences of men," liberation from ancient dogmas came more slowly and haltingly. Man was apparently able to view nature independently and impartially, but not himself. In their thinking about morality and human conduct, most writers, consciously or otherwise, still looked back to Greek and Hebrew sources for enlightenment or authority. Almost without exception they continued to believe unquestioningly in an immutable moral order presided over by a transcendent and benevolent Deity. To be sure, they usually referred to their fundamental moral principles as "laws of nature" — there was good precedent for this, dating back to the Stoics — and they claimed, at least, to discern them, as they also claimed to discern the axioms of Euclid, by pure intellectual insight. But it was no accident that, as many of them insisted, the "light of reason" in human conduct was indistinguishable from the voice of God or — tradition.

The great liberal philosopher, John Locke, provides an excellent illustration of this "cultural lag" of moral and social thought behind the developments in other branches of philosophy and science. Locke is rightly regarded as the father of British Empiricism. His *Essay Concerning Human Understanding*, although a transitional work, stands as a landmark in the progress toward a scientific conception of knowledge. Yet Locke was quite confident that there were "natural laws" of justice and property inscribed upon the human intellect with the same clarity as the laws of logic and mathematics. And his confidence was buttressed by an unquestioning faith that these laws had behind them also the authority of received religion. In short, however liberalizing may have been his influence, Locke still worked, in his ethics and social philosophy, within the framework of the medieval tradition.

This is not the place to undertake an analysis of the reasons for the comparative failure of Locke's social philosophy as an *intellectual* achievement. It must suffice to say that despite this Locke nevertheless succeeded in expressing the attitudes which were becoming increasingly prevalent in his own day. His moral and social philosophy testifies to the growing belief that the moral order is also an order designed to the advantage of man in this world, and that society and its institutions exist solely for the purpose of protecting individuals against the encroachments of others. Locke's *Second Treatise of Civil Government* served to convince generations of men that there *are* certain inherent rights of man and that just government derives its only sanction from a compact with the governed.

Hume's achievement was of a different sort. He belonged to an age of criticism in which the empirical method was gradually extended to the study of human affairs. Now the seventeenth century philosophers, even in the sphere of natural philosophy, had overstressed the role of "reason." It remained for the empirical school, which culminated in Hume, to correct this over-emphasis and to point out that in the sphere of "matters of fact" the ultimate arbiter is observation. "Insight" may give us hypotheses. But since there are no "necessary connections" between matters of fact, any hypothesis remains subject, for its confirmation, to the disclosures of sense experience. There are no self-evident *axioms*, either in natural science *or* in the "sciences of man." So, at least, Hume argued with great brilliance.

But Hume was not content simply to state the empirical method and defend it in general terms. His *primary* purpose was its application to ethical and social philosophy. His work in these fields was not, of course, wholly without precedent. In some respects he had been anticipated by Hobbes; and recent scholarship has increasingly shown the extent of his debt to his elder contemporary and fellow countryman, Francis Hutcheson. By the time Hume began the composition of the *Treatise*, therefore, the opening attacks on "rationalism" in ethics had been made. Yet it remained for Hume, deliberately and with the full weight of his powerful critique of knowledge behind him, to push the attack to its ultimate conclusion, and to carry through without faltering the "experimental" approach to human conduct. It was he who established once and for all the right to explore human nature and conduct "experimentally," uninhibited by the dogmas of the church or the uncritical assumptions of "right reason." He was frequently mistaken in detail. And, superficially, at least, he was often reactionary with respect to specific political issues. Yet, for all this, Hume's work remains perhaps the most powerful intellectual solvent in modern ethical and political philosophy.

III

For some inscrutable reason, Hume's critics have tended to deny that his psychology and theory of knowledge have any bearing upon his moral and social philosophy. In so doing, they refuse to take seriously his avowed purpose in writing the *Treatise*, which was "to introduce the experimental method of reasoning into moral subjects." But more important, they have failed to observe that most of his criticisms of other moral philosophies are based explicitly upon doctrines which he had sought to establish at length in the two earlier books of the *Treatise*. Apart from the latter, much that he says in the ethical parts of that work would appear — as it sometimes does appear in the *Enquiry*, where his conclusions are stated without reference to the rest of his philosophy — merely dogmatic or ill-considered. As we shall see, not merely his refutations of other ethical theories but also his own ethics show the constant application of his epistemological and psychological doctrines. Much the same is true in the case of his social philosophy. *In short, Hume's ethics and social theories are parts of a general philosophy of human nature. To ignore the latter is to miss the power and sweep of the former.*

Historically considered, Hume's psychology is a modification and blend of the "instinct" psychology of the Moral Sense school of Shaftesbury and Hutcheson and the "mechanistic" psychology of Hobbes. Hume resisted the temptation, which must have been very strong in one who was addicted to the principle of "parsimony" and who had hoped to find "some general quality that naturally operates on the mind," to reduce human propensities to some single psychological root such as self-love or the will to power. He acknowledges a plurality of "primary passions," although his list is small. On the whole, however, he was more interested in showing, by means of his principle of association, how the mature and stable sentiments of adult life can be accounted for in terms of a small number of basic drives.

Associationist psychology has been criticized on the grounds both that the principles of association "explain" nothing, and that they invoke non-verifiable "forces" of attraction between ideas. As applied to Hume, these criticisms are misguided in several respects. In the first place, Hume's associationism represents, historically, nothing more than the empirical approach to mental phenomena. It is the eighteenth century ancestor and counterpart of modern scientific psychology. The associationists generally assumed that there are laws of the mind analogous to the laws of physical bodies; and they supposed that such laws are to be verified only by observation of the ways in which minds actually operate. Secondly, in the case of Hume at least, no mysterious "causal efficacy" is attributed to the association of our ideas. On the contrary, his "principles" of association are simply general statements, supported by what he regarded as unimpugnable evidence, of the ways in which various classes of our ideas and impressions, including the passions, are in fact *correlated* or, as he put it, "constantly conjoined." He does not seek to "explain" anything by association, if by this is meant something more than the formulation of verifiable hypotheses concerning the order of occurrence to which certain types of human experience are subject. Thirdly, as we know, Hume much admired and was strongly influenced by "the incomparable Mr. Newton." But careful reading of Hume's work does not indicate any crude misconception of so-called "mechanistic" analogies between the operations of physical bodies and the operations of the human mind. What Newton probably suggested to Hume was the possibility of defining the operations of the mind in experiential terms and the possibility of stating the laws governing those operations without reference to "hidden" or non-observable agencies. Newton himself was explicit in his deprecation of non-empirical "hypotheses." His positive definitions of such conceptions as "force" and "gravitation" are striking in their freedom from any reference to unobservable properties. Similarly, Hume repeatedly rejects any attempt to get "behind" or explain the "reason" for our particular emotional experiences and the objects to which they are addressed. His sole concern is to establish *de facto* associations among our passions, or between our passions and other impressions and ideas. Any "deeper" explanation, if there is one, he eschews as beyond the scope of the empirical method. Rightly understood, therefore, any constant connection between items of experience would exemplify a principle of association, since principles of association are nothing more than general statements of the tendency of certain classes of psychical phenomena to go together. Finally, Hume's associationism is commonly accused of being too "atomic." There is not space to discuss this point fully here. It must suffice to say that Hume, more than most philosophers, was concerned with the *relational* character of experience. His so-called "atomism" is not intended to deny patterns or "gestalts"; it merely implies that they should be regarded as functions of the relations which hold between their parts.

In any case, whatever we may think of associationism — and

certainly it is open to many criticisms — it is important to bear in mind that it is an expression of the belief that the human mind is a natural process whose operations are governed by general laws analogous to, though not identical with, the laws governing the behavior of other natural phenomena. If there were no such laws, thinks Hume, the whole fabric of society, its laws and institutions, would never arise, or, if by a miracle they already existed, would utterly break down. For unless there are laws of behavior, there can be no rules of conduct, no meaningful system of punishments and rewards, no notion of ethical responsibility.

Hume's classification of the passions is of considerable interest, both in itself and in the light it sheds upon his moral philosophy. In the first place, there are, as we have said, certain basic drives or appetites which are present from birth in every normal person. These are "instinctive" in the sense that they antecede all experience of pleasure and pain. They are also without explicit "objects" or goals; that is to say, they are not *initially* mediated by beliefs or judgments as to what will or will not satisfy them. "These passions, properly speaking, *produce* good and evil, and proceed not from them, like the other affections." What may satisfy them must be learned from experience. Nothing is desirable, therefore, independently of experience. This point is of importance, although often overlooked by Hume's critics, since it definitely precludes the possibility of interpreting him as a strict psychological hedonist.

The instinctual responses are distinguished from what Hume calls the "secondary" passions. The latter *are* "founded on pain and pleasure." This expression is somewhat vague. What he seems usually to mean is that the secondary passions are aroused by antecedent impressions of pleasure and pain. In general he accepts what psychologists now call the "law of effect," according to which experiences which are antecedently pleasant or painful tend to be attained and preserved or avoided and removed, respectively.

It is worth observing in this connection that Hume uses the term "desire" more accurately and specifically than most moralists have done. According to him, "desire" is not a general term which refers indiscriminately to all forms of passion, whether instinctual or deliberate. He uses it to refer to a specific *secondary* passion which arises only from the perception or thought of some object which has previously been found to satisfy some instinctual response. Desire thus depends upon (a) a primary impulse, (b) the previous satisfaction of that impulse, and (c) the perception or thought of some object which has afforded that satisfaction. This analysis is important, since it at once emphasizes (a) the dependence of desire upon our basic wants, (b) that particular desires are formed as a *consequence of experience* which has been found pleasing, and (c) that without such experience our passional life would consist largely of random groping and blind drive.

The modernity of this account of the passional life is striking. It stands in sharp contrast to most previous accounts of purpose according to which the ends of human conduct are fixed and predetermined, and the process of self-realization simply the gradual exfoliation of goals "inherent" in human nature. The contrast between Hume and the Greek philosophers on this score is especially instructive. According to the latter, the process of acquiring purposes is essentially one of maturation — like the development of a flower. For Hume the process is one of discovering through experience and interaction with the environment those things which are favorable to the individual organism and those which are not.

Hume devotes a very large part of his analysis of the passions to an elaborate treatment of a special group of secondary passions, which arise when actions which have been previously found to be pleasant or painful are also accompanied by ideas involving a reference to a *self*. These are the passions of "pride" and "humility," "love" and "hatred." The importance of these complicated second-order interests in Hume's moral philosophy has not hitherto been sufficiently noted. Many of his commentators have supposed that Hume's elaborate treatment of them is little more than a display of his ingenuity in accounting in associationist terms for our more complicated sentiments. But this is far from being true.

Hume's treatment of self-regarding and other-regarding passions is briefly as follows (we may take pride as the typical illustration): anything which we find agreeable and is, in one way or another, closely related to the self, excites the passion of pride which is itself agreeable and has the self as its object. There is here what he calls a "double" association of impressions and ideas; that is to say, we are proud of whatever is associated in idea with ourselves, if the quality associated is a pleasure, distinct from but resembling the pleasure of pride itself, and associated with it by an association of *impressions*.

The most important points of Hume's lengthy analysis of these "indirect passions" are briefly as follows: (a) Any object which is in any way agreeable or disagreeable and is connected in our minds with a *person*, whether ourself or another, at once generates a favorable or unfavorable response toward that person. Moreover, because of the concurrence of the two associations mentioned above, both our regard or disregard for the person involved — whether ourselves or others — *and* our feeling toward the related object are mutually reinforced. Those objects which are interesting in themselves become doubly so if connected in our minds with those we like or dislike. (b) "Pride" and "humility," "love" and "hatred" are used by Hume in a more generic sense than is the case in the common usage of these terms. Moreover, he does not, at the outset, impute through their use any eulogistic or dyslogistic significance to the passions which they name. He employs these terms initially to describe those basic attitudes of attraction and revulsion with which we respond to *persons*. But since moral sentiment is *primarily* concerned with questions of character and motive rather than overt action, and since it is concerned with our attitudes toward *persons* rather than with our attitudes toward objects, it follows that the main preoccupation of the moralist must be with such universal and generic self- or other-regarding attitudes as pride, humility, love and hatred. (c) If Hume's use of such terms as "pride" is unconventional, still more so is his view of the appraisals which a disinterested person would make of the passions which these terms are taken to signify. Let us consider the passion of pride. Now there are varieties of pride such as vanity and self-conceit which are "over-weening" and "ill-founded." But there are other varieties which are more properly spoken of simply as "self-value" or the "sense of our own merit." These give us not only a legitimate pleasure but also "confidence and assurance in all our projects and enterprises." In either case, however, the *only* considerations which would affect the moral attitude of a disinterested spectator toward any given specimen of "pride" would be its agreeableness or utility to the persons affected by it. If "conceit" is sometimes vicious, the evil lies in the fact that it is directly or indirectly "disagreeable." But "nothing can be more laudable than to have a value for ourselves" when we really have qualities that are useful or agreeable, and therefore nothing is better entitled to the name of "virtue." Humility, on the other hand, is a "monkish virtue" which, being disagreeable both in itself and in its effects, can give no pleasure to a well-disposed mind. Like Spinoza, Hume rejects the catalogue of virtues which makes a fetish of humiliation, remorse, and a sense of weakness and impotence.

One more point: Hume, in his quiet way, has sought to restore a more truly humane appraisal of our sentiments than has sometimes prevailed in traditional Christian morality. But he accomplishes this without falling into the pitfalls which have attended most of the "transvaluations of values" which have been attempted by moral iconoclasts from Spinoza to Nietzsche. Hume attempts to humanize morality; he nowhere preaches egoism or the will to power as a way of life. Neither in his psychology nor in his ethics does he fall into one-sided conceptions of the nature of man or the good life. He has revised the catalogue of virtues to make a legitimate place for self-esteem and self-regard; but he has not removed from the list the qualities of love and benevolence.

Let us now consider Hume's much discussed theory of sympathy. At the outset an important ambiguity is to be noted. In the *Enquiry* the word "sympathy" is used as a synonym for "benevolence" or the sentiment of "humanity." In the *Treatise*, "sympathy" usually refers to a particular mode of association whereby we come to have *sympathetic* emotions for others. In the latter sense, there is no distinctive *emotion* of "sympathy"; indeed, so regarded, *an* emotion of sympathy would not make sense. *Any* emotion is sympathetic insofar as it is an emotion aroused by the perception or imagination of similar feelings in others. There can be in principle sympathetic love, sympathetic hatred, sympathetic jealousy, sympathetic pride.

In what follows we shall be concerned only with "sympathy" in the latter sense. It should be pointed out, however, that this shift in usage does not necessarily indicate a change in doctrine, as has sometimes been assumed. It is also often held that Hume's theory of sympathy presupposes that all men are alike and that the same things that produce pleasure or pain in one person also produce it in another. But clearly this is a mistake. Sympathy is a *cause* of common attitudes — not an *effect*. We sympathize with those we imagine or believe to be like ourselves, and this no doubt makes for mutual and common interests. But it might be that others did not have the feelings we impute to them. We sympathize also with "dumb animals" (sic); ana yet it is doubtful whether their sentiments resemble our own, or indeed, whether they actually "experience" such sentiments at all. The point is that my sympathy has nothing necessarily to do with what you may be feeling, but only with what you *appear to me* to feel. If we recall what goes on at the theatre, the point will be sufficiently clear. Finally, Hume's theory of sympathy is not an attempt to account for such sentiments as pity in terms of an egoistic psychology. Such a view might be attributed to Hobbes or possibly Adam Smith, but not to Hume. Both in the *Treatise* and in the *Enquiry*, other-regarding attitudes are held to be instinctual. Moreover, no one has ever given a more devastating analysis of the confusions inherent in psychological egoism than Hume himself in the second appendix to the *Enquiry*. Indeed, Hume is so far from holding that all men are egoists that according to him they are in some respects not egoistical enough! According to Hume's shrewd appraisal of human nature, man's fate is plagued as much by stupidity, fanaticism, and quixotic philanthropy, as by overweening self-love.

Hume's doctrine of sympathy is sufficiently simple. Its underlying premise is that our response to other persons is determined by our observation of their bodily behavior. When we perceive any action in another person similar to one which we have encountered in our own lives, we are led by an association of ideas to form an idea of those emotions which were previously correlated with similar action in our own past experience. This idea is transformed into an impression, that is, an actual *passion*, by a second association with our impression of "ourselves." This association of the idea of the emotion with our own egos, however, does not direct the emotion *to* ourselves; rather it simply gives additional *force* to the emotion. Hume is quite explicit on this point. In short, we feel *for* and *with* those beings whose behavior is similar to our own; our feelings are merely reinforced by their association with our awareness of self.

Now sympathetic emotion is strongest in relation to those who most nearly resemble ourselves, weakest in relation to those who seem most dissimilar. Thus the more we come to understand the common fate of our fellow beings and see through the superficial differences of manners, race, or language, the more extensive will be our capacity for sympathetic feeling. But it requires education and imaginative insight into the common character of human behavior and feeling to overcome the universal tendency toward clannishness and "limited benevolence."

It is through sympathy, also, that our passions are aroused toward our own long range "interests." It is not enough that we should be able to plan ahead or to anticipate our future needs. If we were unable sympathetically to *feel* ourselves into that future for which we plan, we would never be able to *act* providently, however prudent our plans.

What Hume is emphasizing in his doctrine of sympathy is that man is pre-eminently a social being, not in the sense of being altruistic or in the sense that the fulfillment of his wants requires the aid of others, but in the more important sense that whatever others do, their joys and sorrows, loves and hates, have an immediate and continuous impact upon our own sentiments. It is this capacity for reciprocity of feeling which renders possible a common moral life.

We come now to perhaps the most crucial of all Hume's psychological theories. This is his famous — or infamous — doctrine that "reason is the slave of the passions."

Since the time of the Greeks, there has been a universal tendency to over-intellectualize man's psychology. The discovery of reason was perhaps the supreme achievement of Greece. But it was not enough for the Greeks and their followers to stress the cognitive employment of reason. They also conceived it as the *opponent* and potential *master* of the appetites. In short, the function of reason was not merely to understand but also to order the "lower" faculties of appetite and will in the light of the true ideal for man, which was itself an ideal of disinterested contemplation or thought.

This doctrine of the psychological and moral supremacy of reason in the sphere of conduct was the standard view until the time of Hume — in many quarters it has remained so. It has been expressed in many ways. One of these, which goes back to the Stoics, is that there exist certain eternal "laws of nature" concerning human conduct, the rational apprehension of which should be sufficient to direct conduct in the line of duty and righteousness. It was in this form that the doctrine was usually expressed by Hume's predecessors.

Let us turn to Hume's criticisms. Reason, according to Hume, is the faculty of understanding or knowledge. But knowledge is one thing; to be *moved* by that knowledge to act is something else. It is a mere confusion to attribute to reason the motivating power which belongs to other faculties, just as it would be a confusion to say that we see with our ears, or smell with our stomachs. It follows that what we know will leave us wholly indifferent unless that knowledge happens to shed light upon some *end* in which we have an *interest*. But interests are functions of our passions, and not of reason alone. In short, no knowledge can move us unless it is related to some end; and there can be no end apart from some want which would be satisfied by achieving it. For example, reason instructs us that meat is nourishing. But unless *we* are hungry it will not serve *us* as *food*. We may know that justice is necessary to the order and stability of society. But unless there is some *concern* on our part for a stable society, that knowledge will have no effect upon our conduct.

All purpose, then, presupposes some purely instinctual response for which no reason can be given. Hence nothing can "oppose" one passion but another passion. Reason can show us the probable consequences of allowing a certain impulse to dominate our lives. But reason alone cannot inhibit that impulse. It can direct; it can throw light on possible sources of our happiness or misery; but the final choice of goals is a function of the passions.

Our passions themselves, as Hume says, are "original existences"; they know nothing, are meaningless, and hence neither true nor false. The heart, in short, has no "reasons" of its own, any more than the reason has independent purposes of *its* own. Conversely, "nothing can be contrary to truth or reason, except what has a reference to it, and the judgments of our understanding only have this reference." Strictly speaking, then, it is nonsensical to speak of a passion as "unreasonable." To be sure, passions may be directed toward illusory objects; but then it is not the "fault" of the passions that this is so, but rather, of the understanding which directs them. "It is not contrary to reason to prefer the destruction of the whole world to the scratching of my finger."

It must be emphasized, however, that Hume is not an irrationalist. Reason may, in a very definite sense, be the "slave of the passions." It is not, as Professor John Laird reminds us, necessarily their dupe. Hume never attributes to our feelings the capacities of the understanding. If reason cannot act independently, no more can the passions think. In this respect, he differs not only from the Romantics of the following century, but also from the Moral Sense school of his own period. To *feel* moral approbation, from Hume's point of view, is not the same thing as to perceive moral truth. If "moral judgment" were, in fact, nothing but an expression of moral approval or sentiment, then it would not be properly speaking a judgment at all, but merely an emotional by-product and sign of benevolence. Whether this *was* Hume's theory regarding moral judgment is a question which we shall have presently to consider. In any case, if reason's wings were cut by Hume, he never denied its authority in the sphere of knowledge.

Moreover, in speaking of reason as "slave," Hume was overstating his own position. Its influence is "oblique," but nonetheless real. Its function is to "mediate" between the passions and their goals. The passions themselves are blind. Only the understanding can shed light on possible objects for their satisfaction or the means by which such objects may be realized. Thus human nature is "composed of two principal parts, which are requisite in all its actions, the affections and the understanding," and "the blind motions of the former, without the direction of the latter, incapacitate men for society."

Hume's doctrine regarding the "influencing motives of the will" may be summarized in a parody of a famous dictum of Kant: "reason without passion is powerless; passion without reason is blind." So conceived, Hume's position is not wholly revolutionary. It is merely an attempt to define and distinguish more clearly than had previously been done the characteristic functions and interrelations of reason and passion. Nevertheless, the consequences of his teaching for moral philosophy generally were of far-reaching influence.

One further consequence of his psychology remains to be considered, because of its important bearing upon the time-honored problem of free-will and moral responsibility. It might be supposed that the philosopher who had demonstrated the absence of any necessary connections in the order of events would side with the proponents of indeterminism and "free" will. But such is not the case. Hume was concerned to show that indeterminism with respect to the will is *incompatible* with moral responsibility, and that freedom in conduct means only freedom from external compulsions. A man is at "liberty" when he can do what he pleases. But this has nothing whatever to do with the question whether there are determinate causes of volition.

No one has ever stated more clearly than Hume many of the confusions in which the free-will problem in ethics is imbedded. He begins by pointing out that experience discloses uniformity in human conduct as well as in other spheres. It is evident, he thinks, that "our actions have a constant conjunction with our motives, tempers, and circumstances." "Liberty" in the sense of absence of cause is thus contrary both to experience and to those principles which are believed by all to underlie the order of nature. As a matter of fact, no one denies that the conduct of *other* persons is to be accounted for in causal terms; one merely "feels" himself to be unconstrained, and hence the exception to the rule.

Why, then, do we suppose *ourselves* to be free from causal determination? In the first place, we confuse "force" with causal connection. Secondly, because we often experience no sense of constraint in pursuing our ends, we mistakenly imagine that this implies absence of cause. But this does not follow, if we bear in mind that the experience of "force" is *not* the same thing as causal necessity. "We feel that our actions are subject to our will on most occasions and imagine that the will itself is subject to nothing." But the *absence* of a feeling of constraint proves nothing, and it has nothing to do with the question whether there are causes which determine the will to act as it does.

Hume is not content to let the matter rest here. He goes on, as usual, to carry the argument into his opponents' camp by showing, not only that they are confused, but also that their doctrine is incompatible with their own notions of morality and religion. "It is indeed certain that all human laws are founded on rewards and punishments, it is supposed as a fundamental principle that these motives have an influence on the mind, and both produce the good and prevent the evil actions." This applies also to divine laws. Moreover, we bestow moral praise and blame only upon those whom we believe to be responsible for their acts, that is, to those whose conduct stems from something "durable and constant" in themselves. When this is not the case, as in the instance of an evil act committed by misadvertence, we regard the individual as unfortunate but not wicked or immoral.

The point is, then, that actions are regarded as moral or immoral

— as distinct from *merely* good or evil — only if they have a motive. If the act performed is deliberately chosen, the individual is said to be morally responsible; if not, not. We do *not* inquire, however, whether the motive *itself* was caused, for this is quite irrelevant to our question.

IV

We come now to Hume's ethical doctrines. Before considering them, it is well to remind ourselves once more that Hume's ethical position is a direct outcome of his theory of knowledge and his psychology. As we will see, his arguments against the ethical "intuitionists" and "rationalists" depends altogether upon these foundational aspects of his philosophy.

Hume's ethics was never adequately formulated in any single one of his writings. The *Treatise*, which contains his profounder and subtler analyses of ethical questions, is often veiled and indecisive as to the ultimate issue. One who sought to determine Hume's final position from the *Treatise* alone would find himself in difficulty from the outset. In this respect, the *Enquiry* is much clearer. There his *position* is much more sharply defined. But the *Enquiry* is a rather facile and elegant work, much less analytical and disputatious than the *Treatise*. Hence it is less satisfactory to anyone seeking the reasons lying behind Hume's rejection of alternative views. In trying to form an adequate conception of Hume's position, therefore, we must work back and forth between the two works. We will draw most of our conclusions concerning Hume's ethics from the *Enquiry*. The reasons lying behind them are usually to be found in the *Treatise*.

This raises a question as to possible differences of doctrine between the two works. It is the view of the present writer that there is no radical difference between the two on any *essential* point. There are differences of emphasis, to be sure, and minor differences in formulation. But these do not imply necessarily any basic theoretical change of view. Such differences as do exist may be stated in the following way: At the time of the writing of the *Treatise*, Hume was much more concerned with the refutation of his opponents' philosophies than with a clear and unequivocal statement of his own positive position in ethics. In that work, for example, he appears to vacillate somewhat with respect to the nature and status of moral judgment, sometimes taking a line which would seem to deny any cognitive import to it, and sometimes not. In the *Enquiry*, his vacillation in this matter largely disappears, and he makes unmistakably clear in that work that he does not consider moral arguments to consist *merely* in attempts and counter-attempts to influence the wills of others. Also, he states much more clearly there the relation of his (broadly speaking) utilitarian theory of value to his moral theory, which is, in many important respects, not utilitarian.[2]

The primary problem in interpreting Hume's ethics can be stated in the following way: If good and evil generally are to be construed in terms of what is "useful or agreeable to ourselves or others," then it would seem to follow that the *criterion* for judging all moral conduct would be something like the greatest happiness principle, according to which the only relevant consideration is the amount of pleasure or pain that results from a given act. This is the usual utilitarian position, according to which moral judgments are concerned solely with the beneficial or ill consequences of conduct. But if so, then motives also must be judged good or bad solely in relation to *their* consequences. This corollary, however, violates a cardinal principle of enlightened morality, namely, that acts are *morally* good or bad if and only if their motives are such; it is a good will which qualifies an act as virtuous and not vice versa. Moreover, when we judge a man as morally *responsible*, and hence as subject to moral praise or blame, our primary concern is with his intentions and not with their consequences. If his purpose can be shown to be blameless or praiseworthy, then he is held to be morally innocent or virtuous, even though the effects of his conduct be unhappy. Thus we seem forced to deny, with respect to moral goodness and virtue at least, that ill or beneficial consequences have anything intrinsically to do with *moral* judgments whatever. In short, Hume seems on the one hand to hold with Mill in judging the value of conduct in terms of its useful or agreeable consequences. But he seems also to hold with Kant in maintaining that nothing is morally good save a good will.

Now in the first place it must be pointed out that there is no *a priori* reason why *moral* goodness and *mere* goodness or value in general should mean the same thing. Certainly we all regard many things as good to which we would never think of ascribing moral

[2] These points are discussed at length below; see p. xxxiv.

goodness or virtue: sunshine, for example. It is increasingly recognized that what Ogden and Richards have aptly called the "one and only one meaning fallacy" applies to ethical as well as to other terms. Nevertheless, morality *is* in some way concerned with values, and any ethical theory according to which moral goodness or virtue had nothing whatever to do with other values would be considered not merely incomplete, but also incompetent. Hence, while it is not logically impossible to be a "utilitarian" with respect to values and an "intentionalist" with respect to virtue, still this does not absolve a person who should hold such a position from showing the positive relations between morality and happiness which we all believe to exist. It is Hume's task to show *how* morality and happiness are related without reducing the former to a system of judgments which are concerned solely with the beneficial or ill consequences of conduct, and without, on the other hand, denying that values are to be construed in terms of what is useful or agreeable.

But before turning to this positive side of Hume's ethics, we must consider his criticisms of the major alternative ethical theories of his predecessors. Here we will find him as trenchant and incisive as he always is in criticism.

His first problem is to dispose of those types of ethical theory which deny any intrinsic connection between moral attributes and human attitudes and feelings. Such theories usually regard moral truths as somehow grounded objectively in "nature" or "reality" on the one hand, or in such purely cognitive terms as "consistency" or "knowledge" on the other.

Prior to Hume it had been widely held that "goodness" is identical either with "reality" itself, or else with some pervasive non-human characteristic of things, such as "order," "normality" or "perfection." And moral propositions were regarded as judgments concerning the "eternal fitness" or "the natural order of things." Similar views were held by the Stoics, and by many of the scholastic followers of Aristotle; and they were widely entertained by the "Cambridge Platonists," a school which flourished in England during the seventeenth and eighteenth centuries. It was also substantially the position of Hume's great predecessor, George Berkeley. Berkeley maintained that, although it was "natural" for men to pursue their own happiness, this could come only from strict obedience to God. "Conformity to His

will," said Berkeley, "is the *sole* rule whereby every man who acts
up to the principles of reason must govern and square his actions.
These rules are also 'eternal rules of reason' which necessarily result
from the nature of things, and may be demonstrated by the infallible
rules of reason." This is the view of the philosopher who had argued
that "It is evident to anyone who takes a survey of the objects of
human knowledge that they are *ideas* actually imprinted on the
senses; or else such as are perceived by attending to the passions and
operations of the mind; or lastly, ideas formed by the help of imagination — either compounding, dividing, or barely representing those
originally perceived in the aforesaid ways." But, in a word, it is the
consistent application of this very theory of knowledge which lies at
the basis of Hume's rejection of just such ethical theories as Berkeley
propounded.

Hume's objections to such "non-naturalistic" theories, as they are
often called, may be grouped under two main heads: (*1*) arguments
from the function or purpose of moral judgments, (*2*) arguments from
the theory of knowledge.

(*1*) Hume drops a remark in the opening paragraph of Section I
of Book III of the *Treatise* which may appear to be merely the innoc-
uous commonplace, the sort of thing with which authors usually begin
a prolonged inquiry: "Morality is a subject that interests us above all
others: We fancy the peace of society to be at stake in every decision
concerning it; and it is evident that this concern must make our speculation appear more real and solid than where the subject is, in great
measure, indifferent to us." This might well seem nothing more than
a casual bit of edification designed to impress the reader sufficiently so
that he will stay awake until the author has warmed up to his task
and the serious discussion begins. Not so with Hume. Actually, this
statement contains in germ one of his two main reasons for rejecting
ethical theories which are "derived from reason."

Morals is a subject about which no one is indifferent. Its judgments,
therefore, are not merely answers to questions of idle curiosity or
speculation. They are "supposed to influence our passions and
actions." This is confirmed by "common experience which informs
us that men are often governed by their duties, and are deterred from
some actions by the opinion of injustice and impelled to others by
that of obligation." This being so, we may assume that no analysis

of ethical judgments and ethical terms can possibly be adequate which involves no reference either explicitly or implicitly to the springs of human action, i.e., the passions. "An active principle can never be founded on an inactive. . . ." We must, therefore, reject such purely intellectual criteria as "rationality," or "consistency," as inadequate, since they fail to account for the "magnetism" of moral judgments. This does not mean, of course, that "rationality" and "consistency" are not good things. It means simply that "moral distinctions" cannot be analyzed in terms of them alone.

Hume's argument can be stated in another and perhaps more striking way. We assume that no person can be held morally responsible for actions which he did not willingly perform. We do not address such judgments as "killing is wrong" to cyclones, not merely because they do not understand, but because the disasters wrought by storms are involuntary. In short, we regard only responsible beings as moral or immoral. But, as we have seen, responsibility *presupposes* a motive for or interest in any act for which a person is held responsible. If this is so, the very notions of "moral" and "immoral" involve a reference to feeling or sentiment; and every moral judgment states or implies such a reference.

This argument cuts even deeper than we have hitherto suggested. It disqualifies all purely "rationalistic" theories, such as that of Kant. But it also disqualifies those "metaphysical" or "theological" theories which set up "order," "naturalness," "perfection," "reality" or "the will of God" as the criteria of moral goodness or virtue. Indeed, it disqualifies all theories whatever which, in the last analysis, deny that moral categories are to be construed in terms of human feeling or interest, and that moral judgments involve an inherent reference to the passions. In brief, conduct, which is the sole interest of morals, is concerned with *ends;* but there can be no end apart from passion.

(2) Hume also raises questions which are of crucial importance concerning the method according to which ethical judgments are to be verified or known. As an empiricist, he is committed to three all-important principles: (a) that no judgment of matters of fact is ever certain, (b) that the evidence for such judgments is grounded in experience alone, (c) that any "true" proposition for which certainty or necessity is claimed must be a statement merely concerning "relations of ideas," i.e., it has nothing whatever to do with matters of fact.

These canons, for the empiricist, are applicable to all statements whatsoever. It follows from this that there can be no necessary *moral* principles which are not also merely statements about the relations of our ideas. This consideration rules out all systems of ethics which claim that there are universal and necessary truths concerning conduct. But it also invalidates those systems according to which moral truths involve a reference to trans-empirical factors which could never be confirmed by experience. Thus, for example, theories which would claim that "killing is wrong" because killing goes against the will of God, or because of some supposedly non-natural quality inherent in the act of killing, must be ruled out as incapable of verification.

In general, two main criteria for any adequate account of ethical judgments emerge from these analyses. First, moral judgments are dynamic, i.e., they influence conduct. They involve, therefore, at least implicitly, some reference to the passions which alone are the "springs of action." All moral suasion has its roots in our sentiments, our *concern* for the satisfaction of our own passions, or, through sympathy, for that of other persons. The other criterion is that any ethical term must have an observable signification, and that any ethical judgment must be capable of an empirical verification. Otherwise we literally know not what we say, nor whether what we say is true.

Now the difficulty with Hume's attack on non-naturalistic ethical theories is that it seems at first to prove too much. And in the *Treatise* — though not in the *Enquiry* — there are indications that Hume has fallen, at least temporarily, into certain positions which appear to be scarcely more tenable than the views which he has attacked. One of these may be characterized as "egoistic approbationism." According to this view, when an individual pronounces an act to be virtuous, he means nothing but that he himself approves it. At one point, Hume expresses this view in so many words. The other view, even more extreme, is what has come to be called the "emotive theory" of ethics. According to this view, ethical judgments are descriptively meaningless. They are, presumably like ejaculations and exclamations, merely *expressions* of feeling. To say that "this is good" is, on this theory, merely to give vent to one's feelings of approval *toward* it, but not to say anything significant *about* it.

In the earlier sections of Book III of the *Treatise*, Hume unquestionably does suggest both of these views. But I think that neither of them can be said to represent his considered position. In the first place, Hume again and again insists that moral judgments possess a stability, impartiality, and universality which would be highly unlikely if every moral judgment merely referred to or expressed the approval of the judger toward an act. Our individual sentiments of praise or blame, he agrees, are variable, "according to our situation of nearness or remoteness with regard to the person blamed or praised, and according to the present disposition of our mind." But this variability does not affect our general view of human conduct. In considering the moral character of any person or act, we adopt the convention of a benevolent impartial spectator; and our expressions of moral praise or blame are expressions of what such a spectator *would* approve or disapprove rather than what we ourselves actually do feel. Hume speaks of this convention as a way of "correcting our sentiments."

Secondly, Hume insists upon what he calls the "reality of moral distinctions," in explicit contradistinction to those "disingenuous" sceptics and cynics who deny that morality has any real basis whatever. It is not, he thinks, "conceivable that any human creature could ever seriously believe that all characters and actions were alike entitled to the affection and regard of every one."

Thirdly, not only do we dispute on occasion concerning the moral qualities of an act or character; we also regard such controversy as cognitively significant. But if moral judgments were merely expressions or statements of personal approval and disapproval, then moral disputes would be meaningless or pointless or both.

Hume's ethical system thus skirts, without actually falling into, the difficulties of egoistic or sentimental relativism or the so-called "emotive theory" of ethical judgments. In the *Treatise*, at least, there are also suggestions of still another view which has sometimes been held to represent his mature position. This is the so-called "Moral Sense" theory. In combatting the rationalists, Hume's predecessors, Shaftesbury and Hutcheson, were led to adopt the view that there is a special moral *sense* analogous to vision or hearing. This view, formally at least, implies that there is a distinctive moral quality, analogous to red, the perception of which supposedly arouses sentiments of approval toward those things which possess it.

Actually, the Moral Sense theory was transitional, and its main historical importance lay in its very trenchant attack on non-naturalistic ethics, to which Hume's own arguments owe much. Now Hume adopted the *terminology* of this school in the section of the *Treatise* entitled "Moral Distinctions derived from a Moral Sense." But careful reading of this section, as well as other parts of the *Treatise* and particularly the *Enquiry*, shows that he did not actually maintain that there is a special cognitive sense through which certain distinctive qualities, which we call "moral," are apprehended. On the contrary, his view, as we shall see, asserts that it is only when a character or act is considered in relation to a certain kind of *feeling* or *sentiment* that we properly "denominate" it as morally good or evil. Indeed, the greater part of his attack on the rationalists, as well as many definite statements which he makes elsewhere in the *Treatise* and the *Enquiry*, are clearly incompatible with the Moral Sense theory.

We turn now to one of the most distinctive characteristics of Hume's ethics. Hume's general theory of value is, broadly speaking, hedonistic and utilitarian. "Whatever is valuable in any kind, so naturally classes itself under the division of *useful* or *agreeable*, the *utile* or the *dulce*, that it is not easy to imagine why we should ever seek further or consider the question as a matter of nice research or inquiry."

But a theory of value is one thing, and a theory of morals is something else. Granted that, on the whole, the moral is closely related to the good, and that what tends to produce the greatest good in a given situation is usually moral *in fact*, it is a serious mistake to *identify* moral goodness, as the utilitarians maintained, with whatever conforms to the so-called greatest happiness principle. In pronouncing a moral judgment, according to Hume, we do *not* look to the *consequences* of an act, but to the motives or character of him who performs it. In short, morality is mainly concerned with questions of virtuous character rather than questions of good behavior. This is confirmed when we consider the question of ethical responsibility. We hold men innocent of "crimes" committed inadvertently. We continue to hold men "virtuous" who, out of benevolent motives, nevertheless bring about a tragic result. Literature is full of such characters, none of whom do we condemn. The ethics of Christianity is regarded as superior to Hebraic or Greek ethics precisely on this point. In this respect, then, Hume tends to hold with Kant that nothing is morally good or virtuous but a "good will."

Unlike Kant, Hume remains a naturalist. Moral sentiment for him is an outgrowth of natural human fellow-feeling, extended by sympathy, and "corrected" and "stabilized" by convention and habit. But he is not content to rest his case with the insistence that there can be no morally virtuous action without a benevolent motive. There still remains the fact that many individuals are evidently impelled solely by a "sense of duty," which, he recognizes, is different from moral sentiment. This Hume must still explain if his ethical theory is to contain an adequate account of obligation. It is here, perhaps, where Hume is at his subtlest and most interesting.

Now, it is an "undoubted maxim" of ethics that "no action can be virtuous or morally good unless there be in human nature some motive to produce it, distinct from the sense of its morality." To suppose otherwise is to involve ourselves in a vicious regress, since every virtuous act presupposes a virtuous motive. Hume is here distinguishing between a moral or virtuous motive and a motive whose purpose is "a regard for virtue." This is not a quibble. A virtuous motive is, briefly, a benevolent motive. A regard for virtue is a regard either for the *approval* of a virtuous or moral person or for the maxims which such a person would approve. The latter is what we call "the sense of duty" or, perhaps, "conscience."

But is Hume entitled to hold that there is such a thing as the sense of duty? He is. He has nowhere argued that there are not derivative sentiments whose *sole* concern is a *regard* for virtue or duty. A person who acts from such a motive may be a formalist, and his motive may not be itself morally virtuous. Nevertheless, the sense of duty is not an illusion; nor is it unimportant in human conduct.

Hume's explanation of the emergence of the sense of duty or obligation is based upon the principles of association. Suppose an act is originally performed for some ulterior end. In time, a part of our feeling is transferred to the act itself, and we come to regard it as worth doing, independently of its result. Or, again, suppose we at first regard a certain type of action as the *sign* of a certain kind of motive. Gradually we will transfer our approval from the motive of which it is a manifestation to the act itself. It is in this way that we build upon compulsive conscientious objections to certain types of behavior whose original, perhaps moral, function we may have quite forgotten. In this way, Hume is affirming the much discussed and newly rediscovered principle of the "autonomy of motives," and applying it to the very important psychological phenomenon of conscience or the "sense of duty." But, to conclude, "though, on some occasions, a person may perform an action merely out of a regard to its moral obligation, yet still this supposes in human nature some distinct principles of producing the action, and whose moral beauty rendered the action meritorious."

Hume's ethics thus achieves a subtle and delicate balance between rationalistic and empirical, universalistic and relativistic, objectivistic and subjectivistic, intentional and utilitarian ethics. In this lies its distinctive merit and persuasiveness. Let us state briefly what this balance is: (a) Hume agrees with the rationalist that ethical distinctions are real and independent of the fluctuations of our momentary and local feelings. Moral judgments are not merely *expressions* of our approval and disapproval; they have descriptive meaning and are capable of truth and falsity; nevertheless they are empirical and hence corrigible. (b) Moral distinctions have a certain objectivity and universality in the sense that they refer to what an impartial and benevolent spectator *would* approve, and not necessarily to what most of us in fact do approve; but there is, even in the doctrine of the impartial spectator, a reference to sentiment; moreover, apart from our own *concern* for morality and its effects — we are all, according to Hume, at least potentially capable of disinterested benevolence — there would be no obligation on our part to act in accordance with the supposed sentiments of such a being. Indeed, apart from our interests, the phenomena of morality and moral judgments would have no human application. (c) Hume agrees with the intentionalist that the application of such terms as "moral" and "virtuous" is limited to motives, and does not properly apply to acts save as signs of certain motives; but his theory of value is hedonistic and utilitarian. Moral values are *values* because they are useful or pleasing to ourselves or others; they are *moral* because they are objects of disinterested approval or benevolence; and, since the concern of moral sentiment is solely with human well-being, every human value is, at least potentially, of interest to morality.

V

The main outlines of Hume's ethics are now, perhaps, reasonably clear. We have still to consider his important treatment of what he calls "artificial virtues." Our present concern is no longer with his analysis of "moral distinctions" but with the conclusions to which he is led with respect to the value and moral justification of actual civic virtues. In order to understand the importance of Hume's argument, however, we must bear in mind that he has denied that there is any value save what is useful or agreeable to ourselves or others, and that there can be, at least initially, no obligation without at least some implicit concern for the end to which the obligatory act is addressed. At the same time, although he sharply opposes the egoistic theory of Hobbes, he holds that there is no purely instinctive "love of mankind" or society "merely as such." Hence it is not possible for him *merely* to fall back on the view of the "sentimentalists," that the basis of obligation is simply man's instinctive good-will toward his fellows. In short, Hume seems to be faced with a dilemma: he cannot account for our duties to society and its laws of justice on non-naturalistic grounds without destroying the whole basis of his ethics; and yet he cannot accept the two main naturalistic alternatives which had hitherto been propounded by Hobbes on the one hand, and the Moral Sense school on the other. Nor, as we shall see, can he agree with such writers as Locke, who argue that our social obligations rest upon a social contract. Hume escapes from these difficulties in the following way.

The rules of society, its customs and precepts, as well as its more formally established laws, are "artificial" in the sense that they are not *objects* of any inherent and natural sentiment. To be sure they are rooted in human nature in the same sense as is the love of tobacco or the preference for brunettes. But no one would speak of the latter as "natural" in the same sense that hunger or the sexual impulse is natural. Without human instincts society would not exist. But human instincts *alone* are not sufficient to account for the complicated social adjustments which man is required to make. At this point Hume introduces a concept which has been increasingly emphasized in ethics and social philosophy generally, namely, "convention."

Before proceeding, however, we must be careful to distinguish, as Hume himself is not always at sufficient pains to do, the reasons which actually induce people to perform socially obligatory acts, and those which ought to induce them to do so. Hume's account of *both* the "natural" and "moral" obligation to acts of justice involves a reference to "conventions."

Consider, following his example, two rowers of a boat who pull the oars together. They do not give promises to one another; nor do they explicitly establish a rule with a view to mutual advantage. They find themselves, by a kind of tacit agreement, rowing together at a certain rate. Again, the duties of a household are not, as a rule, deliberately laid down in advance with a view to common convenience and happiness. Like Topsy, they just grow. Similarly, laws of justice, which determine most of our obligations to other members of society, as Hume said, arise gradually, and acquire force by a slow progression and by our repeated inconveniences in transgressing them. Hume also suggests the interesting comparison of the gradual development of laws of society *and* the sense of interest which binds us to them, with the growth of languages and the development of a sense of language which is "offended" by breaches of common usage. Only in cases of conflict of interest or indecision do we ask for the *justification* of social rules and customs or our obligations to adhere to them. For the most part we adhere to them without question and accept implicitly their utility or value.

There is another point to be remarked upon before we consider Hume's view of the moral justification of justice and the restraints which its laws impose. Hume holds that any *morally* good act is one which, *in the last analysis*, would be approved by an impartial spectator as useful or agreeable to ourselves or others. But it is not to be supposed that in our actual reasoning concerning our conduct toward society this question is usually raised. We do what we do from a variety of motives: particular passions, self-interest, "the sense of duty," habit, or what not. Now *so long* as these motives result in conduct which is in fact useful or agreeable, they would in principle be approved by an impartial spectator. In this sense we are entitled to regard acts performed from self-interest or pride, for example, as indirectly justifiable, even though the persons performing them have only their own welfare in mind. Hume's point is that, if we are candid, we must admit that most men, including many whom we regard as "good," perform their duties and fulfill their commitments from a vast variety of motives, of which the self-regarding ones are on the whole predominant. Such is the fact. But this implies no discredit to human nature, nor does it imply that the moral questions must resolve themselves solely into questions of rational self-interest. So long as what we do is, on the whole, *good*, an enlightened morality need not be offended, even though our motives may be self-regarding. The merely prudent man, like the man who acts from a sense of duty, is, to be sure, not acting from a morally virtuous motive. But if what he does is conducive to the happiness of himself or others, there can be no objection on moral grounds to what he *does*. In such a case we will acknowledge that his conduct is such as a morally enlightened person would approve, even though we may deny him the positive attribute of a virtuous character.

But this merely helps to clear the air of cant and hypocrisy. It still leaves open the question as to the actual *moral* justification for acting in accordance with the laws of justice. Hume's account has much to recommend it. It is his contention that, considered in isolation, individual acts of justice cannot, as a rule, be justified on moral grounds. They often go against the personal interests of the agent, and it is at least doubtful in many cases whether they redound to the well-being either of the individual to whom justice is done or to society as a whole. Consider a case in a small claims court where a poor man is obliged to pay an account to a wealthy corporation. No rational justification could be made of the fulfillment of this obligation on grounds of utility either to the individual, the corporation, or society. Where then lies the value? Hume's answer is that it lies in the maintenance of the whole fabric of rules and customs whereby the stability and order of society is assured. The importance of conventions lies precisely in the fact that as nature provides no natural remedy for the irregularities and anti-social tendencies in human behavior, it is necessary that conventional rules of conduct be established which will be generally observed. The social utility of such conventions lies first of all in their universal observance. In this every man has an enduring interest. This being so, any benevolent mind must disapprove of the violation of rules of justice, and therefore regard himself as morally bound, in his own turn, to adhere to them, regardless of any compulsion or private interest to do so.

To return to questions of fact, it is Hume's belief that as men come to be aware of the social utility of rules of justice they will be led by such moral sentiments as they possess to "concur with interest." And "*this* sentiment imposes a *new* obligation upon mankind." After this sentiment has been brought into operation, Hume maintains, we in turn are likely to transfer our interest from its ultimate goal to the obligation itself, in which case we will thenceforth act from conscience or the "sense of duty."

Hume gives us, then, a kind of natural history of the motives which cause us to adhere to the rules of society: in the beginning common self-interest expresses itself in conventions; then the general utility of such rules in turn evokes moral approbation, when conflict between personal and public interest appears, thus giving rise to a "new" distinctively *moral* obligation; finally our interest is transferred to the maintenance of the rules "for their own sake," from which arises that formalistic "sense of duty" which has forgotten that the rules ever existed for an ulterior end.

What are we to say of Hume's ingenious doctrine? In the first place, I think we must admit that no writer before him adequately appreciated either the importance or the extent of conventions in human conduct. Hume is able to embrace the large degree of truth that there is in "conventionalism" without falling into the position that the laws of justice are *mere* conventional rules of procedure without any deeper moral significance. He thus shows us a way of abandoning the untenable "natural law" theory without embracing the view that there is no reason, other than habit and the preferences bred of habit, for preserving seemingly arbitrary social rules.

There is the further interesting fact about Hume's theory, that it sharply distinguishes between the non-moral obligations to adhere to such rules, which arise from self-interest, the desire for public approval, or even the implicit sense of common interest, and the distinctively *moral* obligation to adhere to them, which has its ground in moral sentiment. He thus accounts for the other important motives which give weight and stability to the fabric of social rules of conduct, without reducing moral attitudes to any of them, and without confusing the obligations to which these several interests give rise. At the same time he gives a plausible account of the general congruity between the approbation of moral sentiment and the other interests which support and are benefited by an orderly system of social rules.

VI

Hume's social and political philosophy is of interest mainly on three scores: first, because of its consistent application of the empirical method to questions of fact concerning the origins and functions of social institutions; secondly, because of its devastating critique of the dominant liberal social philosophies of modern times; and thirdly, because it affords further illustrations and confirmations of his moral theories.

It is a curious irony that the *defense* of liberal ideas in the seventeenth and eighteenth centuries was made in terms of an appeal to precisely the abstract rights, rationally self-evident "laws of nature," or the social contract, which liberals since Hume have generally rejected both on the ground that they are reactionary and on the ground that they require for their defense an untenable theory of knowledge. In attacking the Lockeian foundations of liberalism, he seemed to progressives of his own day to be attacking the foundations of free society itself. Hence the scorn in which, as we have seen, he was held by Jefferson. Actually, Hume's own arguments were primarily an attack upon the terms in which the liberals formulated their social philosophies and the *method* which they used to defend their position rather than disparagement of the substantive position itself. Hume tells us in one place that government by consent is perhaps the best possible. In so far, he agrees with the most radical of the eighteenth century humanitarians. But this is, in a sense, beside the point. His real strength consists in his insistence that if government by consent *is* best, then its moral justification lies in its fruits for those who live under it.

The historical interest of Hume's social theory lies largely in the fact that he and, through him, the Utilitarians subjected the natural rights and natural law theories to a devastating analysis from which, at least in Britain, they have never recovered. Thenceforth the dominant liberal schools of social thought in England, Utilitarianism and Socialism, have been more or less explicitly empirical as well as humanistic in their points of view. In America, partly due to the influence of such writers as Jefferson and Paine, and partly due to the reverence in which such powerfully-written public documents as the *Declaration of Independence* were held, the Lockeian principles retained their persuasiveness long into the nineteenth century. No social philosopher of the first rank in this country until James and Dewey has regarded himself as working explicitly in the tradition of Hume and his nineteenth century disciples, the Philosophical Radicals.

Hume's attack upon the Lockeian position is thoroughgoing. He attacks it on historical, on methodological, and on moral grounds. Factually, he regards the doctrine of the "state of nature" and the "social contract" as "of a piece" with the ancient myth of a "golden age." His own view, like that of many later writers, is that the family is the primordial social unit. But, whatever the origins of society, Hume's important point is that society and its customs are the result of "necessity," "inclination," and "habit," rather than a rational decision on the part of any group to extricate itself from the inconveniences of a state of nature. Only very gradually do men come to recognize the advantages of social life and its institutions. By the time they get around to looking for a justification, the institutions themselves are already on the verge of decay.

It cannot be said, of course, that Hume was fully aware of the importance of the factors of historical change and development which later writers have emphasized. On the whole, his own approach remains "analytical." But he saw more clearly than most of his contemporaries the pitfalls that lie in the path of those who confuse analytical reconstruction with history, and he was saved from the errors of those who seek to justify either existing institutions or their modification on merely historical grounds. Edmund Burke was, perhaps, superior to Hume with respect to his awareness of the historical evolution of such institutions as the British constitution. But Burke's contempt for "abstract principles" led him perilously close to that "historicism" according to which things are right either simply because they already exist, or because they occupy a certain place in the process of historical development. Hume is quite free from this confusion which has so widely prevailed in the nineteenth and twentieth centuries. And he saw, as Burke did not, that, *properly construed*, such notions as the "state of nature" and the doctrine of "consent" are simply ideal constructions by which the philosopher seeks to show not what has occurred in the past, but what of necessity *would* occur if intelligent human beings were capable of making free and intelligent decisions concerning their social arrangements. Such political speculations as those of Hobbes and Locke, however far from historical truth and however faulty in detail, are in reality attempts to discover, by the aid of suppositions contrary to fact, what *justification* there may be either for existing arrangements and the obligations which they entail, or for changing them.

Hume's basic objection to the doctrines of the state of nature and the social contract is that, apart from historical considerations, they are quite utopian. Politics is an art of the possible. If we are to speculate profitably concerning the betterment of society or our obligations to present social institutions, we must not indulge in idle fancies concerning some "happy age" in which "the rivers flowed with wine and milk," and "avarice, ambition, cruelty, and selfishness were never heard of." In such a condition neither government nor justice would have any meaning. Serious thinkers are not concerned with "idle fictions," but with what men can hope for and ought to do, given their present natures and the conditions of scarcity and want in which actually they find themselves.

One of the most important of Hume's contributions to social and political theory is his insistence that a sharp distinction be made between society and the state, and between social and political obligations. It is, he thinks, possible for men to exist without more than a modicum of government. Man is, by habit and interest, a social animal. But the fabric of social life, in Hume's view, depends less upon positive law than upon social convention and habit.

Now all of us are more or less aware of a sense of common interest and destiny with those amongst whom we live. This sense of common interest, as we have seen, is both expressed in terms of, and in turn is determined by, conventions which, although in one sense arbitrary, give order and stability to human life. In time such conventions become habitual, and no question is raised, as a rule, concerning their utility. If such a question *is* raised, Hume thinks it usually sufficient to point out that the "selfishness and confined generosity of men, along with the scanty provision nature has made for his wants" is such that any individual must see that the universal observance of the laws of society is necessary to every member. "Every individual person must find himself a gainer, on balancing the account; since without justice, society must immediately dissolve, and every one must fall into that savage and solitary condition, which is infinitely worse than the worst situation that can possibly be supposed in society." This may seem a bit disingenuous in Hume, especially since, like Plato, he is aware that to the egoist, considering only his own personal advantage, the desirable thing is that *others* should observe rules of justice, while he himself remains free to violate them as he pleases. It is also evident in this passage that Hume was closer to Hobbes than he may sometimes have supposed. Nevertheless, at its worst, Hume's position has the merit of recognizing that actually the basis of social life is convention and habit rather than deliberate agreement or calculated self-interest.

A more interesting point is Hume's discussion of the reason why we "annex the idea of virtue to justice and vice to injustice." It is, he contends, our "sympathy with the public interest" which is "the source of the moral approbation which attends that virtue." Here he clearly parts company with Hobbes. For the latter, there is neither justice nor social morality apart from the laws of the Sovereign; indeed, for Hobbes, terms such as "honorable" and "dishonorable" have no *meaning* apart from the commands and sanctions of the State. For Hume, morality is independent of the sanctions of government, and moral obligations to adhere to the rules of justice do not cease when the arm of the law is broken. "The utmost politicians can perform is to extend the natural sentiments beyond their original bounds; but still nature must furnish the materials and give us some notion of moral distinction."

Government, like society, is an "invention, very advantageous, and even in some circumstances absolutely necessary to mankind." But the origin of government, Hume agrees with Plato, is due primarily to the necessity of organized defense against external aggression. Later, in the Essay on the "Origin of Government," he argues somewhat differently that governments are usually founded by conquest or usurpation. Rather more important is Hume's contention that even *if* it were true that originally governments were the result of a common agreement, the *actual* authority of the sovereign depends upon habitual submission. The problem of *maintaining* that authority, however, is one of compelling obedience. But this is a problem of *power*. Actual obedience and respect arise from fear of punishment, from necessity and habit, rather than from active consent or a sense of moral obligation.

Hume's main interest, however, is neither in the question of origins nor in the question as to why men do in fact give allegiance to government. Rather it is in the central problems of normative political philosophy: what are the ends of *government*, and what is the moral basis of political obligation or "allegiance."

In a sense it would not be inaccurate to say that for Hume the end of government, like that of all institutions, is the alleviation of the common evil and the promotion of the common good. But while this is the general end, it does not define the specific function of government. The peculiar characteristic of political as opposed to merely civil society is the fact that in the case of the latter, violation of customs is not attended as a rule by physical reprisals. The essence of political authority lies in the fact that it may not be ignored without incurring a penalty that normal persons are usually unwilling to incur. In short, in so far as government is effective, there is for most people no practicable alternative to submission to its will. To be sure, society has its own ways of securing conformity. But its sanctions are not deliberate; nor are they by any means sufficient to *compel* the individual in the face of a counter-interest of fairly great intensity. The political use of force, however, is deliberate, and the continual *threat* of its employment is usually sufficient to reduce any potential violator to submission without overtly invoking it. Were this not the case, government would simply cease to function in any practical sense.

What, then, is the *function* which is served by this deliberate use of physical sanctions by one group against another? And what is the justification of this function itself? To the first question Hume's answer is similar to, but goes beyond, that of Locke. Were "social justice" always sufficient to restrain men, there would be no need of positive law. Without "disorder and inequity," magistrates would be merely useless and oppressive. The prime virtue of politically organized society is the establishment of *laws* which *impose* restraints upon its members which otherwise they would not willingly or habitually accept.

But granted that restraint is "advantageous," why is it *necessary?* Here we must bring to bear Hume's psychology. The two greatest *natural* enemies of order and restraint are certain ineradicable tendencies toward partiality and vacillation. We may recall Hume's doctrine that reason will not move us, either to our own or society's advantage, in the absence of passion. But most of our passions are directed toward particular objects rather than our total good. Indeed, it is of the essence of most passions that they should be preoccupied with *particular* ends regardless of their usefulness in the total economy of life. Moreover, Hume believes, there is a general tendency in man to be more influenced by immediate rather than remote values. The *propinquity* of a satisfaction for most persons enhances its appeal. Both of these characteristics are inimical to our own long range interests or those of society at large. Furthermore, our "calm passions" of prudence and good-will, although very real, are not sufficiently constant or intense to make it possible to rely upon them as constant restraints upon our other passions.

The great social vices, then, may be summarized in the words "purposelessness" and "faction." It is because of them, and the inability to remove them by other means, that the existence of government is necessary. In short, the primary function of the State is to supply man with motives and habits which will offset those ineradicable weaknesses which would otherwise destroy him. An important corollary of this view, incidentally, is that the main function of government is to prevent or remove evil rather than to institute positive good. Like most of his contemporaries, Hume still regards the utility of government as extremely limited. He does not seriously entertain the notion of a state which shall perform positive services to increase social well-being. However, many enlightened theorists in our own day would defend Hume's position on the general ground that the service state has an inherent tendency to become totalitarian.

We have yet to consider Hume's theory of the *moral* limits of political obligation. The other side of this question is the right to rebellion. Again, this question must be carefully distinguished from questions concerning the actual motives which impel men either to submit to authority or to revolt. As we have seen, interest, necessity, habit, and, ultimately, fear, are the usual guarantors of allegiance.

The moral basis of the political obligation cannot be a prior promise or contract. Hume does not impugn the social ideals of those writers, such as Locke or Rousseau, "who have had recourse to a promise or original contract as the source of our allegiance to government." They intend to establish a principle which is "perfectly just and reasonable." It is their *reasoning* which is "fallacious and sophistical." In the first place, the "natural law" concerning the performance of promises or the keeping of covenants, even when interpreted in empirical terms, is only one among many, not prior to the rest. The keeping of covenants is merely one part of the system of "artificial" virtues subsumed under the principles of justice. It is no more fundamental than any other. Moreover, government is *equally* as necessary to the execution of promises as it is to the observance of other necessary conditions of civil society. Actually, the basis of our obligation to "magistrates" must be wider and deeper than our obligation to any *single* rule of justice. It is not the fact that we have given our word — even granted that we have done so — which alone morally binds us to the state; rather, our obligation is derived from the total fabric of ordered social relationships which government ensures.

Secondly, the obligation to comply with the will of government is not inferior to or dependent on the obligation to accept any of the rules of civil society. Both "natural justice" *and* positive law are artificial and conventional. Once we grasp this point, and recall that the principal advantage of laws of *any* sort derives from the order and stability that comes from their general observance, we see that the moral obligation to the one is on the same footing as the obligation to the other. "How fruitless" is it, therefore, to try "to resolve the one into the other and seek in the laws of nature a stronger foundation for our political duties than interest and human conventions, while these laws are built on the very same foundations."

Hume has other arguments to muster against the contract theory of political obligation, of which only one need detain us further here. A contract derives its own justification from the *advantages* which accrue from its observance. But men often bind themselves by promises to the performance of acts which it would have been to their interest to perform quite *independently* of those promises. The advantage of government is such that, independently of any contract, it is usually to our common interest to obey it. If this is so, we may conclude that the *moral* basis of political obligation lies in its all-pervasive utility in human life and not in some fictitious promise which, even in democratic societies, is neither asked nor given.

The question of revolution is a difficult one for any political philosophy. Hume's doctrine is at least consistent. On the contract theory, the only justifiable basis of revolution is the violation of the contract by the government. But aside from the extreme difficulties in which Locke and others found themselves concerning the question as to who is to *decide* when a violation of the terms of the contract has been perpetrated, they were logically bound to regard any government as right and proper so long as the letter of the agreement was observed, no matter how oppressive or inconvenient its rule might be. Hume, on the other hand, regards the criterion of justifiable revolution *solely* as one of common interest. Where the interests which government should serve no longer are served, the obligation of allegiance ceases, contract or no contract; and "whenever the evil magistrate carries his oppression so far as to render his authority perfectly intolerable, we are no longer bound to submit to it. The cause ceases; the effect must cease also."

It is of interest to observe in this connection Hume's views on the subject of passive obedience, which many writers, including Luther, have held to be a moral and even religious obligation even when the ruler is tyrannical. No morally enlightened mind, Hume says, has had anything but respect for "those who took up arms against Dionysius, or Nero, or Philip the Second . . . and nothing but the most violent perversion of common sense can ever lead us to condemn them." In such instances, he maintains, to argue for passive obedience is a patent "absurdity."

But Hume is very far from urging revolution against every petty abuse of authority. He is quite clear that the justification both of allegiance and revolution lies in utility; but he also believes that it is in fact rarely the case that any sufficiently beneficial outcome results from revolution. As he grew older, moreover, his conviction on this score tended to increase. The dissolution of government, he maintains, is one of the most terrible things that can happen to men, and it ought, therefore, to be contemplated only in dire extremity.

A related question, which Hume considers at length in the *Treatise*, concerns the proper *object* of our political allegiance. Granted that government is a necessity, and our obligations to it very great, still it may be asked, *who* has the right to rule? What constitutes a rightful title to governmental authority? Again, Hume discounts the contract theory, although he admits that of all systems of government, government by consent is the best. But it is not the only basis. Here, again, Hume resembles Burke, who also rejects the contract theory and the doctrine of natural rights. Like Hume, Burke contends that "government is a contrivance of human wisdom to provide for human wants." But the means to the satisfaction of human wants is not something to be determined *a priori*. Nor is a viable constitution the product of abstract speculation concerning "rights." It is the cumulative expression of the wisdom of a people. It may be modified, but modified gradually and in a spirit of "reverence" — a favorite word with Burke — and according to necessity rather than "speculative right." Hume is less rhetorical than Burke, and less given to the latter's affected blandishments, when he speaks of the "classes." But he shares Burke's belief that a great part of the secret of domestic tranquility, whose greatest enemy is "faction," lies in the immemorial habits of respect for government and its laws, which come only with a "legitimate" ruler. Legitimacy is not a matter of consent, for the latter is equally present and absent, whether the ruler be legitimate or a usurper. It is, primarily, a matter of tradition and custom. There is no single criterion: original contract, long possession, present possession, succession, and continuously operating positive laws, all contribute to the title of sovereignty. If a government has remained in power for a considerable period of time, and has established itself as the unquestioned authority, so that it governs without having constantly to invoke the active exercise of force, it may be presumed, on the whole, to be governing "rightfully." Like Burke, Hume tends to believe that the fact that a people accepts without protest an existing authority is evidence that the rule of the latter is not unduly oppressive. It may be added that Hume lived before the era of concentration camps and goon squads. In any case, although in *general* it is true that government is "a mere human invention for mutual advantage and security . . . it is certainly impossible . . . to establish any particular rules by which we may know when resistance is lawful."

Some readers may find this aspect of Hume's political philosophy less attractive than the thoroughgoing naturalism and humanism of his leading principles. Yet he remains singularly free from any of the tendencies toward totalitarianism and statism which may be discerned in such of his contemporaries as Rousseau or even Burke.

One final consideration requires mention if we are to grasp the philosophical and historical importance of Hume's social doctrines. From his analysis there emerges a new conception of the relations between rights and government and between rights and society. The followers of Locke had emphasized, in the theory of natural rights, that just government must be founded on rights which are antecedent to government or even society itself. It is, according to them, the function of society and government to protect these rights, and the jurisdictional *limits* of government are determined by this alone. Whatever the merits of this doctrine, it is decided in advance what the purpose and limits of government should be. Hume's political philosophy has none of this rigidity. For him there are no inherent "natural" rights or obligations. They are "artificial" in the sense that they presuppose a system of rules which is the product of society rather than individual will. Let there be no mistake: the *justification* of such rules, or society itself, for that matter, lies in the interests which are thereby served. But individual interest alone does not create a right; nor does the pristine nature of man alone determine his obligations. Rights are opportunities which are functions partly of individual interest and partly of the occasions which society can afford or will permit; similarly, obligations are functions partly of our interests and partly of the conditions which society imposes as the price of their satisfaction.

Both rights and duties, then, remain in effect only so long as there is a stable social framework in which they can operate. This does not mean that one society is as "good" as another, or that we are thereby committed to moral relativism. Hume's criteria of good and evil, of vice and virtue, always remain the same. It means that a man's valid *claims* exist only in relation to a system of social rules and positive laws which alone can determine what a man may "unalterably enjoy."

As one of his critics has said, "the enquiring spirit of Hume never reaches an end." And this is as it should be. Whatever his shortcomings, and they are many, few philosophers have been less inclined to confuse what is with what ought to be; and none has understood more thoroughly than he that we cannot know what ought to be until we know what is, however disagreeable. His concern is not to edify but to inquire, not to exhort but to consider. This is a spirit rarely exemplified in moral philosophy.

HENRY DAVID AIKEN

HARVARD UNIVERSITY

SELECTED BIBLIOGRAPHY

A. Hume's Works and Letters

A Treatise of Human Nature (1739).
Essays, Moral and Political (vol. I: 1741; vol. II: 1742).
An Enquiry Concerning Human Understanding (1748).
   (First published as *Philosophical Essays Concerning Human Understanding*.) Second edition with additions and corrections, 1750.
An Enquiry Concerning the Principles of Morals (1751).
Political Discourses (1752).
History of England (1754–62).
Four Dissertations (1757):
   (1) Natural History of Religion
   (2) Of the Passions
   (3) Of Tragedy
   (4) Of the Standard of Taste
Dialogues Concerning Natural Religion (1779).
The Letters of David Hume, edited by J. T. Greig. Oxford, 1932.

B. Works on Hume[1]

Broad, C. D., *Five Types of Ethical Theory*. London, 1930. (Chapter 4 is on Hume.)

Burton, J. H., *Life and Correspondence of David Hume*. 2 Volumes. Edinburgh, 1846.

Hedenius, I., *Studies in Hume's Ethics*. Upsala and Stockholm, 1935.

Hendel, C. W., *Studies in the Philosophy of David Hume*. Princeton, 1925.

Huxley, T. H., *Hume*. London, 1879.

Jessup, T. E., *Bibliography of David Hume and of Scottish Philosophy*. London, 1938.

Kuypers, M. S., *Studies in the Eighteenth Century Background of Hume's Empiricism*. Minneapolis, 1930.

Kydd, R. M., *Reason and Conduct in Hume's Treatise*. Oxford, 1946.

Laing, B. M., *David Hume*. London, 1932.

Laird, J., *Hume's Philosophy of Human Nature*. London, 1932.

Morris, C. R., *Locke, Berkeley, Hume*. Oxford, 1931.

Shearer, E. A., *Hume's Place in Ethics*. Bryn Mawr, 1915.

Smith, N. K., *The Philosophy of David Hume*. New York, 1941.

Stephen, L., *History of English Thought in the Eighteenth Century*. London, 1876.

[1] Only works dealing, at least in part, with Hume's Moral Philosophy are listed.

NOTE ON THE TEXT

Hume's moral and social philosophy is embodied in his *Treatise of Human Nature*, Book III: "Of Morals," and the *Enquiry Concerning the Principles of Morals*. Both texts, which are reprinted entire, have been complemented by relevant sections of Book II ("Of the Passions") of the *Treatise* and essays selected from the *Essays, Moral and Political* (edition 1777). Their position in the complete edition has been stated in a footnote to each section or essay. With the exception of Section II of Book II of the *Treatise*, where the opening paragraph has been omitted, all complementary material is unabridged. Spelling and punctuation have been revised in accordance with present-day usage. Brackets indicate notes contributed by the editor.

I

A TREATISE OF HUMAN NATURE

*Being an Attempt to Introduce the Experimental
Method of Reasoning into Moral Subjects*

BOOK III

OF MORALS

PRECEDED BY SELECTIONS FROM

BOOK II: OF THE PASSIONS

BOOK II

OF THE PASSIONS

SECTION I

DIVISION OF THE SUBJECT[1]

As ALL the perceptions of the mind may be divided into *impressions* and *ideas*, so the impressions admit of another division into *original* and *secondary*. This division of the impressions is the same with that which I formerly made use of when I distinguished them into impressions of *sensation* and *reflection*.[2] Original impressions, or impressions of sensation, are such as, without any antecedent perception, arise in the soul, from the constitution of the body, from the animal spirits, or from the application of objects to the external organs. Secondary or reflective impressions are such as proceed from some of these original ones, either immediately or by the interposition of its idea. Of the first kind are all the impressions of the senses and all bodily pains and pleasures; of the second are the passions and other emotions resembling them.

It is certain that the mind in its perceptions must begin somewhere; and that since the impressions precede their correspondent ideas there must be some impressions which, without any introduction, make their appearance in the soul. As these depend upon natural and physical causes, the examination of them would lead me too far from my present subject, into the sciences of anatomy and natural philosophy. For this reason I shall here confine myself to those other impressions, which I have called secondary and reflective, as arising either from the original impressions or from their ideas. Bodily pains and pleasures are the source of many passions, both when felt and considered by the mind; but arise originally in the soul, or in the body,

[1] [Book II. Part I. Sect. 1.]
[2] Book I. Part I. Sect. 2.

3

whichever you please to call it, without any preceding thought or perception. A fit of the gout produces a long train of passions, as grief, hope, fear; but is not derived immediately from any affection or idea.

The reflective impressions may be divided into two kinds, viz., the *calm* and the *violent*. Of the first kind is the sense of beauty and deformity in action, composition, and external objects. Of the second are the passions of love and hatred, grief and joy, pride and humility. This division is far from being exact. The raptures of poetry and music frequently rise to the greatest height; while those other impressions, properly called *passions*, may decay into so soft an emotion as to become in a manner imperceptible. But as in general the passions are more violent than the emotions arising from beauty and deformity, these impressions have been commonly distinguished from each other. The subject of the human mind being so copious and various, I shall here take advantage of this vulgar and specious division, that I may proceed with the greater order; and having said all I thought necessary concerning our ideas, shall now explain those violent emotions or passions, their nature, origin, causes, and effects.

When we take a survey of the passions, there occurs a division of them into *direct* and *indirect*. By direct passions I understand such as arise immediately from good or evil, from pain or pleasure. By indirect, such as proceed from the same principles, but by the conjunction of other qualities. This distinction I cannot at present justify or explain any further. I can only observe in general that under the indirect passions I comprehend pride, humility, ambition, vanity, love, hatred, envy, pity, malice, generosity, with their dependents. And under the direct passions, desire, aversion, grief, joy, hope, fear, despair, and security. I shall begin with the former.

SECTION II

OF THE LOVE OF FAME[1]

.   .   .   .

No QUALITY of human nature is more remarkable, both in itself and in its consequences, than that propensity we have to sympathize

[1] [Book II. Part I. Sect. 11]

with others, and to receive by communication their inclinations and sentiments, however different from, or even contrary to, our own. This is not only conspicuous in children, who implicitly embrace every opinion proposed to them, but also in men of the greatest judgment and understanding, who find it very difficult to follow their own reason or inclination in opposition to that of their friends and daily companions. To this principle we ought to ascribe the great uniformity we may observe in the humours and turn of thinking of those of the same nation; and it is much more probable that this resemblance arises from sympathy than from any influence of the soil and climate which, though they continue invariably the same, are not able to preserve the character of a nation the same for a century together. A good-natured man finds himself in an instant of the same humour with his company; and even the proudest and most surly take a tincture from their countrymen and acquaintance. A cheerful countenance infuses a sensible complacency and serenity into my mind, as an angry or sorrowful one throws a sudden damp upon me. Hatred, resentment, esteem, love, courage, mirth, and melancholy; all these passions I feel more from communication than from my own natural temper and disposition. So remarkable a phenomenon merits our attention and must be traced up to its first principles.

When any affection is infused by sympathy, it is at first known only by its effects and by those external signs in the countenance and conversation which convey an idea of it. This idea is presently converted into an impression and acquires such a degree of force and vivacity as to become the very passion itself and produce an equal emotion as an original affection. However instantaneous this change of the idea into an impression may be, it proceeds from certain views and reflections which will not escape the strict scrutiny of a philosopher, though they may the person himself who makes them.

It is evident that the idea or rather impression of ourselves is always intimately present with us, and that our consciousness gives us so lively a conception of our own person that it is not possible to imagine that anything can in this particular go beyond it. Whatever object, therefore, is related to ourselves must be conceived with a like vivacity of conception, according to the foregoing principles; and though this relation should not be so strong as that of causation, it must still have a considerable influence. Resemblance and contiguity are relations not to be neglected, especially when by an inference from cause and effect and by the observation of external signs we are informed of the real existence of the object which is resembling or contiguous.

Now it is obvious that nature has preserved a great resemblance among all human creatures, and that we never remark any passion or principle in others of which, in some degree or other, we may not find a parallel in ourselves. The case is the same with the fabric of the mind as with that of the body. However the parts may differ in shape or size, their structure and composition are in general the same. There is a very remarkable resemblance which preserves itself amidst all their variety; and this resemblance must very much contribute to make us enter into the sentiments of others and embrace them with facility and pleasure. Accordingly we find that where, beside the general resemblance of our natures, there is any peculiar similarity in our manners, or character, or country, or language, it facilitates the sympathy. The stronger the relation is betwixt ourselves and any object, the more easily does the imagination make the transition, and convey to the related idea the vivacity of conception with which we always form the idea of our own person.

Nor is resemblance the only relation which has this effect, but receives new force from other relations that may accompany it. The sentiments of others have little influence when far removed from us and require the relation of contiguity to make them communicate themselves entirely. The relations of blood, being a species of causation, may sometimes contribute to the same effect, as also acquaintance which operates in the same manner with education and custom, as we shall see more fully afterwards.[2] All these relations, when united together, convey the impression or consciousness of our own person to the idea of the sentiments or passions of others, and makes us conceive them in the strongest and most lively manner.

It has been remarked in the beginning of this Treatise that all ideas are borrowed from impressions, and that these two kinds of perceptions differ only in the degrees of force and vivacity with which they strike upon the soul. The component parts of ideas and impressions are precisely alike. The manner and order of their appearance may be the same. The different degrees of their force and vivacity are, therefore, the only particulars that distinguish them; and as this difference

[2] Book II. Part II. Sect. 4.

may be removed, in some measure, by a relation betwixt the impressions and ideas, it is no wonder an idea of a sentiment or passion may by this means be so enlivened as to become the very sentiment or passion. The lively idea of any objects always approaches its impression; and it is certain we may feel sickness and pain from the mere force of imagination, and make a malady real by often thinking of it. But this is most remarkable in the opinions and affections; and it is there principally that a lively idea is converted into an impression. Our affections depend more upon ourselves and the internal operations of the mind than any other impressions; for which reason they arise more naturally from the imagination, and from every lively idea we form of them. This is the nature and cause of sympathy; and it is after this manner we enter so deep into the opinions and affections of others whenever we discover them.

What is principally remarkable in this whole affair is the strong confirmation these phenomena give to the foregoing system concerning the understanding, and consequently to the present one concerning the passions, since these are analogous to each other. It is indeed evident that when we sympathize with the passions and sentiments of others, these movements appear at first in *our* mind as mere ideas, and are conceived to belong to another person, as we conceive any other matter of fact. It is also evident that the ideas of the affections of others are converted into the very impressions they represent, and that the passions arise in conformity to the images we form of them. All this is an object of the plainest experience, and depends not on any hypothesis of philosophy. That science can only be admitted to explain the phenomena; though at the same time it must be confessed they are so clear of themselves that there is but little occasion to employ it. For besides the relation of cause and effect by which we are convinced of the reality of the passion with which we sympathize — besides this, I say, we must be assisted by the relations of resemblance and contiguity in order to feel the sympathy in its full perfection. And since these relations can entirely convert an idea into an impression, and convey the vivacity of the latter into the former so perfectly as to lose nothing of it in the transition, we may easily conceive how the relation of cause and effect alone may serve to strengthen and enliven an idea. In sympathy there is an evident conversion of an idea into an impression. This conversion arises from the relation of objects to ourselves. Ourself is always intimately present to us. Let us compare all these circumstances, and we shall find that sympathy is exactly correspondent to the operations of our understanding; and even contains something more surprising and extraordinary.

It is now time to turn our view from the general consideration of sympathy to its influence on pride and humility, when these passions arise from praise and blame, from reputation and infamy. We may observe that no person is ever praised by another for any quality which would not, if real, produce of itself a pride in the person possessed of it. The eulogiums either turn upon his power, or riches, or family, or virtue; all of which are subjects of vanity that we have already explained and accounted for. It is certain, then, that if a person considered himself in the same light in which he appears to his admirer, he would first receive a separate pleasure, and afterwards a pride or self-satisfaction, according to the hypothesis above explained. Now, nothing is more natural than for us to embrace the opinions of others in this particular, both from *sympathy*, which renders all their sentiments intimately present to us, and from *reasoning*, which makes us regard their judgment as a kind of argument for what they affirm. These two principles of authority and sympathy influence almost all our opinions, but must have a peculiar influence when we judge of our own worth and character. Such judgments are always attended with passion;[3] and nothing tends more to disturb our understanding, and precipitate us into any opinions, however unreasonable, than their connection with passion, which diffuses itself over the imagination and gives an additional force to every related idea. To which we may add that, being conscious of great partiality in our own favour, we are peculiarly pleased with anything that confirms the good opinion we have of ourselves, and are easily shocked with whatever opposes it.

All this appears very probable in theory; but in order to bestow a full certainty on this reasoning, we must examine the phenomena of the passions and see if they agree with it.

Among these phenomena we may esteem it a very favourable one to our present purpose that though fame in general be agreeable, yet we receive a much greater satisfaction from the approbation of those whom we ourselves esteem and approve of than of those whom we hate and despise. In like manner we are principally mortified with the

[3] Book I. Part III. Sect. 10.

contempt of persons upon whose judgment we set some value, and are, in a great measure, indifferent about the opinions of the rest of mankind. But if the mind received from any original instinct a desire of fame and aversion to infamy, fame and infamy would influence us without distinction; and every opinion, according as it were favourable or unfavourable, would equally excite that desire or aversion. The judgment of a fool is the judgment of another person, as well as that of a wise man, and is only inferior in its influence on our own judgment.

We are not only better pleased with the approbation of a wise man than with that of a fool, but receive an additional satisfaction from the former when it is obtained after a long and intimate acquaintance. This is accounted for after the same manner.

The praises of others never give us much pleasure, unless they concur with our own opinion and extol us for those qualities in which we chiefly excel. A mere soldier little values the character of eloquence; a gownman, of courage; a bishop, of humour; or a merchant, of learning. Whatever esteem a man may have for any quality, abstractedly considered, when he is conscious he is not possessed of it, the opinions of the whole world will give him little pleasure in that particular, and that because they never will be able to draw his own opinion after them.

Nothing is more usual than for men of good families, but narrow circumstances, to leave their friends and country, and rather seek their livelihood by mean and mechanical employments among strangers than among those who are acquainted with their birth and education. We shall be unknown, say they, where we go. Nobody will suspect from what family we are sprung. We shall be removed from all our friends and acquaintance, and our poverty and meanness will by that means sit more easy upon us. In examining these sentiments, I find they afford many very convincing arguments for my present purpose.

First, we may infer from them that the uneasiness of being contemned depends on sympathy, and that sympathy depends on the relation of objects to ourselves, since we are most uneasy under the contempt of persons who are both related to us by blood and contiguous in place. Hence we seek to diminish this sympathy and uneasiness by separating these relations, and placing ourselves in a contiguity to strangers and at a distance from relations.

Secondly, we may conclude that relations are requisite to sympathy, not absolutely considered as relations, but by their influence in converting our ideas of the sentiments of others into the very sentiments by means of the association betwixt the idea of their persons and that of our own. For here the relations of kindred and contiguity both subsist, but not being united in the same persons, they contribute in a less degree to the sympathy.

Thirdly, this very circumstance of the diminution of sympathy by the separation of relations is worthy of our attention. Suppose I am placed in a poor condition among strangers, and consequently am but lightly treated; I yet find myself easier in that situation than when I was every day exposed to the contempt of my kindred and countrymen. Here I feel a double contempt; from my relations, but they are absent; from those about me, but they are strangers. This double contempt is likewise strengthened by the two relations of kindred and contiguity. But as the persons are not the same who are connected with me by those two relations, this difference of ideas separates the impressions arising from the contempt, and keeps them from running into each other. The contempt of my neighbours has a certain influence as has also that of my kindred; but these influences are distinct and never unite as when the contempt proceeds from persons who are at once both my neighbours and kindred. This phenomenon is analogous to the system of pride and humility above explained, which may seem so extraordinary to vulgar apprehensions.

Fourthly, a person in these circumstances naturally conceals his birth from those among whom he lives, and is very uneasy if any one suspects him to be of a family much superior to his present fortune and way of living. Everything in this world is judged of by comparison. What is an immense fortune for a private gentleman is beggary for a prince. A peasant would think himself happy in what cannot afford necessaries for a gentleman. When a man has either been accustomed to a more splendid way of living, or thinks himself entitled to it by his birth and quality, everything below is disagreeable and even shameful; and it is with the greatest industry he conceals his pretensions to a better fortune. Here he himself knows his misfortunes; but as those with whom he lives are ignorant of them, he has the disagreeable reflection and comparison suggested only by his own thoughts, and never receives it by a sympathy with others; which must contribute very much to his ease and satisfaction.

If there be any objections to this hypothesis *that the pleasure which we receive from praise arises from a communication of sentiments,* we shall find, upon examination, that these objections, when taken in a proper light, will serve to confirm it. Popular fame may be agreeable even to a man who despises the vulgar; but it is because their multitude gives them additional weight and authority. Plagiaries are delighted with praises, which they are conscious they do not deserve; but this is a kind of castle-building where the imagination amuses itself with its own fictions, and tries to render them firm and stable by a sympathy with the sentiments of others. Proud men are most shocked with contempt, though they do not most readily assent to it; but it is because of the opposition betwixt the passion which is natural to them and that received by sympathy. A violent lover, in like manner, is very much displeased when you blame and condemn his love; though it is evident your opposition can have no influence but by the hold it takes of himself, and by his sympathy with you. If he despises you, or perceives you are in jest, whatever you say has no effect upon him.

SECTION III

OF LIBERTY AND NECESSITY[1]

WE COME now to explain the *direct* passions or the impressions which arise immediately from good or evil, from pain or pleasure. Of this kind are *desire and aversion, grief and joy, hope and fear.*

Of all the immediate effects of pain and pleasure there is none more remarkable than the *will;* and though, properly speaking, it be not comprehended among the passions, yet, as the full understanding of its nature and properties is necessary to the explanation of them, we shall here make it the subject of our inquiry. I desire it may be observed that by the *will* I mean nothing but *the internal impression we feel and are conscious of, when we knowingly give rise to any new motion of our body, or new perception of our mind.* This impression, like the preceding ones of pride and humility, love and hatred, it is impossible to define, and needless to describe any further; for which

[1] [Book II. Part III. Sect. 1]

reason we shall cut off all those definitions and distinctions with which philosophers are wont to perplex rather than clear up this question; and entering at first upon the subject, shall examine that long-disputed question concerning *liberty and necessity*, which occurs so naturally in treating of the will.

It is universally acknowledged that the operations of external bodies are necessary; and that in the communication of their motion, in their attraction and mutual cohesion, there are not the least traces of indifference or liberty. Every object is determined by an absolute fate to a certain degree and direction of its motion, and can no more depart from that precise line in which it moves than it can convert itself into an angel, or spirit, or any superior substance. The actions, therefore, of matter are to be regarded as instances of necessary actions; and whatever is in this respect on the same footing with matter must be acknowledged to be necessary. That we may know whether this be the case with the actions of the mind, we shall begin with examining matter, and considering on what the idea of a necessity in its operations are founded, and why we conclude one body or action to be the infallible cause of another.

It has been observed already that in no single instance the ultimate connection of any objects is discoverable either by our senses or reason, and that we can never penetrate so far into the essence and construction of bodies as to perceive the principle on which their mutual influence depends. It is their constant union alone with which we are acquainted; and it is from the constant union the necessity arises. If objects had not an uniform and regular conjunction with each other, we should never arrive at any idea of cause and effect; and even after all, the necessity which enters into that idea is nothing but a determination of the mind to pass from one object to its usual attendant, and infer the existence of one from that of the other. Here then are two particulars which we are to consider as essential to necessity, viz., the constant *union* and the *inference* of the mind; and wherever we discover these, we must acknowledge a necessity. As the actions of matter have no necessity but what is derived from these circumstances, and it is not by any insight into the essence of bodies we discover their connection, the absence of this insight, while the union and inference remain, will never, in any case, remove the necessity. It is the observation of the union which pro-

OF LIBERTY AND NECESSITY

duces the inference; for which reason it might be thought sufficient, if we prove a constant union in the actions of the mind in order to establish the inference along with the necessity of these actions. But that I may bestow a greater force on my reasoning, I shall examine these particulars apart and shall first prove from experience that our actions have a constant union with our motives, tempers, and circumstances, before I consider the inferences we draw from it.

To this end a very slight and general view of the common course of human affairs will be sufficient. There is no light in which we can take them that does not confirm this principle. Whether we consider mankind according to the difference of sexes, ages, governments, conditions, or methods of education, the same uniformity and regular operation of natural principles are discernible. Like causes still produce like effects, in the same manner as in the mutual action of the elements and powers of nature.

There are different trees which regularly produce fruit whose relish is different from each other; and this regularity will be admitted as an instance of necessity and causes in external bodies. But are the products of Guienne and of Champagne more regularly different than the sentiments, actions, and passions of the two sexes of which the one are distinguished by their force and maturity, the other by their delicacy and softness?

Are the changes of our body from infancy to old age more regular and certain than those of our mind and conduct? And would a man be more ridiculous who would expect that an infant of four years old will raise a weight of three hundred pounds than one who, from a person of the same age, would look for a philosophical reasoning or a prudent and well concerted action?

We must certainly allow that the cohesion of the parts of matter arises from natural and necessary principles, whatever difficulty we may find in explaining them: and for a like reason we must allow that human society is founded on like principles; and our reason in the latter case is better than even that in the former, because we not only observe that men *always* seek society, but can also explain the principles on which this universal propensity is founded. For is it more certain that two flat pieces of marble will unite together than two young savages of different sexes will copulate? Do the children arise from this copulation more uniformly than does the parents' care for their safety and preservation? And after they have arrived at years of discretion by the care of their parents, are the inconveniences attending their separation more certain than their foresight of these inconveniences, and their care of avoiding them by a close union and confederacy?

The skin, pores, muscles, and nerves of a day-labourer are different from those of a man of quality; so are his sentiments, actions, and manners. The different stations of life influence the whole fabric, external and internal; and these different stations arise necessarily, because uniformly, from the necessary and uniform principles of human nature. Men cannot live without society and cannot be associated without government. Government makes a distinction of property and establishes the different ranks of men. This produces industry, traffic, manufactures, law-suits, war, leagues, alliances, voyages, travels, cities, fleets, ports, and all those other actions and objects which cause such a diversity, and at the same time maintain such an uniformity in human life.

Should a traveler, returning from a far country, tell us that he had seen a climate in the fiftieth degree of northern latitude where all the fruits ripen and come to perfection in the winter and decay in the summer, after the same manner as in England they are produced and decay in the contrary seasons, he would find few so credulous as to believe him. I am apt to think a traveller would meet with as little credit who should inform us of people exactly of the same character with those in Plato's *Republic* on the one hand, or those in Hobbes's *Leviathan* on the other. There is a general course of nature in human actions as well as in the operations of the sun and the climate. There are also characters peculiar to different nations and particular persons as well as common to mankind. The knowledge of these characters is founded on the observation of an uniformity in the actions that flow from them; and this uniformity forms the very essence of necessity.

I can imagine only one way of eluding this argument, which is by denying that uniformity of human actions on which it is founded. As long as actions have a constant union and connection with the situation and temper of the agent, however we may in words refuse to acknowledge the necessity, we really allow the thing. Now, some may perhaps find a pretext to deny this regular union and connection. For what is more capricious than human actions? What more inconstant than the desires of man? And what creature departs more widely, not only from right reason, but from his own character and disposition? An hour, a moment is sufficient to make him change from one extreme to another and overturn what cost the greatest pain and labour to establish. Necessity is regular and certain. Human conduct is irregular and uncertain. The one therefore proceeds not from the other.

To this I reply that in judging of the actions of men we must proceed upon the same maxims as when we reason concerning external objects. When any phenomena are constantly and invariably conjoined together, they acquire such a connection in the imagination that it passes from one to the other without any doubt or hesitation. But below this there are many inferior degrees of evidence and probability; nor does one single contrariety of experiment entirely destroy all our reasoning. The mind balances the contrary experiments and, deducting the inferior from the superior, proceeds with that degree of assurance or evidence which remains. Even when these contrary experiments are entirely equal, we remove not the notion of causes and necessity; but supposing that the usual contrariety proceeds from the operation of contrary and concealed causes, we conclude that the chance or indifference lies only in our judgment on account of our imperfect knowledge, not in the things themselves, which are in every case equally necessary, though, to appearance, not equally constant or certain. No union can be more constant and certain than that of some actions with some motives and characters; and if, in other cases, the union is uncertain, it is no more than what happens in the operations of body; nor can we conclude anything from the one irregularity which will not follow equally from the other.

It is commonly allowed that madmen have no liberty. But were we to judge by their actions, these have less regularity and constancy than the actions of wise men, and consequently are further removed from necessity. Our way of thinking in this particular is, therefore, absolutely inconsistent; but is a natural consequence of these confused ideas and undefined terms which we so commonly make use of in our reasonings, especially on the present subject.

We must now show that, as the *union* betwixt motives and actions has the same constancy as that in any natural operations, so its influence on the understanding is also the same in *determining* us to infer the existence of one from that of another. If this shall appear, there is no known circumstance that enters into the connection and production of the actions of matter that is not to be found in all the operations of the mind; consequently we cannot without a manifest absurdity attribute necessity to the one, and refuse it to the other.

There is no philosopher whose judgment is so riveted to this fantastical system of liberty as not to acknowledge the force of *moral evidence*, and both in speculation and practice proceed upon it as upon a reasonable foundation. Now, moral evidence is nothing but a conclusion concerning the actions of men, derived from the consideration of their motives, temper, and situation. Thus, when we see certain characters or figures described upon paper, we infer that the person who produced them would affirm such facts: the death of Cæsar, the success of Augustus, the cruelty of Nero; and remembering many other concurrent testimonies we conclude that those facts were once really existent, and that so many men, without any interest, would never conspire to deceive us; especially since they must, in the attempt, expose themselves to the derision of all their contemporaries when these facts were asserted to be recently and universally known. The same kind of reasoning runs through politics, war, commerce, economy, and indeed mixes itself so entirely in human life that it is impossible to act or subsist a moment without having recourse to it. A prince who imposes a tax upon his subjects expects their compliance. A general who conducts an army makes account of a certain degree of courage. A merchant looks for fidelity and skill in his factor or supercargo. A man who gives orders for his dinner doubts not of the obedience of his servants. In short, as nothing more nearly interests us than our own actions and those of others, the greatest part of our reasonings is employed in judgments concerning them. Now I assert that whoever reasons after this manner does *ipso facto* believe the actions of the will to arise from necessity, and that he knows not what he means when he denies it.

All those objects of which we call the one *cause* and the other *effect*, considered in themselves, are as distinct and separate from each other as any two things in nature; nor can we ever, by the most accurate survey of them, infer the existence of the one from that of the other. It is only from experience and the observation of their constant union that we are able to form this inference; and even after all, the inference is nothing but the effects of custom on the imagination. We must not here be content with saying that the idea of cause and effect arises from objects constantly united; but must affirm that it is the very same with the idea of these objects, and that the *necessary connection* is not discovered by a conclusion of the understanding, but is merely a perception of the mind. Wherever, therefore, we observe the same union, and wherever the union operates in the same manner upon the belief and opinion, we have the idea of cause and necessity, though perhaps we may avoid those expressions. Motion in one body, in all past instances that have fallen under our observation, is followed upon impulse by motion in another. It is impossible for the mind to penetrate further. From this constant union it *forms* the idea of cause and effect, and by its influence *feels* the necessity. As there is the same constancy and the same influence in what we call moral evidence, I ask no more. What remains can only be a dispute of words.

And indeed, when we consider how aptly *natural* and *moral* evidence cement together and form only one chain of argument betwixt them, we shall make no scruple to allow that they are of the same nature and derived from the same principles. A prisoner who has neither money nor interest discovers the impossibility of his escape as well from the obstinacy of the gaoler as from the walls and bars with which he is surrounded; and in all attempts for his freedom chooses rather to work upon the stone and iron of the one than upon the inflexible nature of the other. The same prisoner, when conducted to the scaffold, foresees his death as certainly from the constancy and fidelity of his guards as from the operation of the axe or wheel. His mind runs along a certain train of ideas: the refusal of the soldiers to consent to his escape; the action of the executioner; the separation of the head and body, bleeding, convulsive motions, and death. Here is a connected chain of natural causes and voluntary actions; but the mind feels no difference betwixt them in passing from one link to another; nor is less certain of the future event than if it were connected with the present impressions of the memory and senses by a train of causes cemented together by what we are pleased to call a *physical necessity*. The same experienced union has the same effect on the mind, whether the united objects be motives, volitions, and actions, or figure and motion. We may change the names of things, but their nature and their operation on the understanding never change.

I dare be positive no one will ever endeavour to refute these reasonings otherwise than by altering my definitions, and assigning a different meaning to the terms of *cause, and effect, and necessity, and liberty, and chance.* According to my definitions, necessity makes an essential part of causation; and consequently liberty, by removing necessity, removes all causes and is the very same thing with chance. As chance is commonly thought to imply a contradiction and is at least directly contrary to experience, there are always the same arguments against liberty or free-will. If any one alters the definitions, I cannot pretend to argue with him till I know the meaning he assigns to these terms.

SECTION IV

THE SAME SUBJECT CONTINUED[1]

I BELIEVE we may assign the three following reasons for the prevalence of the doctrine of liberty, however absurd it may be in one sense, and unintelligible in any other. First, after we have performed any action, though we confess we were influenced by particular views and motives, it is difficult for us to persuade ourselves we were governed by necessity, and that it was utterly impossible for us to have acted otherwise, the idea of necessity seeming to imply something of force, and violence, and constraint, of which we are not sensible. Few are capable of distinguishing betwixt the liberty of *spontaneity*, as it is called in the schools, and the liberty of *indifference;* betwixt that which is opposed to violence, and that which means a negation of necessity and causes. The first is even the most common sense of the word; and as it is only that species of liberty which it concerns us to preserve, our thoughts have been principally turned towards it, and have almost universally confounded it with the other.

Secondly, there is a *false sensation* or *experience* even of the liberty of indifference, which is regarded as an argument for its real existence. The necessity of any action, whether of matter or of mind, is not properly a quality in the agent, but in any thinking or intelligent being who may consider the action, and consists in the determination of

[1] [Book II. Part III. Sect. 2]

his thought to infer its existence from some preceding objects; as liberty or chance, on the other hand, is nothing but the want of that determination and a certain looseness which we feel in passing or not passing from the idea of one to that of the other. Now, we may observe that, though in reflecting on human actions we seldom feel such a looseness or indifference, yet it very commonly happens that, in performing the actions themselves, we are sensible of something like it; and as all related or resembling objects are readily taken for each other, this has been employed as a demonstrative, or even an intuitive proof of human liberty. We feel that our actions are subject to our will on most occasions, and imagine we feel that the will itself is subject to nothing; because when, by a denial of it, we are provoked to try, we feel that it moves easily every way and produces an image of itself even on that side on which it did not settle. This image or faint motion, we persuade ourselves, could have been completed into the thing itself; because, should that be denied, we find, upon a second trial, that it can. But these efforts are all in vain; and whatever capricious and irregular actions we may perform, as the desire of showing our liberty is the sole motive of our actions, we can never free ourselves from the bonds of necessity. We may imagine we feel a liberty within ourselves, but a spectator can commonly infer our actions from our motives and character; and even where he cannot, he concludes in general that he might, were he perfectly acquainted with every circumstance of our situation and temper, and the most secret springs of our complexion and disposition. Now, this is the very essence of necessity, according to the foregoing doctrine.

A third reason why the doctrine of liberty has generally been better received in the world than its antagonist, proceeds from *religion*, which has been very unnecessarily interested in this question. There is no method of reasoning more common, and yet none more blamable, than in philosophical debates to endeavour to refute any hypothesis by a pretext of its dangerous consequences to religion and morality. When any opinion leads us into absurdities, it is certainly false; but it is not certain an opinion is false because it is of dangerous consequence. Such topics, therefore, ought entirely to be forborne, as serving nothing to the discovery of truth, but only to make the person of an antagonist odious. This I observe in general, without pretending to draw any advantage from it. I submit myself frankly to an examination of this kind, and dare venture to affirm that the doctrine of necessity, according to my explication of it, is not only innocent but even advantageous to religion and morality.

I define necessity two ways, conformable to the two definitions of *cause*, of which it makes an essential part. I place it either in the constant union and conjunction of like objects, or in the inference of the mind from the one to the other. Now, necessity, in both these senses, has universally, though tacitly, in the schools, in the pulpit, and in common life, been allowed to belong to the will of man; and no one has ever pretended to deny that we can draw inferences concerning human actions, and that those inferences are founded on the experienced union of like actions with like motives and circumstances. The only particular in which any one can differ from me is either that perhaps he will refuse to call this necessity — but as long as the meaning is understood, I hope the word can do no harm — or that he will maintain there is something else in the operations of matter. Now, whether it be so or not is of no consequence to religion, whatever it may be to natural philosophy. I may be mistaken in asserting that we have no idea of any other connection in the actions of body, and shall be glad to be further instructed on that head: but sure I am I ascribe nothing to the actions of the mind but what must readily be allowed of. Let no one, therefore, put an invidious construction on my words by saying simply that I assert the necessity of human actions and place them on the same footing with the operations of senseless matter. I do not ascribe to the will that unintelligible necessity which is supposed to lie in matter. But I ascribe to matter that intelligible quality, call it necessity or not, which the most rigorous orthodoxy does or must allow to belong to the will. I change, therefore, nothing in the received systems with regard to the will, but only with regard to material objects.

Nay, I shall go further and assert that this kind of necessity is so essential to religion and morality that without it there must ensue an absolute subversion of both, and that every other supposition is entirely destructive to all laws, both *divine* and *human*. It is indeed certain that as all human laws are founded on rewards and punishments, it is supposed as a fundamental principle that these motives have an influence on the mind and both produce the good and prevent the evil actions. We may give to this influence what name we please;

but as it is usually conjoined with the action, common sense requires it should be esteemed a cause, and be looked upon as an instance of that necessity which I would establish.

This reasoning is equally solid when applied to *divine* laws, so far as the Deity is considered as a legislator, and is supposed to inflict punishment and bestow rewards with a design to produce obedience. But I also maintain that even where he acts not in his magisterial capacity, but is regarded as the avenger of crimes merely on account of their odiousness and deformity, not only it is impossible without the necessary connection of cause and effect in human actions that punishments could be inflicted compatible with justice and moral equity; but also that it could ever enter into the thoughts of any reasonable being to inflict them. The constant and universal object of hatred or anger is a person or creature endowed with thought and consciousness; and when any criminal or injurious actions excite that passion, it is only by their relation to the person or connection with him. But according to the doctrine of liberty or chance, this connection is reduced to nothing, nor are men more accountable for those actions which are designed and premeditated than for such as are the most casual and accidental. Actions are, by their very nature, temporary and perishing; and where they proceed not from some cause in the characters and dispositions of the person who performed them, they infix not themselves upon him, and can neither redound to his honour, if good, nor infamy, if evil. The action itself may be blamable; it may be contrary to all the rules of morality and religion: but the person is not responsible for it; and as it proceeded from nothing in him that is durable or constant, and leaves nothing of that nature behind it, it is impossible he can, upon its account, become the object of punishment or vengeance. According to the hypothesis of liberty, therefore a man is as pure and untainted after having committed the most horrid crimes as at the first moment of his birth, nor is his character any way concerned in his actions, since they are derived from it, and the wickedness of the one can never be used as a proof of the depravity of the other. It is only upon the principles of necessity that a person acquires any merit or demerit from his actions, however the common opinion may incline to the contrary.

But so inconsistent are men with themselves that though they often assert that necessity utterly destroys all merit and demerit either towards mankind or superior powers, yet they continue still to reason upon these very principles of necessity in all their judgments concerning this matter. Men are not blamed for such evil actions as they perform ignorantly and casually, whatever may be their consequences. Why? but because the causes of these actions are only momentary and terminate in them alone. Men are less blamed for such evil actions as they perform hastily and unpremeditately than for such as proceed from thought and deliberation. For what reason? but because a hasty temper, though a constant cause in the mind, operates only by intervals and infects not the whole character. Again, repentance wipes off every crime, especially if attended with an evident reformation of life and manners. How is this to be accounted for? but by asserting that actions render a person criminal, merely as they are proofs of criminal passions or principles in the mind; and when, by any alteration of these principles, they cease to be just proofs, they likewise cease to be criminal. But according to the doctrine of *liberty* or *chance*, they never were just proofs, and consequently never were criminal.

Here then I turn to my adversary, and desire him to free his own system from these odious consequences before he charges them upon others. Or if he rather chooses that this question should be decided by fair arguments before philosophers than by declamations before the people, let him return to what I have advanced to prove, that liberty and chance are synonymous; and concerning the nature of moral evidence and the regularity of human actions. Upon a review of these reasonings, I cannot doubt of an entire victory; and, therefore, having proved that all actions of the will have particular causes, I proceed to explain what these causes are and how they operate.

SECTION V

OF THE INFLUENCING MOTIVES OF THE WILL[1]

NOTHING IS MORE usual in philosophy, and even in common life, than to talk of the combat of passion and reason, to give the preference to reason, and assert that men are only so far virtuous as they conform themselves to its dictates. Every rational creature, it is said, is obliged to regulate his actions by reason; and if any other motive or principle challenge the direction of his conduct, he ought to oppose it till it be entirely subdued or at least brought to a conformity with that superior principle. On this method of thinking the greatest part of moral philosophy, ancient and modern, seems to be founded; nor is there an ampler field as well for metaphysical arguments as popular declamations than this supposed pre-eminence of reason above passion. The eternity, invariableness, and divine origin of the former have been displayed to the best advantage; the blindness, inconstancy, and deceitfulness of the latter have been as strongly insisted on. In order to show the fallacy of all this philosophy, I shall endeavour to prove, *first*, that reason alone can never be a motive to any action of the will; and, *secondly*, that it can never oppose passion in the direction of the will.

The understanding exerts itself after two different ways, as it judges from demonstration or probability; as it regards the abstract relations of our ideas, or those relations of objects of which experience only gives us information. I believe it scarce will be asserted that the first species of reasoning alone is ever the cause of any action. As its proper province is the world of ideas, and as the will always places us in that of realities, demonstration and volition seem upon that account to be totally removed from each other. Mathematics, indeed, are useful in all mechanical operations, and arithmetic in almost every art and profession: but it is not of themselves they have any influence. Mechanics are the art of regulating the motions of bodies *to some designed end* or *purpose;* and the reason why we employ arithmetic in fixing the proportions of numbers is only that we may discover the proportions of their influence and operation. A merchant is desirous of knowing the sum total of his accounts with any person: why? but

[1] [Book II. Part III. Sect. 3]

that he may learn what sum will have the same *effects* in paying his debt, and going to market, as all the particular articles taken together. Abstract or demonstrative reasoning, therefore, never influences any of our actions, but only as it directs our judgment concerning causes and effects; which leads us to the second operation of the understanding.

It is obvious that when we have the prospect of pain or pleasure from any object, we feel a consequent emotion of aversion or propensity, and are carried to avoid or embrace what will give us this uneasiness or satisfaction. It is also obvious that this emotion rests not here, but, making us cast our view on every side, comprehends whatever objects are connected with its original one by the relation of cause and effect. Here then reasoning takes place to discover this relation; and according as our reasoning varies, our actions receive a subsequent variation. But it is evident in this case that the impulse arises not from reason, but is only directed by it. It is from the prospect of pain or pleasure that the aversion or propensity arises towards any object: and these emotions extend themselves to the causes and effects of that object, as they are pointed out to us by reason and experience. It can never in the least concern us to know that such objects are causes, and such others effects, if both the causes and effects be indifferent to us. Where the objects themselves do not affect us, their connection can never give them any influence; and it is plain that, as reason is nothing but the discovery of this connection, it cannot be by its means that the objects are able to affect us.

Since reason alone can never produce any action or give rise to volition, I infer that the same faculty is as incapable of preventing volition or of disputing the preference with any passion or emotion. This consequence is necessary. It is impossible reason could have the latter effect of preventing volition, but by giving an impulse in a contrary direction to our passions; and that impulse, had it operated alone, would have been ample to produce volition. Nothing can oppose or retard the impulse of passion but a contrary impulse; and if this contrary impulse ever arises from reason, that latter faculty must have an original influence on the will and must be able to cause as well as hinder any act of volition. But if reason has no original influence, it is impossible it can withstand any principle which has such an efficacy, or ever keep the mind in suspense a moment. Thus it appears that the principle which opposes our passion cannot be the same with reason, and is only called so in an improper sense. We speak not strictly and philosophically when we talk of the combat of passion and of reason. Reason is, and ought only to be, the slave of the passions, and can never pretend to any other office than to serve and obey them. As this opinion may appear somewhat extraordinary, it may not be improper to confirm it by some other considerations.

A passion is an original existence or, if you will, modification of existence, and contains not any representative quality which renders it a copy of any other existence or modification. When I am angry, I am actually possessed with the passion, and in that emotion have no more a reference to any other object than when I am thirsty, or sick, or more than five feet high. It is impossible, therefore, that this passion can be opposed by, or be contradictory to, truth and reason; since this contradiction consists in the disagreement of ideas, considered as copies, with those objects which they represent.

What may at first occur on this head is that as nothing can be contrary to truth or reason, except what has a reference to it, and as the judgments of our understanding only have this reference, it must follow that passions can be contrary to reason only so far as they are *accompanied* with some judgment or opinion. According to this principle, which is so obvious and natural, it is only in two senses that any affection can be called unreasonable. First, when a passion, such as hope or fear, grief or joy, despair or security, is founded on the supposition of the existence of objects which really do not exist. Secondly, when, in exerting any passion in action, we choose means sufficient for the designed end, and deceive ourselves in our judgment of causes and,effects. Where a passion is neither founded on false suppositions, nor chooses means insufficient for the end, the understanding can neither justify nor condemn it. It is not contrary to reason to prefer the destruction of the whole world to the scratching of my finger. It is not contrary to reason for me to choose my total ruin to prevent the least uneasiness of an Indian, or person wholly unknown to me. It is as little contrary to reason to prefer even my own acknowledged lesser good to my greater, and have a more ardent affection for the former than the latter. A trivial good may, from certain circumstances, produce a desire superior to what arises from the greatest and most valuable enjoyment; nor is there anything more extraordinary in this than in mechanics to see one pound weight raise up a hundred by the advantage of its situation. In short, a passion must be accompanied with some false judgment in order to its being unreasonable; and even then it is not the passion, properly speaking, which is unreasonable, but the judgment.

The consequences are evident. Since a passion can never, in any sense, be called unreasonable but when founded on a false supposition, or when it chooses means insufficient for the designed end, it is impossible that reason and passion can ever oppose each other, or dispute for the government of the will and actions. The moment we perceive the falsehood of any supposition or the insufficiency of any means, our passions yield to our reason without any opposition. I may desire any fruit as of an excellent relish; but whenever you convince me of my mistake, my longing ceases. I may will the performance of certain actions as means of obtaining any desired good; but as my willing of these actions is only secondary, and founded on the supposition that they are causes of the proposed effect; as soon as I discover the falsehood of that supposition, they must become indifferent to me.

It is natural for one that does not examine objects with a strict philosophic eye to imagine that those actions of the mind are entirely the same, which produce not a different sensation, and are not immediately distinguishable to the feeling and perception. Reason, for instance, exerts itself without producing any sensible emotions; and except in the more sublime disquisitions of philosophy, or in the frivolous subtilties of the schools, scarce ever conveys any pleasure or uneasiness. Hence it proceeds that every action of the mind which operates with the same calmness and tranquillity is confounded with reason by all those who judge of things from the first view and appearance. Now it is certain there are certain calm desires and tendencies which, though they be real passions, produce little emotion in the mind, and are more known by their effects than by the immediate feeling or sensation. These desires are of two kinds; either certain instincts originally implanted in our natures, such as benevolence and resentment, the love of life, and kindness to children; or the general appetite to good, and aversion to evil, considered merely as such. When any of these passions are calm, and cause no disorder in the soul, they are very readily taken for the determinations of reason, and are supposed to proceed from the same faculty with that which judges of truth and falsehood. Their nature and principles have been supposed the same, because their sensations are not evidently different.

Beside these calm passions, which often determine the will, there are certain violent emotions of the same kind which have likewise a great influence on that faculty. When I receive any injury from another, I often feel a violent passion of resentment which makes me desire his evil and punishment independent of all considerations of pleasure and advantage to myself. When I am immediately threatened with any grievous ill, my fears, apprehensions, and aversions rise to a great height, and produce a sensible emotion.

The common error of metaphysicians has lain in ascribing the direction of the will entirely to one of these principles, and supposing the other to have no influence. Men often act knowingly against their interest; for which reason the view of the greatest possible good does not always influence them. Men often counteract a violent passion in prosecution of their interests and designs; it is not, therefore, the present uneasiness alone which determines them. In general we may observe that both these principles operate on the will; and where they are contrary, that either of them prevails, according to the *general* character or *present* disposition of the person. What we call strength of mind implies the prevalence of the calm passions above the violent, though we may easily observe there is no man so constantly possessed of this virtue as never on any occasion to yield to the solicitations of passion and desire. From these variations of temper proceeds the great difficulty of deciding concerning the actions and resolutions of men, where there is any contrariety of motives and passions.

BOOK III
OF MORALS

PART I

OF VIRTUE AND VICE IN GENERAL

SECTION I

MORAL DISTINCTIONS NOT DERIVED FROM REASON

THERE IS an inconvenience which attends all abstruse reasoning, that it may silence without convincing an antagonist, and requires the same intense study to make us sensible of its force that was at first requisite for its invention. When we leave our closet and engage in the common affairs of life, its conclusions seem to vanish like the phantoms of the night on the appearance of the morning; and it is difficult for us to retain even that conviction which we had attained with difficulty. This is still more conspicuous in a long chain of reasoning, where we must preserve to the end the evidence of the first propositions, and where we often lose sight of all the most received maxims, either of philosophy or common life. I am not, however, without hopes that the present system of philosophy will acquire new force as it advances, and that our reasonings concerning *morals* will corroborate whatever has been said concerning the *understanding* and the *passions*. Morality is a subject that interests us above all others; we fancy the peace of society to be at stake in every decision concerning it; and it is evident that this concern must make our speculations appear more real and solid than where the subject is in a great measure indifferent to us. What affects us, we conclude, can never be a chimera; and, as our passion is engaged on the one side or the other, we naturally think that the question lies within human comprehension; which, in other cases of this nature, we are apt to entertain some doubt of. Without this advantage, I never should have ventured upon a third volume of such abstruse philosophy, in an age wherein the greatest part of men seem agreed to convert reading into an amusement, and to reject everything that requires any considerable degree of attention to be comprehended.

It has been observed that nothing is ever present to the mind but its perceptions; and that all the actions of seeing, hearing, judging, loving, hating, and thinking, fall under this denomination. The mind can never exert itself in any action which we may not comprehend under the term of *perception;* and consequently that term is no less applicable to those judgments by which we distinguish moral good and evil, than to every other operation of the mind. To approve of one character, to condemn another, are only so many different perceptions.

Now, as perceptions resolve themselves into two kinds, viz., *impressions* and *ideas*, this distinction gives rise to a question, with which we shall open up our present inquiry concerning morals, whether it is by means of our *ideas* or *impressions* we distinguish betwixt vice and virtue, and pronounce an action blamable or praiseworthy? This will immediately cut off all loose discourses and declamations, and reduce us to something precise and exact on the present subject.

Those who affirm that virtue is nothing but a conformity to reason; that there are eternal fitnesses and unfitnesses of things which are the same to every rational being that considers them; that the immutable measure of right and wrong impose an obligation, not only on human creatures, but also on the Deity himself: all these systems concur in the opinion that morality, like truth, is discerned merely by ideas, and by their juxtaposition and comparison. In order, therefore, to judge of these systems, we need only consider whether it be possible from reason alone to distinguish betwixt moral good and evil, or whether there must concur some other principles to enable us to make that distinction.

If morality had naturally no influence on human passions and actions, it were in vain to take such pains to inculcate it; and nothing would be more fruitless than that multitude of rules and precepts with which all moralists abound. Philosophy is commonly divided into *speculative* and *practical;* and as morality is always comprehended under the latter division, it is supposed to influence our passions and actions, and to go beyond the calm and indolent judgments of the understanding. And this is confirmed by common experience, which informs us that men are often governed by their duties, and are deterred from some actions by the opinion of injustice, and impelled to others by that of obligation.

Since morals, therefore, have an influence on the actions and affections, it follows that they cannot be derived from reason, and that because reason alone, as we have already proved, can never have any such influence. Morals excite passions, and produce or prevent actions. Reason of itself is utterly impotent in this particular. The rules of morality, therefore, are not conclusions of our reason.

No one, I believe, will deny the justness of this inference; nor is there any other means of evading it than by denying that principle on which it is founded. As long as it is allowed that reason has no influence on our passions and actions, it is in vain to pretend that morality is discovered only by a deduction of reason. An active principle can never be founded on an inactive; and if reason be inactive in itself, it must remain so in all its shapes and appearances, whether it exerts itself in natural or moral subjects, whether it considers the powers of external bodies or the actions of rational beings.

It would be tedious to repeat all the arguments by which I have proved[1] that reason is perfectly inert and can never either prevent or produce any action or affection. It will be easy to recollect what has been said upon that subject. I shall only recall on this occasion one of these arguments, which I shall endeavour to render still more conclusive and more applicable to the present subject.

Reason is the discovery of truth or falsehood. Truth or falsehood consists in an agreement or disagreement either to the *real* relations of ideas, or to *real* existence and matter of fact. Whatever, therefore, is not susceptible of this agreement or disagreement is incapable of being true or false, and can never be an object of our reason. Now, it is evident our passions, volitions, and actions, are not susceptible of any such agreement or disagreement; being original facts and realities, complete in themselves, and implying no reference to other passions, volitions, and actions. It is impossible, therefore, they can be pronounced either true or false and be either contrary or conformable to reason.

This argument is of double advantage to our present purpose. For it proves *directly* that actions do not derive their merit from a conformity to reason, nor their blame from a contrariety to it; and it proves the same truth more *indirectly*, by showing us that as reason can never immediately prevent or produce any action by contradicting

[1] Book II. Part III. Sect. 3.

or approving of it, it cannot be the source of moral good and evil, which are found to have that influence. Actions may be laudable or blamable, but they cannot be reasonable or unreasonable: laudable or blamable, therefore, are not the same with reasonable or unreasonable. The merit and demerit of actions frequently contradict, and sometimes control our natural propensities. But reason has no such influence. Moral distinctions, therefore, are not the offspring of reason. Reason is wholly inactive, and can never be the source of so active a principle as conscience, or a sense of morals.

But, perhaps, it may be said that though no will or action can be immediately contradictory to reason, yet we may find such a contradiction in some of the attendants of the actions, that is, in its causes or effects. The action may cause a judgment, or may be *obliquely* caused by one, when the judgment concurs with a passion; and by an abusive way of speaking, which philosophy will scarce allow of, the same contrariety may, upon that account, be ascribed to the action. How far this truth or falsehood may be the source of morals, it will now be proper to consider.

It has been observed that reason, in a strict and philosophical sense, can have an influence on our conduct only after two ways: either when it excites a passion by informing us of the existence of something which is a proper object of it; or when it discovers the connection of causes and effects so as to afford us means of exerting any passion. These are the only kinds of judgment which can accompany our actions, or can be said to produce them in any manner; and it must be allowed that these judgments may often be false and erroneous. A person may be affected with passion, by supposing a pain or pleasure to lie in an object which has no tendency to produce either of these sensations, or which produces the contrary to what is imagined. A person may also take false measures for the attaining of his end, and may retard by his foolish conduct instead of forwarding the execution of any object. These false judgments may be thought to affect the passions and actions, which are connected with them, and may be said to render them unreasonable, in a figurative and improper way of speaking. But though this be acknowledged, it is easy to observe that these errors are so far from being the source of all immorality that they are commonly very innocent, and draw no manner of guilt upon the person who is so unfortunate as to fall into them. They extend not beyond a mistake of *fact*, which moralists have not generally supposed criminal, as being perfectly involuntary. I am more to be lamented than blamed if I am mistaken with regard to the influence of objects in producing pain or pleasure, or if I know not the proper means of satisfying my desires. No one can ever regard such errors as a defect in my moral character. A fruit, for instance, that is really disagreeable appears to me at a distance, and, through mistake, I fancy it to be pleasant and delicious. Here is one error. I choose certain means of reaching this fruit which are not proper for my end. Here is a second error; nor is there any third one which can ever possibly enter into our reasonings concerning actions. I ask, therefore, if a man in this situation, and guilty of these two errors, is to be regarded as vicious and criminal, however unavoidable they might have been? Or if it be possible to imagine that such errors are the sources of all immorality?

And here it may be proper to observe that if moral distinctions be derived from the truth or falsehood of those judgments, they must take place wherever we form the judgments; nor will there be any difference, whether the question be concerning an apple or a kingdom, or whether the error be avoidable or unavoidable.

For as the very essence of morality is supposed to consist in an agreement or disagreement to reason, the other circumstances are entirely arbitrary, and can never either bestow on any action the character of virtuous or vicious, or deprive it of that character. To which we may add that this agreement or disagreement, not admitting of degrees, all virtues and vices would of course be equal.

Should it be pretended that, though a mistake of *fact* be not criminal, yet a mistake of *right* often is, and that this may be the source of immorality: I would answer that it is impossible such a mistake can ever be the original source of immorality, since it supposes a real right and wrong, that is, a real distinction in morals, independent of these judgments. A mistake, therefore, of right may become a species of immorality; but it is only a secondary one, and is founded on some other antecedent to it.

As to those judgments which are the *effects* of our actions, and which, when false, give occasion to pronounce the actions contrary to truth and reason, we may observe that our actions never cause any judgment, either true or false, in ourselves, and that it is only on others they have such an influence. It is certain that an action, on many occasions, may give rise to false conclusions in others; and that a person who through a window sees any lewd behaviour of mine with my neighbour's wife may be so simple as to imagine she is certainly my own. In this respect my action resembles somewhat a lie or falsehood; only with this difference, which is material, that I perform not the action with any intention of giving rise to a false judgment in another, but merely to satisfy my lust and passion. It causes, however, a mistake and false judgment by accident; and the falsehood of its effects may be ascribed, by some odd figurative way of speaking, to the action itself. But still I can see no pretext of reason for asserting that the tendency to cause such an error is the first spring or original source of all immorality.[2]

[2] One might think it were entirely superfluous to prove this, if a late author who has had the good fortune to obtain some reputation had not seriously affirmed that such a falsehood is the foundation of all guilt and moral deformity. That we may discover the fallacy of his hypothesis, we need only consider that a false conclusion is drawn from an action only by means of an obscurity of natural principles, which makes a cause be secretly interrupted in its operation, by contrary causes, and renders the connection betwixt two objects uncertain and variable. Now, as a like uncertainty and variety of causes take place even in natural objects, and produce a like error in our judgment, if that tendency to produce error were the very essence of vice and immorality, it should follow that even inanimate objects might be vicious and immoral.

It is in vain to urge that inanimate objects act without liberty and choice. For as liberty and choice are not necessary to make an action produce in us an erroneous conclusion, they can be, in no respect, essential to morality; and I do not readily perceive, upon this system, how they can ever come to be regarded by it. If the tendency to cause error be the origin of immorality, that tendency and immorality would in every case be inseparable.

Add to this that if I had used the precaution of shutting the window, while I indulged myself in those liberties with my neighbour's wife, I should have been guilty of no immorality; and that because my action, being perfectly concealed, would have had no tendency to produce any false conclusion.

For the same reason, a thief who steals in by a ladder at a window and takes all imaginable care to cause no disturbance is in no respect criminal. For either he will not be perceived, or if he be, it is impossible he can produce any error, nor will any one, from these circumstances, take him to be other than what he really is.

It is well known that those who are squint-sighted do very readily cause mistakes in others, and that we imagine they salute or are talking to one person while they address themselves to another. Are they, therefore, upon that account, immoral?

Besides, we may easily observe that in all those arguments there is an evident reasoning in a circle. A person who takes possession of *another's* goods and uses them as his *own*, in a manner declares them to be his own; and this falsehood is the

Thus, upon the whole, it is impossible that the distinction betwixt moral good and evil can be made by reason; since that distinction has an influence upon our actions, of which reason alone is incapable. Reason and judgment may, indeed, be the mediate cause of an action, by prompting or by directing a passion; but it is not pretended that a judgment of this kind, either in its truth or falsehood, is attended with virtue or vice. And as to the judgments which are caused by our judgments, they can still less bestow those moral qualities on the actions which are their causes.

But, to be more particular, and to show that those eternal immutable fitnesses and unfitnesses of things cannot be defended by sound philosophy, we may weigh the following considerations.

If the thought and understanding were alone capable of fixing the boundaries of right and wrong, the character of virtuous and vicious either must lie in some relations of objects, or must be a matter of fact which is discovered by our reasoning. This consequence is evident. As the operations of human understanding divide themselves into two kinds — the comparing of ideas and the inferring of matter of fact — were virtue discovered by the understanding, it must be an object of one of these operations; nor is there any third operation

source of the immorality of injustice. But is property, or right, or obligation, intelligible without an antecedent morality?

A man that is ungrateful to his benefactor in a manner affirms that he never received any favours from him. But in what manner? Is it because it is his duty to be grateful? But this supposes that there is some antecedent rule of duty and morals. Is it because human nature is generally grateful, and makes us conclude that a man who does any harm never receives any favour from the person he harmed? But human nature is not so generally grateful as to justify such a conclusion; or, if it were, is an exception to a general rule in every case criminal, for no other reason than because it is an exception?

But what may suffice entirely to destroy this whimsical system is that it leaves us under the same difficulty to give a reason why truth is virtuous and falsehood vicious, as to account for the merit or turpitude of any other action. I shall allow, if you please, that all immorality is derived from this supposed falsehood in action, provided you can give me any plausible reason why such a falsehood is immoral. If you consider rightly of the matter, you will find yourself in the same difficulty as at the beginning.

This last argument is very conclusive; because, if there be not an evident merit or turpitude annexed to this species of truth or falsehood, it can never have any influence upon our actions. For who ever thought of forbearing any action, because others might possibly draw false conclusions from it? Or who ever performed any, that he might give rise to true conclusions?

of the understanding which can discover it. There has been an opinion very industriously propagated by certain philosophers that morality is susceptible of demonstration; and though no one has ever been able to advance a single step in those demonstrations, yet it is taken for granted that this science may be brought to an equal certainty with geometry or algebra. Upon this supposition vice and virtue must consist in some relations, since it is allowed on all hands that no matter of fact is capable of being demonstrated. Let us therefore begin with examining this hypothesis and endeavour, if possible, to fix those moral qualities which have been so long the objects of our fruitless researches, point out distinctly the relations which constitute morality or obligation, that we may know wherein they consist, and after what manner we must judge of them.

If you assert that vice and virtue consist in relations susceptible of certainty and demonstration, you must confine yourself to those *four* relations which alone admit of that degree of evidence; and in that case you run into absurdities from which you will never be able to extricate yourself. For as you make the very essence of morality to lie in the relations, and as there is no one of these relations but what is applicable not only to an irrational but also to an inanimate object, it follows that even such objects must be susceptible of merit or demerit. *Resemblance, contrariety, degrees in quality*, and *proportions in quantity and number;* all these relations belong as properly to matter as to our actions, passions, and volitions. It is unquestionable, therefore, that morality lies not in any of these relations, nor the sense of it in their discovery.[3]

[3] As a proof how confused our way of thinking on this subject commonly is, we may observe that those who assert that morality is demonstrable do not say that morality lies in the relations, and that the relations are distinguishable by reason. They only say that reason can discover such an action in such relations to be virtuous, and such another vicious. It seems they thought it sufficient if they could bring the word "relation" into the proposition, without troubling themselves whether it was to the purpose or not. But here, I think, is plain argument. Demonstrative reason discovers only relations. But that reason, according to this hypothesis, discovers also vice and virtue. These moral qualities, therefore, must be relations. When we blame any action, in any situation, the whole complicated object of action and situation must form certain relations, wherein the essence of vice consists. This hypothesis is not otherwise intelligible. For what does reason discover, when it pronounces any action vicious? Does it discover a relation or a matter of fact? These questions are decisive, and must not be eluded.

Should it be asserted that the sense of morality consists in the discovery of some relation distinct from these, and that our enumeration was not complete when we comprehended all demonstrable relations under four general heads; to this I know not what to reply, till some one be so good as to point out to me this new relation. It is impossible to refute a system which has never yet been explained. In such a manner of fighting in the dark, a man loses his blows in the air and often places them where the enemy is not present.

I must therefore, on this occasion, rest contented with requiring the two following conditions of any one that would undertake to clear up this system. *First*, as moral good and evil belong only to the actions of the mind, and are derived from our situation with regard to external objects, the relations from which these moral distinctions arise must lie only betwixt internal actions and external objects, and must not be applicable either to internal actions, compared among themselves, or to external objects, when placed in opposition to other external objects. For as morality is supposed to attend certain relations, if these relations could belong to internal actions considered singly, it would follow that we might be guilty of crimes in ourselves, and independent of our situation with respect to the universe; and in like manner, if these moral relations could be applied to external objects, it would follow that even inanimate beings would be susceptible of moral beauty and deformity. Now, it seems difficult to imagine that any relation can be discovered betwixt our passions, volitions, and actions, compared to external objects, which relation might not belong either to these passions and volitions, or to these external objects, compared among *themselves*.

But it will be still more difficult to fulfil the *second* condition requisite to justify this system. According to the principles of those who maintain an abstract rational difference betwixt moral good and evil, and a natural fitness and unfitness of things, it is not only supposed that these relations, being eternal and immutable, are the same when considered by every rational creature, but their *effects* are also supposed to be necessarily the same; and it is concluded they have no less, or rather a greater, influence in directing the will of the Deity than in governing the rational and virtuous of our own species. These two particulars are evidently distinct. It is one thing to know virtue, and another to conform the will to it. In order, therefore, to prove that the measures of right and wrong are eternal laws, *obligatory* on every rational mind, it is not sufficient to show the relations upon which they are founded; we must also point out the connection betwixt the relation and the will, and must prove that this connection is so necessary that in every well-disposed mind it must take place and have its influence, though the difference betwixt these minds be in other respects immense and infinite. Now, besides what I have already proved, that even in human nature no relation can ever alone produce any action — besides this, I say, it has been shown, in treating of the understanding, that there is no connection of cause and effect, such as this is supposed to be, which is discoverable otherwise than by experience, and of which we can pretend to have any security by the simple consideration of the objects. All beings in the universe, considered in themselves, appear entirely loose and independent of each other. It is only by experience we learn their influence and connection; and this influence we ought never to extend beyond experience.

Thus it will be impossible to fulfil the *first* condition required to the system of eternal rational measures of right and wrong, because it is impossible to show those relations upon which such a distinction may be founded; and it is as impossible to fulfil the *second* condition, because we cannot prove a *priori* that these relations, if they really existed and were perceived, would be universally forcible and obligatory.

But to make these general reflections more clear and convincing, we may illustrate them by some particular instances, wherein this character of moral good or evil is the most universally acknowledged. Of all crimes that human creatures are capable of committing, the most horrid and unnatural is ingratitude, especially when it is committed against parents, and appears in the more flagrant instances of wounds and death. This is acknowledged by all mankind, philosophers as well as the people. The question only arises among philosophers, whether the guilt or moral deformity of this action be discovered by demonstrative reasoning, or be felt by an internal sense and by means of some sentiment which the reflecting on such an action naturally occasions. This question will soon be decided against the former opinion, if we can show the same relations in other objects without the notion of any guilt or iniquity attending them. Reason or science is nothing but the comparing of ideas, and the discovery of their relations; and if the same relations have different characters it must evidently follow that those characters are not discovered merely by reason. To put the affair, therefore, to this trial, let us choose any inanimate object, such as an oak or elm, and let us suppose that by the dropping of its seed it produces a sapling below it which, springing up by degrees, at last overtops and destroys the parent tree: I ask if in this instance there be wanting any relation which is discoverable in parricide or ingratitude? Is not the one tree the cause of the other's existence; and the latter the cause of the destruction of the former in the same manner as when a child murders his parent? It is not sufficient to reply that a choice or will is wanting. For in the case of parricide, a will does not give rise to any *different* relations, but is only the cause from which the action is derived; and consequently produces the *same* relations that in the oak or elm arise from some other principles. It is a will or choice that determines a man to kill his parent; and they are the laws of matter and motion that determine a sapling to destroy the oak from which it sprung Here then the same relations have different causes; but still the relations are the same; and as their discovery is not in both cases attended with a notion of immorality, it follows that that notion does not arise from such a discovery.

But to choose an instance still more resembling; I would fain ask anyone why incest in the human species is criminal, and why the very same action and the same relations in animals have not the smallest moral turpitude and deformity? If it be answered that this action is innocent in animals, because they have not reason sufficient to discover its turpitude, but that man being endowed with that faculty which *ought* to restrain him to his duty, the same action instantly becomes criminal to him. Should this be said, I would reply that this is evidently arguing in a circle. For before reason can perceive this turpitude, the turpitude must exist, and consequently is independent of the decisions of our reason, and is their object more properly than their effect. According to this system, then, every animal that has sense, and appetite, and will, that is, every animal must be susceptible of all the same virtues and vices for which we ascribe praise and blame to human creatures. All the difference is that our superior reason may serve to discover the vice or virtue, and by that means may augment the blame or praise; but still this discovery supposes a separate being in these moral distinctions, and a being which depends only on the will and appetite, and which, both in thought and reality, may be distinguished from reason. Animals are susceptible of the same relations with respect to each other as the human species, and therefore would also be susceptible of the same morality if the essence of morality consisted in these relations. Their want of a sufficient degree of reason may hinder them from perceiving the duties and obligations of morality, but can never hinder these duties from existing; since they must antecedently exist in order to their being perceived. Reason must find them, and can never produce them. This argument deserves to be weighed as being, in my opinion, entirely decisive.

Nor does this reasoning only prove that morality consists not in any relations that are the objects of science; but, if examined, will prove with equal certainty that it consists not in any *matter of fact* which can be discovered by the understanding. This is the *second* part of our argument; and if it can be made evident, we may conclude that morality is not an object of reason. But can there be any difficulty in proving that vice and virtue are not matters of fact whose existence we can infer by reason? Take any action allowed to be vicious — wilful murder, for instance. Examine it in all lights, and see if you can find that matter of fact or real existence which you call *vice*. In whichever way you take it, you find only certain passions, motives, volitions, and thoughts. There is no other matter of fact in the case. The vice entirely escapes you, as long as you consider the object. You never can find it till you turn your reflection into your own breast and find a sentiment of disapprobation which arises in you towards this action. Here is a matter of fact; but it is the object of feeling, not of reason. It lies in yourself, not in the object. So that when you pronounce any action or character to be vicious, you mean nothing, but that from the constitution of your nature you have a feeling or sentiment of blame from the contemplation of it Vice and virtue, therefore, may be compared to sounds, colours, heat, and cold, which, according to modern philosophy, are not qualities in objects but perceptions in the mind: and this discovery in morals, like that other in physics, is to be regarded as a considerable advancement of the speculative sciences; though, like that too, it has little or no influence on practice. Nothing can be more real, or concern us more, than our own sentiments of pleasure and uneasiness; and if these be favourable to virtue, and unfavourable to vice, no more can be requisite to the regulation of our conduct and behaviour.

I cannot forbear adding to these reasonings an observation which may, perhaps, be found of some importance. In every system of morality which I have hitherto met with, I have always remarked that the author proceeds for some time in the ordinary way of reasoning, and establishes the being of a god, or makes observations concerning human affairs; when of a sudden I am surprised to find that instead of the usual copulations of propositions *is* and *is not*, I meet with no proposition that is not connected with an *ought* or an *ought not*. This change is imperceptible, but is, however, of the last consequence. For as this *ought* or *ought not* expresses some new relation or affirmation, it is necessary that it should be observed and explained; and at the same time that a reason should be given for what seems altogether inconceivable, how this new relation can be a deduction from others which are entirely different from it. But as authors do not commonly use this precaution, I shall presume to recommend it to the readers; and am persuaded that this small attention would subvert all the vulgar systems of morality and let us see that the distinction of vice and virtue is not founded merely on the relations of objects, nor is perceived by reason.

SECTION II

MORAL DISTINCTIONS DERIVED FROM A MORAL SENSE

THUS THE COURSE of the argument leads us to conclude that since vice and virtue are not discoverable merely by reason, or the comparison of ideas, it must be by means of some impression or sentiment they occasion, that we are able to mark the difference betwixt them. Our decisions concerning moral rectitude and depravity are evidently perceptions; and as all perceptions are either impressions or ideas, the exclusion of the one is a convincing argument for the other. Morality, therefore, is more properly felt than judged of; though this feeling or sentiment is commonly so soft and gentle that we are apt to confound it with an idea, according to our common custom of taking all things for the same which have any near resemblance to each other.

The next question is of what nature are these impressions, and after what manner do they operate upon us? Here we cannot remain long in suspense, but must pronounce the impression arising from virtue to be agreeable, and that proceeding from vice to be uneasy. Every moment's experience must convince us of this. There is no spectacle so fair and beautiful as a noble and generous action; nor any which gives us more abhorrence than one that is cruel and treacherous. No enjoyment equals the satisfaction we receive from the company of those we love and esteem; as the greatest of all punishments is to be obliged to pass our lives with those we hate or contemn. A very play or romance may afford us instances of this pleasure which virtue conveys to us; and pain which arises from vice.

Now, since the distinguishing impressions by which moral good or evil is known are nothing but *particular* pains or pleasures, it follows that in all inquiries concerning these moral distinctions it will be sufficient to show the principles which make us feel a satisfaction or uneasiness from the survey of any character, in order to satisfy us why the character is laudable or blamable. An action, or sentiment, or character, is virtuous or vicious; why? because its view causes a pleasure or uneasiness of a particular kind. In giving a reason, therefore, for the pleasure or uneasiness, we sufficiently explain the vice or virtue. To have the sense of virtue is nothing but to *feel* a satisfaction of a particular kind from the contemplation of a character. The very *feeling* constitutes our praise or admiration. We go no further; nor do we inquire into the cause of the satisfaction. We do not infer a character to be virtuous because it pleases; but in feeling that it pleases after such a particular manner we in effect feel that it is virtuous. The case is the same as in our judgments concerning all kinds of beauty, and tastes, and sensations. Our approbation is implied in the immediate pleasure they convey to us.

I have objected to the system which establishes eternal rational measures of right and wrong, that it is impossible to show in the actions of reasonable creatures any relations which are not found in external objects; and therefore, if morality always attended these relations, it were possible for inanimate matter to become virtuous or vicious. Now it may, in like manner, be objected to the present system, that if virtue and vice be determined by pleasure and pain, these qualities must in every case arise from the sensations; and consequently any object, whether animate or inanimate, rational or irrational, might become morally good or evil, provided it can excite a satisfaction or uneasiness. But though this objection seems to be the very same, it has by no means the same force in the one case as in the other. For, *first*, it is evident that under the term *pleasure* we comprehend sensations which are very different from each other, and which have only such a distant resemblance as is requisite to make them be expressed by the same abstract term. A good composition of music and a bottle of good wine equally produce pleasure; and, what is more, their goodness is determined merely by the pleasure. But shall we say, upon that account, that the wine is harmonious, or the music of a good flavour? In like manner, an inanimate object and the character or sentiments of any person may, both of them, give satisfaction; but, as the satisfaction is different, this keeps our sentiments concerning them from being confounded, and makes us ascribe virtue to the one and not to the other. Nor is every sentiment of pleasure or pain, which arises from characters and actions, of that *peculiar* kind which makes us praise or condemn. The good qualities of an enemy are hurtful to us, but may still command our esteem and respect. It is only when a character is considered in general, without reference to our particular interest, that it causes such a feeling or sentiment as denominates it morally good or evil. It is true, those sentiments from interest and morals are apt to be confounded, and naturally run into one another. It seldom happens that we do not think an enemy vicious, and can distinguish betwixt his opposition to our interest and real villainy or baseness. But this hinders not but that the sentiments are in themselves distinct, and a man of temper and judgment may preserve himself from these illusions. In like manner, though it is certain a musical voice is nothing but one that naturally gives a *particular* kind of pleasure, yet it is difficult for a man to be sensible that the voice of an enemy is agreeable, or to allow it to be musical. But a person of a fine ear, who has the command of himself, can separate these feelings and give praise to what deserves it.

Secondly, we may call to remembrance the preceding system of the passions, in order to remark a still more considerable difference among our pains and pleasures. Pride and humility, love and hatred, are excited when there is anything presented to us that both bears a relation to the object of the passion and produces a separate sensation related to the sensation of the passion. Now, virtue and vice are attended with these circumstances. They must necessarily be placed either in ourselves or others, and excite either pleasure or uneasiness; and therefore must give rise to one of these four passions, which clearly distinguishes them from the pleasure and pain arising from inanimate objects that often bear no relation to us; and this is, perhaps, the most considerable effect that virtue and vice have upon the human mind.

It may now be asked *in general* concerning this pain or pleasure that distinguishes moral good and evil, *from what principle is it derived, and whence does it arise in the human mind?* To this I reply, *first,* that it is absurd to imagine that, in every particular instance, these sentiments are produced by an *original* quality and *primary* constitution. For as the number of our duties is in a manner infinite, it is impossible that our original instincts should extend to each of them, and from our very first infancy impress on the human mind all that multitude of precepts which are contained in the completest system of ethics. Such a method of proceeding is not conformable to the usual maxims by which nature is conducted, where a few principles produce all that variety we observe in the universe, and everything is carried on in the easiest and most simple manner. It is necessary, therefore, to abridge these primary impulses and find some more general principles upon which all our notions of morals are founded.

But, in the *second* place, should it be asked, whether we ought to search for these principles in *nature,* or whether we must look for them in some other origin? I would reply that our answer to this question depends upon the definition of the word *nature,* than which there is none more ambiguous and equivocal. If *nature* be opposed to miracles, not only the distinction betwixt vice and virtue is natural, but also every event which has ever happened in the world, *excepting those miracles on which our religion is founded.* In saying, then, that the sentiments of vice and virtue are natural in this sense, we make no very extraordinary discovery.

But *nature* may also be opposed to rare and unusual; and in this sense of the word, which is the common one, there may often arise disputes concerning what is natural or unnatural; and one may in general affirm that we are not possessed of any very precise standard by which these disputes can be decided. Frequent and rare depend upon the number of examples we have observed; and as this number may gradually increase or diminish, it will be impossible to fix any exact boundaries betwixt them. We may only affirm on this head that if ever there was anything which could be called natural in this sense, the sentiments of morality certainly may; since there never was any nation of the world, nor any single person in any nation, who was utterly deprived of them, and who never, in any instance, showed the least approbation or dislike of manners. These sentiments are so rooted in our constitution and temper that, without entirely confounding the human mind by disease or madness, it is impossible to extirpate and destroy them.

But *nature* may also be opposed to artifice as well as to what is rare and unusual; and in this sense it may be disputed whether the notions of virtue be natural or not. · We readily forget that the designs, and projects, and views of men are principles as necessary in their operation as heat and cold, moist and dry; but, taking them to be free and entirely our own, it is usual for us to set them in opposition to the other principles of nature. Should it therefore be demanded whether the sense of virtue be natural or artificial, I am of opinion that it is impossible for me at present to give any precise answer to this question. Perhaps it will appear afterwards that our sense of some virtues is artificial, and that of others natural. The discussion of this question will be more proper, when we enter upon an exact detail of each particular vice and virtue.[1]

Meanwhile, it may not be amiss to observe from these definitions of *natural* and *unnatural* that nothing can be more unphilosophical than those systems which assert that virtue is the same with what is natural, and vice with what is unnatural. For in the first sense of the word "nature," as opposed to miracles, both vice and virtue are equally natural; and in the second sense, as opposed to what is unusual, perhaps virtue will be found to be the most unnatural. At least it must be owned that heroic virtue, being as unusual, is as little natural as the most brutal barbarity. As to the third sense of the word, it is certain that both vice and virtue are equally artificial and out of nature. For, however it may be disputed whether the notion of a

[1] In the following discourse, *natural* is also opposed sometimes to *civil*, sometimes to *moral*. The opposition will always discover the sense in which it is taken.

merit or demerit in certain actions be natural or artificial, it is evident that the actions themselves are artificial, and performed with a certain design and intention; otherwise they could never be ranked under any of these denominations. It is impossible, therefore, that the character of natural and unnatural can ever, in any sense, mark the boundaries of vice and virtue.

Thus we are still brought back to our first position that virtue is distinguished by the pleasure, and vice by the pain, that any action, sentiment, or character, gives us by the mere view and contemplation. This decision is very commodious; because it reduces us to this simple question, *why any action or sentiment, upon the general view or survey, gives a certain satisfaction or uneasiness*, in order to show the origin of its moral rectitude or depravity, without looking for any incomprehensible relations and qualities which never did exist in nature, nor even in our imagination, by any clear and distinct conception? I flatter myself I have executed a great part of my present design by a state of the question which appears to me so free from ambiguity and obscurity.

PART II

OF JUSTICE AND INJUSTICE

SECTION I

JUSTICE, WHETHER A NATURAL OR ARTIFICIAL VIRTUE?

I HAVE ALREADY HINTED that our sense of every kind of virtue is not natural, but that there are some virtues that produce pleasure and approbation by means of an artifice or contrivance, which arises from the circumstances and necessity of mankind. Of this kind I assert *justice* to be; and shall endeavour to defend this opinion by a short and, I hope, convincing argument, before I examine the nature of the artifice from which the sense of that virtue is derived.

It is evident that, when we praise any actions, we regard only the motives that produced them, and consider the actions as signs or indications of certain principles in the mind and temper. The external performance has no merit. We must look within to find the moral quality. This we cannot do directly; and therefore fix our attention on actions, as on external signs. But these actions are still considered as signs, and the ultimate object of our praise and approbation is the motive that produced them.

After the same manner, when we require any action, or blame a person for not performing it, we always suppose that one in that situation should be influenced by the proper motive of that action, and we esteem it vicious in him to be regardless of it. If we find upon inquiry that the virtuous motive was still powerful over his breast, though checked in its operation by some circumstances unknown to us, we retract our blame and have the same esteem for him as if he had actually performed the action which we require of him.

It appears, therefore, that all virtuous actions derive their merit only from virtuous motives, and are considered merely as signs of those motives. From this principle I conclude that the first virtuous

49

motive which bestows a merit on any action can never be a regard to the virtue of that action, but must be some other natural motive or principle. To suppose that the mere regard to the virtue of the action may be the first motive which produced the action and rendered it virtuous, is to reason in a circle. Before we can have such a regard, the action must be really virtuous; and this virtue must be derived from some virtuous motive; and, consequently, the virtuous motive must be different from the regard to the virtue of the action. A virtuous motive is requisite to render an action virtuous. An action must be virtuous before we can have a regard to its virtue. Some virtuous motive, therefore, must be antecedent to that regard.

Nor is this merely a metaphysical subtilty; but enters into all our reasonings in common life, though, perhaps, we may not be able to place it in such distinct philosophical terms. We blame a father for neglecting his child. Why? Because it shows a want of natural affection which is the duty of every parent. Were not natural affection a duty, the care of children could not be a duty; and it were impossible we could have the duty in our eye in the attention we give to our offspring. In this case, therefore, all men suppose a motive to the action distinct from a sense of duty.

Here is a man that does many benevolent actions: relieves the distressed, comforts the afflicted, and extends his bounty even to the greatest strangers. No character can be more amiable and virtuous. We regard these actions as proofs of the greatest humanity. This humanity bestows a merit on the actions. A regard to this merit is, therefore, a secondary consideration and derived from the antecedent principles of humanity, which is meritorious and laudable.

In short, it may be established as an undoubted maxim that *no action can be virtuous or morally good, unless there be in human nature some motive to produce it distinct from the sense of its morality.*

But may not the sense of morality or duty produce an action without any other motive? I answer, it may; but this is no objection to the present doctrine. When any virtuous motive or principle is common in human nature, a person who feels his heart devoid of that motive may hate himself upon that account, and may perform the action without the motive, from a certain sense of duty, in order to acquire by practice that virtuous principle, or at least to disguise to himself as much as possible his want of it. A man that really feels no gratitude in his temper is still pleased to perform grateful actions, and thinks he has by that means fulfilled his duty. Actions are at first only considered as signs of motives; but it is usual in this case as in all others to fix our attention on the signs, and neglect in some measure the thing signified. But though, on some occasions, a person may perform an action merely out of regard to its moral obligation, yet still this supposes in human nature some distinct principles which are capable of producing the action, and whose moral beauty renders the action meritorious.

Now, to apply all this to the present case, I suppose a person to have lent me a sum of money on condition that it be restored in a few days; and also suppose that after the expiration of the term agreed on he demands the sum; I ask, *What reason or motive have I to restore the money?* It will perhaps be said that my regard to justice, and abhorrence of villainy and knavery, are sufficient reasons for me if I have the least grain of honesty or sense of duty and obligation. And this answer, no doubt, is just and satisfactory to man in his civilized state, and when trained up according to a certain discipline and education. But in his rude and more *natural* condition, if you are pleased to call such a condition natural, this answer would be rejected as perfectly unintelligible and sophistical. For one in that situation would immediately ask you, *Wherein consists this honesty and justice, which you find in restoring a loan and abstaining from the property of others?* It does not surely lie in the external action. It must, therefore, be placed in the motive from which the external action is derived. This motive can never be a regard to the honesty of the action. For it is a plain fallacy to say that a virtuous motive is requisite to render an action honest, and, at the same time, that a regard to the honesty is the motive of the action. We can never have a regard to the virtue of an action, unless the action be antecedently virtuous. No action can be virtuous, but so far as it proceeds from a virtuous motive. A virtuous motive, therefore, must precede the regard to the virtue; and it is impossible that the virtuous motive and the regard to the virtue can be the same.

It is requisite, then, to find some motive to acts of justice and honesty, distinct from our regard to the honesty; and in this lies the great difficulty. For should we say that a concern for our private interest or reputation is the legitimate motive to all honest actions:

it would follow that wherever that concern ceases, honesty can no longer have place. But it is certain that self-love, when it acts at its liberty instead of engaging us to honest actions, is the source of all injustice and violence; nor can a man ever correct those vices without correcting and restraining the *natural* movements of that appetite.

But should it be affirmed that the reason or motive of such actions is the *regard to public interest*, to which nothing is more contrary than examples of injustice and dishonesty — should this be said, I would propose the three following considerations as worthy of our attention. *First*, public interest is not naturally attached to the observation of the rules of justice, but is only connected with it, after an artificial convention for the establishment of these rules, as shall be shown more at large hereafter. *Secondly*, if we suppose that the loan was secret, and that it is necessary for the interest of the person that the money be restored in the same manner (as when the lender would conceal his riches), in that case the example ceases, and the public is no longer interested in the actions of the borrower, though I suppose there is no moralist who will affirm that the duty and obligation ceases. *Thirdly*, experience sufficiently proves that men in the ordinary conduct of life look not so far as the public interest, when they pay their creditors, perform their promises, and abstain from theft, and robbery, and injustice of every kind. That is a motive too remote and too sublime to affect the generality of mankind, and operate with any force in actions so contrary to private interest as are frequently those of justice and common honesty.

In general, it may be affirmed that there is no such passion in human minds as the love of mankind, merely as such, independent of personal qualities, of services, or of relation to ourself. It is true, there is no human and indeed no sensible creature whose happiness or misery does not in some measure affect us when brought near us and represented in lively colours; but this proceeds merely from sympathy, and is no proof of such an universal affection to mankind, since this concern extends itself beyond our own species. An affection betwixt the sexes is a passion evidently implanted in human nature; and this passion not only appears in its peculiar symptoms, but also in inflaming every other principle of affection, and raising a stronger love from beauty, wit, kindness, than what would otherwise flow from them. Were there an universal love among all human creatures, it would appear after the same manner. Any degree of a good quality would cause a stronger affection than the same degree of a bad quality would cause hatred; contrary to what we find by experience. Men's tempers are different, and some have a propensity to the tender, and others to the rougher affections; but in the main, we may affirm that man in general, or human nature, is nothing but the object both of love and hatred, and requires some other cause which, by a double relation of impressions and ideas, may excite these passions. In vain would we endeavour to elude this hypothesis. There are no phenomena that point out any such kind affection to men, independent of their merit and every other circumstance. We love company in general; but it is as we love any other amusement. An Englishman in Italy is a friend; an European in China; and perhaps a man would be beloved as such, were we to meet him in the moon. But this proceeds only from the relation to ourselves, which in these cases gathers force by being confined to a few persons.

If public benevolence, therefore, or a regard to the interests of mankind, cannot be the original motive to justice, much less can *private benevolence* or a *regard to the interests of the party concerned* be this motive. For what if he be my enemy and has given me just cause to hate him? What if he be a vicious man and deserves the hatred of all mankind? What if he be a miser and can make no use of what I would deprive him of? What if he be a profligate debauchee and would rather receive harm than benefit from large possessions? What if I be in necessity and have urgent motives to acquire something to my family? In all these cases, the original motive to justice would fail, and, consequently, the justice itself, and along with it all property, right, and obligation.

A rich man lies under a moral obligation to communicate to those in necessity a share of his superfluities. Were private benevolence the original motive to justice a man would not be obliged to leave others in the possession of more than he is obliged to give them. At least, the difference would be very inconsiderable. Men generally fix their affections more on what they are possessed of than on what they never enjoyed; for this reason it would be greater cruelty to dispossess a man of anything than not to give it him. But who will assert that this is the only foundation of justice?

Besides, we must consider that the chief reason why men attach themselves so much to their possessions is that they consider them as their property, and as secured to them inviolably by the laws of society. But this is a secondary consideration and dependent on the preceding notions of justice and property.

A man's property is supposed to be fenced against every mortal, in every possible case. But private benevolence is, and ought to be, weaker in some persons than in others, and in many or indeed in most persons must absolutely fail. Private benevolence, therefore, is not the original motive of justice.

From all this it follows that we have no real or universal motive for observing the laws of equity but the very equity and merit of that observance; and as no action can be equitable or meritorious, where it cannot arise from some separate motive, there is here an evident sophistry and reasoning in a circle. Unless, therefore, we will allow that nature has established a sophistry, and rendered it necessary and unavoidable, we must allow that the sense of justice and injustice is not derived from nature, but arises artificially, though necessarily, from education and human conventions.

I shall add, as a corollary to this reasoning, that since no action can be laudable or blamable, without some motives or impelling passions distinct from the sense of morals, these distinct passions must have a great influence on that sense. It is according to their general force in human nature that we blame or praise. In judging of the beauty of animal bodies, we always carry in our eye the economy of a certain species; and where the limbs and features observe that proportion which is common to the species, we pronounce them handsome and beautiful. In like manner, we always consider the *natural* and *usual* force of the passions, when we determine concerning vice and virtue; and if the passions depart very much from the common measures on either side, they are always disapproved as vicious. A man naturally loves his children better than his nephews, his nephews better than his cousins, his cousins better than strangers, where everything else is equal. Hence arise our common measures of duty, in preferring the one to the other. Our sense of duty always follows the common and natural course of our passions.

To avoid giving offence, I must here observe that when I deny justice to be a natural virtue, I make use of the word *natural* only as opposed to *artificial*. In another sense of the word, as no principle of the human mind is more natural than a sense of virtue, so no virtue is more natural than justice. Mankind is an inventive species; and where an invention is obvious and absolutely necessary, it may as properly be said to be natural as anything that proceeds immediately from original principles, without the intervention of thought or reflection. Though the rules of justice be *artificial*, they are not *arbitrary*. Nor is the expression improper to call them *laws of nature*, if by *natural* we understand what is common to any species, or even if we confine it to mean what is inseparable from the species.

SECTION II

OF THE ORIGIN OF JUSTICE AND PROPERTY

WE NOW PROCEED to examine two questions, viz., *concerning the manner in which the rules of justice are established by the artifice of men;* and *concerning the reasons which determine us to attribute to the observance or neglect of these rules a moral beauty and deformity.* These questions will appear afterwards to be distinct. We shall begin with the former.

Of all the animals with which this globe is peopled there is none towards whom nature seems, at first sight, to have exercised more cruelty than towards man, in the numberless wants and necessities with which she has loaded him, and in the slender means which she affords to the relieving these necessities. In other creatures, these two particulars generally compensate each other. If we consider the lion as a voracious and carnivorous animal, we shall easily discover him to be very necessitous; but if we turn our eye to his make and temper, his agility, his courage, his arms, and his force, we shall find that his advantages hold proportion with his wants. The sheep and ox are deprived of all these advantages; but their appetites are moderate and their food is of easy purchase. In man alone this unnatural conjunction of infirmity and of necessity may be observed in its greatest perfection. Not only the food which is required for his sustenance flies his search and approach, or at least requires his labour to be produced, but he must be possessed of clothes and lodging to defend him against the injuries of the weather; though, to consider him only in himself, he is provided neither with arms, nor force, nor other natural abilities which are in any degree answerable to so many necessities.

It is by society alone he is able to supply his defects, and raise himself up to an equality with his fellow creatures, and even acquire a superiority above them. By society all his infirmities are compensated; and though in that situation his wants multiply every moment upon him, yet his abilities are still more augmented, and leave him in every respect more satisfied and happy than it is possible for him in his savage and solitary condition ever to become. When every individual person labours apart and only for himself, his force is too small to execute any considerable work; his labour being employed in supplying all his different necessities, he never attains a perfection in any particular art; and as his force and success are not at all times equal, the least failure in either of these particulars must be attended with inevitable ruin and misery. Society provides a remedy for these *three* inconveniences. By the conjunction of forces our power is augmented; by the partition of employments our ability increases; and by mutual succour we are less exposed to fortune and accidents. It is by this additional *force*, *ability*, and *security*, that society becomes advantageous.

But in order to form society, it is requisite not only that it be advantageous, but also that men be sensible of these advantages; and it is impossible in their wild uncultivated state that by study and reflection alone they should ever be able to attain this knowledge. Most fortunately, therefore, there is conjoined to those necessities whose remedies are remote and obscure, another necessity which, having a present and more obvious remedy, may justly be regarded as the first and original principle of human society. This necessity is no other than that natural appetite betwixt the sexes which unites them together and preserves their union till a new tie takes place in their concern for their common offspring. This new concern becomes also a principle of union betwixt the parents and offspring and forms a more numerous society where the parents govern by the advantage of their superior strength and wisdom, and at the same time are restrained in the exercise of their authority by that natural affection which they bear their children. In a little time, custom and habit, operating on the tender minds of the children, makes them sensible of the advantages which they may reap from society, as well as fashions them by degrees for it by rubbing off those rough corners and untoward affections which prevent their coalition.

For it must be confessed that however the circumstances of human nature may render a union necessary, and however those passions of lust and natural affection may seem to render it unavoidable, yet there are other particulars in our *natural temper* and in our *outward circumstances* which are very incommodious, and are even contrary to the requisite conjunction. Among the former we may justly esteem our *selfishness* to be the most considerable. I am sensible that, generally speaking, the representations of this quality have been carried much too far; and that the descriptions which certain philosophers delight so much to form of mankind in this particular are as wide of nature as any accounts of monsters which we meet with in fables and romances. So far from thinking that men have no affection for anything beyond themselves, I am of opinion that, though it be rare to meet with one who loves any single person better than himself, yet it is as rare to meet with one in whom all the kind affections, taken together, do not overbalance all the selfish. Consult common experience; do you not see that, though the whole expense of the family be generally under the direction of the master of it, yet there are few that do not bestow the largest part of their fortunes on the pleasures of their wives and the education of their children, reserving the smallest portion for their own proper use and entertainment? This is what we may observe concerning such as have those endearing ties; and may presume that the case would be the same with others, were they placed in a like situation.

But though this generosity must be acknowledged to the honour of human nature, we may at the same time remark that so noble an affection, instead of fitting men for large societies, is almost as contrary to them as the most narrow selfishness. For while each person loves himself better than any other single person, and in his love to others bears the greatest affection to his relations and acquaintance, this must necessarily produce an opposition of passions, and a consequent opposition of actions which cannot but be dangerous to the new-established union.

It is, however, worth while to remark that this contrariety of passions would be attended with but small danger, did it not concur with a peculiarity in our *outward circumstances* which affords it an opportunity of exerting itself. There are three different species of goods which we are possessed of: the internal satisfaction of our minds, the external advantages of our body, and the enjoyment of such possessions as we have acquired by our industry and good fortune. We are perfectly secure in the enjoyment of the first. The second may be ravished from us, but can be of no advantage to him who deprives us of them. The last only are both exposed to the violence of others, and may be transferred without suffering any loss or alteration; while at the same time there is not a sufficient quantity of them to supply every one's desires and necessities. As the improvement, therefore, of these goods is the chief advantage of society, so the *instability* of their possession, along with their *scarcity*, is the chief impediment.

In vain should we expect to find in *uncultivated nature* a remedy to this inconvenience; or hope for any inartificial principle of the human mind which might control those partial affections, and make us overcome the temptations arising from our circumstances. The idea of justice can never serve to this purpose, or be taken for a natural principle capable of inspiring men with an equitable conduct towards each other. That virtue, as it is now understood, would never have been dreamed of among rude and savage men. For the notion of injury or injustice implies an immorality or vice committed against some other person. And as every immorality is derived from some defect or unsoundness of the passions, and as this defect must be judged of, in a great measure, from the ordinary course of nature in the constitution of the mind, it will be easy to know whether we be guilty of any immorality with regard to others, by considering the natural and usual force of those several affections which are directed towards them. Now, it appears that in the original frame of our mind our strongest attention is confined to ourselves; our next is extended to our relations and acquaintance; and it is only the weakest which reaches to strangers and indifferent persons. This partiality, then, and unequal affection must not only have an influence on our behaviour and conduct in society, but even on our ideas of vice and virtue; so as to make us regard any remarkable transgression of such a degree of partiality, either by too great an enlargement or contraction of the affections, as vicious and immoral. This we may observe in our common judgments concerning actions, where we blame a person who either centers all his affections in his family, or is so regardless of them as, in any opposition of interest, to give the preference to a stranger or mere chance acquaintance. From all which it follows that our natural uncultivated ideas of morality, instead of providing a remedy for the partiality of our affections, do rather conform themselves to that partiality and give it an additional force and influence.

The remedy, then, is not derived from nature but from *artifice;* or, more properly speaking, nature provides a remedy in the judgment and understanding for what is irregular and incommodious in the affections. For when men, from their early education in society, have become sensible of the infinite advantages that result from it, and have besides acquired a new affection to company and conversation, and when they have observed that the principal disturbance in society arises from those goods which we call external, and from their looseness and easy transition from one person to another, they must seek for a remedy by putting these goods as far as possible on the same footing with the fixed and constant advantages of the mind and body. This can be done after no other manner than by a convention entered into by all the members of the society to bestow stability on the possession of those external goods, and leave every one in the peaceable enjoyment of what he may acquire by his fortune and industry. By this means every one knows what he may safely possess; and the passions are restrained in their partial and contradictory motions Nor is such a restraint contrary to these passions; for if so, it could never be entered into nor maintained; but it is only contrary to their heedless and impetuous movement. Instead of departing from our own interest, or from that of our nearest friends, by abstaining from the possessions of others, we cannot better consult both these interests than by such a convention; because it is by that means we maintain society, which is so necessary to their well-being and subsistence as well as to our own.

This convention is not of the nature of a *promise;* for even promises themselves, as we shall see afterwards, arise from human conventions. It is only a general sense of common interest; which sense all the members of the society express to one another, and which induces them to regulate their conduct by certain rules. I observe that it will be for my interest to leave another in the possession of his goods, *provided* he will act in the same manner with regard to me. He is sensible of a like interest in the regulation of his conduct. When this common sense of interest is mutually expressed and is known to both, it produces a suitable resolution and behaviour. And this may properly enough be called a convention or agreement betwixt us, though without the interposition of a promise; since the actions of each of us have a reference to those of the other, and are performed upon the supposition that something is to be performed on the other part. Two men who pull the oars of a boat do it by an agreement or convention, though they have never given promises to each other. Nor is the rule concerning the stability of possessions the less derived from human conventions, that it arises gradually, and acquires force by a slow progression and by our repeated experience of the inconveniences of transgressing it. On the contrary, this experience assures us still more that the sense of interest has become common to all our fellows, and gives us a confidence of the future regularity of their conduct; and it is only on the expectation of this that our moderation and abstinence are founded. In like manner are languages gradually established by human conventions, without any promise. In like manner do gold and silver become the common measures of exchange, and are esteemed sufficient payment for what is of a hundred times their value.

After this convention concerning abstinence from the possessions of others is entered into, and every one has acquired a stability in his possessions, there immediately arise the ideas of justice and injustice; as also those of *property, right*, and *obligation*. The latter are altogether unintelligible without first understanding the former. Our property is nothing but those goods whose constant possession is established by the laws of society — that is, by the laws of justice. Those, therefore, who make use of the words *property*, or *right*, or *obligation*, before they have explained the origin of justice, or even make use of them in that explication, are guilty of a very gross fallacy, and can never reason upon any solid foundation. A man's property is some object related to him. This relation is not natural but moral, and founded on justice. It is very preposterous, therefore, to imagine that we can have any idea of property without fully comprehending the nature of justice, and showing its origin in the artifice and contrivance of men. The origin of justice explains that of property. The same artifice gives rise to both. As our first and most natural sentiment of morals is founded on the nature of our passions, and gives the perference to ourselves and friends above strangers, it is impossible there can be naturally any such thing as a fixed right or property, while the opposite passions of men impel them in contrary directions, and are not restrained by any convention or agreement.

No one can doubt that the convention for the distinction of property and for the stability of possession is of all circumstances the most necessary to the establishment of human society, and that after the agreement for the fixing and observing of this rule there remains little or nothing to be done towards settling a perfect harmony and concord. All the other passions, beside this of interest, are either easily restrained, or are not of such pernicious consequence when indulged. *Vanity* is rather to be esteemed a social passion and a bond of union among men. *Pity* and *love* are to be considered in the same light. And as to *envy* and *revenge*, though pernicious, they operate only by intervals, and are directed against particular persons whom we consider as our superiors or enemies. This avidity alone of acquiring goods and possessions for ourselves and our nearest friends is insatiable, perpetual, universal, and directly destructive of society. There scarce is any one who is not actuated by it; and there is no one who has not reason to fear from it, when it acts without any restraint and gives way to its first and most natural movements. So that, upon the whole, we are to esteem the difficulties in the establishment of society to be greater or less, according to those we encounter in regulating and restraining this passion.

It is certain that no affection of the human mind has both a sufficient force and a proper direction to counterbalance the love of gain, and render men fit members of society by making them abstain from the possessions of others. Benevolence to strangers is too weak for this purpose; and as to the other passions, they rather inflame this avidity, when we observe that the larger our possessions are, the more ability we have of gratifying all our appetites. There is no passion, therefore, capable of controlling the interested affection but the very affection itself, by an alteration of its direction. Now, this alteration must necessarily take place upon the least reflection; since it is evident that the passion is much better satisfied by its restraint than by its liberty, and that, in preserving society, we make much greater advances in the acquiring possessions than in the solitary and forlorn condition which must follow upon violence and an universal licence. The question, therefore, concerning the wickedness or goodness of human nature enters not in the least into that other question concerning the origin of society; nor is there anything to be considered but the degrees of men's sagacity or folly. For whether the passion of self-interest be esteemed vicious or virtuous, it is all a case, since itself alone restrains it; so that if it be virtuous, men become social by their virtue; if vicious, their vice has the same effect.

Now, as it is by establishing the rule for the stability of possession that this passion restrains itself, if that rule be very abstruse and of difficult invention, society must be esteemed in a manner accidental and the effect of many ages. But if it be found that nothing can be more simple and obvious than that rule; that every parent, in order to preserve peace among his children, must establish it; and that these first rudiments of justice must every day be improved, as the society enlarges — if all this appear evident, as it certainly must, we may conclude that it is utterly impossible for men to remain any considerable time in that savage condition which precedes society, but that his very first state and situation may justly be esteemed social. This, however, hinders not but that philosophers may, if they please, extend their reasoning to the supposed *state of nature;* provided they allow it to be a mere philosophical fiction, which never had and never could have any reality. Human nature being composed of two principal parts which are requisite in all its actions — the affections and understanding — it is certain that the blind motions of the former, without the direction of the latter, incapacitate men for society; and it may be allowed us to consider separately the effects that result from the separate operations of these two component parts of the mind. The same liberty may be permitted to moral, which is allowed to natural philosophers; and it is very usual with the latter to consider any motion as compounded and consisting of two parts separate from each other, though at the same time they acknowledge it to be in itself uncompounded and inseparable.

This *state of nature*, therefore, is to be regarded as a mere fiction, not unlike that of the *golden age*, which poets have invented; only with this difference, that the former is described as full of war, violence, and injustice, whereas the latter is painted out to us as the most charming and most peaceable condition that can possibly be imagined. The seasons in that first age of nature were so temperate, if we may believe the poets, that there was no necessity for men to provide themselves with clothes and houses as a security against the violence of heat and cold. The rivers flowed with wine and milk, the oaks yielded honey, and nature spontaneously produced her greatest delicacies. Nor were these the chief advantages of that happy age. The storms and tempests were not alone removed from nature; but those more furious tempests were unknown to human breasts, which now cause such uproar and engender such confusion. Avarice, ambition, cruelty, selfishness, were never heard of; cordial affection, compassion, sympathy, were the only movements with which the human mind was yet acquainted. Even the distinction of *mine* and *thine* was banished from that happy race of mortals, and carried with them the very notions of property and obligation, justice and injustice.

This, no doubt, is to be regarded as an idle fiction, but yet deserves our attention because nothing can more evidently show the origin of those virtues which are the subjects of our present inquiry. I have already observed that justice takes its rise from human conventions, and that these are intended as a remedy to some inconveniences which proceed from the concurrence of certain *qualities* of the human mind with the *situation* of external objects. The qualities of the mind are *selfishness* and *limited generosity;* and the situation of external objects is their *easy change,* joined to their *scarcity* in comparison of the wants and desires of men. But however philosophers may have been bewildered in those speculations, poets have been guided more infallibly by a certain taste or common instinct which, in most kinds of reasoning, goes further than any of that art and philosophy with which we have been yet acquainted. They easily perceived, if every man had a tender regard for another, or if nature supplied abundantly all our wants and desires, that the jealousy of interest, which justice supposes, could no longer have place; nor would there be any occasion for those distinctions and limits of property and possession which at present are in use among mankind. Increase to a sufficient degree the benevolence of men, or the bounty of nature, and you render justice useless by supplying its place with much nobler virtues and more valuable blessings. The selfishness of men is animated by the few possessions we have in proportion to our wants; and it is to restrain this selfishness that men have been obliged to separate themselves from the community, and to distinguish betwixt their own goods and those of others.

Nor need we have recourse to the fictions of poets to learn this, but, beside the reason of the thing, may discover the same truth by common experience and observation. It is easy to remark that a cordial affection renders all things common among friends, and that married people in particular mutually lose their property and are unacquainted with the *mine* and *thine*, which are so necessary and yet cause such disturbance in human society. The same effect arises from any alteration in the circumstances of mankind; as when there is such a plenty of anything as satisfies all the desires of men; in which case the distinction of property is entirely lost, and everything remains in common. This we may observe with regard to air and water, though the most valuable of all external objects; and may easily conclude that if men were supplied with everything in the same abundance, or if *every one* had the same affection and tender regard for *every one* as for himself, justice and injustice would be equally unknown among mankind.

Here then is a proposition which, I think, may be regarded as certain, *that it is only from the selfishness and confined generosity of man, along with the scanty provision nature has made for his wants that justice derives its origin.* If we look backward we shall find that this proposition bestows an additional force on some of those observations which we have already made on this subject.

First, we may conclude from it that a regard to public interest, or a strong extensive benevolence, is not our first and original motive for the observation of the rules of justice, since it is allowed that if men were endowed with such a benevolence, these rules would never have been dreamed of.

Secondly, we may conclude from the same principle that the sense of justice is not founded on reason, or on the discovery of certain connections and relations of ideas which are eternal, immutable, and universally obligatory. For since it is confessed that such an alteration as that above mentioned, in the temper and circumstances of mankind, would entirely alter our duties and obligations, it is necessary upon the common system *that the sense of virtue is derived from reason,* to show the change which this must produce in the relations and ideas. But it is evident that the only cause why the extensive generosity of man and the perfect abundance of everything would destroy the very idea of justice is because they render it useless; and that, on the other hand, his confined benevolence and his necessitous condition give rise to that virtue only by making it requisite to the public interest and to that of every individual. It was therefore a concern for our own and the public interest which made us establish the laws of justice; and nothing can be more certain than that it is not any relation of ideas which gives us this concern, but our impressions and sentiments, without which everything in nature is perfectly indifferent to us, and can never in the least affect us. The sense of justice, therefore, is not founded on our ideas but on our impressions.

Thirdly, we may further confirm the foregoing proposition *that those impressions, which give rise to this sense of justice, are not natural to the mind of man, but arise from artifice and human conventions.* For since any considerable alteration of temper and circumstances destroys equally justice and injustice, and since such an alteration has an effect only by changing our own and the public interest, it follows that the first establishment of the rules of justice depends on these different interests. But if men pursued the public interest naturally, and with a hearty affection, they would have never dreamed of restraining each other by these rules; and if they pursued their own interest, without any precaution, they would run headlong into every kind of injustice and violence. These rules, therefore, are artificial and seek their end in an oblique and indirect manner; nor is the interest which gives rise to them of a kind that could be pursued by the natural and inartificial passions of men.

To make this more evident, consider that, though the rules of justice are established merely by interest, their connection with interest is somewhat singular, and is different from what may be observed on other occasions. A single act of justice is frequently contrary to *public interest;* and were it to stand alone, without being followed by other acts, may in itself be very prejudicial to society. When a man of merit, of a beneficent disposition, restores a great fortune to a miser or a seditious bigot, he has acted justly and laudably; but the public is a real sufferer. Nor is every single act of justice, considered apart, more conducive to private interest than to public; and it is easily conceived how a man may impoverish himself by a single instance of integrity, and have reason to wish that, with regard to that single act, the laws of justice were for a moment suspended in the universe. But however single acts of justice may be contrary either to public or private interest, it is certain that the whole plan or scheme is highly conducive, or indeed absolutely requisite, both to the support of society and the well-being of every individual. It is impossible to separate the good from the ill. Property must be stable, and must be fixed by general rules. Though in one instance the public be a sufferer, this momentary ill is amply compensated by the steady prosecution of the rule and by the peace and order which it establishes in society. And even every individual person must find himself a gainer on balancing the account; since without justice society must immediately dissolve, and every one must fall into that savage and solitary condition which is infinitely worse than the worst situation that can possibly be supposed in society. When, therefore, men have had experience enough to observe that, whatever may be the consequence of any single act of justice performed by a single person, yet the whole system of actions concurred in by the whole society is infinitely advantageous to the whole and to every part, it is not long before justice and property take place. Every member of society is sensible of this interest; every one expresses this sense to his fellows along with the resolution he has taken of squaring his actions by it, on condition that others will do the same. No more is requisite to induce any one of them to perform an act of justice, who has the first opportunity. This becomes an example to others; and thus justice establishes itself by a kind of convention or agreement, that is, by a sense of interest, supposed to be common to all, and where every single act is performed in expectation that others are to perform the like. Without such a convention no one would ever have dreamed that there was such a virtue as justice, or have been induced to conform his actions to it. Taking any single act, my justice may be pernicious in every respect; and it is only upon the supposition that others are to imitate my example that I can be induced to embrace that virtue; since nothing but this combination can render justice advantageous, or afford me any motives to conform myself to its rules.

We come now to the *second* question we proposed, viz., *Why we annex the idea of virtue to justice, and of vice to injustice.* This question will not detain us long after the principles which we have already established. All we can say of it at present will be dispatched in a few words; and for further satisfaction the reader must wait till we come to the third part of this book. The *natural* obligation to justice, viz., interest, has been fully explained; but as to the *moral* obligation, or the sentiment of right and wrong, it will first be requisite to examine the natural virtues before we can give a full and satisfactory account of it.

After men have found by experience that their selfishness and confined generosity, acting at their liberty, totally incapacitate them for society, and at the same time have observed that society is necessary to the satisfaction of those very passions, they are naturally induced to lay themselves under the restraint of such rules as may render their commerce more safe and commodious. To the imposition, then, and observance of these rules, both in general and in every particular instance, they are at first induced only by a regard to interest; and this motive, on the first formation of society, is sufficiently strong and forcible. But when society has become numerous and has increased to a tribe or nation, this interest is more remote; nor do men so readily perceive that disorder and confusion follow upon every breach of these rules, as in a more narrow and contracted society. But though in our own actions we may frequently lose sight of that interest which we have in maintaining order, and may follow a lesser and more present interest, we never fail to observe the prejudice we receive either mediately or immediately from the injustice of others, as not being in that case either blinded by passion or biassed by any contrary temptation. Nay, when the injustice is so distant from us as no way to affect our interest, it still displeases us, because we consider it as prejudicial to human society and pernicious to every one that approaches the person guilty of it. We partake of their uneasiness by *sympathy;* and as everything which gives uneasiness in human actions, upon the general survey, is called *vice*, and whatever produces satisfaction, in the same manner, is denominated *virtue*, this is the reason why the sense of moral good and evil follows upon justice and injustice. And though this sense in the present case be derived only from contemplating the actions of others, yet we fail not to extend it even to our own actions. The *general rule* reaches beyond those instances from which it arose; while at the same time we naturally *sympathize* with others in the sentiments they entertain of us.

Though this progress of the sentiments be *natural* and even necessary, it is certain that it is here forwarded by the artifice of politicians who, in order to govern men more easily and preserve peace in human society, have endeavoured to produce an esteem for justice and an abhorrence of injustice. This, no doubt, must have its effect; but nothing can be more evident than that the matter has been carried too far by certain writers on morals, who seem to have employed their utmost efforts to extirpate all sense of virtue from among mankind. Any artifice of politicians may assist nature in the producing of those sentiments which she suggests to us, and may even, on some occasions, produce alone an approbation or esteem for any particular action; but it is impossible it should be the sole cause of the distinction we make betwixt vice and virtue; for if nature did not aid us in this particular, it would be in vain for politicians to talk of *honourable* or *dishonourable, praiseworthy* or *blamable*. These words would be perfectly unintelligible and would no more have any idea annexed to them than if they were of a tongue perfectly unknown to us. The utmost politicians can perform is to extend the natural sentiments beyond their original bounds; but still nature must furnish the materials and give us some notion of moral distinctions.

As public praise and blame increase our esteem for justice, so private education and instruction contribute to the same effect. For as parents easily observe that a man is the more useful both to himself and others, the greater degree of probity and honour he is endowed with, and that those principles have greater force when custom and education assist interest and reflection; for these reasons they are induced to inculcate on their children from their earliest infancy the principles of probity, and teach them to regard the observance of those rules by which society is maintained as worthy and honourable, and their violation as base and infamous. By this means the sentiments of honour may take root in their tender minds, and acquire such firmness and solidity that they may fall little short of those principles which are the most essential to our natures, and the most deeply radicated in our internal constitution.

What further contributes to increase their solidity is the interest of our reputation, after the opinion *that a merit or demerit attends justice or injustice* is once firmly established among mankind. There is nothing which touches us more nearly than our reputation, and nothing on which our reputation more depends than our conduct with relation to the property of others. For this reason every one who has any regard to his character, or who intends to live on good terms with mankind, must fix an inviolable law to himself never by any temptation to be induced to violate those principles which are essential to a man of probity and honour.

I shall make only one observation before I leave this subject, viz., that though I assert that in the *state of nature* or that imaginary state which preceded society there be neither justice nor injustice, yet I assert not that it was allowable in such a state to violate the property of others. I only maintain that there was no such thing as property, and, consequently, could be no such thing as justice or injustice. I shall have occasion to make a similar reflection with regard to *promises*, when I come to treat of them; and I hope this reflection, when duly weighed, will suffice to remove all odium from the foregoing opinions with regard to justice and injustice.

SECTION III

OF THE RULES WHICH DETERMINE PROPERTY

THOUGH THE ESTABLISHMENT of the rule concerning the stability of possession be not only useful but even absolutely necessary to human society, it can never serve to any purpose while it remains in such general terms. Some method must be shown by which we may distinguish what particular goods are to be assigned to each particular person, while the rest of mankind are excluded from their possession and enjoyment. Our next business, then, must be to discover the reasons which modify this general rule and fit it to the common use and practice of the world.

It is obvious that those reasons are not derived from any utility or advantage, which either the *particular* person or the public may reap from his enjoyment of any *particular* goods, beyond what would result from the possession of them by any other person. It were better, no doubt, that every one were possessed of what is most suitable to him and proper for his use; but besides that this relation of fitness may be common to several at once, it is liable to so many controversies, and men are so partial and passionate in judging of these controversies that such a loose and uncertain rule would be absolutely incompatible with the peace of human society. The convention concerning the stability of possession is entered into, in order to cut off all occasions of discord and contention; and this end would never be attained were we allowed to apply this rule differently in every particular case, according to every particular utility which might be discovered in such an application. Justice, in her decisions, never regards the fitness or unfitness of objects to particular persons, but conducts herself by more extensive views. Whether a man be generous or a miser, he is equally well received by her, and obtains with the same facility a decision in his favour, even for what is entirely useless to him.

It follows, therefore, that the general rule that *possession must be stable* is not applied by particular judgments, but by other general rules which must extend to the whole society, and be inflexible either by spite or favour. To illustrate this I propose the following instance. I first consider men in their savage and solitary condition; and suppose that, being sensible of the misery of that state and foreseeing the advantages that would result from society, they seek each other's company and make an offer of mutual protection and assistance. I also suppose that they are endowed with such sagacity as immediately to perceive that the chief impediment to this project of society and partnership lies in the avidity and selfishness of their natural temper; to remedy which they enter into a convention for the stability of possession and for mutual restraint and forbearance. I am sensible that this method of proceeding is not altogether natural; but besides that, I here only suppose those reflections to be formed at once which, in fact, arise insensibly and by degrees — besides this, I say, it is very possible that several persons, being by different accidents separated from the societies to which they formerly belonged, may be obliged to form a new society among themselves; in which case they are entirely in the situation above mentioned.

It is evident, then, that their first difficulty in this situation, after the general convention for the establishment of society and for the constancy of possession, is how to separate their possessions and assign to each his particular portion which he must for the future unalterably enjoy. This difficulty will not detain them long; but it must immediately occur to them as the most natural expedient that every one continue to enjoy what he is at present master of, and that property or constant possession be conjoined to the immediate possession. Such is the effect of custom that it not only reconciles us to anything we have long enjoyed, but even gives us an affection for it, and makes us prefer it to other objects which may be more valuable, but are less known to us. What has long lain under our eye and has often been employed to our advantage, *that* we are always the most unwilling to part with; but can easily live without possessions which we never have enjoyed and are not accustomed to.   It is evident, therefore, that men would easily acquiesce in this expedient that *every one continue to enjoy what he is at present possessed of;* and this is the reason why they would so naturally agree in preferring it.[1]

[1] No questions in philosophy are more difficult than when a number of causes present themselves for the same phenomenon, to determine which is the principal and predominant. There seldom is any very precise argument to fix our choice, and men must be contented to be guided by a kind of taste or fancy, arising from analogy and a comparison of similar instances. Thus, in the present case, there are, no doubt, motives of public interest for most of the rules which determine property; but still I suspect that these rules are principally fixed by the imagination, or the more frivolous properties of our thought and conception.   I shall continue to explain these causes, leaving it to the reader's choice whether he will prefer those derived from public utility, or those derived from the imagination.   We shall begin with the right of the present possessor.

It is a quality which I have already observed* in human nature, that when two objects appear in a close relation to each other, the mind is apt to ascribe to them any additional relation, in order to complete the union; and this inclination is so strong as often to make us run into errors (such as that of the conjunction of thought and matter) if we find that they can serve to that purpose. Many of our impressions are incapable of place or local position; and yet those very impressions we suppose to have a local conjunction with the impressions of sight and touch, merely because they are conjoined by causation, and are already united in the imagination. Since, therefore, we can feign a new relation, and even an absurd one, in order to complete any union, it will easily be imagined that if there be any relations which depend on the mind, it will readily conjoin them to any preceding relation and unite by a new bond such objects as have already an union in the fancy. Thus, for instance, we never fail in our arrangement of bodies to place those which are *resembling* in *contiguity* to each other, or at least in *correspondent* points of view; because we feel a satisfaction in joining the relation of contiguity to that of resemblance, or the resemblance of situation to that of qualities. And this is easily accounted for from the known properties of human nature. When

*Book I. Part IV. Sect. 5.

But we may observe that, though the rule of the assignment of property to the present possessor be natural and by that means useful, yet its utility extends not beyond the first formation of society; nor would anything be more pernicious than the constant observance of it; by which restitution would be excluded and every injustice would be authorized and rewarded. We must, therefore, seek for some other circumstance that may give rise to property after society is once established; and of this kind I find four most considerable, viz., *occupation, prescription, accession,* and *succession.* We shall briefly examine each of these, beginning with occupation.

The possession of all external goods is changeable and uncertain; which is one of the most considerable impediments to the establishment of society, and is the reason why by universal agreement, express or tacit, men restrain themselves by what we now call the rules of justice and equity. The misery of the condition which precedes this restraint is the cause why we submit to that remedy as quickly as possible; and this affords us an easy reason why we annex the idea of property to the first possession or to *occupation.* Men are unwilling to leave property in suspense even for the shortest time, or open the least door to violence and disorder. To which we may add that the first possession always engages the attention most; and did we neglect it, there would be no colour of reason for assigning property to any succeeding possession.[2]

the mind is determined to join certain objects but undetermined in its choice of the particular objects, it naturally turns its eye to such as are related together. They are already united in the mind: they present themselves at the same time to the conception; and instead of requiring any new reason for their conjunction, it would require a very powerful reason to make us overlook this natural affinity. This we shall have occasion to explain more fully afterwards, when we come to treat of *beauty.* In the meantime, we may content ourselves with observing that the same love of order and uniformity which arranges the books in a library, and the chairs in a parlour, contributes to the formation of society and to the well-being of mankind, by modifying the general rule concerning the stability of possession. And as property forms a relation betwixt a person and an object, it is natural to found it on some preceding relation; and, as property is nothing but a constant possession, secured by the laws of society, it is natural to add it to the present possession which is a relation that resembles it. For this also has its influence. If it be natural to conjoin all sorts of relations, it is more so to conjoin such relations as are resembling and are related together.

[2] Some philosophers account for the right of occupation by saying that every one has a property in his own labour; and when he joins that labour to anything, it

There remains nothing but to determine exactly what is meant by possession; and this is not so easy as may at first sight be imagined. We are said to be in possession of anything, not only when we immediately touch it, but also when we are so situated with respect to it as to have it in our power to use it and may move, alter, or destroy it, according to our present pleasure or advantage. This relation, then, is a species of cause and effect; and as property is nothing but a stable possession, derived from the rules of justice, or the conventions of men, it is to be considered as the same species of relation. But here we may observe that, as the power of using any object becomes more or less certain, according as the interruptions we may meet with are more or less probable, and as this probability may increase by insensible degrees, it is in many cases impossible to determine when possession begins or ends; nor is there any certain standard by which we can decide such controversies. A wild boar that falls into our snares is deemed to be in our possession if it be impossible for him to escape. But what do we mean by impossible? How do we separate this impossibility from an improbability? And how distinguish that exactly from a probability? Mark the precise limits of the one and the other, and show the standard by which we may decide all disputes that may arise and, as we find by experience, frequently do arise upon this subject.[3]

gives him the property of the whole: but, 1. There are several kinds of occupation where we cannot be said to join our labour to the object we acquire: as when we possess a meadow by grazing our cattle upon it. 2. This accounts for the matter by means of *accession*, which is taking a needless circuit. 3. We cannot be said to join our labour to anything but in a figurative sense. Properly speaking, we only make an alteration on it by our labour. This forms a relation betwixt us and the object; and thence arises the property, according to the preceding principles.

[3] If we seek a solution of these difficulties in reason and public interest, we never shall find satisfaction; and if we look for it in the imagination, it is evident that the qualities which operate upon that faculty run so insensibly and gradually into each other that it is impossible to give them any precise bounds or termination. The difficulties on this head must increase, when we consider that our judgment alters very sensibly according to the subject, and that the same power and proximity will be deemed possession in one case, which is not esteemed such in another. A person who has hunted a hare to the last degree of weariness would look upon it as an injustice for another to rush in before him and seize his prey. But the same person, advancing to pluck an apple that hangs within his reach, has no reason to complain if another, more alert, passes him and takes possession. What is the reason of this difference, but that immobility, not being natural to the hare,

But such disputes may not only arise concerning the real existence of property and possession, but also concerning their extent; and these disputes are often susceptible of no decision, or can be decided by no other faculty than the imagination. A person who lands on the shore of a small island that is desert and uncultivated is deemed but the effect of industry, forms in that case a strong relation with the hunter, which is wanting in the other?

Here, then, it appears that a certain and infallible power of enjoyment, without touch or some other sensible relation, often produces not property: and I further observe that a sensible relation, without any present power, is sometimes sufficient to give a title to any object. The sight of a thing is seldom a considerable relation, and is only regarded as such when the object is hidden or very obscure; in which case we find that the view alone conveys a property; according to that maxim *that even a whole continent belongs to the nation which first discovered it.* It is however remarkable that both in the case of discovery and that of possession, the first discoverer and possessor must join to the relation an intention of rendering himself proprietor; otherwise the relation will not have its effect; and that because the connection in our fancy betwixt the property and the relation is not so great but that it requires to be helped by such an intention.

From all these circumstances it is easy to see how perplexed many questions may become concerning the acquisition of property by occupation; and the least effort of thought may present us with instances which are not susceptible of any reasonable decision. If we prefer examples which are real to such as are feigned, we may consider the following one, which is to be met with in almost every writer that has treated of the laws of nature. Two Grecian colonies, leaving their native country in search of new seats, were informed that a city near them was deserted by its inhabitants. To know the truth of this report they dispatched at once two messengers, one from each colony, who finding on their approach that the information was true begun a race together with an intention to take possession of the city, each of them for his countrymen. One of these messengers, finding that he was not an equal match for the other, launched his spear at the gates of the city, and was so fortunate as to fix it there before the arrival of his companion. This produced a dispute betwixt the two colonies, which of them was the proprietor of the empty city; and this dispute still subsists among philosophers. For my part, I find the dispute impossible to be decided, and that because the whole question hangs upon the fancy, which in this case is not possessed of any precise or determinate standard upon which it can give sentence. To make this evident, let us consider that if these two persons had been simply members of the colonies, and not messengers or deputies, their actions would not have been of any consequence; since in that case their relation to the colonies would have been but feeble and imperfect. Add to this that nothing determined them to run to the gates rather than the walls or any other part of the city, but that the gates, being the most obvious and remarkable part, satisfy the fancy best in taking them for the whole, as we find by the poets who frequently draw their images and metaphors its possessor from the very first moment, and acquires the property of the whole; because the object is there bounded and circumscribed in the fancy, and at the same time is proportioned to the new possessor. The same person landing on a desert island as large as Great Britain extends his property no further than his immediate possession, though a numerous colony are esteemed the proprietors of the whole from the instant of their debarkment.

But if it often happens that the title of first possession becomes obscure through time, and that it is impossible to determine many controversies which may arise concerning it; in that case, long possession or *prescription* naturally takes place and gives a person a sufficient property in anything he enjoys. The nature of human society admits not of any great accuracy; nor can we always remount to the first origin of things in order to determine their present condition. Any considerable space of time sets objects at such a distance that they seem in a manner to lose their reality, and have as little influence on the mind as if they never had been in being. A man's title that is clear and certain at present will seem obscure and doubtful fifty years hence, even though the facts on which it is founded should be proved with the greatest evidence and certainty. The same facts have not the same influence after so long an interval of time. And this may be received as a convincing argument for our preceding doctrine with regard to property and justice. Possession during a long tract of time conveys a title to any object. But as it is certain that, however everything be produced *in time*, there is nothing real that is produced *by time*, it follows that property being produced by time is not anything real in the objects, but is the offspring of the sentiments on which alone time is found to have any influence.[4]

from them. Besides, we may consider that the touch or contact of the one messenger is not properly possession, no more than the piercing the gates with the spear, but only forms a relation; and there is a relation in the other case equally obvious, though not perhaps of equal force. Which of these relations, then conveys a right and property, or whether any of them be sufficient for that effect, I leave to the decision of such as are wiser than myself.

[4] Present possession is plainly a relation betwixt a person and an object; but is not sufficient to counterbalance the relation of first possession, unless the former be long and uninterrupted; in which case the relation is increased on the side of the present possession by the extent of time, and diminished on that of first possession by the distance. This change in the relation produces a consequent change in the property.

We acquire the property of objects by *accession* when they are connected in an intimate manner with objects that are already our property and, at the same time, are inferior to them. Thus the fruits of our garden, the offspring of our cattle, and the work of our slaves, are all of them esteemed our property, even before possession. Where objects are connected together in the imagination, they are apt to be put on the same footing, and are commonly supposed to be endowed with the same qualities. We readily pass from one to the other and make no difference in our judgments concerning them, especially if the latter be inferior to the former.[b]

[b] This source of property can never be explained but from the imagination; and one may affirm that the causes are here unmixed. We shall proceed to explain them more particularly, and illustrate them by examples from common life and experience.

It has been observed above that the mind has a natural propensity to join relations, especially resembling ones, and finds a kind of fitness and uniformity in such an union. From this propensity are derived these laws of nature *that upon the first formation of society property always follows the present possession; and afterwards, that it arises from first or from long possession.* Now, we may easily observe that relation is not confined merely to one degree; but that from an object that is related to us, we acquire a relation to every other object which is related to it, and so on, till the thought loses the chain by too long a progress. However the relation may weaken by each remove, it is not immediately destroyed, but frequently connects two objects by means of an immediate one which is related to both. And this principle is of such force as to give rise to the right of *accession*, and causes us to acquire the property, not only of such objects as we are immediately possessed of, but also of such as are closely connected with them.

Suppose a German, a Frenchman, and a Spaniard, to come into a room where there are placed upon the table three bottles of wine, Rhenish, Burgundy, and Port; and suppose they should fall a quarrelling about the division of them, a person who was chosen for umpire would naturally, to show his impartiality, give every one the product of his own country; and this from a principle which, in some measure, is the source of those laws of nature that ascribe property to occupation, prescription, and accession.

In all these cases, and particularly that of accession, there is first a *natural* union betwixt the idea of the person and that of the object, and afterwards a new and *moral* union produced by that right or property which we ascribe to the person. But here there occurs a difficulty which merits our attention, and may afford us an opportunity of putting to trial that singular method of reasoning which has been employed on the present subject. I have already observed that the imagination passes with greater facility from little to great than from great to little, and that the transition of ideas is always easier and smoother in the former case than in the latter. Now, as the right of accession arises from the easy transition

The right of *succession* is a very natural one, from the presumed consent of the parent or near relation, and from the general interest of ideas by which related objects are connected together, it should naturally be imagined that the right of accession must increase in strength, in proportion as the transition of ideas is performed with greater facility. It may therefore be thought that when we have acquired the property of any small object, we shall readily consider any great object related to it as an accession, and as belonging to the proprietor of the small one; since the transition is in that case very easy from the small object to the great one, and should connect them together in the closest manner. But, in fact, the case is always found to be otherwise. The empire of Great Britain seems to draw along with it the dominion of the Orkneys, the Hebrides, the Isle of Man, and the Isle of Wight; but the authority over those lesser islands does not naturally imply any title to Great Britain. In short, a small object naturally follows a great one as its accession; but a great one is never supposed to belong to the proprietor of a small one related to it, merely on account of that property and relation. Yet in this latter case the transition of ideas is smoother from the proprietor to the small object which is his property, and from the small object to the great one, than in the former case from the proprietor to the great object, and from the great one to the small. It may, therefore, be thought that these phenomena are objections to the foregoing hypothesis *that the ascribing of property to accession is nothing but an effect of the relations of ideas, and of the smooth transition of the imagination.*

It will be easy to solve this objection if we consider the agility and unsteadiness of the imagination with the different views in which it is continually placing its objects. When we attribute to a person a property in two objects, we do not always pass from the person to one object, and from that to the other related to it. The objects being here to be considered as the property of the person, we are apt to join them together, and place them in the same light. Suppose, therefore, a great and a small object to be related together, if a person be strongly related to the great object, he will likewise be strongly related to both the objects considered together, because he is related to the most considerable part. On the contrary, if he be only related to the small object, he will not be strongly related to both considered together, since his relation lies only with the most trivial part, which is not apt to strike us in any great degree when we consider the whole. And this is the reason why small objects become accessions to great ones, and not great to small.

It is the general opinion of philosophers and civilians that the sea is incapable of becoming the property of any nation; and that because it is impossible to take possession of it, or form any such distinct relation with it as may be the foundation of property. Where this reason ceases, property immediately takes place. Thus the most strenuous advocates for the liberty of the seas universally allow that friths and bays naturally belong as an accession to the proprietors of the surrounding continent. These have properly no more bond or union with the land than the *Pacific* ocean would have; but having an union in the fancy, and being at the same time *inferior*, they are of course regarded as an accession.

of mankind which requires that men's possessions should pass to those who are dearest to them in order to render them more industrious

The property of rivers, by the laws of most nations, and by the natural turn of our thought, is attributed to the proprietors of their banks, excepting such vast rivers as the Rhine or the Danube, which seem too large to the imagination to follow as an accession the property of the neighbouring fields. Yet even these rivers are considered as the property of that nation through whose dominions they run; the idea of a nation being a suitable bulk to correspond with them, and bear them such a relation in the fancy.

The accessions which are made to lands bordering upon rivers follow the land, say the civilians, provided it be made by what they call *alluvion*, that is, insensibly and imperceptibly; which are circumstances that mightily assist the imagination in the conjunction. Where there is any considerable portion torn at once from one bank, and joined to another, it becomes not his property whose land it falls on, till it unite with the land, and till the trees or plants have spread their roots into both. Before that, the imagination does not sufficiently join them.

There are other cases which somewhat resemble this of accession, but which, at the bottom, are considerably different, and merit our attention. Of this kind is the conjunction of the properties of different persons, after such a manner as not to admit of *separation*. The question is to whom the united mass must belong.

Where this conjunction is of such a nature as to admit of *division*, but not of *separation*, the decision is natural and easy. The whole mass must be supposed to be common betwixt the proprietors of the several parts, and afterwards must be divided according to the proportions of these parts. But here I cannot forbear taking notice of a remarkable subtility of the Roman law, in distinguishing betwixt *confusion* and *commixtion*. Confusion is a union of two bodies, such as different liquors, where the parts become entirely undistinguishable. Commixtion is the blending of two bodies, such as two bushels of corn, where the parts remain separate in an obvious and visible manner. As in the latter case the imagination discovers not so entire a union as in the former, but is able to trace and preserve a distinct idea of the property of each; this is the reason why the *civil* law, though it established an entire community in the case of *confusion*, and after that a proportional division, yet in the case of *commixtion* supposes each of the proprietors to maintain a distinct right; however, necessity may at last force them to submit to the same division.

Quod si frumentum Titii frumento tuo mistum fuerit: siquidem ex voluntate vestra, commune est: quia singula corpora, id est, singula grana, quæ cujusque propria fuerunt, ex consensu vestro communicata sunt. Quod si casu id mistum fuerit, vel Titius id miscuerit sine tua voluntate, non videtur id commune esse; quia singula corpora in sua substantia durant. Sed nec magis istis casibus commune sit frumentum quam grex intelligitur esse communis, si pecora Titii tuis pecoribus mista fuerint. Sed si ab alterutro vestrum totum id frumentum retineatur, in rem quidem actio pro modo frumenti cujusque competit. Arbitrio autem judicis, ut ipse æstimet quale cujusque frumentum fuerit. Inst. Lib. II, Tit. 1, §28.

Where the properties of two persons are united after such a manner as neither and frugal. Perhaps these causes are seconded by the influence of *relation*, or the association of ideas, by which we are naturally to admit of *division* nor *separation*, as when one builds a house on another's ground, in that case the whole must belong to one of the proprietors; and here I assert that it naturally is conceived to belong to the proprietor of the most considerable part. For, however the compound object may have a relation to two different persons, and carry our view at once to both of them, yet, as the most considerable part principally engages our attention, and by the strict union draws the inferior along it, for this reason, the whole bears a relation to the proprietor of that part and is regarded as his property. The only difficulty is what we shall be pleased to call *the most considerable part*, and most attractive to the imagination.

This quality depends on several different circumstances which have little connection with each other. One part of a compound object may become more considerable than another, either because it is more constant and durable; because it is of greater value; because it is more obvious and remarkable; because it is of greater extent; or because its existence is more separate and independent. It will be easy to conceive that, as these circumstances may be conjoined and opposed in all the different ways, and according to all the different degrees which can be imagined, there will result many cases where the reasons on both sides are so equally balanced that it is impossible for us to give any satisfactory decision. Here, then, is the proper business of municipal laws, to fix what the principles of human nature have left undetermined.

The superficies yields to the soil, says the civil law; the writing to the paper; the canvas to the picture. These decisions do not well agree together, and are a proof of the contrariety of those principles from which they are derived.

But of all the questions of this kind, the most curious is that which for so many ages divided the disciples of Proculus and Sabinus. Suppose a person should make a cup from the metal of another, or a ship from his wood, and suppose the proprietor of the metal or wood should demand his goods, the question is whether he acquires a title to the cup or ship. Sabinus maintained the affirmative, and asserted that the substance or matter is the foundation of all the qualities; that it is incorruptible and immortal, and therefore superior to the form, which is casual and dependent. On the other hand Proculus observed that the form is the most obvious and remarkable part, and that from it bodies are denominated of this or that particular species. To which he might have added that the matter or substance is in most bodies so fluctuating and uncertain that it is utterly impossible to trace it in all its changes. For my part, I know not from what principles such a controversy can be certainly determined. I shall therefore content myself with observing that the decision of Trebonian seems to me pretty ingenious; that the cup belongs to the proprietor of the metal, because it can be brought back to its first form; but that the ship belongs to the author of its form, for a contrary reason. But however ingenious this reason may seem, it plainly depends upon the fancy which, by the possibility of such a reduction, finds a closer connection and relation betwixt a cup and the proprietor of its metal than betwixt a ship and the proprietor of its wood where the substance is more fixed and unalterable.

directed to consider the son after the parent's decease, and ascribe to him a title to his father's possessions. Those goods must become the property of somebody: but *of whom* is the question. Here it is evident the person's children naturally present themselves to the mind; and being already connected to those possessions by means of their deceased parent, we are apt to connect them still further by the relation of property. Of this there are many parallel instances.[6]

SECTION IV

OF THE TRANSFERENCE OF PROPERTY BY CONSENT

HOWEVER useful or even necessary the stability of possession may be to human society, it is attended with very considerable inconveniences. The relation of fitness or suitableness ought never to enter into consideration in distributing the properties of mankind; but we must govern ourselves by rules which are more general in their application, and more free from doubt and uncertainty. Of this kind is *present* possession upon the first establishment of society; and afterwards *occupation, prescription, accession,* and *succession.* As these depend very much on chance, they must frequently prove contradictory both to men's wants and desires; and persons and possessions must often be very ill adjusted. This is a grand inconvenience which

[6] In examining the different titles to authority in government, we shall meet with many reasons to convince us that the right of succession depends, in a great measure, on the imagination. Meanwhile I shall rest contented with observing one example which belongs to the present subject. Suppose that a person die without children, and that a dispute arises among his relations concerning his inheritance; it is evident that if his riches be derived partly from his father, partly from his mother, the most natural way of determining such a dispute is to divide his possessions, and assign each part to the family from whence it is derived. Now, as the person is supposed to have been once the full and entire proprietor of those goods, I ask, what is it makes us find a certain equity and natural reason in this partition, except it be the imagination? His affection to these families does not depend upon his possessions; for which reason his consent can never be presumed precisely for such a partition. And as to the public interest, it seems not to be in the least concerned on the one side or the other.

calls for a remedy. To apply one directly, and allow every man to seize by violence what he judges to be fit for him, would destroy society; and therefore the rules of justice seek some medium betwixt a rigid stability and this changeable and uncertain adjustment. But there is no medium better than that obvious one that possession and property should always be stable, except when the proprietor consents to bestow them in some other person. This rule can have no ill consequence in occasioning wars and dissensions, since the proprietor's consent, who alone is concerned, is taken along in the alienation; and it may serve to many good purposes in adjusting property to persons. Different parts of the earth produce different commodities; and not only so, but different men both are by nature fitted for different employments and attain to greater perfection in any one when they confine themselves to it alone. All this requires a mutual exchange and commerce; for which reason the translation of property by consent is founded on a law of nature, as well as its stability without such a consent.

So far is determined by a plain utility and interest. But, perhaps, it is from more trivial reasons that *delivery* or a sensible transference of the object is commonly required by civil laws, and also by the laws of nature, according to most authors, as a requisite circumstance in the translation of property. The property of an object, when taken for something real, without any reference to morality or the sentiments of the mind, is a quality perfectly insensible, and even inconceivable; nor can we form any distinct notion, either of its stability or translation. This imperfection of our ideas is less sensibly felt with regard to its stability, as it engages less our attention, and is easily passed over by the mind, without any scrupulous examination. But as the translation of property from one person to another is a more remarkable event, the defect of our ideas becomes more sensible on that occasion and obliges us to turn ourselves on every side in search of some remedy. Now, as nothing more enlivens any idea than a present impression and a relation betwixt that impression and the idea, it is natural for us to seek some false light from this quarter. In order to aid the imagination in conceiving the transference of property, we take the sensible object and actually transfer its possession to the person on whom we would bestow the property. The supposed resemblance of the actions and the presence of this sensible delivery deceive the mind, and make it fancy that it conceives the mysterious transition of the property. And that this explication of the matter is just appears hence, that men have invented a *symbolical* delivery to satisfy the fancy where the real one is impracticable. Thus the giving the keys of a granary is understood to be the delivery of the corn contained in it; the giving of stone and earth represents the delivery of a manor. This is a kind of superstitious practice in civil laws and in the laws of nature, resembling the *Roman Catholic* superstition in religion. As the *Roman Catholics* represent the inconceivable mysteries of the *Christian* religion and render them more present to the mind by a taper, or habit, or grimace which is supposed to resemble them, so lawyers and moralists have run into like inventions for the same reason, and have endeavoured by those means to satisfy themselves concerning the transference of property by consent.

SECTION V

OF THE OBLIGATION OF PROMISES

THAT THE RULE of morality, which enjoins the performance of promises, is not *natural*, will sufficiently appear from these two propositions which I proceed to prove, viz., *that a promise would not be intelligible before human conventions had established it;* and *that even if it were intelligible, it would not be attended with any moral obligation.*

I say, *first*, that a promise is not intelligible naturally, nor antecedent to human conventions; and that a man, unacquainted with society, could never enter into any engagements with another, even though they could perceive each other's thoughts by intuition. If promises be natural and intelligible, there must be some act of the mind attending these words, *I promise;* and on this act of the mind must the obligation depend. Let us therefore run over all the faculties of the soul, and see which of them is exerted in our promises.

The act of the mind, expressed by a promise, is not a *resolution* to perform anything; for that alone never imposes any obligation. Nor is it a *desire* of such a performance; for we may bind ourselves without such a desire, or even with an aversion, declared and avowed. Neither is it the *willing* of that action which we promise to perform; for a promise always regards some future time, and the will has an influence only on present actions. It follows, therefore, that since the act of the mind which enters into a promise and produces its obligation, is neither the resolving, desiring, nor willing, any particular performance, it must necessarily be the *willing* of that *obligation* which arises from the promise. Nor is this only a conclusion of philosophy, but is entirely conformable to our common ways of thinking and of expressing ourselves, when we say that we are bound by our own consent, and that the obligation arises from our mere will and pleasure. The only question then is whether there be not a manifest absurdity in supposing this act of the mind, and such an absurdity as no man could fall into whose ideas are not confounded with prejudice and the fallacious use of language.

All morality depends upon our sentiments; and when any action or quality of the mind pleases us *after a certain manner*, we say it is virtuous; and when the neglect or non-performance of it displeases us *after a like manner*, we say that we lie under an obligation to perform it. A change of the obligation supposes a change of the sentiment; and a creation of a new obligation supposes some new sentiment to arise. But it is certain we can naturally no more change our own sentiments than the motions of the heavens; nor by a single act of our will — that is, by a promise — render any action agreeable or disagreeable, moral or immoral, which, without that act, would have produced contrary impressions, or have been endowed with different qualities. It would be absurd, therefore, to will any new obligation — that is, any new sentiment of pain or pleasure; nor is it possible that men could naturally fall into so gross an absurdity. A promise, therefore, is *naturally* something altogether unintelligible, nor is there any act of the mind belonging to it.[1]

---

[1] Were morality discoverable by reason, and not by sentiment, it would be still more evident that promises could make no alteration upon it. Morality is supposed to consist in relation. Every new imposition of morality, therefore, must arise from some new relation of objects; and consequently the will could not produce *immediately* any change in the morals, but could have that effect only by producing a change upon the objects. But as the moral obligation of a promise is the pure effect of the will, without the least change in any part of the universe, it follows that promises have no *natural* obligation.

Should it be said that this act of the will, being in effect a new object, produces

But, *secondly*, if there was any act of the mind belonging to it, it could not *naturally* produce any obligation. This appears evidently from the foregoing reasoning. A promise creates a new obligation. A new obligation supposes new sentiments to arise. The will never creates new sentiments. There could not naturally, therefore, arise any obligation from a promise, even supposing the mind could fall into the absurdity of willing that obligation.

The same truth may be proved still more evidently by that reasoning which proved justice in general to be an artificial virtue. No action can be required of us as our duty, unless there be implanted in human nature some actuating passion or motive capable of producing the action. This motive cannot be the sense of duty. A sense of duty supposes an antecedent obligation; and where an action is not required by any natural passion, it cannot be required by any natural obligation; since it may be omitted without proving any defect or imperfection in the mind and temper, and consequently without any vice. Now, it is evident we have no motive leading us to the performance of promises, distinct from a sense of duty. If we thought that promises had no moral obligation, we never should feel any inclination to observe them. This is not the case with the natural virtues. Though there was no obligation to relieve the miserable, our humanity would lead us to it; and when we omit that duty, the immorality of the omission arises from its being a proof that we want the natural sentiments of humanity. A father knows it to be his duty to take care of his children, but he has also a natural inclination to it. And if no human creature had that inclination, no one could lie under any such obligation. But as there is naturally no inclination to observe promises distinct from a sense of their obligation, it follows that fidelity is no natural virtue,

new relations and new duties, I would answer that this is a pure sophism, which may be detected by a very moderate share of accuracy and exactness. To will a new obligation is to will a new relation of objects; and therefore, if this new relation of objects were formed by the volition itself, we should, in effect, will the volition, which is plainly absurd and impossible. The will has here no object to which it could tend, but must return upon itself *in infinitum*. The new obligation depends upon new relations. The new relations depend upon a new volition. The new volition has for object a new obligation, and consequently new relations, and consequently a new volition; which volition, again, has in view a new obligation, relation, and volition, without any termination. It is impossible, therefore, we could ever will a new obligation; and consequently it is impossible the will could ever accompany a promise, or produce a new obligation of morality.

and that promises have no force antecedent to human conventions.

If any one dissent from this, he must give a regular proof of these two propositions, viz., *that there is a peculiar act of the mind annexed to promises;* and *that consequent to this act of the mind there arises an inclination to perform, distinct from a sense of duty.* I presume that it is impossible to prove either of these two points; and therefore I venture to conclude that promises are human inventions, founded on the necessities and interests of society.

In order to discover these necessities and interests, we must consider the same qualities of human nature which we have already found to give rise to the preceding laws of society. Men being naturally selfish or endowed only with a confined generosity, they are not easily induced to perform any action for the interest of strangers, except with a view to some reciprocal advantage, which they had no hope of obtaining but by such a performance. Now, as it frequently happens that these mutual performances cannot be finished at the same instant, it is necessary that one party be contented to remain in uncertainty, and depend upon the gratitude of the other for a return of kindness. But so much corruption is there among men that, generally speaking, this becomes but a slender security; and as the benefactor is here supposed to bestow his favours with a view to self-interest, this both takes off from the obligation and sets an example of selfishness which is the true mother of ingratitude. Were we, therefore, to follow the natural course of our passions and inclinations, we should perform but few actions for the advantage of others from disinterested views, because we are naturally very limited in our kindness and affection; and we should perform as few of that kind out of regard to interest, because we cannot depend upon their gratitude. Here, then, is the mutual commerce of good offices in a manner lost among mankind, and every one reduced to his own skill and industry for his well-being and subsistence. The invention of the law of nature concerning the *stability* of possession has already rendered men tolerable to each other; that of the *transference* of property and possession by consent has begun to render them mutually advantageous; but still these laws of nature, however strictly observed, are not sufficient to render them so serviceable to each other as by nature they are fitted to become. Though possession be *stable*, men may often reap but small advantage from it, while they are possessed of a greater quantity of any species of goods than they have occasion for, and at the same time suffer by the want of others. The *transference* of property, which is the proper remedy for this inconvenience, cannot remedy it entirely; because it can only take place with regard to such objects as are *present* and *individual*, but not to such as are *absent* or *general*. One cannot transfer the property of a particular house, twenty leagues distant, because the consent cannot be attended with delivery, which is a requisite circumstance. Neither can one transfer the property of ten bushels of corn or five hogsheads of wine by the mere expression and consent because these are only general terms, and have no distinct relation to any particular heap of corn or barrels of wine. Besides, the commerce of mankind is not confined to the barter of commodities, but may extend to services and actions which we may exchange to our mutual interest and advantage. Your corn is ripe to-day; mine will be so tomorrow. It is profitable for us both that I should labour with you today, and that you should aid me tomorrow. I have no kindness for you, and know you have as little for me. I will not, therefore, take any pains upon your account; and should I labour with you upon my own account, in expectation of a return, I know I should be disappointed, and that I should in vain depend upon your gratitude. Here, then, I leave you to labour alone: you treat me in the same manner. The seasons change; and both of us lose our harvests for want of mutual confidence and security.

All this is the effect of the natural and inherent principles and passions of human nature; and as these passions and principles are unalterable, it may be thought that our conduct, which depends on them, must be so too, and that it would be in vain either for moralists or politicians to tamper with us, or attempt to change the usual course of our actions, with a view to public interest. And, indeed, did the success of their designs depend upon their success in correcting the selfishness and ingratitude of men, they would never make any progress, unless aided by Omnipotence, which is alone able to new-mould the human mind and change its character in such fundamental articles. All they can pretend to is to give a new direction to those natural passions, and teach us that we can better satisfy our appetites in an oblique and artificial manner than by their headlong and impetuous motion. Hence I learn to do a service to another, without bearing him any real kindness, because I foresee that he will return my service in expectation of another of the same kind, and in order to maintain the same correspondence of good offices with me or with others. And accordingly, after I have served him, and he is in possession of the advantage arising from my action, he is induced to perform his part as foreseeing the consequences of his refusal.

But though this self-interested commerce of men begins to take place and to predominate in society, it does not entirely abolish the more generous and noble intercourse of friendship and good offices. I may still do services to such persons as I love and am more particularly acquainted with, without any prospect of advantage; and they may make me a return in the same manner, without any view but that of recompensing my past services. In order, therefore, to distinguish those two different sorts of commerce, the interested and the disinterested, there is a *certain form of word* invented for the former, by which we bind ourselves to the performance of any action. This form of words constitutes what we call a *promise*, which is the sanction of the interested commerce of mankind. When a man says *he promises anything*, he in effect expresses a *resolution* of performing it; and along with that, by making use of this *form of words*, subjects himself to the penalty of never being trusted again in case of failure. A resolution is the natural act of the mind, which promises express; but were there no more than a resolution in the case, promises would only declare our former motives, and would not create any new motive or obligation. They are the conventions of men which create a new motive when experience has taught us that human affairs would be conducted much more for mutual advantage, were there certain *symbols* or *signs* instituted by which we might give each other security of our conduct in any particular incident. After these signs are instituted, whoever uses them is immediately bound by his interest to execute his engagements, and must never expect to be trusted any more if he refuse to perform what he promised.

Nor is that knowledge, which is requisite to make mankind sensible of this interest in the *institution* and *observance* of promises, to be esteemed superior to the capacity of human nature, however savage and uncultivated. There needs but a very little practice of the world to make us perceive all these consequences and advantages. The shortest experience of society discovers them to every mortal; and when each individual perceives the same sense of interest in all his fellows, he immediately performs his part of any contract, as being assured that they will not be wanting in theirs. All of them, by concert, enter into a scheme of actions calculated for common benefit, and agree to be true to their word; nor is there anything requisite to form this concert or convention, but that every one have a sense of interest in the faithful fulfilling of engagements and express that sense to other members of the society. This immediately causes that interest to operate upon them; and interest is the *first* obligation to the performance of promises.

Afterwards a sentiment of morals concurs with interest, and becomes a new obligation upon mankind. This sentiment of morality in the performance of promises arises from the same principles as that in the abstinence from the property of others. *Public interest, education,* and *the artifices of politicians,* have the same effect in both cases. The difficulties that occur to us in supposing a moral obligation to attend promises, we either surmount or elude. For instance, the expression of a resolution is not commonly supposed to be obligatory; and we cannot readily conceive how the making use of a certain form of words should be able to cause any material difference. Here, therefore, we *feign* a new act of the mind, which we call the *willing* an obligation; and on this we suppose the morality to depend. But we have proved already that there is no such act of the mind, and, consequently, that promises impose no natural obligation.

To confirm this, we may subjoin some other reflections concerning that will which is supposed to enter into a promise and to cause its obligation. It is evident that the will alone is never supposed to cause the obligation, but must be expressed by words or signs in order to impose a tie upon any man. The expression, being once brought in as subservient to the will, soon becomes the principal part of the promise; nor will a man be less bound by his word, though he secretly give a different direction to his intention, and withhold himself both from a resolution and from willing an obligation. But though the expression makes on most occasions the whole of the promise, yet it does not always so; and one who should make use of any expression of which he knows not the meaning, and which he uses without any intention of binding himself, would not certainly be bound by it. Nay, though he knows its meaning, yet if he uses it in jest only and with such signs as show evidently he has no serious intention of binding himself, he would not lie under any obligation of performance; but it is necessary that the words be a perfect expression of the will, without any contrary signs. Nay, even this we must not carry so far as to imagine that one whom by our quickness of understanding we conjecture from certain signs to have an intention of deceiving us, is not bound by his expression or verbal promise if we accept of it; but must limit this conclusion to those cases where the signs are of a different kind from those of deceit. All these contradictions are easily accounted for if the obligation of promises be merely a human invention for the convenience of society, but will never be explained if it be something *real* and *natural*, arising from any action of the mind or body.

I shall further observe that, since every new promise imposes a new obligation of morality on the person who promises, and since this new obligation arises from his will, it is one of the most mysterious and incomprehensible operations that can possibly be imagined, and may even be compared to *transubstantiation* or *holy orders*,[2] where a certain form of words, along with a certain intention, changes entirely the nature of an external object, and even of a human creature. But though these mysteries be so far alike, it is very remarkable that they differ widely in other particulars, and that this difference may be regarded as a strong proof of the difference of their origins. As the obligation of promises is an invention for the interest of society, it is warped into as many different forms as that interest requires, and even runs into direct contradictions, rather than lose sight of its object. But as those other monstrous doctrines are mere priestly inventions and have no public interest in view, they are less disturbed in their progress by new obstacles; and it must be owned that after the first absurdity they follow more directly the current of reason and good sense. Theologians clearly perceived that the external form of words, being mere sound, require an intention to make them have any efficacy; and that this intention being once considered as a requisite circumstance, its absence must equally prevent the effect, whether avowed or concealed, whether sincere or deceitful. Accordingly, they have commonly determined that the intention of the priest makes the sacrament, and that when he secretly withdraws his intention, he is

[2] I mean so far as holy orders are supposed to produce the *indelible character*. In other respects they are only a legal qualification.

highly criminal in himself, but still destroys the baptism, or communion, or holy orders. The terrible consequences of this doctrine were not able to hinder its taking place, as the inconvenience of a similar doctrine, with regard to promises, have prevented that doctrine from establishing itself. Men are always more concerned about the present life than the future; and are apt to think the smallest evil which regards the former more important than the greatest which regards the latter.

We may draw the same conclusion concerning the origin of promises from the *force* which is supposed to invalidate all contracts and to free us from their obligation. Such a principle is a proof that promises have no natural obligation, and are mere artificial contrivances for the convenience and advantage of society. If we consider aright of the matter, force is not essentially different from any other motive of hope or fear which may induce us to engage our word and lay ourselves under any obligation. A man, dangerously wounded, who promises a competent sum to a surgeon to cure him, would certainly be bound to performance, though the case be not so much different from that of one who promises a sum to a robber, as to produce so great a difference in our sentiments of morality if these sentiments were not built entirely on public interest and convenience.

SECTION VI

SOME FURTHER REFLECTIONS CONCERNING JUSTICE AND INJUSTICE

WE HAVE NOW run over the three fundamental laws of nature, *that of the stability of possession, of its transference by consent,* and *of the performance of promises.* It is on the strict observance of those three laws that the peace and security of human society entirely depend; nor is there any possibility of establishing a good correspondence among men, where these are neglected. Society is absolutely necessary for the well-being of men; and these are as necessary to the support of society. Whatever restraint they may impose on the passions of men, they are the real offspring of those passions, and are only a more artful and more refined way of satisfying them. Nothing is more vigilant and inventive than our passions; and nothing is more obvious than the convention for the observance of these rules. Nature has, therefore, trusted this affair entirely to the conduct of men, and has not placed in the mind any peculiar original principles to determine us to a set of actions into which the other principles of our frame and constitution were sufficient to lead us. And to convince us the more fully of this truth, we may here stop a moment, and, from a review of the preceding reasonings, may draw some new arguments to prove that those laws, however necessary, are entirely artificial and of human invention; and, consequently, that justice is an artificial, and not a natural virtue.

I. The first argument I shall make use of is derived from the vulgar definition of justice. Justice is commonly defined to be *a constant and perpetual will of giving every one his due.* In this definition it is supposed that there are such things as right and property, independent of justice, and antecedent to it; and that they would have subsisted, though men had never dreamt of practising such a virtue. I have already observed, in a cursory manner, the fallacy of this opinion, and shall here continue to open up, a little more distinctly, my sentiments on that subject.

I shall begin with observing that this quality which we call *property* is like many of the imaginary qualities of the *Peripatetic* philosophy, and vanishes upon a more accurate inspection into the subject, when considered apart from our moral sentiments. It is evident property does not consist in any of the sensible qualities of the object. For these may continue invariably the same, while the property changes. Property, therefore, must consist in some relation of the object. But it is not in its relation with regard to other external and inanimate objects. For these may also continue invariably the same, while the property changes. This quality, therefore, consists in the relations of objects to intelligent and rational beings. But it is not the external and corporeal relation which forms the essence of property. For that relation may be the same betwixt inanimate objects, or with regard to brute creatures; though in those cases it forms no property. It is therefore in some internal relation that the property consists; that is, in some influence which the external relations of the object have on the mind and actions. Thus the external relation which we call *occupation* or first possession is not of itself imagined to be the property of the object, but only to cause its property. Now, it is evident this external relation causes nothing in external objects, and has only an influence on the mind by giving us a sense of duty in abstaining from that object, and in restoring it to the first possessor. These actions are properly what we call *justice;* and consequently it is on that virtue that the nature of property depends, and not the virtue on the property.

If any one, therefore, would assert that justice is a natural virtue, and injustice a natural vice, he must assert that, abstracting from the notions of *property* and *right* and *obligation,* a certain conduct and train of actions in certain external relations of objects has naturally a moral beauty or deformity, and causes an original pleasure or uneasiness. Thus the restoring a man's goods to him is considered as virtuous, not because nature has annexed a certain sentiment of pleasure to such a conduct with regard to the property of others, but because she has annexed that sentiment to such a conduct with regard to those external objects of which others have had the first or long possession, or which they have received by the consent of those who have had first or long possession. If nature has given us no such sentiment, there is not naturally, nor antecedent to human conventions, any such thing as property. Now, though it seems sufficiently evident in this dry and accurate consideration of the present subject that nature has annexed no pleasure or sentiment of approbation to such a conduct, yet that I may leave as little room for doubt as possible, I shall subjoin a few more arguments to confirm my opinion.

First, if nature had given us a pleasure of this kind, it would have been as evident and discernible as on every other occasion; nor should we have found any difficulty to perceive that the consideration of such actions in such a situation gives a certain pleasure and sentiment of approbation. We should not have been obliged to have recourse to notions of property in the definition of justice, and at the same time make use of the notions of justice in the definition of property. This deceitful method of reasoning is a plain proof that there are contained in the subject some obscurities and difficulties which we are not able to surmount, and which we desire to evade by this artifice.

Secondly, those rules by which properties, rights, and obligations, are determined have in them no marks of a natural origin, but many of artifice and contrivance. They are too numerous to have proceeded from nature; they are changeable by human laws; and have all of them a direct and evident tendency to public good and the support of civil society. This last circumstance is remarkable upon two accounts. *First*, because, though the cause of the establishment of these laws had been a *regard* for the public good as much as the public good is their natural tendency, they would still have been artificial as being purposely contrived and directed to a certain end. *Secondly*, because, if men had been endowed with such a strong regard for public good, they would never have restrained themselves by these rules; so that the laws of justice arise from natural principles, in a manner still more oblique and artificial. It is self-love which is their real origin; and as the self-love of one person is naturally contrary to that of another, these several interested passions are obliged to adjust themselves after such a manner as to concur in some system of conduct and behaviour. This system, therefore, comprehending the interest of each individual, is of course advantageous to the public, though it be not intended for that purpose by the inventors.

II. In the second place we may observe that all kinds of vice and virtue run insensibly into each other, and may approach by such imperceptible degrees as will make it very difficult, if not absolutely impossible, to determine when the one ends and the other begins; and from this observation we may derive a new argument for the foregoing principle. For whatever may be the case with regard to all kinds of vice and virtue, it is certain that rights, and obligations, and property, admit of no such insensible gradation, but that a man either has a full and perfect property or none at all; and is either entirely obliged to perform any action, or lies under no manner of obligation. However civil laws may talk of a perfect *dominion*, and of an imperfect, it is easy to observe that this arises from a fiction which has no foundation in reason, and can never enter into our notions of natural justice and equity. A man that hires a horse, though but for a day, has as full a right to make use of it for that time, as he whom we call its proprietor has to make use of it any other day; and it is evident that, however the use may be bounded in time or degree, the right itself is not susceptible of any such gradation, but is absolute and entire so far as it extends. Accordingly, we may observe that this right both arises and perishes in an instant; and that a man entirely acquires the property of any object by occupation or the consent of the proprietor, and loses it by his own consent, without any of that insensible gradation which is remarkable in other qualities and relations. Since, therefore, this is the case with regard to property, and rights, and obligations, I ask how it stands with regard to justice and injustice? After whatever manner you answer this question, you run into inextricable difficulties. If you reply that justice and injustice admit of degree and run insensibly into each other, you expressly contradict the foregoing position that obligation and property are not susceptible of such a gradation. These depend entirely upon justice and injustice and follow them in all their variations. Where the justice is entire, the property is also entire; where the justice is imperfect, the property must also be imperfect. And *vice versa*, if the property admit of no such variations, they must also be incompatible with justice. If you assent, therefore, to this last proposition, and assert that justice and injustice are not susceptible of degrees, you in effect assert that they are not *naturally* either vicious or virtuous; since vice and virtue, moral good and evil, and indeed all *natural* qualities, run insensibly into each other and are on many occasions undistinguishable.

And here it may be worth while to observe that, though abstract reasoning and the general maxims of philosophy and law establish this position *that property, and right, and obligation admit not of degrees*, yet in our common and negligent way of thinking we find great difficulty to entertain that opinion, and do even *secretly* embrace the contrary principle. An object must either be in the possession of one person or another. An action must either be performed or not. The necessity there is of choosing one side in these dilemmas, and the impossibility there often is of finding any just medium, oblige us, when we reflect on the matter, to acknowledge that all property and obligations are entire. But on the other hand, when we consider the origin of property and obligation, and find that they depend on public utility and sometimes on the propensity of the imagination, which are seldom entire on any side, we are naturally inclined to imagine that these moral relations admit of an insensible gradation. Hence it is that in references, where the consent of the parties leave the referees entire masters of the subject, they commonly discover so much equity and justice on both sides as induces them to strike a medium, and divide the difference betwixt the parties. Civil judges, who have not this liberty, but are obliged to give a decisive sentence on some one side, are often at a loss how to determine, and are necessitated to proceed on the most frivolous reasons in the world. Half rights and obligations, which seem so natural in common life, are perfect absurdities in their tribunal; for which reason they are often obliged to take half arguments for whole ones in order to terminate the affair one way or the other.

III. The third argument of this kind I shall make use of may be explained thus. If we consider the ordinary course of human actions, we shall find that the mind restrains not itself by any general and universal rules, but acts on most occasions as it is determined by its present motives and inclination. As each action is a particular individual event, it must proceed from particular principles, and from our immediate situation within ourselves, and with respect to the rest of the universe. If on some occasions we extend our motives beyond those very circumstances which gave rise to them, and form something like *general rules* for our conduct, it is easy to observe that these rules are not perfectly inflexible, but allow of many exceptions. Since, therefore, this is the ordinary course of human actions, we may conclude that the laws of justice, being universal and perfectly inflexible, can never be derived from nature, nor be the immediate offspring of any natural motive or inclination. No action can be either morally good or evil, unless there be some natural passion or motive to impel us to it, or deter us from it; and it is evident that the morality must be susceptible of all the same variations which are natural to the passion. Here are two persons who dispute for an estate; of whom one is rich, a fool, and a bachelor; the other poor, a man of sense, and has a numerous family: the first is my enemy; the second my friend. Whether I be actuated in this affair by a view to public or private interest, by friendship or enmity, I must be induced to do my utmost to procure the estate to the latter. Nor would any consideration of the right and property of the persons be able to restrain me, were I actuated only by natural motives, without any combination or convention with others. For as all property depends on morality, and as all morality depends on the ordinary course of our passions and actions, and as these again are only directed by particular motives, it is evident such a partial conduct must be suitable to the strictest morality, and could never be a violation of property. Were men, therefore, to take the liberty of acting with regard to the laws of society, as they do in every other affair, they would conduct themselves on most occasions by particular judgments, and would take into consideration the characters and circumstances of the persons as well as the general nature of the question. But it is easy to observe that this would produce an infinite confusion in human society, and that the avidity and partiality of men would quickly bring disorder into the world, if not restrained by some general and inflexible principles. It was therefore with a view to this inconvenience that men have established those principles and have agreed to restrain themselves by general rules which are unchangeable by spite and favour and by particular views of private or public interest. These rules, then, are artificially invented for a certain purpose, and are contrary to the common principles of human nature which accommodate themselves to circumstances and have no stated invariable method of operation.

Nor do I perceive how I can easily be mistaken in this matter. I see, evidently, that when any man imposes on himself general inflexible rules in his conduct with others, he considers certain objects as their property, which he supposes to be sacred and inviolable. But no proposition can be more evident than that property is perfectly unintelligible without first supposing justice and injustice; and that these virtues and vices are as unintelligible, unless we have motives, independent of the morality, to impel us to just actions, and deter us from unjust ones. Let those motives, therefore, be what they will, they must accommodate themselves to circumstances, and must admit of all the variations which human affairs in their incessant revolutions are susceptible of. They are, consequently, a very improper foundation for such rigid inflexible rules as the laws of nature; and it is evident these laws can only be derived from human conventions, when men have perceived the disorders that result from following their natural and variable principles.

Upon the whole, then, we are to consider this distinction betwixt justice and injustice as having two different foundations, viz., that of *interest*, when men observe that it is impossible to live in society without restraining themselves by certain rules; and that of *morality*, when this interest is once observed and men receive a pleasure from the view of such actions as tend to the peace of society, and an uneasiness from such as are contrary to it. It is the voluntary convention and artifice of men which makes the first interest take place; and therefore those laws of justice are so far to be considered as *artificial*.

After that interest is once established and acknowledged, the sense of morality in the observance of these rules follows *naturally*, and of itself; though it is certain that it is also augmented by a new *artifice*, and that the public instructions of politicians and the private education of parents contribute to the giving us a sense of honour and duty in the strict regulation of our actions with regard to the properties of others.

SECTION VII

OF THE ORIGIN OF GOVERNMENT

NOTHING IS MORE certain than that men are in a great measure governed by interest, and that, even when they extend their concern beyond themselves, it is not to any great distance; nor is it usual for them in common life to look further than their nearest friends and acquaintance. It is no less certain that it is impossible for men to consult their interest in so effectual a manner as by an universal and inflexible observance of the rules of justice by which alone they can preserve society, and keep themselves from falling into that wretched and savage condition which is commonly represented as the *state of nature*. And as this interest which all men have in the upholding of society and the observation of the rules of justice is great, so is it palpable and evident, even to the most rude and uncultivated of the human race; and it is almost impossible for any one who has had experience of society to be mistaken in this particular. Since, therefore, men are so sincerely attached to their interest, and their interest is so much concerned in the observance of justice, and this interest is so certain and avowed, it may be asked how any disorder can ever arise in society, and what principle there is in human nature so *powerful* as to overcome so strong a passion, or so *violent* as to obscure so clear a knowledge?

It has been observed, in treating of the passions, that men are mightily governed by the imagination, and proportion their affections more to the light under which any object appears to them than to its real and intrinsic value. What strikes upon them with a strong and lively idea commonly prevails above what lies in a more obscure light;

and it must be a great superiority of value that is able to compensate this advantage. Now, as everything that is contiguous to us, either in space or time, strikes upon us with such an idea, it has a proportional effect on the will and passions, and commonly operates with more force than any object that lies in a more distant and obscure light. Though we may be fully convinced that the latter object excels the former, we are not able to regulate our actions by this judgment, but yield to the solicitations of our passions, which always plead in favour of whatever is near and contiguous.

This is the reason why men so often act in contradiction to their known interest; and, in particular, why they prefer any trivial advantage that is present to the maintenance of order in society, which so much depends on the observance of justice. The consequences of every breach of equity seem to lie very remote, and are not liable to counterbalance any immediate advantage that may be reaped from it. They are, however, nevertheless real for being remote; and as all men are in some degree subject to the same weakness, it necessarily happens that the violations of equity must become very frequent in society, and the commerce of men by that means be rendered very dangerous and uncertain. You have the same propension that I have in favour of what is contiguous above what is remote. You are, therefore, naturally carried to commit acts of injustice as well as me. Your example both pushes me forward in this way by imitation, and also affords me a new reason for any breach of equity by showing me that I should be the cully of my integrity if I alone should impose on myself a severe restraint amidst the licentiousness of others.

This quality, therefore, of human nature, not only is very dangerous to society, but also seems, on a cursory view, to be incapable of any remedy. The remedy can only come from the consent of men; and if men be incapable of themselves to prefer remote to contiguous, they will never consent to anything which would oblige them to such a choice and contradict in so sensible a manner their natural principles and propensities. Whoever chooses the means, chooses also the end; and if it be impossible for us to prefer what is remote, it is equally impossible for us to submit to any necessity which would oblige us to such a method of acting.

But here it is observable that this infirmity of human nature becomes a remedy to itself, and that we provide against our negligence about remote objects, merely because we are naturally inclined to that negligence. When we consider any objects at a distance, all their minute distinctions vanish, and we always give the preference to whatever is in itself preferable, without considering its situation and circumstances. This gives rise to what, in an improper sense, we call *reason*, which is a principle that is often contradictory to those propensities that display themselves upon the approach of the object. In reflecting on any action which I am to perform a twelvemonth hence, I always resolve to prefer the greater good, whether at that time it will be more contiguous or remote; nor does any difference in that particular make a difference in my present intentions and resolutions. My distance from the final determination makes all those minute differences vanish, nor am I affected by anything but the general and more discernible qualities of good and evil. But on my nearer approach, those circumstances which I at first overlooked begin to appear, and have an influence on my conduct and affections. A new inclination to the present good springs up, and makes it difficult for me to adhere inflexibly to my first purpose and resolution. This natural infirmity I may very much regret, and I may endeavour by all possible means to free myself from it. I may have recourse to study and reflection within myself, to the advice of friends, to frequent meditation and repeated resolution, and having experienced how ineffectual all these are, I may embrace with pleasure any other expedient by which I may impose a restraint upon myself and guard against this weakness.

The only difficulty, therefore, is to find out this expedient by which men cure their natural weakness and lay themselves under the necessity of observing the laws of justice and equity, notwithstanding their violent propension to prefer contiguous to remote. It is evident such a remedy can never be effectual without correcting this propensity; and as it is impossible to change or correct anything material in our nature, the utmost we can do is to change our circumstances and situation, and render the observance of the laws of justice our nearest interest, and their violation our most remote. But this being impracticable with respect to all mankind, it can only take place with respect to a few whom we thus immediately interest in the execution of justice. These are the persons whom we call civil magistrates, kings and their ministers, our governors and rulers, who, being indifferent persons to the greatest part of the state, have no interest, or but a remote one, in any act of injustice; and, being satisfied with their present condition and with their part in society, have an immediate interest in every execution of justice which is so necessary to the upholding of society. Here, then, is the origin of civil government and society. Men are not able radically to cure either in themselves or others that narrowness of soul which makes them prefer the present to the remote. They cannot change their natures. All they can do is to change their situation and render the observance of justice the immediate interest of some particular persons, and its violation their more remote. These persons, then, are not only induced to observe those rules in their own conduct, but also to constrain others to a like regularity, and enforce the dictates of equity through the whole society. And if it be necessary, they may also interest others more immediately in the execution of justice, and create a number of officers, civil and military, to assist them in their government.

But this execution of justice, though the principal, is not the only advantage of government. As violent passion hinders men from seeing distinctly the interest they have in an equitable behaviour towards others, so it hinders them from seeing that equity itself, and gives them a remarkable partiality in their own favours. This inconvenience is corrected in the same manner as that above mentioned. The same persons who execute the laws of justice will also decide all controversies concerning them; and, being indifferent to the greatest part of the society, will decide them more equitably than every one would in his own case.

By means of these two advantages in the *execution* and *decision* of justice, men acquire a security against each other's weakness and passion as well as against their own, and, under the shelter of their governors, begin to taste at ease the sweets of society and mutual assistance. But government extends further its beneficial influence; and not contented to protect men in those conventions they make for their mutual interest, it often obliges them to make such conventions and forces them to seek their own advantage by a concurrence in some common end or purpose. There is no quality in human nature which causes more fatal errors in our conduct than that which leads us to prefer whatever is present to the distant and remote, and makes us desire objects more according to their situation than their intrinsic value. Two neighbours may agree to drain a meadow which they possess in common, because it is easy for them to know each other's mind; and each must perceive that the immediate consequence of his failing in his part is the abandoning the whole project. But it is very difficult, and indeed impossible, that a thousand persons should agree in any such action; it being difficult for them to concert so complicated a design, and still more difficult for them to execute it; while each seeks a pretext to free himself of the trouble and expense and would lay the whole burden on others. Political society easily remedies both these inconveniences. Magistrates find an immediate interest in the interest of any considerable part of their subjects. They need consult nobody but themselves to form any scheme for the promoting of that interest. And as the failure of any one piece in the execution is connected, though not immediately, with the failure of the whole, they prevent that failure because they find no interest in it, either immediate or remote. Thus bridges are built, harbours opened, ramparts raised, canals formed, fleets equipped, and armies disciplined, everywhere, by the care of government which, though composed of men subject to all human infirmities, becomes by one of the finest and most subtile inventions imaginable a composition which is in some measure exempted from all these infirmities.

SECTION VIII

OF THE SOURCE OF ALLEGIANCE

THOUGH GOVERNMENT be an invention very advantageous and even in some circumstances absolutely necessary to mankind, it is not necessary in all circumstances; nor is it impossible for men to preserve society for some time without having recourse to such an invention. Men, it is true, are always much inclined to prefer present interest to distant and remote; nor is it easy for them to resist the temptation of any advantage that they may immediately enjoy, in apprehension of an evil that lies at a distance from them; but still this weakness is less conspicuous where the possessions and the pleasures of life are few and of little value, as they always are in the infancy of society. An

Indian is but little tempted to dispossess another of his hut, or to steal his bow, as being already provided of the same advantages; and as to any superior fortune which may attend one above another in hunting and fishing, it is only casual and temporary, and will have but small tendency to disturb society. And so far am I from thinking with some philosophers that men are utterly incapable of society without government that I assert the first rudiments of government to arise from quarrels, not among men of the same society, but among those of different societies. A less degree of riches will suffice to this latter effect than is requisite for the former. Men fear nothing from public war and violence but the resistance they meet with, which, because they share it in common, seems less terrible, and, because it comes from strangers, seems less pernicious in its consequences than when they are exposed singly against one whose commerce is advantageous to them, and without whose society it is impossible they can subsist. Now, foreign war, to a society without government, necessarily produces civil war. Throw any considerable goods among men, they instantly fall a quarrelling, while each strives to get possession of what pleases him, without regard to the consequences. In a foreign war the most considerable of all goods, life and limbs, are at stake; and as every one shuns dangerous ports, seizes the best arms, seeks excuse for the slightest wounds, the laws, which may be well enough observed while men were calm, can now no longer take place when they are in such commotion.

This we find verified in the American tribes, where men live in concord and amity among themselves, without any established government, and never pay submission to any of their fellows, except in time of war, when their captain enjoys a shadow of authority, which he loses after their return from the field and the establishment of peace with the neighbouring tribes. This authority, however, instructs them in the advantages of government and teaches them to have recourse to it when either by the pillage of war, by commerce, or by any fortuitous inventions, their riches and possessions have become so considerable as to make them forget, on every emergency, the interest they have in the preservation of peace and justice. Hence we may give a plausible reason, among others, why all governments are at first monarchical, without any mixture and variety; and why republics arise only from the abuses of monarchy and despotic power. Camps are the true mothers of cities; and as war cannot be administered, by reason of the suddenness of every exigency, without some authority in a single person, the same kind of authority naturally takes place in that civil government which succeeds the military. And this reason I take to be more natural than the common one derived from patriarchal government, or the authority of a father, which is said first to take place in one family, and to accustom the members of it to the government of a single person. The state of society without government is one of the most natural states of men, and must subsist with the conjunction of many families, and long after the first generation. Nothing but an increase of riches and possessions could oblige men to quit it; and so barbarous and uninstructed are all societies on their first formation that many years must elapse before these can increase to such a degree as to disturb men in the enjoyment of peace and concord.

But though it be possible for men to maintain a small uncultivated society without government, it is impossible they should maintain a society of any kind without justice, and the observance of those three fundamental laws concerning the stability of possession, its translation by consent, and the performance of promises. These are, therefore, antecedent to government, and are supposed to impose an obligation before the duty of allegiance to civil magistrates has once been thought of. Nay, I shall go further and assert that government, *upon its first establishment*, would naturally be supposed to derive its obligation from those laws of nature and in particular from that concerning the performance of promises. When men have once perceived the necessity of government to maintain peace and execute justice, they would naturally assemble together, would choose magistrates, determine their power, and *promise* them obedience. As a promise is supposed to be a bond or security already in use and attended with a moral obligation, it is to be considered as the original sanction of government, and as the source of the first obligation to obedience. This reasoning appears so natural that it has become the foundation of our fashionable system of politics, and is in a manner the creed of a party amongst us, who pride themselves, with reason, on the soundness of their philosophy and their liberty of thought. "All men," say they, "are born free and equal: government and superiority can only be established by consent: the consent of men in establishing government imposes on them a new obligation, unknown to the laws of nature. Men, therefore, are bound to obey their magistrates only because they promise it; and if they had not given their word either expressly or tacitly to preserve allegiance, it would never have become a part of their moral duty." This conclusion, however, when carried so far as to comprehend government in all its ages and situations, is entirely erroneous; and I maintain that though the duty of allegiance be at first grafted on the obligation of promises and be for some time supported by that obligation, yet it quickly takes root of itself and has an original obligation and authority, independent of all contracts. This is a principle of moment, which we must examine with care and attention before we proceed any further.

It is reasonable for those philosophers who assert justice to be a natural virtue, and antecedent to human conventions, to resolve all civil allegiance into the obligation of a promise, and assert that it is our own consent alone which binds us to any submission to magistracy. For as all government is plainly an invention of men, and the origin of most governments is known in history, it is necessary to mount higher in order to find the source of our political duties, if we would assert them to have any *natural* obligation of morality. These philosophers, therefore, quickly observe that society is as ancient as the human species, and those three fundamental laws of nature as ancient as society; so that, taking advantage of the antiquity and obscure origin of these laws, they first deny them to be artificial and voluntary inventions of men, and then seek to ingraft on them those other duties which are more plainly artificial. But being once undeceived in this particular, and having found that *natural* as well as *civil* justice derives its origin from human conventions, we shall quickly perceive how fruitless it is to resolve the one into the other and seek in the laws of nature a stronger foundation for our political duties than interest and human conventions, while these laws themselves are built on the very same foundation. On whichever side we turn this subject, we shall find that these two kinds of duties are exactly on the same footing and have the same source both of their *first invention* and *moral obligation*. They are contrived to remedy like inconveniences, and acquire their moral sanction in the same manner from their remedying those inconveniences. These are two points which we shall endeavour to prove as distinctly as possible.

We have already shown that men *invented* the three fundamental laws of nature when they observed the necessity of society to their mutual subsistence, and found that it was impossible to maintain any correspondence together without some restraint on their natural appetites. The same self-love, therefore, which renders men so incommodious to each other, taking a new and more convenient direction, produces the rules of justice, and is the *first* motive of their observance. But when men have observed that though the rules of justice be sufficient to maintain any society, yet it is impossible for them, of themselves, to observe those rules in large and polished societies, they establish government as a new invention to attain their ends, and preserve the old or procure new advantages by a more strict execution of justice. So far, therefore, our *civil* duties are connected with our *natural*, that the former are invented chiefly for the sake of the latter; and that the principal object of government is to constrain men to observe the laws of nature. In this respect, however, that law of nature concerning the performance of promises is only comprised along with the rest; and its exact observance is to be considered as an effect of the institution of government, and not the obedience to government as an effect of the obligation of a promise. Though the object of our civil duties be the enforcing of our natural, yet the *first* [1] motive of the invention, as well as performance of both, is nothing but self-interest; and since there is a separate interest in the obedience to government from that in the performance of promises, we must also allow of a separate obligation. To obey the civil magistrate is requisite to preserve order and concord in society. To perform promises is requisite to beget mutual trust and confidence in the common offices of life. The ends as well as the means are perfectly distinct; nor is the one subordinate to the other.

To make this more evident, let us consider that men will often bind themselves by promises to the performance of what it would have been their interest to perform independent of these promises; as when they would give others a fuller security by superadding a new obligation of interest to that which they formerly lay under. The interest in the performance of promises, besides its moral obligation, is general, avowed, and of the last consequence in life. Other interests may be more particular and doubtful; and we are apt to entertain a greater

[1] First in time, not in dignity or force.

suspicion that men may indulge their humour or passion in acting contrary to them. Here, therefore, promises come naturally in play, and are often required for fuller satisfaction and security. But supposing those other interests to be as general and avowed as the interest in the performance of a promise, they will be regarded as on the same footing, and men will begin to repose the same confidence in them. Now this is exactly the case with regard to our civil duties or obedience to the magistrate; without which no government could subsist, nor any peace or order be maintained in large societies, where there are so many possessions on the one hand, and so many wants, real or imaginary, on the other. Our civil duties, therefore, must soon detach themselves from our promises and acquire a separate force and influence. The interest in both is of the very same kind: it is general, avowed, and prevails in all times and places. There is, then, no pretext of reason for founding the one upon the other, while each of them has a foundation peculiar to itself. We might as well resolve the obligation to abstain from the possessions of others into the obligation of a promise, as that of allegiance. The interests are not more distinct in the one case than in the other. A regard to property is not more necessary to natural society than obedience is to civil society or government; nor is the former society more necessary to the being of mankind than the latter to their well-being and happiness. In short, if the performance of promises be advantageous, so is obedience to government; if the former interest be general, so is the latter; if the one interest be obvious and avowed, so is the other. And as these two rules are founded on like obligations of interest, each of them must have a peculiar authority, independent of the other.

But it is not only the *natural* obligations of interest which are distinct in promises and allegiance; but also the *moral* obligations of honour and conscience: nor does the merit or demerit of the one depend in the least upon that of the other. And, indeed, if we consider the close connection there is betwixt the natural and moral obligations, we shall find this conclusion to be entirely unavoidable. Our interest is always engaged on the side of obedience to magistracy; and there is nothing but a great present advantage that can lead us to rebellion, by making us overlook the remote interest which we have in the preserving of peace and order in society. But though a present interest may thus blind us with regard to our own actions, it takes not place with regard to those of others; nor hinders them from appearing in their true colours, as highly prejudicial to public interest and to our own in particular. This naturally gives us an uneasiness in considering such seditious and disloyal actions, and makes us attach to them the idea of vice and moral deformity. It is the same principle which causes us to disapprove of all kinds of private injustice, and in particular of the breach of promises. We blame all treachery and breach of faith, because we consider that the freedom and extent of human commerce depend entirely on a fidelity with regard to promises. We blame all disloyalty to magistrates, because we perceive that the execution of justice in the stability of possession, its translation by consent, and the performance of promises, is impossible without submission to government. As there are here two interests entirely distinct from each other, they must give rise to two moral obligations, equally separate and independent. Though there was no such thing as a promise in the world, government would still be necessary in all large and civilized societies; and if promises had only their own proper obligation, without the separate sanction of government, they would have but little efficacy in such societies. This separates the boundaries of our public and private duties, and shows that the latter are more dependent on the former than the former on the latter. *Education* and *the artifice of politicians* concur to bestow a further morality on loyalty, and to brand all rebellion with a greater degree of guilt and infamy. Nor is it a wonder that politicians should be very industrious in inculcating such notions where their interest is so particularly concerned.

Lest those arguments should not appear entirely conclusive — as I think they are — I shall have recourse to authority, and shall prove from the universal consent of mankind that the obligation of submission to government is not derived from any promise of the subjects. Nor need any one wonder that though I have all along endeavoured to establish my system on pure reason, and have scarce ever cited the judgment even of philosophers or historians on any article, I should now appeal to popular authority and oppose the sentiments of the rabble to any philosophical reasoning. For it must be observed that the opinions of men in this case carry with them a peculiar authority, and are, in a great measure, infallible. The distinction of moral good and evil is founded on the pleasure or pain which results from the view of any sentiment or character; and as that pleasure or pain cannot be unknown to the person who feels it, it follows[2] that there is just so much vice or virtue in any character as every one places in it, and that it is impossible in this particular we can ever be mistaken. And though our judgments concerning the *origin* of any vice or virtue be not so certain as those concerning their *degrees*, yet, since the question in this case regards not any philosophical origin of an obligation but a plain matter of fact, it is not easily conceived how we can fall into an error. A man who acknowledges himself to be bound to another for a certain sum must certainly know whether it be by his own bond or that of his father; whether it be of his mere good-will or for money lent him; and under what conditions and for what purposes he has bound himself. In like manner, it being certain that there is a moral obligation to submit to government because every one thinks so; it must be as certain that this obligation arises not from a promise, since no one whose judgment has not been led astray by too strict adherence to a system of philosophy has ever yet dreamt of ascribing it to that origin. Neither magistrates nor subjects have formed this idea of our civil duties.

We find that magistrates are so far from deriving their authority and the obligation to obedience in their subjects from the foundation of a promise or original contract, that they conceal as far as possible from their people, especially from the vulgar, that they have their origin from thence. Were this the sanction of government, our rulers would never receive it tacitly, which is the utmost that can be pretended; since what is given tacitly and insensibly can never have such influence on mankind as what is performed expressly and openly. A tacit promise is where the will is signified by other more diffuse signs than those of speech; but a will there must certainly be in the case, and that can never escape the person's notice who exerted it, however silent or tacit. But were you to ask the far greatest part of the nation whether they had ever consented to the authority of their rulers or promised to obey them, they would be inclined to think very strangely of you, and would certainly reply that the affair depended not on their

[2] This proposition must hold strictly true with regard to every quality that is determined merely by sentiment. In what sense we can talk either of a *right* or a *wrong* taste in morals, eloquence, or beauty, shall be considered afterwards. In the meantime it may be observed that there is such an uniformity in the *general* sentiments of mankind as to render such questions of but small importance.

consent, but that they were born to such an obedience. In consequence of this opinion we frequently see them imagine such persons to be their natural rulers, as are at that time deprived of all power and authority, and whom no man, however foolish, would voluntarily choose; and this merely because they are in that line which ruled before, and in that degree of it which used to succeed, though perhaps in so distant a period that scarce any man alive could ever have given any promise of obedience. Has a government, then, no authority over such as these because they never consented to it and would esteem the very attempt of such a free choice a piece of arrogance and impiety? We find by experience that it punishes them very freely for what it calls treason and rebellion which, it seems, according to this system reduces itself to common injustice. If you say that by dwelling in its dominions they in effect consented to the established government, I answer that this can only be where they think the affair depends on their choice, which few or none beside those philosophers have ever yet imagined. It never was pleaded as an excuse for a rebel that the first act he performed, after he came to years of discretion, was to levy war against the sovereign of the state; and that, while he was a child he could not bind himself by his own consent, and, having become a man, showed plainly by the first act he performed that he had no design to impose on himself any obligation to obedience. We find, on the contrary, that civil laws punish this crime at the same age as any other which is criminal of itself, without our consent, that is, when the person is come to the full use of reason; whereas to this crime it ought in justice to allow some intermediate time in which a tacit consent at least might be supposed. To which we may add that a man living under an absolute government would owe it no allegiance; since by its very nature it depends not on consent. But as that is as *natural* and *common* a government as any, it must certainly occasion some obligation; and it is plain from experience that men who are subjected to it do always think so. This is a clear proof that we do not commonly esteem our allegiance to be derived from our consent or promise; and a further proof is that when our promise is upon any account expressly engaged, we always distinguish exactly betwixt the two obligations, and believe the one to add more force to the other than in a repetition of the same promise. Where no promise is given, a man looks not on his faith as broken in private matters, upon account of rebellion, but keeps those two duties of honour and allegiance perfectly distinct and separate. As the uniting of them was thought by these philosophers a very subtile invention, this is a convincing proof that it is not a true one, since no man can either give a promise or be restrained by its sanction and obligation unknown to himself.

SECTION IX

OF THE MEASURES OF ALLEGIANCE

THOSE POLITICAL WRITERS who have had recourse to a promise or original contract as the source of our allegiance to government intended to establish a principle which is perfectly just and reasonable; though the reasoning upon which they endeavoured to establish it was fallacious and sophistical. They would prove that our submission to government admits of exceptions, and that an egregious tyranny in the rulers is sufficient to free the subjects from all ties of allegiance. Since men enter into society, say they, and submit themselves to government by their free and voluntary consent, they must have in view certain advantages which they propose to reap from it, and for which they are contented to resign their native liberty. There is therefore something mutual engaged on the part of the magistrate, viz., protection and security; and it is only by the hopes he affords of these advantages that he can ever persuade men to submit to him. But when, instead of protection and security, they meet with tyranny and oppression, they are freed from their promises — as happens in all conditional contracts — and return to that state of liberty which preceded the institution of government. Men would never be so foolish as to enter into such engagements as should turn entirely to the advantage of others, without any view of bettering their own condition. Whoever proposes to draw any profit from our submission must engage himself, either expressly or tacitly, to make us reap some advantage from his authority; nor ought he to expect that without the performance of his part we will ever continue in obedience.

I repeat it: this conclusion is just, though the principles be erroneous; and I flatter myself that I can establish the same conclusion on more reasonable principles. I shall not take such a compass in establishing our political duties as to assert that men perceive the advantages of government, that they institute government with a view to those advantages, that this institution requires a promise of obedience which imposes a moral obligation to a certain degree, but, being conditional, ceases to be binding whenever the other contracting party performs not his part of the engagement. I perceive that a promise itself arises entirely from human conventions, and is invented with a view to a certain interest. I seek, therefore, some such interest more immediately connected with government, and which may be at once the original motive to its institution and the source of our obedience to it. This interest I find to consist in the security and protection which we enjoy in political society, and which we can never attain when perfectly free and independent. As the interest, therefore, is the immediate sanction of government, the one can have no longer being than the other; and whenever the civil magistrate carries his oppression so far as to render his authority perfectly intoler-able, we are no longer bound to submit to it. The cause ceases; the effect must cease also.

So far the conclusion is immediate and direct concerning the *natural obligation* which we have to allegiance. As to the *moral* obligation, we may observe that the maxim would here be false, that *when the cause ceases the effect must cease also.* For there is a principle of human nature, which we have frequently taken notice of, that men are mightily addicted to *general rules*, and that we often carry our maxims beyond those reasons which first induced us to establish them. Where cases are similar in many circumstances, we are apt to put them on the same footing, without considering that they differ in the most material circumstances, and that the resemblance is more apparent than real. It may therefore be thought that in the case of allegiance our moral obligation of duty will not cease, even though the natural obligation of interest, which is its cause, has ceased; and that men may be bound by *conscience* to submit to a tyrannical government, against their own and the public interest. And indeed, to the force of this argument I so far submit as to acknowledge that general rules commonly extend beyond the principles on which they are founded; and that we seldom make any exception to them, unless that exception have the qualities of a general rule and be founded on very numerous and common instances. Now, this I assert to be entirely the present case. When men submit to the authority of others, it is to procure themselves some security against the wickedness and injustice of men who are perpetually carried by their unruly passions and by their present and immediate interest to the violation of all the laws of society. But as this imperfection is inherent in human nature, we know that it must attend men in all their states and conditions; and that those whom we choose for rulers do not immediately become of a superior nature to the rest of mankind, upon account of their superior power and authority. What we expect from them depends not on a change of their nature but of their situation, when they acquire a more immediate interest in the preservation of order and the execution of justice. But besides that this interest is only more immediate in the execution of justice among their subjects — besides this, I say, we may often expect from the irregularity of human nature that they will neglect even this immediate interest and be transported by their passions into all the excesses of cruelty and ambition. Our general knowledge of human nature, our observation of the past history of mankind, our experience of present times — all these causes must induce us to open the door of exceptions, and must make us conclude that we may resist the more violent effects of supreme power without any crime or injustice.

Accordingly we may observe that this is both the general practice and principle of mankind, and that no nation that could find any remedy ever yet suffered the cruel ravages of a tyrant, or were blamed for their resistance. Those who took up arms against Dionysius, or Nero, or Philip the Second, have the favour of every reader in the perusal of their history; and nothing but the most violent perversion of common sense can ever lead us to condemn them. It is certain, therefore, that in all our notions of morals we never entertain such an absurdity as that of passive obedience, but make allowances for resistance in the more flagrant instances of tyranny and oppression. The general opinion of mankind has some authority in all cases; but in this of morals it is perfectly infallible. Nor is it less infallible because men cannot distinctly explain the principles on which it is founded. Few persons can carry on this train of reasoning: "Government is a mere human invention for the interest of society. Where the tyranny of the governor removes this interest, it also removes the natural obligation to obedience. The moral obligation is founded on the natural, and therefore must cease where *that* ceases; especially where the subject is such as makes us foresee very many occasions wherein the natural obligation may cease, and causes us to form a kind of general rule for the regulation of our conduct in such occurrences." But though this train of reasoning be too subtle for the vulgar, it is certain that all men have an implicit notion of it, and are sensible that they owe obedience to government merely on account of the public interest; and at the same time, that human nature is so subject to frailties and passions, as may easily pervert this institution and change their governors into tyrants and public enemies. If the sense of public interest were not our original motive to obedience, I would fain ask, what other principle is there in human nature capable of subduing the natural ambition of men and forcing them to such a submission? Imitation and custom are not sufficient. For the question still recurs what motive first produces those instances of submission which we imitate, and that train of actions which produces the custom? There evidently is no other principle than public interest; and if interest first produces obedience to government, the obligation to obedience must cease whenever the interest ceases in any great degree and in a considerable number of instances.

SECTION X

OF THE OBJECTS OF ALLEGIANCE

But though on some occasions it may be justifiable, both in sound politics and morality, to resist supreme power, it is certain that in the ordinary course of human affairs nothing can be more pernicious and criminal; and that, besides the convulsions which always attend revolutions, such a practice tends directly to the subversion of all government and the causing a universal anarchy and confusion among mankind. As numerous and civilized societies cannot subsist without government, so government is entirely useless without an exact obedience. We ought always to weigh the advantages which we reap from authority against the disadvantages; and by this means we shall become more scrupulous of putting in practice the doctrine of resistance. The common rule requires submission; and it is only in cases of grievous tyranny and oppression that the exception can take place.

Since, then, such a blind submission is commonly due to magistracy, the next question is, *to whom it is due, and whom we are to regard as our lawful magistrates?* In order to answer this question, let us recollect what we have already established concerning the origin of government and political society. When men have once experienced the impossibility of preserving any steady order in society, while every one is his own master and violates or observes the laws of interest according to his present interest or pleasure, they naturally run into the invention of government and put it out of their own power as far as possible to transgress the laws of society. Government, therefore, arises from the voluntary convention of men; and it is evident that the same convention which establishes government will also determine the persons who are to govern, and will remove all doubt and ambiguity in this particular. And the voluntary consent of men must here have the greater efficacy, that the authority of the magistrate does *at first* stand upon the foundation of a promise of the subjects by which they bind themselves to obedience as in every other contract or engagement. The same promise, then, which binds them to obedience ties them down to a particular person, and makes him the object of their allegiance.

But when government has been established on this footing for some considerable time, and the separate interests which we have in submission has produced a separate sentiment of morality, the case is entirely altered, and a promise is no longer able to determine the particular magistrate; since it is no longer considered as the foundation of government. We naturally suppose ourselves born to submission; and imagine that such particular persons have a right to command, as we on our part are bound to obey. These notions of right and obligation are derived from nothing but the *advantage* we reap from government, which gives us a repugnance to practise resistance ourselves and makes us displeased with any instance of it in others. But here it is remarkable that in this new state of affairs the original sanction of government, which is *interest*, is not admitted to determine the persons whom we are to obey, as the original sanction did at first when affairs were on the footing of a *promise*. A *promise* fixes and determines the persons without any uncertainty: but it is evident that if men were to regulate their conduct in this particular by the view of a peculiar *interest*, either public or private, they would involve themselves in endless confusion and would render all government in a great measure ineffectual. The private interest of every one is different; and though the public interest in itself be always one and the same, yet it becomes the source of as great dissensions, by reason of the different opinions of particular persons concerning it. The same interest, therefore, which causes us to submit to magistracy, makes us renounce itself in the choice of our magistrates, and binds us down to a certain form of government and to particular persons, without allowing us to aspire to the utmost perfection in either. The case is here the same as in that law of nature concerning the stability of possession. It is highly advantageous, and even absolutely necessary to society, that possession should be stable; and this leads us to the establishment of such a rule. But we find that were we to follow the same advantage in assigning particular possessions to particular persons, we should disappoint our end and perpetuate the confusion which that rule is intended to prevent. We must therefore proceed by general rules, and regulate ourselves by general interests, in modifying the law of nature concerning the stability of possession. Nor need we fear that our attachment to this law will diminish upon account of the seeming frivolousness of those interests by which it is determined. The impulse of the mind is derived from a very strong interest; and those other more minute interests serve only to direct the motion, without adding anything to it or diminishing from it. It is the same case with government. Nothing is more advantageous to society than such an invention; and this interest is sufficient to make us embrace it with ardour and alacrity, though we are obliged afterwards to regulate and direct our devotion to government by several considerations which are not of the same importance, and to choose our magistrates without having in view any particular advantage from the choice.

The first of those principles I shall take notice of as a foundation of the right of magistracy, is that which gives authority to all the most established governments of the world, without exception: I mean *long possession* in any one form of government or succession of princes. It is certain that if we remount to the first origin of every nation, we shall find that there scarce is any race of kings or form of a commonwealth that is not primarily founded on usurpation and rebellion, and whose title is not at first worse than doubtful and uncertain. Time alone gives solidity to their right, and, operating gradually on the minds of men, reconciles them to any authority, and makes it seem just and reasonable. Nothing causes any sentiment to have a greater influence upon us than custom, or turns our imagination more strongly to any object. When we have been long accustomed to obey any set of men, that general instinct or tendency which we have to suppose a moral obligation attending loyalty takes easily this direction and chooses that set of men for its object. It is interest which gives the general instinct; but it is custom which gives the particular direction.

And here it is observable that the same length of time has a different influence on our sentiments of morality, according to its different influence on the mind. We naturally judge of everything by comparison; and since, in considering the fate of kingdoms and republics, we embrace a long extent of time, a small duration has not, in this case, a like influence on our sentiments as when we consider any other object. One thinks he acquires a right to a horse, or a suit of clothes, in a very short time; but a century is scarce sufficient to establish any new government, or remove all scruples in the minds of the subjects concerning it. Add to this that a shorter period of time will suffice to give a prince a title to any additional power he may usurp than will serve to fix his right, where the whole is an usurpation. The kings of France have not been possessed of absolute power for above two reigns; and yet nothing will appear more extravagant to Frenchmen than to talk of their liberties. If we consider what has been said concerning *accession*, we shall easily account for this phenomenon.

When there is no form of government established by *long* possession, the *present* possession is sufficient to supply its place and may be regarded as the *second* source of all public authority. Right to authority is nothing but the constant possession of authority, maintained by the laws of society and the interests of mankind; and nothing can be more natural than to join this constant possession to the present one, according to the principles above mentioned. If the same principles did not take place with regard to the property of private persons, it was because these principles were counterbalanced by very strong considerations of interest, when we observed that all restitution would by that means be prevented, and every violence be authorized and protected. And, though the same motives may seem to have force with regard to public authority, yet they are opposed by a contrary interest; which consists in the preservation of peace, and the avoiding of all changes which, however they may be easily produced in private affairs, are unavoidably attended with bloodshed and confusion where the public is interested.

Any one who, finding the impossibility of accounting for the right of the present possessor by any received system of ethics, should resolve to deny absolutely that right and assert that it is not authorized by morality, would be justly thought to maintain a very extravagant paradox, and to shock the common sense and judgment of mankind. No maxim is more conformable, both to prudence and morals, than to submit quietly to the government which we find established in the country where we happen to live, without inquiring too curiously into its origin and first establishment. Few governments will bear being examined so rigorously. How many kingdoms are there at present in the world, and how many more do we find in history, whose governors have no better foundation for their authority than that of present possession! To confine ourselves to the Roman and Grecian empire; is it not evident that the long succession of emperors, from the dissolution of the Roman liberty to the final extinction of that empire by the Turks, could not so much as pretend to any other title to the empire? The election of the senate was a mere form, which always followed the choice of the legions; and these were almost always divided in the different provinces, and nothing but the sword was able to terminate the difference. It was by the sword, therefore, that every emperor acquired as well as defended his right; and we must either say that all the known world for so many ages had no government and owed no allegiance to any one, or must allow that the right of the stronger in public affairs is to be received as legitimate and authorized by morality when not opposed by any other title.

The right of *conquest* may be considered as a *third* source of the title of sovereigns. This right resembles very much that of present possession, but has rather a superior force, being seconded by the notions of glory and honour which we ascribe to *conquerors*, instead of the sentiments of hatred and detestation which attend *usurpers*.

Men naturally favour those they love; and therefore are more apt to ascribe a right to successful violence betwixt one sovereign and another than to the successful rebellion of a subject against his sovereign.[1]

When neither long possession, nor present possession, nor conquest, take place, as when the first sovereign who founded any monarchy dies; in that case the right of *succession* naturally prevails in their stead, and men are commonly induced to place the son of their late monarch on the throne, and suppose him to inherit his father's authority. The presumed consent of the father, the imitation of the succession to private families, the interest which the state has in choosing the person who is most powerful and has the most numerous followers — all these reasons lead men to prefer the son of their late monarch to any other person.[2]

These reasons have some weight; but I am persuaded that to one who considers impartially of the matter, it will appear that there concur some principles of the imagination along with those views of interest. The royal authority seems to be connected with the young prince even in his father's lifetime, by the natural transition of the thought, and still more after his death; so that nothing is more natural than to complete this union by a new relation, and by putting him actually in possession of what seems so naturally to belong to him.

To confirm this we may weigh the following phenomena which are pretty curious in their kind. In elective monarchies the right of succession has no place by the laws and settled custom; and yet its influence is so natural that it is impossible entirely to exclude it from the imagination, and render the subjects indifferent to the son of their deceased monarch. Hence in some governments of this kind the choice commonly falls on one or other of the royal family; and in some governments they are all excluded. Those contrary phenomena proceed from the same principle. Where the royal family is excluded, it

---

[1] It is not here asserted that *present possession* or *conquest* are sufficient to give a title against *long possession* and *positive laws:* but only that they have some force, and will be able to cast the balance where the titles are otherwise equal, and will even be sufficient *sometimes* to sanctify the weaker title. What degree of force they have is difficult to determine. I believe all moderate men will allow that they have great force in all disputes concerning the rights of princes.

[2] To prevent mistakes I must observe that this case of succession is not the same with that of hereditary monarchies, where custom has fixed the right of succession. These depend upon the principle of long possession above explained.

is from a refinement in politics, which makes people sensible of their propensity to choose a sovereign in that family, and gives them a jealousy of their liberty, lest their new monarch, aided by this propensity, should establish his family and destroy the freedom of elections for the future.

The history of Artaxerxes and the younger Cyrus may furnish us with some reflections to the same purpose. Cyrus pretended a right to the throne above his elder brother, because he was born after his father's accession. I do not pretend that this reason was valid. I would only infer from it that he would never have made use of such a pretext, were it not for the qualities of the imagination above mentioned, by which we are naturally inclined to unite by a new relation whatever objects we find already united. Artaxerxes had an advantage above his brother, as being the eldest son and the first in succession; but Cyrus was more closely related to the royal authority, as being begot after his father was invested with it.

Should it here be pretended that the view of convenience may be the source of all the right of succession, and that men gladly take advantage of any rule by which they can fix the successor of their late sovereign, and prevent that anarchy and confusion which attends all new elections; to this I would answer that I readily allow that this motive may contribute something to the effect; but at the same time I assert that without another principle it is impossible such a motive should take place. The interest of a nation requires that the succession to the crown should be fixed one way or other; but it is the same thing to its interest in what way it be fixed; so that if the relation of blood had not an effect independent of public interest, it would never have been regarded without a positive law; and it would have been impossible that so many positive laws of different nations could ever have concurred precisely in the same views and intentions.

This leads us to consider the *fifth* source of authority, viz., *positive laws*, when the legislature establishes a certain form of government and succession of princes. At first sight it may be thought that this must resolve into some of the preceding titles of authority. The legislative power, whence the positive law is derived, must either be established by original contract, long possession, present possession, conquest, or succession; and, consequently, the positive law must derive its force from some of those principles. But here it is remarkable that though a positive law can only derive its force from these principles, yet it acquires not all the force of the principle from whence it is derived, but loses considerably in the transition, as it is natural to imagine. For instance, a government is established for many centuries on a certain system of laws, forms, and methods of succession. The legislative power established by this long succession changes all on a sudden the whole system of government, and introduces a new constitution in its stead. I believe few of the subjects will think themselves bound to comply with this alteration, unless it have an evident tendency to the public good, but will think themselves still at liberty to return to the ancient government. Hence the notion of *fundamental laws*, which are supposed to be unalterable by the will of the sovereign; and of this nature the Salic law is understood to be in France. How far these fundamental laws extend is not determined in any government, nor is it possible it ever should. There is such an insensible gradation from the most material laws to the most trivial, and from the most ancient laws to the most modern, that it will be impossible to set bounds to the legislative power, and determine how far it may innovate in the principles of government. That is the work more of imagination and passion than of reason.

Whoever considers the history of the several nations of the world, their revolutions, conquests, increase, and diminution, the manner in which their particular governments are established, and the successive right transmitted from one person to another, will soon learn to treat very lightly all disputes concerning the rights of princes, and will be convinced that a strict adherence to any general rules, and the rigid loyalty to particular persons and families on which some people set so high a value, are virtues that hold less of reason than of bigotry and superstition. In this particular, the study of history confirms the reasonings of true philosophy which, showing us the original qualities of human nature, teaches us to regard the controversies in politics as incapable of any decision in most cases, and as entirely subordinate to the interests of peace and liberty. Where the public good does not evidently demand a change, it is certain that the concurrence of all those titles, *original contract*, *long possession*, *present possession*, *succession*, and *positive laws*, forms the strongest title to sovereignty and is justly regarded as sacred and inviolable. But when these titles are mingled and opposed in different degrees, they often occasion perplexity, and are less capable of solution from the arguments of lawyers and philosophers than from the swords of the soldiery. Who shall tell me, for instance, whether Germanicus or Drusus ought to have succeeded Tiberius, had he died while they were both alive without naming any of them for his successor? Ought the right of adoption to be received as equivalent to that of blood in a nation where it had the same effect in private families, and had already in two instances taken place in the public? Ought Germanicus to be esteemed the eldest son, because he was born before Drusus; or the younger, because he was adopted after the birth of his brother? Ought the right of the elder to be regarded in a nation where the eldest brother had no advantage in the succession to private families? Ought the Roman empire at that time to be esteemed hereditary, because of two examples; or ought it, even so early, to be regarded as belonging to the stronger or the present possessor, as being founded on so recent an usurpation? Upon whatever principles we may pretend to answer these and such like questions, I am afraid we shall never be able to satisfy an impartial inquirer who adopts no party in political controversies and will be satisfied with nothing but sound reason and philosophy.

But here an English reader will be apt to inquire concerning that famous *revolution* which has had such a happy influence on our constitution, and has been attended with such mighty consequences. We have already remarked that in the case of enormous tyranny and oppression it is lawful to take arms even against supreme power; and that, as government is a mere human invention for mutual advantage and security, it no longer imposes any obligation, either natural or moral, when once it ceases to have that tendency. But though this *general* principle be authorized by common sense and the practice of all ages, it is certainly impossible for the laws, or even for philosophy, to establish any *particular* rules by which we may know when resistance is lawful, and decide all controversies which may arise on that subject. This may not only happen with regard to supreme power, but it is possible even in some constitutions, where the legislative authority is not lodged in one person, that there may be a magistrate so eminent and powerful as to oblige the laws to keep silence in this particular. Nor would this silence be an effect only of their *respect*, but also of their *prudence;* since it is certain that in the vast variety of circumstances which occur in all governments, an exercise of power in so great a magistrate may at one time be beneficial to the public, which at another time would be pernicious and tyrannical. But notwithstanding this silence of the laws in limited monarchies, it is certain that the people still retain the right of resistance; since it is impossible, even in the most despotic governments, to deprive them of it. The same necessity of self-preservation, and the same motive of public good, give them the same liberty in the one case as in the other. And we may further observe that in such mixed governments the cases wherein resistance is lawful must occur much oftener, and greater indulgence be given to the subjects to defend themselves by force of arms than in arbitrary governments. Not only where the chief magistrate enters into measures in themselves extremely pernicious to the public, but even when he would encroach on the other parts of the constitution and extend his power beyond the legal bounds, it is allowable to resist and dethrone him; though such resistance and violence may in the general tenor of the laws be deemed unlawful and rebellious. For besides that nothing is more essential to public interest than the preservation of public liberty, it is evident that if such a mixed government be once supposed to be established, every part or member of the constitution must have a right of self-defence and of maintaining its ancient bounds against the encroachment of every other authority. As matter would have been created in vain, were it deprived of a power of resistance, without which no part of it could preserve a distinct existence, and the whole might be crowded up into a single point; so it is a gross absurdity to suppose in any government a right without a remedy, or allow that the supreme power is shared with the people, without allowing that it is lawful for them to defend their share against every invader. Those, therefore, who would seem to respect our free government, and yet deny the right of resistance, have renounced all pretensions to common sense and do not merit a serious answer.

It does not belong to my present purpose to show that these general principles are applicable to the late *revolution;* and that all the rights and privileges which ought to be sacred to a free nation were at that time threatened with the utmost danger. I am better pleased to leave this controverted subject, if it really admits of controversy, and to indulge myself in some philosophical reflections which naturally arise from that important event.

First, we may observe that should the *lords* and *commons* in our constitution, without any reason from public interest, either depose the king in being, or after his death exclude the prince who by laws and settled custom ought to succeed, no one would esteem their proceedings legal, or think themselves bound to comply with them. But should the king by his unjust practices or his attempts for a tyrannical and despotic power justly forfeit his legal, it then not only becomes morally lawful and suitable to the nature of political society to dethrone him; but what is more, we are apt likewise to think that the remaining members of the constitution acquire a right of excluding his next heir, and of choosing whom they please for his successor. This is founded on a very singular quality of our thought and imagination. When a king forfeits his authority, his heir ought naturally to remain in the same situation as if the king were removed by death, unless by mixing himself in the tyranny he forfeit it for himself. But though this may seem reasonable, we easily comply with the contrary opinion. The deposition of a king in such a government as ours is certainly an act beyond all common authority; and an illegal assuming a power for public good which, in the ordinary course of government, can belong to no member of the constitution. When the public good is so great and so evident as to justify the action, the commendable use of this licence causes us naturally to attribute to the *parliament* a right of using further licences; and the ancient bounds of the laws being once transgressed with approbation, we are not apt to be so strict in confining ourselves precisely within their limits. The mind naturally runs on with any train of action which it has begun; nor do we commonly make any scruple concerning our duty, after the first action of any kind which we perform. Thus at the *revolution* no one who thought the deposition of the father justifiable esteemed themselves to be confined to his infant son; though, had that unhappy monarch died innocent at that time, and had his son by any accident been conveyed beyond seas, there is no doubt but a regency would have been appointed till he should come to age and could be restored to his dominions. As the slightest properties of the imagination have an effect on the judgments of the people, it shows the wisdom of the laws and of the parliament to take advantage of such properties, and to choose the magistrates either in or out of a line, according as the vulgar will most naturally attribute authority and right to them.

Secondly, though the accession of the Prince of Orange to the throne might at first give occasion to many disputes, and his title be contested, it ought not now to appear doubtful, but must have acquired a sufficient authority from those three princes who have succeeded him upon the same title. Nothing is more usual, though nothing may at first sight appear more unreasonable than this way of thinking. Princes often *seem* to acquire a right from their successors as well as from their ancestors; and a king who during his lifetime might justly be deemed a usurper will be regarded by posterity as a lawful prince, because he has had the good fortune to settle his family on the throne and entirely change the ancient form of government. Julius Cæsar is regarded as the first Roman emperor; while Sulla and Marius, whose titles were really the same as his, are treated as tyrants and usurpers. Time and custom give authority to all forms of government and all successions of princes; and that power which at first was founded only on injustice and violence, becomes in time legal and obligatory. Nor does the mind rest there; but returning back upon its footsteps, transfers to their predecessors and ancestors that right which it naturally ascribes to the posterity as being related together and united in the imagination. The present King of France makes Hugh Capet a more lawful prince than Cromwell; as the established liberty of the Dutch is no inconsiderable apology for their obstinate resistance to Philip the Second.

SECTION XI

OF THE LAWS OF NATIONS

WHEN CIVIL government has been established over the greatest part of mankind, and different societies have been formed contiguous to each other, there arises a new set of duties among the neighbouring states, suitable to the nature of that commerce which they carry on with each other. Political writers tell us that in every kind of intercourse a body politic is to be considered as one person; and, indeed, this assertion is so far just that different nations as well as private persons require mutual assistance, at the same time that their selfishness and ambition are perpetual sources of war and discord. But though nations in this particular resemble individuals, yet as they are very different in other respects, no wonder they regulate themselves by different maxims, and give rise to a new set of rules which we call *the laws of nations*. Under this head we may comprise the sacredness of the persons of ambassadors, the declaration of war, the abstaining from poisoned arms, with other duties of that kind which are evidently calculated for the commerce that is peculiar to different societies.

But though these rules be superadded to the laws of nature, the former do not entirely abolish the latter; and one may safely affirm that the three fundamental rules of justice, the stability of possession, its transference by consent, and the performance of promises, are duties of princes as well as of subjects. The same interest produces the same effect in both cases. Where possession has no stability, there must be perpetual war. Where property is not transferred by consent, there can be no commerce. Where promises are not observed, there can be no leagues nor alliances. The advantages, therefore, of peace, commerce, and mutual succour make us extend to different kingdoms the same notions of justice which take place among individuals.

There is a maxim very current in the world, which few politicians are willing to avow, but which has been authorized by the practice of all ages, *that there is a system of morals calculated for princes, much more free than that which ought to govern private persons*. It is evident this is not to be understood of the lesser *extent* of public duties and obligations; nor will any one be so extravagant as to assert that the most solemn treaties ought to have no force among princes. For as princes do actually form treaties among themselves, they must propose some advantage from the execution of them; and the prospect of such advantage for the future must engage them to perform their part, and must establish that law of nature. The meaning, therefore, of this political maxim is that though the morality of princes has the same *extent*, yet it has not the same *force* as that of private persons, and may lawfully be transgressed from a more trivial motive. However shocking such a proposition may appear to certain philosophers, it will be easy to defend it upon those principles by which we have accounted for the origin of justice and equity.

When men have found by experience that it is impossible to subsist without society, and that it is impossible to maintain society while they give free course to their appetites, so urgent an interest quickly restrains their actions and imposes an obligation to observe those rules which we call *the laws of justice*. This obligation of interest rests not here; but by the necessary course of the passions and sentiments gives rise to the moral obligation of duty, while we approve of such actions as tend to the peace of society, and disapprove of such as tend to its disturbance. The same *natural* obligation of interest takes place among independent kingdoms and gives rise to the same *morality;* so that no one of ever so corrupt morals will approve of a prince who voluntarily and of his own accord breaks his word or violates any treaty. But here we may observe that though the intercourse of different states be advantageous and even sometimes necessary, yet it is not so necessary nor advantageous as that among individuals, without which it is utterly impossible for human nature ever to subsist. Since, therefore, the *natural* obligation to justice among different states is not so strong as among individuals, the *moral* obligation which arises from it must partake of its weakness; and we must necessarily give a greater indulgence to a prince or minister who deceives another than to a private gentleman who breaks his word of honour.

Should it be asked *what proportion these two species of morality bear to each other?* I would answer that this is a question to which we can never give any precise answer, nor is it possible to reduce to numbers the proportion which we ought to fix betwixt them. One may safely affirm that this proportion finds itself without any art or study of men, as we may observe on many other occasions. The practice of the world goes further in teaching us the degrees of our duty than the most subtile philosophy which was ever yet invented. And this may serve as a convincing proof that all men have an implicit notion of the foundation of those moral rules concerning natural and civil justice, and are sensible that they arise merely from human conventions and from the interest which we have in the preservation of peace and order. For otherwise the diminution of the interest would never produce a relaxation of the morality, and reconcile us more easily to any transgression of justice among princes and republics than in the private commerce of one subject with another.

SECTION XII

OF CHASTITY AND MODESTY

IF ANY DIFFICULTY attend this system concerning the laws of nature and nations, it will be with regard to the universal approbation or blame which follows their observance or transgression, and which some may not think sufficiently explained from the general interests of society. To remove as far as possible all scruples of this kind, I shall here consider another set of duties, viz., the *modesty* and *chastity* which belong to the fair sex: and I doubt not but these virtues will be found to be still more conspicuous instances of the operation of those principles which I have insisted on.

There are some philosophers who attack the female virtues with great vehemence, and fancy they have gone very far in detecting popular errors when they can show that there is no foundation in nature for all that exterior modesty which we require in the expressions, and dress, and behaviour of the fair sex. I believe I may spare myself the trouble of insisting on so obvious a subject, and may proceed without further preparation to examine after what manner such notions arise from education, from the voluntary conventions of men, and from the interest of society.

Whoever considers the length and feebleness of human infancy with the concern which both sexes naturally have for their offspring will easily perceive that there must be a union of male and female for the education of the young, and that this union must be of considerable duration. But in order to induce the men to impose on themselves this restraint, and undergo cheerfully all the fatigues and expenses to which it subjects them, they must believe that their children are their own, and that their natural instinct is not directed to a wrong object when they give loose to love and tenderness. Now, if we examine the structure of the human body, we shall find that this security is very difficult to be attained on our part; and that, since in the copulation of the sexes the principle of generation goes from the man to the woman, an error may easily take place on the side of the former, though it be utterly impossible with regard to the latter. From this trivial and anatomical observation is derived that vast difference betwixt the education and duties of the two sexes.

Were a philosopher to examine the matter *a priori*, he would reason after the following manner. Men are induced to labour for the maintenance and education of their children by the persuasion that they are really their own; and therefore it is reasonable and even necessary to give them some security in this particular. This security cannot consist entirely in the imposing of severe punishments on any transgressions of conjugal fidelity on the part of the wife; since these public punishments cannot be inflicted without legal proof, which it is difficult to meet with in this subject. What restraint, therefore, shall we impose on women in order to counterbalance so strong a temptation as they have to infidelity? There seems to be no restraint possible but in the punishment of bad fame or reputation — a punishment which has a mighty influence on the human mind, and at the same time is inflicted by the world upon surmises, and conjectures, and proofs, that would never be received in any court of judicature. In order, therefore, to impose a due restraint on the female sex, we must attach a peculiar degree of shame to their infidelity, above what arises merely from its injustice, and must bestow proportionable praises on their chastity.

But though this be a very strong motive to fidelity, our philosopher would quickly discover that it would not alone be sufficient to that purpose. All human creatures, especially of the female sex, are apt to overlook remote motives in favour of any present temptation: the temptation is here the strongest imaginable; its approaches are insensible and seducing; and a woman easily finds, or flatters herself she shall find certain means of securing her reputation and preventing all the pernicious consequences of her pleasures. It is necessary, therefore, that besides the infamy attending such licences there should be some preceding backwardness or dread, which may prevent their first approaches and may give the female sex a repugnance to all expressions, and postures, and liberties, that have immediate relation to that enjoyment.

Such would be the reasonings of our speculative philosopher; but I am persuaded that, if he had not a perfect knowledge of human nature, he would be apt to regard them as mere chimerical speculations, and would consider the infamy attending infidelity, and backwardness to all its approaches, as principles that were rather to be wished than hoped for in the world. For what means, would he say, of persuading mankind that the transgressions of conjugal duty are more infamous than any other kind of injustice, when it is evident they are more excusable upon account of the greatness of the temptation? And what possibility of giving a backwardness to the approaches of a pleasure to which nature has inspired so strong a propensity, and a propensity that it is absolutely necessary in the end to comply with for the support of the species?

But speculative reasonings, which cost so much pains to philosophers, are often formed by the world naturally and without reflection; as difficulties which seem unsurmountable in theory are easily got over in practice. Those who have an interest in the fidelity of women naturally disapprove of their infidelity, and all the approaches to it. Those who have no interest are carried along with the stream. Education takes possession of the ductile minds of the fair sex in their infancy. And when a general rule of this kind is once established, men are apt to extend it beyond those principles from which it first arose. Thus bachelors, however debauched, cannot choose but be shocked with any instance of lewdness or impudence in woman. And though all these maxims have a plain reference to generation, yet women past child-bearing have no more privilege in this respect than those who are in the flower of their youth and beauty. Men have undoubtedly an implicit notion that all those ideas of modesty and decency have a regard to generation; since they impose not the same laws *with the same force* on the male sex, where that reason takes not place. The exception is there obvious and extensive, and founded on a remarkable difference which produces a clear separation and disjunction of ideas. But as the case is not the same with regard to the different ages of women, for this reason, though men know that these notions are founded on the public interest, yet the general rule carries us beyond the original principle and makes us extend the notions of modesty over the whole sex, from their earliest infancy to their extremest old age and infirmity.

Courage, which is the point of honour among men, derives its merit in a great measure from artifice, as well as the chastity of women, though it has also some foundation in nature, as we shall see afterwards.

As to the obligations which the male sex lie under with regard to chastity, we may observe that, according to the general notions of the world, they bear nearly the same proportion to the obligations of women, as the obligations of the law of nations do to those of the law of nature. It is contrary to the interest of civil society that men should have an *entire* liberty of indulging their appetites in venereal enjoyment; but as this interest is weaker than in the case of the female sex, the moral obligation arising from it must be proportionably weaker. And to prove this we need only appeal to the practice and sentiments of all nations and ages.

PART III

OF THE OTHER VIRTUES AND VICES

SECTION I

OF THE ORIGIN OF THE NATURAL VIRTUES AND VICES

WE COME NOW to the examination of such virtues and vices as are entirely natural, and have no dependence on the artifice and contrivance of men. The examination of these will conclude this system of morals.

The chief spring or actuating principle of the human mind is pleasure or pain; and when these sensations are removed, both from our thought and feeling, we are in a great measure incapable of passion or action, of desire or volition. The most immediate effects of pleasure and pain are the propense and averse motions of the mind; which are diversified into volition, into desire and aversion, grief and joy, hope and fear, according as the pleasure or pain changes its situation and becomes probable or improbable, certain or uncertain, or is considered as out of our power for the present moment. But when, along with this, the objects that cause pleasure or pain acquire a relation to ourselves or others, they still continue to excite desire and aversion, grief and joy; but cause at the same time the indirect passions of pride or humility, love or hatred, which in this case have a double relation of impressions and ideas to the pain or pleasure.

We have already observed that moral distinctions depend entirely on certain peculiar sentiments of pain and pleasure, and that whatever mental quality in ourselves or others gives us a satisfaction by the survey or reflection is of course virtuous; as everything of this nature that gives uneasiness is vicious. Now, since every quality in ourselves or others which gives pleasure always causes pride or love, as every one that produces uneasiness excites humility or hatred, it follows that these two particulars are to be considered as equivalent with regard to our mental qualities; *virtue* and the power of producing love or pride; *vice* and the power of producing humility or hatred. In every case, therefore, we must judge of the one by the other, and may pronounce any *quality* of the mind virtuous which causes love or pride, and any one vicious which causes hatred or humility.

If any *action* be either virtuous or vicious, it is only as a sign of some quality or character. It must depend upon durable principles of the mind which extend over the whole conduct and enter into the personal character. Actions themselves, not proceeding from any constant principle, have no influence on love or hatred, pride or humility; and consequently are never considered in morality.

This reflection is self-evident and deserves to be attended to as being of the utmost importance in the present subject. We are never to consider any single action in our inquiries concerning the origin of morals, but only the quality or character from which the action proceeded. These alone are *durable* enough to affect our sentiments concerning the person. Actions are indeed better indications of a character than words, or even wishes and sentiments; but it is only so far as they are such indications that they are attended with love or hatred, praise or blame.

To discover the true origin of morals, and of that love or hatred which arises from mental qualities, we must take the matter pretty deep and compare some principles which have been already examined and explained.

We may begin with considering anew the nature and force of *sympathy*. The minds of all men are similar in their feelings and operations; nor can any one be actuated by any affection of which all others are not in some degree susceptible. As in strings equally wound up the motion of one communicates itself to the rest, so all the affections readily pass from one person to another, and beget correspondent movements in every human creature. When I see the *effects* of passion in the voice and gesture of any person, my mind immediately passes from these effects to their causes, and forms such a lively idea of the passion as is presently converted into the passion itself. In like manner, when I perceive the *causes* of any emotion, my mind is conveyed to the effects, and is actuated with a like emotion. Were I present at any of the more terrible operations of surgery, it is certain that, even before it begun, the preparation of the instruments, the laying of the bandages in order, the heating of the irons, with all the signs of anxiety and concern in the patient and assistants, would have a great effect upon my mind, and excite the strongest sentiments of pity and terror. No passion of another discovers itself immediately to the mind. We are only sensible of its causes or effects. From *these* we infer the passion; and consequently, *these* give rise to our sympathy.

Our sense of beauty depends very much on this principle; and where any object has a tendency to produce pleasure in its possessor, it is always regarded as beautiful; as every object that has a tendency to produce pain is disagreeable and deformed. Thus the convenience of a house, the fertility of a field, the strength of a horse, the capacity, security, and swift-sailing of a vessel, form the principal beauty of these several objects. Here the object, which is denominated *beautiful*, pleases only by its tendency to produce a certain effect. That effect is the pleasure or advantage of some other person. Now, the pleasure of a stranger for whom we have no friendship pleases us only by sympathy. To this principle, therefore, is owing the beauty which we find in everything that is useful. How considerable a part this is of beauty will easily appear upon reflection. Wherever an object has a tendency to produce pleasure in the possessor, or, in other words, is the proper *cause* of pleasure, it is sure to please the spectator by a delicate sympathy with the possessor. Most of the works of art are esteemed beautiful in proportion to their fitness for the use of man; and even many of the productions of nature derive their beauty from that source. Handsome and beautiful, on most occasions, is not an absolute but a relative quality, and pleases us by nothing but its tendency to produce an end that is agreeable.[1]

The same principle produces in many instances our sentiments of morals as well as those of beauty. No virtue is more esteemed than justice, and no vice more detested than injustice; nor are there any qualities which go further to the fixing the character, either as amiable or odious. Now, justice is a moral virtue, merely because it has that tendency to the good of mankind, and indeed is nothing but an artificial invention to that purpose. The same may be said of allegiance,

---

[1] Decentior equus cujus astricta sunt ilia; sed idem velocior. Pulcher aspectu sit athleta, cujus lacertos exercitatio expressit; idem certamini paratior. Nunquam vero *species* ab *utilitate* dividitur. Sed hoc quidem discernere, modici judicii est. — *Quinct.* lib. 8.

of the laws of nations, of modesty, and of good manners. All these are mere human contrivances for the interest of society. And since there is a very strong sentiment of morals, which in all nations and all ages has attended them, we must allow that the reflecting on the tendency of characters and mental qualities is sufficient to give us the sentiments of approbation and blame. Now, as the means to an end can only be agreeable where the end is agreeable, and as the good of society, where our own interest is not concerned or that of our friends, pleases only by sympathy, it follows that sympathy is the source of the esteem which we pay to all the artificial virtues.

Thus it appears that *sympathy* is a very powerful principle in human nature, that it has a great influence on our taste of beauty, and that it produces our sentiment of morals in all the artificial virtues. From thence we may presume that it also gives rise to many of the other virtues, and that qualities acquire our approbation because of their tendency to the good of mankind. This presumption must become a certainty, when we find that most of those qualities which we *naturally* approve of have actually that tendency and render a man a proper member of society; while the qualities which we *naturally* disapprove of have a contrary tendency and render any intercourse with the person dangerous or disagreeable. For having found that such tendencies have force enough to produce the strongest sentiment of morals, we can never reasonably, in these cases, look for any other cause of approbation or blame; it being an inviolable maxim in philosophy that where any particular cause is sufficient for an effect, we ought to rest satisfied with it, and ought not to multiply causes without necessity. We have happily attained experiments in the artificial virtues, where the tendency of qualities to the good of society is the *sole* cause of our approbation, without any suspicion of the concurrence of another principle. From thence we learn the force of that principle. And where that principle may take place, and the quality approved of is really beneficial to society, a true philosopher will never require any other principle to account for the strongest approbation and esteem.

That many of the natural virtues have this tendency to the good of society, no one can doubt of. Meekness, beneficence, charity, generosity, clemency, moderation, equity, bear the greatest figure among the moral qualities, and are commonly denominated the *social* virtues, to mark their tendency to the good of society. This goes so far that some philosophers have represented all moral distinctions as the effect of artifice and education, when skilful politicians endeavoured to restrain the turbulent passions of men, and make them operate to the public good, by the notions of honour and shame. This system, however, is not consistent with experience. For, *first*, there are other virtues and vices beside those which have this tendency to the public advantage and loss. *Secondly*, had not men a natural sentiment of approbation and blame, it could never be excited by politicians; nor would the words *laudable* and *praiseworthy*, *blamable* and *odious*, be any more intelligible than if they were a language perfectly unknown to us, as we have already observed. But though this system be erroneous, it may teach us that moral distinctions arise in a great measure from the tendency of qualities and characters to the interests of society, and that it is our concern for that interest which makes us approve or disapprove of them. Now, we have no such extensive concern for society but from sympathy; and consequently it is that principle which takes us so far out of ourselves as to give us the same pleasure or uneasiness in the characters of others, as if they had a tendency to our own advantage or loss.

The only difference betwixt the natural virtues and justice lies in this, that the good which results from the former rises from every single act, and is the object of some natural passion; whereas a single act of justice, considered in itself, may often be contrary to the public good; and it is only the concurrence of mankind in a general scheme or system of action which is advantageous. When I relieve persons in distress, my natural humanity is my motive; and so far as my succour extends, so far have I promoted the happiness of my fellow creatures. But if we examine all the questions that come before any tribunal of justice, we shall find that, considering each case apart, it would as often be an instance of humanity to decide contrary to the laws of justice as conformable to them. Judges take from a poor man to give to a rich; they bestow on the dissolute the labour of the industrious; and put into the hands of the vicious the means of harming both themselves and others. The whole scheme, however, of law and justice is advantageous to the society; and it was with a view to this advantage that men, by their voluntary conventions, established it. After it is once established by these conventions, it is *naturally* attended with a strong sentiment of morals which can proceed from nothing but our sympathy with the interests of society. We need no other explication of that esteem which attends such of the natural virtues as have a tendency to the public good.

I must further add that there are several circumstances which render this hypothesis much more probable with regard to the natural than the artificial virtues. It is certain that the imagination is more affected by what is particular than by what is general; and that the sentiments are always moved with difficulty, where their objects are in any degree loose and undetermined. Now, every particular act of justice is not beneficial to society, but the whole scheme or system; and it may not perhaps be any individual person for whom we are concerned, who receives benefit from justice, but the whole society alike. On the contrary, every particular act of generosity or relief of the industrious and indigent is beneficial, and is beneficial to a particular person who is not undeserving of it. It is more natural, therefore, to think that the tendencies of the latter virtue will affect our sentiments and command our approbation than those of the former; and therefore, since we find that the approbation of the former arises from their tendencies, we may ascribe, with better reason, the same cause to the approbation of the latter. In any number of similar effects, if a cause can be discovered for one, we ought to extend that cause to all the other effects which can be accounted for by it; but much more, if these other effects be attended with peculiar circumstances which facilitate the operation of that cause.

Before I proceed further, I must observe two remarkable circumstances in this affair which may seem objections to the present system. The first may be thus explained. When any quality or character has a tendency to the good of mankind, we are pleased with it and approve of it because it presents the lively idea of pleasure; which idea affects us by sympathy, and is itself a kind of pleasure. But as this sympathy is very variable, it may be thought that our sentiments of morals must admit of all the same variations. We sympathize more with persons contiguous to us than with persons remote from us; with our acquaintance, than with strangers; with our countrymen, than with foreigners. But notwithstanding this variation of our sympathy, we give the same approbation to the same moral qualities in China as in England. They appear equally virtuous and recommend themselves equally to the esteem of a judicious spectator. The sympathy varies without a variation in our esteem. Our esteem, therefore, proceeds not from sympathy.

To this I answer, the approbation of moral qualities most certainly is not derived from reason or any comparison of ideas; but proceeds entirely from a moral taste and from certain sentiments of pleasure or disgust which arise upon the contemplation and view of particular qualities or characters. Now, it is evident that those sentiments, whenever they are derived, must vary according to the distance or contiguity of the objects; nor can I feel the same lively pleasure from the virtues of a person who lived in Greece two thousand years ago that I feel from the virtues of a familiar friend and acquaintance. Yet I do not say that I esteem the one more than the other; and therefore, if the variation of the sentiment without a variation of the esteem be an objection, it must have equal force against every other system, as against that of sympathy. But to consider the matter aright, it has no force at all; and it is the easiest matter in the world to account for it. Our situation with regard both to persons and things is in continual fluctuation; and a man that lies at a distance from us may in a little time become a familiar acquaintance. Besides, every particular man has a peculiar position with regard to others; and it is impossible we could ever converse together on any reasonable terms, were each of us to consider characters and persons only as they appear from his peculiar point of view. In order, therefore, to prevent those continual *contradictions* and arrive at a more *stable* judgment of things, we fix on some *steady* and *general* points of view, and always, in our thoughts, place ourselves in them, whatever may be our present situation. In like manner, external beauty is determined merely by pleasure; and it is evident a beautiful countenance cannot give so much pleasure when seen at a distance of twenty paces as when it is brought nearer us. We say not, however, that it appears to us less beautiful; because we know what effect it will have in such a position, and by that reflection we correct its momentary appearance.

In general, all sentiments of blame or praise are variable, according to our situation of nearness or remoteness with regard to the person blamed or praised, and according to the present disposition of our mind. But these variations we regard not in our general decisions, but still apply the terms expressive of our liking or dislike in the same manner as if we remained in one point of view. Experience soon teaches us this method of correcting our sentiments, or at least of correcting our language, where the sentiments are more stubborn and unalterable. Our servant, if diligent and faithful, may excite stronger sentiments of love and kindness than Marcus Brutus, as represented in history; but we say not upon that account that the former character is more laudable than the latter. We know that, were we to approach equally near to that renowned patriarch, he would command a much higher degree of affection and admiration. Such corrections are common with regard to all the senses; and, indeed, it were impossible we could ever make use of language or communicate our sentiments to one another, did we not correct the momentary appearances of things and overlook our present situation.

It is therefore from the influence of characters and qualities upon those who have an intercourse with any person that we blame or praise him. We consider not whether the persons affected by the qualities be our acquaintance or strangers, countrymen or foreigners. Nay, we overlook our own interest in those general judgments, and blame not a man for opposing us in any of our pretensions when his own interest is particularly concerned. We make allowance for a certain degree of selfishness in men because we know it to be inseparable from human nature and inherent in our frame and constitution. By this reflection we correct those sentiments of blame which so naturally arise upon any opposition.

But however the general principle of our blame or praise may be corrected by those other principles, it is certain they are not altogether efficacious, nor do our passions often correspond entirely to the present theory. It is seldom men heartily love what lies at a distance from them; and what no way redounds to their particular benefit; as it is no less rare to meet with persons who can pardon another any opposition he makes to their interest, however justifiable that opposition may be by the general rules of morality. Here we are contented with saying that reason requires such an impartial conduct, but that it is seldom we can bring ourselves to it, and that our passions do not readily follow the determination of our judgment. This language will be easily understood if we consider what we formerly said concerning that *reason* which is able to oppose our passion, and which we have found to be nothing but a general calm determination of the passions, founded on some distant view or reflection. When we form our judgments of persons merely from the tendency of their characters to our own benefit, or to that of our friends, we find so many contradictions to our sentiments in society and conversation, and such an uncertainty from the incessant changes of our situation, that we seek some other standard of merit and demerit which may not admit of so great variation. Being thus loosened from our first station, we cannot afterwards fix ourselves so commodiously by any means as by a sympathy with those who have any commerce with the person we consider. This is far from being as lively as when our own interest is concerned, or that of our particular friends; nor has it such an influence on our love and hatred; but being equally conformable to our calm and general principles, it is said to have an equal authority over our reason, and to command our judgment and opinion. We blame equally a bad action which we read of in history, with one performed in our neighbourhood the other day; the meaning of which is that we know from reflection that the former action would excite as strong sentiments of disapprobation as the latter, were it placed in the same position.

I now proceed to the *second* remarkable circumstance which I propose to take notice of. Where a person is possessed of a character that in its natural tendency is beneficial to society, we esteem him virtuous, and are delighted with the view of his character, even though particular accidents prevent its operation and incapacitate him from being serviceable to his friends and country. Virtue in rags is still virtue; and the love which it procures attends a man into a dungeon or desert, where the virtue can no longer be exerted in action and is lost to all the world. Now, this may be esteemed an objection to the present system. Sympathy interests us in the good of mankind; and if sympathy were the source of our esteem for virtue, that sentiment of approbation could only take place where the virtue actually attained its end and was beneficial to mankind. Where it fails of its end, it is only an imperfect means and, therefore, can never acquire any merit from that end. The goodness of an end can bestow a merit on such means alone as are complete and actually produce the end.

To this we may reply that, where any object, in all its parts, is fitted to attain any agreeable end, it naturally gives us pleasure and is esteemed beautiful, even though some external circumstances be wanting to render it altogether effectual. It is sufficient if everything be complete in the object itself. A house that is contrived with great judgment for all the commodities of life pleases us upon that account, though perhaps we are sensible that no one will ever dwell in it. A fertile soil and a happy climate delight us by a reflection on the happiness which they would afford the inhabitants, though at present the country be desert and uninhabited. A man whose limbs and shape promise strength and activity is esteemed handsome, though condemned to perpetual imprisonment. The imagination has a set of passions belonging to it upon which our sentiments of beauty much depend. These passions are moved by degrees of liveliness and strength, which are inferior to *belief*, and independent of the real existence of their objects. Where a character is in every respect fitted to be beneficial to society, the imagination passes easily from the cause to the effect, without considering that there are still some circumstances wanting to render the cause a complete one. *General rules* create a species of probability which sometimes influences the judgment, and always the imagination.

It is true, when the cause is complete and a good disposition is attended with good fortune which renders it really beneficial to society, it gives a stronger pleasure to the spectator, and is attended with a more lively sympathy. We are more affected by it; and yet we do not say that it is more virtuous, or that we esteem it more. We know that an alteration of fortune may render the benevolent disposition entirely impotent; and therefore we separate as much as possible the fortune from the disposition. The case is the same as when we correct the different sentiments of virtue which proceed from its different distances from ourselves. The passions do not always follow our corrections; but these corrections serve sufficiently to regulate our abstract notions, and are alone regarded when we pronounce in general concerning the degrees of vice and virtue.

It is observed by critics that all words or sentences which are difficult to the pronunciation are disagreeable to the ear. There is no difference, whether a man hear them pronounced or read them silently to himself. When I run over a book with my eye, I imagine I hear it all; and also by the force of imagination enter into the uneasiness which the delivery of it would give the speaker. The uneasiness is not real; but as such a composition of words has a natural tendency to produce it, this is sufficient to affect the mind with a painful sentiment and render the discourse harsh and disagreeable. It is a similar case, where any real quality is by accidental circumstances rendered impotent and is deprived of its natural influence on society.

Upon these principles we may easily remove any contradiction which may appear to be betwixt the *extensive sympathy* on which our sentiments of virtue depend, and that *limited generosity* which I have frequently observed to be natural to men, and which justice and property suppose, according to the precedent reasoning. My sympathy with another may give me the sentiment of pain and disapprobation, when any object is presented that has a tendency to give him uneasiness, though I may not be willing to sacrifice anything of my own interest, or cross any of my passions for his satisfaction. A house may displease me by being ill-contrived for the convenience of the owner; and yet I may refuse to give a shilling towards the rebuilding of it. Sentiments must touch the heart to make them control our passions; but they need not extend beyond the imagination to make them influence our taste. When a building seems clumsy and tottering to the eye, it is ugly and disagreeable, though we may be fully assured of the solidity of the workmanship. It is a kind of fear which causes this sentiment of disapprobation; but the passion is not the same with that which we feel when obliged to stand under a wall that we really think tottering and insecure. The *seeming tendencies* of objects affect the mind; and the emotions they excite are of a like species with those which proceed from the *real consequences* of objects, but their feeling is different. Nay, these emotions are so different in their feeling that they may often be contrary, without destroying each other; as when the fortifications of a city belonging to an enemy are esteemed beautiful upon account of their strength, though we could wish that they were entirely destroyed. The imagination adheres to the *general* views of things, and distinguishes the feelings they produce from those which arise from our particular and momentary situation.

If we examine the panegyrics that are commonly made of great men, we shall find that most of the qualities which are attributed to them may be divided into two kinds, viz., such as make them perform their part in society; and such as render them serviceable to themselves and enable them to promote their own interest. Their *prudence, temperance, frugality, industry, assiduity, enterprise, dexterity*, are celebrated as well as their *generosity* and *humanity*. If we ever give an indulgence to any quality that disables a man from making a figure in life, it is to that of *indolence* which is not supposed to deprive one of his parts and capacity, but only suspends their exercise; and that without any inconvenience to the person himself, since it is, in some measure, from his own choice. Yet indolence is always allowed to be a fault, and a very great one if extreme: nor do a man's friends ever acknowledge him to be subject to it but in order to save his character in more material articles. He could make a figure, say they, if he pleased to give application. His understanding is sound, his conception quick, and his memory tenacious; but he hates business, and is indifferent about his fortune. And this a man sometimes may make even a subject of vanity, though with the air of confessing a fault; because he may think that this incapacity for business implies much more noble qualities, such as a philosophical spirit, a fine taste, a delicate wit, or a relish for pleasure and society. But take any other case: suppose a quality that, without being an indication of any other good qualities, incapacitates a man *always* for business, and is destructive to his interest; such as a blundering understanding and a wrong judgment of everything in life; inconstancy and irresolution; or a want of address in the management of men and business: these are all allowed to be imperfections in a character; and many men would rather acknowledge the greatest crimes than have it suspected that they are in any degree subject to them.

It is very happy, in our philosophical researches, when we find the same phenomenon diversified by a variety of circumstances, and, by discovering what is common among them, can the better assure ourselves of the truth of any hypothesis we may make use of to explain it. Were nothing esteemed virtue but what were beneficial to society, I am persuaded that the foregoing explication of the moral sense ought still to be received, and that upon sufficient evidence. But this evidence must grow upon us when we find other kinds of virtue which will not admit of any explication except from that hypothesis. Here is a man who is not remarkably defective in his social qualities; but what principally recommends him is his dexterity in business by which he has extricated himself from the greatest difficulties and conducted the most delicate affairs with a singular address and prudence. I find an esteem for him immediately to arise in me: his company is a satisfaction to me; and before I have any further acquaintance with him, I would rather do him a service than another whose character is in every other respect equal, but is deficient in that particular. In this case, the qualities that please me are all considered as useful to the person, and as having a tendency to promote his interest and satisfaction. They are only regarded as means to an end, and please me in proportion to their fitness for that end. The end, therefore, must be agreeable to me. But what makes the end agreeable? The person is a stranger: I am no way interested in him, nor lie under any obligation to him; his happiness concerns not me further than the happiness of every human and indeed of every sensible creature; that is, it affects me only by sympathy. From that principle, whenever I discover his happiness and good, whether in its causes or effects, I enter so deeply into it that it gives me a sensible emotion. The appearance of qualities that have a *tendency* to promote it have an agreeable effect upon my imagination and command my love and esteem.

This theory may serve to explain why the same qualities, in all cases, produce both pride and love, humility and hatred; and the same man is always virtuous or vicious, accomplished or despicable to others, who is so to himself. A person in whom we discover any passion or habit which originally is only incommodious to himself becomes always disagreeable to us merely on its account; as, on the other hand, one whose character is only dangerous and disagreeable to others can never be satisfied with himself as long as he is sensible of that disadvantage. Nor is this observable only with regard to characters and manners, but may be remarked even in the most minute circumstances. A violent cough in another gives us uneasiness, though in itself it does not in the least affect us. A man will be mortified if you tell him he has a stinking breath, though it is evidently no annoyance to himself. Our fancy easily changes its situation; and, either surveying ourselves as we appear to others or considering others as they feel themselves, we enter by that means into sentiments which no way belong to us, and in which nothing but sympathy is able to interest us. And this sympathy we sometimes carry so far as even to be displeased with a quality commodious to us, merely because it displeases others and makes us disagreeable in their eyes, though, perhaps, we never can have any interest in rendering ourselves agreeable to them.

There have been many systems of morality advanced by philosophers in all ages; but if they are strictly examined, they may be reduced to two which alone merit our attention. Moral good and evil are certainly distinguished by our *sentiments*, not by *reason:* but these sentiments may arise either from the mere species or appearance of characters and passions, or from reflections on their tendency to the happiness of mankind and of particular persons. My opinion is that both these causes are intermixed in our judgments or morals, after the same manner as they are in our decisions concerning most kinds of external beauty: though I am also of opinion that reflections on the tendencies of actions have by far the greatest influence and determine all the great lines of our duty. There are, however, instances in cases of less moment, wherein this immediate taste or sentiment produces our approbation. Wit and a certain easy and disengaged behaviour are qualities *immediately agreeable* to others and command their love and esteem. Some of these qualities produce satisfaction in others by particular *original* principles of human nature, which cannot be accounted for: others may be resolved into principles which are more general. This will best appear upon a particular inquiry.

As some qualities acquire their merit from their being *immediately agreeable* to others, without any tendency to public interest, so some are denominated virtuous from their being *immediately agreeable* to the person himself who possesses them. Each of the passions and operations of the mind has a particular feeling, which must be either agreeable or disagreeable. The first is virtuous, the second vicious. This particular feeling constitutes the very nature of the passions, and therefore needs not be accounted for.

But however directly the distinction of vice and virtue may seem to flow from the immediate pleasure or uneasiness, which particular qualities cause to ourselves or others, it is easy to observe that it has also a considerable dependence on the principle of *sympathy* so often insisted on. We approve of a person who is possessed of qualities *immediately agreeable* to those with whom he has any commerce, though perhaps we ourselves never reaped any pleasure from them. We also approve of one who is possessed of qualities that are *immediately agreeable* to himself, though they be of no service to any mortal. To account for this, we must have recourse to the foregoing principles.

Thus to take a general review of the present hypothesis: Every quality of the mind is denominated virtuous which gives pleasure by the mere survey, as every quality which produces pain is called vicious. This pleasure and this pain may arise from four different sources. For we reap a pleasure from the view of a character which is naturally fitted to be useful to others or to the person himself, or which is agreeable to others or to the person himself. One may perhaps be surprised that amidst all these interests and pleasures we should forget our own which touch us so nearly on every other occasion. But we shall easily satisfy ourselves on this head when we consider that every particular person's pleasure and interest being different, it is impossible men could ever agree in their sentiments and judgments, unless they chose some common point of view from which they might survey their object, and which might cause it to appear the same to all of them. Now, in judging of characters, the only interest or pleasure which appears the same to every spectator is that of the person himself whose character is examined, or that of persons who have a connection with him. And though such interests and pleasures touch us more faintly than our own, yet, being more constant and universal, they counterbalance the latter even in practice and are alone admitted in speculation as the standard of virtue and morality. They alone produce that particular feeling or sentiment on which moral distinctions depend.

As the good or ill desert of virtue or vice, it is an evident consequence of the sentiments of pleasure or uneasiness. These sentiments produce love or hatred; and love or hatred, by the original constitution of human passion, is attended with benevolence or anger; that is, with a desire of making happy the person we love, and miserable the person we hate. We have treated of this more fully on another occasion.

SECTION II

OF GREATNESS OF MIND

IT MAY NOW be proper to illustrate this general system of morals by applying it to particular instances of virtue and vice, and showing how their merit or demerit arises from the four sources here explained. We shall begin with examining the passions of *pride* and *humility*, and shall consider the vice or virtue that lies in their excesses or just proportion. An excessive pride or overweening conceit of ourselves is always esteemed vicious and is universally hated, as modesty or a just sense of our weakness is esteemed virtuous, and procures the good-will of every one. Of the four sources of moral distinctions this is to be ascribed to the *third*, viz., the immediate agreeableness and disagreeableness of a quality to others, without any reflections on the tendency of that quality.

In order to prove this, we must have recourse to two principles which are very conspicuous in human nature. The first of these is the *sympathy* and communication of sentiments and passions above mentioned. So close and intimate is the correspondence of human souls that no sooner any person approaches me, than he diffuses on me all his opinions, and draws along my judgment in a greater or lesser degree. And though on many occasions my sympathy with him goes not so far as entirely to change my sentiments and way of thinking, yet it seldom is so weak as not to disturb the easy course of my thought, and give an authority to that opinion which is recommended to me by his assent and approbation. Nor is it any way material upon what subject he and I employ our thoughts. Whether we judge of an indifferent person or of my own character, my sympathy gives equal force to his decision; and even his sentiments of his own merit make me consider him in the same light in which he regards himself.

This principle of sympathy is of so powerful and insinuating a nature that it enters into most of our sentiments and passions, and often takes place under the appearance of its contrary. For it is remarkable that when a person opposes me in anything which I am strongly bent upon, and rouses up my passion by contradiction, I have always a degree of sympathy with him, nor does my commotion proceed from any other origin. We may here observe an evident conflict or rencounter of opposite principles and passions. On the one side, there is that passion or sentiment which is natural to me; and it is observable that the stronger this passion is, the greater is the commotion. There must also be some passion or sentiment on the other side; and this passion can proceed from nothing but sympathy. The sentiments of others can never affect us but by becoming in some measure our own; in which case they operate upon us by opposing and increasing our passions in the very same manner as if they had been originally derived from our own temper and disposition. While they remain concealed in the minds of others, they can never have any influence upon us: and even when they are known, if they went no further than the imagination or conception, that faculty is so accustomed to objects of every different kind that a mere idea, though contrary to our sentiments and inclinations, would never alone be able to affect us.

The second principle I shall take notice of is that of *comparison*, or the variation of our judgments concerning objects, according to the proportion they bear to those with which we compare them. We judge more of objects by comparison than by their intrinsic worth and value; and regard everything as mean when set in opposition to what is superior of the same kind. But no comparison is more obvious than that with ourselves; and hence it is that on all occasions it takes place and mixes with most of our passions. This kind of comparison is directly contrary to sympathy in its operation, as we have observed in treating of *compassion* and *malice*.[1] *In all kinds of compassion, an object makes us always receive from another to which it is compared a sensation contrary to what arises from itself in its direct and immediate survey. The direct survey of another's pleasure naturally gives us pleasure, and therefore produces pain when compared with our own. His pain, considered in itself, is painful, but augments the idea of our own happiness and gives us pleasure.*

Since, then, those principles of sympathy, and a comparison with ourselves, are directly contrary, it may be worth while to consider what general rules can be formed, besides the particular temper of the person, for the prevalence of the one or the other. Suppose I am now in safety at land and would willingly reap some pleasure from

[1] Book II. Part II. Sect. 8.

this consideration, I must think on the miserable condition of those who are at sea in a storm, and must endeavour to render this idea as strong and lively as possible in order to make me more sensible of my own happiness. But whatever pains I may take, the comparison will never have an equal efficacy, as if I were really on the shore,[2] and saw a ship at a distance tossed by a tempest and in danger every moment of perishing on a rock or sand-bank. But suppose this idea to become still more lively. Suppose the ship to be driven so near me that I can perceive distinctly the horror painted on the countenances of the seamen and passengers, hear their lamentable cries, see the dearest friends give their last adieu or embrace with a resolution to perish in each other's arms: no man has so savage a heart as to reap any pleasure from such a spectacle, or withstand the motions of the tenderest compassion and sympathy. It is evident, therefore, there is a medium in this case; and that, if the idea be too faint, it has no influence by comparison; and on the other hand, if it be too strong, it operates on us entirely by sympathy, which is the contrary to comparison. Sympathy being the conversion of an idea into an impression demands a greater force and vivacity in the idea than is requisite to comparison.

All this is easily applied to the present subject. We sink very much in our own eyes when in the presence of a great man or one of a superior genius; and this humility makes a considerable ingredient in that *respect* which we pay our superiors, according to our foregoing reasonings on that passion.[3] Sometimes even envy and hatred arise from the comparison; but in the greatest part of men it rests at respect and esteem. As sympathy has such a powerful influence on the human mind, it causes pride to have in some measure the same effect as merit, and, by making us enter into those elevated sentiments which the proud man entertains of himself, presents that comparison which is so mortifying and disagreeable. Our judgment does not entirely accompany him in the flattering conceit in which he pleases himself; but still is so shaken as to receive the idea it presents, and to give it an influence above the loose conceptions of the imagination. A man who, in an idle humour, would form a notion of a person of a merit

[2] Suavi mari magno turbantibus æquora ventis
   E terra magnum alterius spectare laborem;
   Non quia vexari quenquam est jucunda voluptas,
   Sed quibus ipse malis careas quia cerene suav' est. — *Lucret.*

[3] Book II. Part II. Sect. 10.

very much superior to his own, would not be mortified by that fiction; but when a man whom we are really persuaded to be of inferior merit is presented to us, if we observe in him any extraordinary degree of pride and self-conceit, the firm persuasion he has of his own merit takes hold of the imagination and diminishes us in our own eyes in the same manner as if he were really possessed of all the good qualities which he so literally attributes to himself. Our idea is here precisely in that medium which is requisite to make it operate on us by comparison. Were it accompanied with belief, and did the person appear to have the same merit which he assumes to himself, it would have a contrary effect and would operate on us by sympathy. The influence of that principle would then be superior to that of comparison, contrary to what happens where the person's merit seems below his pretensions.

The necessary consequence of these principles is that pride or an overweening conceit of ourselves must be vicious; since it causes uneasiness in all men, and presents them every moment with a disagreeable comparison. It is a trite observation in philosophy, and even in common life and conversation, that it is our own pride which makes us so much displeased with the pride of other people; and that vanity becomes insupportable to us merely because we are vain. The gay naturally associate themselves with the gay, and the amorous with the amorous; but the proud never can endure the proud and rather seek the company of those who are of an opposite disposition. As we are all of us proud in some degree, pride is universally blamed and condemned by all mankind as having a natural tendency to cause uneasiness in others by means of comparison. And this effect must follow the more naturally that those who have an ill-grounded conceit of themselves are for ever making those comparisons; nor have they any other method of supporting their vanity. A man of sense and merit is pleased with himself, independent of all foreign considerations; but a fool must always find some person that is more foolish in order to keep himself in good humour with his own parts and understanding.

But though an overweening conceit of our own merit be vicious and disagreeable, nothing can be more laudable than to have a value for ourselves where we really have qualities that are valuable. The utility and advantage of any quality to ourselves is a source of virtue, as well as its agreeableness to others; and it is certain that nothing is

more useful to us in the conduct of life than a due degree of pride
which makes us sensible of our own merit and gives us a confidence
and assurance in all our projects and enterprises. Whatever capacity
any one may be endowed with, it is entirely useless to him if he be not
acquainted with it and form not designs suitable to it. It is requisite
on all occasions to know our own force; and were it allowable to err
on either side, it would be more advantageous to overrate our merit
than to form ideas of it below its just standard. Fortune commonly
favours the bold and enterprising; and nothing inspires us with more
boldness than a good opinion of ourselves.

Add to this that, though pride or self-applause be sometimes disagreeable to others, it is always agreeable to ourselves; as, on the other
hand, modesty, though it give pleasure to every one who observes it,
produces often uneasiness in the person endowed with it. Now, it
has been observed that our own sensations determine the vice and
virtue of any quality as well as those sensations which it may excite
in others.

Thus self-satisfaction and vanity may not only be allowable, but
requisite in a character. It is however certain that good-breeding
and decency require that we should avoid all signs and expressions
which tend directly to show that passion. We have, all of us, a
wonderful partiality for ourselves, and were we always to give vent
to our sentiments in this particular, we should mutually cause the
greatest indignation in each other, not only by the immediate presence
of so disagreeable a subject of comparison, but also by the contrariety
of our judgments. In like manner, therefore, as we establish the
laws of nature in order to secure property in society and prevent the
opposition of self-interest, we establish the *rules of good-breeding* in
order to prevent the opposition of men's pride and render conversation
agreeable and inoffensive. Nothing is more disagreeable than a man's
overweening conceit of himself. Every one almost has a strong propensity to this vice. No one can well distinguish *in himself* betwixt
the vice and virtue, or be certain that his esteem of his own merit is
well founded; for these reasons all direct expressions of this passion
are condemned; nor do we make any exception to this rule in favour
of men of sense and merit. They are not allowed to do themselves
justice openly in words, no more than other people; and even if they
show a reserve and secret doubt in doing themselves justice in their

own thoughts, they will be more applauded. That impertinent and almost universal propensity of men to overvalue themselves has given us such a *prejudice* against self-applause that we are apt to condemn it by a *general rule* wherever we meet with it; and it is with some difficulty we give a privilege to men of sense, even in their most secret thoughts. At least, it must be owned that some disguise in this particular is absolutely requisite, and that, if we harbour pride in our breasts, we must carry a fair outside and have the appearance of modesty and mutual deference in all our conduct and behaviour. We must on every occasion be ready to prefer others to ourselves; to treat them with a kind of deference, even though they be our equals; to seem always the lowest and least in the company where we are not very much distinguished above them; and if we observe these rules in our conduct, men will have more indulgence for our secret sentiments, when we discover them in an oblique manner.

I believe no one who has any practice of the world, and can penetrate into the inward sentiments of men, will assert that the humility which good-breeding and decency require of us goes beyond the outside, or that a thorough sincerity in this particular is esteemed a real part of our duty. On the contrary, we may observe that a genuine and hearty pride or self-esteem, if well concealed and well founded, is essential to the character of a man of honour, and that there is no quality of the mind which is more indispensably requisite to procure the esteem and approbation of mankind. There are certain deferences and mutual submissions which custom requires of the different ranks of men towards each other; and whoever exceeds in this particular, if through interest, is accused of meanness, if through ignorance, of simplicity. It is necessary, therefore, to know our rank and station in the world, whether it be fixed by our birth, fortune, employments, talents, or reputation. It is necessary to feel the sentiment and passion of pride in conformity to it, and to regulate our actions accordingly. And should it be said that prudence may suffice to regulate our actions in this particular, without any real pride, I would observe that here the object of prudence is to conform our actions to the general usage and custom; and that it is impossible those tacit airs of superiority should ever have been established and authorized by custom, unless men were generally proud, and unless that passion were generally approved when well grounded.

If we pass from common life and conversation to history, this reasoning acquires new force when we observe that all those great actions and sentiments which have become the admiration of mankind are founded on nothing but pride and self-esteem. "Go," says Alexander the Great to his soldiers, when they refused to follow him to the Indies, "go, tell your countrymen that you left Alexander completing the conquest of the world." This passage was always particularly admired by the prince of Conde, as we learn from St. Evremond. "Alexander," said that prince, "abandoned by his soldiers, among barbarians not yet fully subdued, felt in himself such a dignity and right of empire that he could not believe it possible any one could refuse to obey him. Whether in Europe or in Asia, among Greeks or Persians, all was indifferent to him; wherever he found men he fancied he had found subjects."

In general we may observe that whatever we call *heroic virtue*, and admire under the character of greatness and elevation of mind, is either nothing but a steady and well-established pride and self-esteem or partakes largely of that passion. Courage, intrepidity, ambition, love of glory, magnanimity, and all the other shining virtues of that kind, have plainly a strong mixture of self-esteem in them and derive a great part of their merit from that origin. Accordingly we find that many religious declaimers decry those virtues as purely pagan and natural, and represent to us the excellence of the *Christian* religion, which places humility in the rank of virtues and corrects the judgment of the world, and even of philosophers who so generally admire all the efforts of pride and ambition. Whether this virtue of humility has been rightly understood, I shall not pretend to determine. I am content with the concession that the world naturally esteems a well-regulated pride which secretly animates our conduct without breaking out into such indecent expressions of vanity as may offend the vanity of others.

The merit of pride or self-esteem is derived from two circumstances, viz., its utility and its agreeableness to ourselves; by which it capacitates us for business, and at the same time gives us an immediate satisfaction. When it goes beyond its just bounds, it loses the first advantage and even becomes prejudicial; which is the reason why we condemn an extravagant pride and ambition, however regulated by the decorums of good-breeding and politeness. But as such a passion is still agreeable and conveys an elevated and sublime sensation to the person who is actuated by it, the sympathy with that satisfaction diminishes considerably the blame which naturally attends its dangerous influence on our conduct and behaviour. Accordingly we may observe that an excessive courage and magnanimity, especially when it displays itself under the frowns of fortune, contributes in a great measure to the character of a hero, and will render a person the admiration of posterity at the same time that it ruins his affairs, and leads him into dangers and difficulties with which otherwise he would never have been acquainted.

Heroism or military glory is much admired by the generality of mankind. They consider it as the most sublime kind of merit. Men of cool reflection are not so sanguine in their praises of it. The infinite confusions and disorder which it has caused in the world diminish much of its merit in their eyes. When they would oppose the popular notions on this head, they always paint out the evils which this supposed virtue has produced in human society: the subversion of empires, the devastation of provinces, the sack of cities. As long as these are present to us, we are more inclined to hate than admire the ambition of heroes. But when we fix our view on the person himself who is the author of all this mischief, there is something so dazzling in his character, the mere contemplation of it so elevates the mind that we cannot refuse it our admiration. The pain which we receive from its tendency to the prejudice of society is overpowered by a stronger and more immediate sympathy.

Thus our explication of the merit or demerit which attends the degrees of pride or self esteem may serve as a strong argument for the preceding hypothesis by showing the effects of those principles above explained in all the variations of our judgments concerning that passion. Nor will this reasoning be advantageous to us only by showing that the distinction of vice and virtue arises from the *four* principles of the *advantage* and of the *pleasure* of the *person himself* and of *others*, but may also afford us a strong proof of some under-parts of that hypothesis.

No one who duly considers of this matter will make any scruple of allowing that any piece of ill-breeding, or any expression of pride and haughtiness, is displeasing to us merely because it shocks our own pride and leads us by sympathy into a comparison which causes the disagreeable passion of humility. Now, as an insolence of this kind is blamed even in a person who has always been civil to ourselves in particular, nay, in one whose name is only known to us in history, it follows that our disapprobation proceeds from a sympathy with others, and from the reflection that such a character is highly displeasing and odious to every one who converses or has any intercourse with the person possessed of it. We sympathize with those people in their uneasiness; and as their uneasiness proceeds in part from a sympathy with the person who insults them, we may here observe a double rebound of the sympathy, which is a principle very similar to what we have observed on another occasion.[4]

SECTION III

OF GOODNESS AND BENEVOLENCE

HAVING THUS explained the origin of that praise and approbation which attends everything we call *great* in human affections, we now proceed to give an account of their *goodness*, and show whence its merit is derived.

When experience has once given us a competent knowledge of human affairs, and has taught us the proportion they bear to human passion, we perceive that the generosity of men is very limited, and that it seldom extends beyond their friends and family, or, at most, beyond their native country. Being thus acquainted with the nature of man, we expect not any impossibilities from him, but confine our view to that narrow circle in which any person moves, in order to form a judgment of his moral character. When the natural tendency of his passions leads him to be serviceable and useful within his sphere, we approve of his character and love his person, by a sympathy with the sentiments of those who have a more particular connection with him. We are quickly obliged to forget our own interest in our judgments of this kind, by reason of the perpetual contradictions we meet with in society and conversation from persons that are not placed in the same situation and have not the same interest with ourselves. The only point of view in which our sentiments concur with those of others

[4] Book II. Part II. Sect. 5.

is when we consider the tendency of any passion to the advantage or harm of those who have any immediate connection or intercourse with the person possessed of it. And though this advantage or harm be often very remote from ourselves, yet sometimes it is very near us and interests us strongly by sympathy. This concern we readily extend to other cases that are resembling; and when these are very remote, our sympathy is proportionably weaker, and our praise or blame fainter and more doubtful. The case is here the same as in our judgments concerning external bodies. All objects seem to diminish by their distance; but though the appearance of objects to our senses be the original standard by which we judge of them, yet we do not say that they actually diminish by the distance; but, correcting the appearance by reflection, arrive at a more constant and established judgment concerning them. In like manner, though sympathy be much fainter than our concern for ourselves, and a sympathy with persons remote from us much fainter than that with persons near and contiguous, yet we neglect all these differences in our calm judgments concerning the characters of men. Besides that we ourselves often change our situation in this particular, we every day meet with persons who are in a different situation from ourselves, and who could never converse with us on any reasonable terms, were we to remain constantly in that situation and point of view which is peculiar to us. The intercourse of sentiments, therefore, in society and conversation makes us form some general unalterable standard by which we may approve or disapprove of characters and manners. And though the *heart* does not always take part with those general notions or regulate its love and hatred by them, yet are they sufficient for discourse, and serve all our purposes in company, in the pulpit, on the theatre, and in the schools.

From these principles we may easily account for that merit which is commonly ascribed to *generosity, humanity, compassion, gratitude, friendship, fidelity, zeal, disinterestedness, liberality,* and all those other qualities which form the character of good and benevolent. A propensity to the tender passions makes a man agreeable and useful in all the parts of life, and gives a just direction to all his other qualities which otherwise may become prejudicial to society. Courage and ambition, when not regulated by benevolence, are fit only to make a tyrant and public robber. It is the same case with judgment and capacity, and all the qualities of that kind. They are indifferent in themselves to the interests of society, and have a tendency to the good or ill of mankind, according as they are directed by these other passions.

As love is *immediately agreeable* to the person who is actuated by it, and hatred *immediately disagreeable*, this may also be a considerable reason why we praise all the passions that partake of the former, and blame all those that have any considerable share of the latter. It is certain we are infinitely touched with a tender sentiment as well as with a great one. The tears naturally start in our eyes at the conception of it; nor can we forbear giving a loose to the same tenderness towards the person who exerts it. All this seems to me a proof that our approbation has in these cases an origin different from the prospect of utility and advantage, either to ourselves or others. To which we may add that men naturally, without reflection, approve of that character which is most like their own. The man of a mild disposition and tender affections, in forming a notion of the most perfect virtue, mixes in it more of benevolence and humanity than the man of courage and enterprise who naturally looks upon a certain elevation of the mind as the most accomplished character. This must evidently proceed from an *immediate* sympathy which men have with characters similar to their own. They enter with more warmth into such sentiments and feel more sensibly the pleasure which arises from them.

It is remarkable that nothing touches a man of humanity more than any instance of extraordinary delicacy in love or friendship, where a person is attentive to the smallest concerns of his friend, and is willing to sacrifice to them the most considerable interest of his own. Such delicacies have little influence on society because they make us regard the greatest trifles; but they are the more engaging, the more minute the concern is, and are a proof of the highest merit in any one who is capable of them. The passions are so contagious that they pass with the greatest facility from one person to another and produce correspondent movements in all human breasts. Where friendship appears in very signal instances, my heart catches the same passion and is warmed by those warm sentiments that display themselves before me. Such agreeable movements must give me an affection to every one that excites them. This is the case with everything that is agreeable in any person. The transition from pleasure to love is easy; but the transition must here be still more easy, since the agreeable sentiment which is excited by sympathy is love itself, and there is nothing required but to change the object.

Hence the peculiar merit of benevolence in all its shapes and appearances. Hence even its weaknesses are virtuous and amiable; and a person whose grief upon the loss of a friend were excessive would be esteemed upon that account. His tenderness bestows a merit, as it does a pleasure, on his melancholy.

We are not, however, to imagine that all the angry passions are vicious, though they are disagreeable. There is a certain indulgence due to human nature in this respect. Anger and hatred are passions inherent in our very frame and constitution. The want of them on some occasions may even be a proof of weakness and imbecility. And where they appear only in a low degree, we not only excuse them because they are natural, but even bestow our applauses on them because they are inferior to what appears in the greatest part of mankind.

Where these angry passions rise up to cruelty, they form the most detested of all vices. All the pity and concern which we have for the miserable sufferers by this vice turns against the person guilty of it and produces a stronger hatred than we are sensible of on any other occasion.

Even when the vice of inhumanity rises not to this extreme degree, our sentiments concerning it are very much influenced by reflections on the harm that results from it. And we may observe in general that if we can find any quality in a person which renders him incommodious to those who live and converse with him, we always allow it to be a fault or blemish, without any further examination. On the other hand, when we enumerate the good qualities of any person, we always mention those parts of his character which render him a safe companion, an easy friend, a gentle master, an agreeable husband, or an indulgent father. We consider him with all his relations in society; and love or hate him according as he affects those who have any immediate intercourse with him. And it is a most certain rule that if there be no relation of life in which I could not wish to stand to a particular person, his character must so far be allowed to be perfect. If he be as little wanting to himself as to others, his character is entirely perfect. This is the ultimate test of merit and virtue.

SECTION IV

OF NATURAL ABILITIES

No DISTINCTION is more usual in all systems of ethics than that betwixt *natural abilities* and *moral virtues;* where the former are placed on the same footing with bodily endowments, and are supposed to have no merit or moral worth annexed to them. Whoever considers the matter accurately will find that a dispute upon this head would be merely a dispute of words, and that though these qualities are not altogether of the same kind, yet they agree in the most material circumstances. They are both of them equally mental qualities, and both of them equally produce pleasure, and have of course an equal tendency to procure the love and esteem of mankind. There are few who are not as jealous of their character with regard to sense and knowledge as to honour and courage; and much more than with regard to temperance and sobriety. Men are even afraid of passing for good-natured, lest *that* should be taken for want of understanding; and often boast of more debauches than they have been really engaged in, to give themselves airs of fire and spirit. In short, the figure a man makes in the world, the reception he meets with in company, the esteem paid him by his acquaintance — all these advantages depend almost as much upon his good sense and judgment as upon any other part of his character. Let a man have the best intentions in the world, and be the furthest from all injustice and violence, he will never be able to make himself be much regarded without a moderate share, at least, of parts and understanding. Since then natural abilities, though perhaps inferior, yet are on the same footing, both as to their causes and effects, with those qualities which we call moral virtues, why should we make any distinction betwixt them?

Though we refuse to natural abilities the title of virtues, we must allow that they procure the love and esteem of mankind; that they give a new lustre to the other virtues; and that a man possessed of them is much more entitled to our good-will and services than one entirely void of them. It may indeed be pretended that the sentiment of approbation which those qualities produce, besides its being *inferior,* is also somewhat *different* from that which attends the other virtues. But this, in my opinion, is not a sufficient reason for excluding them from the catalogue of virtues.   Each of the virtues, even benevolence, justice, gratitude, integrity, excites a different sentiment or feeling in the spectator.   The characters of Cæsar and Cato, as drawn by Sallust, are both of them virtuous in the strictest sense of the word, but in a different way; nor are the sentiments entirely the same which arise from them.   The one produces love, the other esteem; the one is amiable, the other awful; we could wish to meet with the one character in a friend, the other character we would be ambitious of in ourselves. In like manner, the approbation which attends natural abilities may be somewhat different to the feeling from that which arises from the other virtues, without making them entirely of a different species. And indeed we may observe that the natural abilities, no more than the other virtues, produce not, all of them, the same kind of approbation. Good sense and genius beget esteem; wit and humour excite love.[1]

Those who represent the distinction betwixt natural abilities and moral virtues as very material may say that the former are entirely involuntary, and have therefore no merit attending them, as having no dependence on liberty and free will   But to this I answer, *first*, that many of those qualities which all moralists, especially the ancients, comprehend under the title of moral virtues, are equally involuntary and necessary with the qualities of the judgment and imagination. Of this nature are constancy, fortitude, magnanimity, and, in short, all the qualities which form the *great* man.   I might say the same, in some degree, of the others; it being almost impossible for the mind to change its character in any considerable article, or cure itself of a passionate or splenetic temper, when they are natural to it.   The greater degree there is of these blamable qualities, the more vicious they become, and yet they are the less voluntary.   *Secondly*, I would have any one give me a reason why virtue and vice may not be involuntary, as well as beauty and deformity.   These moral distinctions arise from the natural distinctions of pain and pleasure; and when we receive those feelings from the general consideration of any quality or

---

[1] Love and esteem are at the bottom the same passions, and arise from like causes.   The qualities that produce both are agreeable, and give pleasure.   But where this pleasure is severe and serious; or where its object is great, and makes a strong impression; or where it produces any degree of humility and awe: in all these cases the passion which arises from the pleasure is more properly denominated esteem than love.   Benevolence attends both, but is connected with love in a more eminent degree.

character, we denominate it vicious or virtuous. Now I believe no one will assert that a quality can never produce pleasure or pain to the person who considers it, unless it be perfectly voluntary in the person who possesses it. *Thirdly*, as to free will, we have shown that it has no place with regard to the actions, no more than the qualities of men. It is not a just consequence that what is voluntary is free. Our actions are more voluntary than our judgments; but we have not more liberty in the one than in the other.

But though this distinction betwixt voluntary and involuntary be not sufficient to justify the distinction betwixt natural abilities and moral virtues, yet the former distinction will afford us a plausible reason why moralists have invented the latter. Men have observed that, though natural abilities and moral qualities be in the main on the same footing, there is, however, this difference betwixt them, that the former are almost invariable by any art or industry, while the latter, or at least the actions that proceed from them, may be changed by the motives of rewards and punishment, praise and blame. Hence legislators and divines and moralists have principally applied themselves to the regulating these voluntary actions and have endeavoured to produce additional motives for being virtuous in that particular. They knew that to punish a man for folly, or exhort him to be prudent and sagacious, would have but little effect, though the same punishments and exhortations with regard to justice and injustice might have a considerable influence. But as men in common life and conversation do not carry those ends in view, but naturally praise or blame whatever pleases or displeases them, they do not seem much to regard this distinction, but consider prudence under the character of virtue as well as benevolence, and penetration as well as justice. Nay, we find that all moralists, whose judgment is not perverted by a strict adherence to a system, enter into the same way of thinking; and that the ancient moralists, in particular, made no scruple of placing prudence at the head of the cardinal virtues. There is a sentiment of esteem and approbation which may be excited, in some degree, by any faculty of the mind in its perfect state and condition; and to account for this sentiment is the business of *philosophers*. It belongs to *grammarians* to examine what qualities are entitled to the denomination of *virtue;* nor will they find, upon trial, that this is so easy a task as at first sight they may be apt to imagine.

The principal reason why natural abilities are esteemed is because of their tendency to be useful to the person who is possessed of them. It is impossible to execute any design with success where it is not conducted with prudence and discretion; nor will the goodness of our intentions alone suffice to procure us a happy issue to our enterprises. Men are superior to beasts principally by the superiority of their reason; and they are the degrees of the same faculty which set such an infinite difference betwixt one man and another. All the advantages of art are owing to human reason; and where fortune is not very capricious, the most considerable part of these advantages must fall to the share of the prudent and sagacious.

When it is asked whether a quick or a slow apprehension be most valuable; whether one that at first view penetrates into a subject but can perform nothing upon study; or a contrary character which must work out everything by dint of application; whether a clear head, or a copious invention; whether a profound genius, or a sure judgment; in short, what character or peculiar understanding is more excellent than another? It is evident we can answer none of these questions without considering which of those qualities capacitates a man best for the world and carries him furthest in any of his undertakings.

There are many other qualities of the mind whose merit is derived from the same origin. *Industry, perseverance, patience, activity, vigilance, application, constancy,* with other virtues of that kind which it will be easy to recollect, are esteemed valuable upon no other account than their advantage in the conduct of life. It is the same case with *temperance, frugality, economy, resolution;* as, on the other hand, *prodigality, luxury, irresolution, uncertainty,* are vicious merely because they draw ruin upon us and incapacitate us for business and action.

As wisdom and good sense are valued because they are *useful* to the person possessed of them, so *wit* and *eloquence* are valued because they are *immediately agreeable* to others. On the other hand, *good humour* is loved and esteemed because it is *immediately agreeable* to the person himself. It is evident that the conversation of a man of wit is very satisfactory; as a cheerful good-humoured companion diffuses a joy over the whole company from a sympathy with his gaiety. These qualities, therefore, being agreeable, they naturally beget love and esteem and answer to all the characters of virtue.

It is difficult to tell, on many occasions, what it is that renders one man's conversation so agreeable and entertaining, and another's so insipid and distasteful. As conversation is a transcript of the mind as well as books, the same qualities which render the one valuable must give us an esteem for the other. This we shall consider afterwards. In the meantime, it may be affirmed in general that all the merit a man may derive from his conversation — which, no doubt, may be very considerable — arises from nothing but the pleasure it conveys to those who are present.

In this view, *cleanliness* is also to be regarded as a virtue, since it naturally renders us agreeable to others, and is a very considerable source of love and affection. No one will deny that a negligence in this particular is a fault; and as faults are nothing but smaller vices, and this fault can have no other origin than the uneasy sensations which it excites in others, we may in this instance, seemingly so trivial, clearly discover the origin of the moral distinction of vice and virtue in other instances.

Besides all those qualities which render a person lovely or valuable, there is also a certain *je-ne-sçai-quoi* of agreeable and handsome that concurs to the same effect. In this case, as well as in that of wit and eloquence, we must have recourse to a certain sense which acts without reflection and regards not the tendencies of qualities and characters. Some moralists account for all the sentiments of virtue by this sense. Their hypothesis is very plausible. Nothing but a particular inquiry can give the preference to any other hypothesis. When we find that almost all the virtues have such particular tendencies, and also find that these tendencies are sufficient alone to give a strong sentiment of approbation, we cannot doubt, after this, that qualities are approved of in proportion to the advantage which results from them.

The *decorum* or *indecorum* of a quality with regard to the age, or character, or station, contributes also to its praise or blame. This decorum depends in a great measure upon experience. It is usual to see men lose their levity as they advance in years. Such a degree of gravity, therefore, and such years are connected together in our thoughts. When we observe them separated in any person's character, this imposes a kind of violence on our imagination and is disagreeable.

That faculty of the soul which, of all others, is of the least consequence to the character, and has the least virtue or vice in its several degrees, at the same time that it admits of a great variety of degrees,

is the *memory*. Unless it rise up to that stupendous height as to surprise us, or sink so low as in some measure to affect the judgment, we
commonly take no notice of its variations, nor ever mention them to
the praise or dispraise of any person. It is so far from being a virtue
to have a good memory that men generally affect to complain of a
bad one; and, endeavouring to persuade the world that what they say
is entirely of their own invention, sacrifice it to the praise of genius
and judgment. Yet to consider the matter abstractedly, it would be
difficult to give a reason why the faculty of recalling past ideas with
truth and clearness should not have as much merit in it as the faculty
of placing our present ideas in such an order as to form true propositions and opinions. The reason of the difference certainly must be
that the memory is exerted without any sensation of pleasure or pain,
and in all its middling degrees serves almost equally well in business
and affairs. But the least variations in the judgment are sensibly felt
in their consequences, while at the same time that faculty is never
exerted in any eminent degree without an extraordinary delight and
satisfaction. The sympathy with this utility and pleasure bestows
a merit on the understanding; and the absence of it makes us consider
the memory as a faculty very indifferent to blame or praise.

Before I leave this subject of *natural abilities*, I must observe that
perhaps one source of the esteem and affection which attends them is
derived from the *importance* and *weight* which they bestow on the
person possessed of them. He becomes of greater consequence in life.
His resolutions and actions affect a greater number of his fellow-
creatures. Both his friendship and enmity are of moment. And it is
easy to observe that whoever is elevated, after this manner, above the
rest of mankind must excite in us the sentiments of esteem and approbation. Whatever is important engages our attention, fixes our
thought, and is contemplated with satisfaction. The histories of
kingdoms are more interesting than domestic stories; the histories of
great empires more than those of small cities and principalities; and
the histories of wars and revolutions more than those of peace and
order. We sympathize with the persons that suffer in all the various
sentiments which belong to their fortunes. The mind is occupied by
the multitude of the objects and by the strong passions that display
themselves. And this occupation or agitation of the mind is commonly
agreeable and amusing. The same theory accounts for the esteem and

regard we pay to men of extraordinary parts and abilities. The good and ill of multitudes are connected with their actions. Whatever they undertake is important and challenges our attention. Nothing is to be overlooked and despised that regards them. And where any person can excite these sentiments, he soon acquires our esteem unless other circumstances of his character render him odious and disagreeable.

SECTION V

SOME FURTHER REFLECTIONS CONCERNING THE NATURAL VIRTUES

IT HAS BEEN observed, in treating of the passions, that pride and humility, love and hatred, are excited by any advantages or disadvantages of the *mind, body*, or *fortune;* and that these advantages or disadvantages have that effect by producing a separate impression of pain or pleasure. The pain or pleasure which arises from the general survey or view of any action or quality of the *mind*, constitutes its vice or virtue, and gives rise to our approbation or blame, which is nothing but a fainter and more imperceptible love or hatred. We have assigned four different sources of this pain and pleasure; and in order to justify more fully that hypothesis, it may here be proper to observe that the advantages or disadvantages of the *body* and of *fortune* produce a pain or pleasure from the very same principles. The tendency of any object to be *useful* to the person possessed of it or to others, to convey *pleasure* to him or to others; all these circumstances convey an immediate pleasure to the person who considers the object, and command his love and approbation.

To begin with the advantages of the *body;* we may observe a phenomenon which might appear somewhat trivial and ludicrous, if anything could be trivial which fortified a conclusion of such importance, or ludicruous, which was employed in a philosophical reasoning. It is a general remark that those we call good *women's men*, who have either signalized themselves by their amorous exploits, or whose make of body promises any extraordinary vigour of that kind, are well received by the fair sex and naturally engage the affections even of those whose virtue prevents any design of ever giving employment to those talents.

Here it is evident that the ability of such a person to give enjoyment is the real source of that love and esteem he meets with among the females; at the same time that the women who love and esteem him have no prospect of receiving that enjoyment themselves, and can only be affected by means of their sympathy with one that has a commerce of love with him. This instance is singular and merits our attention.

Another source of the pleasure we receive from considering bodily advantages is their utility to the person himself who is possessed of them. It is certain that a considerable part of the beauty of men as well as of other animals consists in such a conformation of members as we find by experience to be attended with strength and agility, and to capacitate the creature for any action or exercise. Broad shoulders, a lank belly, firm joints, taper legs — all these are beautiful in our species because they are signs of force and vigour which, being advantages we naturally sympathize with, they convey to the beholder a share of that satisfaction they produce in the possessor.

So far as to the *utility* which may attend any quality of the body. As to the immediate *pleasure*, it is certain that an air of health as well as of strength and agility makes a considerable part of beauty; and that a sickly air in another is always disagreeable upon account of that idea of pain and uneasiness which it conveys to us. On the other hand, we are pleased with the regularity of our own features, though it be neither useful to ourselves nor others; and it is necessary for us in some measure to set ourselves at a distance, to make it convey to us any satisfaction. We commonly consider ourselves as we appear in the eyes of others, and sympathize with the advantageous sentiments they entertain with regard to us.

How far the advantages of *fortune* produce esteem and approbation from the same principles, we may satisfy ourselves by reflecting on our precedent reasoning on that subject. We have observed that our approbation of those who are possessed of the advantages of fortune may be ascribed to three different causes. *First*, to that immediate pleasure which a rich man gives us by the view of the beautiful clothes, equipage, gardens, or houses, which he possesses. *Secondly*, to the advantage which we hope to reap from him by his generosity and liberality. *Thirdly*, to the pleasure and advantage which he himself reaps from his possessions, and which produce an agreeable sympathy in us. Whether we ascribe our esteem of the rich and great to one or all of these causes, we may clearly see the traces of those principles which give rise to the sense of vice and virtue. I believe most people, at first sight, will be inclined to ascribe our esteem of the rich to self-interest and the prospect of advantage. But as it is certain that our esteem or deference extends beyond any prospect of advantage to ourselves, it is evident that that sentiment must proceed from a sympathy with those who are dependent on the person we esteem and respect, and who have an immediate connection with him. We consider him as a person capable of contributing to the happiness or enjoyment of his fellow-creatures whose sentiments with regard to him we naturally embrace. And this consideration will serve to justify my hypothesis in preferring the *third* principle to the other two, and ascribing our esteem of the rich to a sympathy with the pleasure and advantage which they themselves receive from their possessions. For as even the other two principles cannot operate to a due extent, or account for all the phenomena without having recourse to a sympathy of one kind or other, it is much more natural to choose that sympathy which is immediate and direct than that which is remote and indirect. To which we may add that where the riches or power are very great, and render the person considerable and important in the world, the esteem attending them may in part be ascribed to another source, distinct from these three, viz., their interesting the mind by a prospect of the multitude and importance of their consequences, though, in order to account for the operation of this principle, we must also have recourse to *sympathy*, as we have observed in the preceding section.

It may not be amiss, on this occasion, to remark the flexibility of our sentiments, and the several changes they so readily receive from the objects with which they are conjoined. All the sentiments of approbation which attend any particular species of objects have a great resemblance to each other, though derived from different sources; and, on the other hand, those sentiments, when directed to different objects, are different to the feeling, though derived from the same source. Thus the beauty of all visible objects causes a pleasure pretty much the same, though it be sometimes derived from the mere *species* and appearance of the objects, sometimes from sympathy and an idea of their utility. In like manner, whenever we survey the actions and characters of men, without any particular interest in them, the pleasure or pain which arises from the survey (with some minute differences) is in the main of the same kind, though perhaps there be a great diversity in the causes from which it is derived. On the other hand, a convenient house and a virtuous character cause not the same feeling of approbation, even though the source of our approbation be the same, and flow from sympathy and an idea of their utility. There is something very inexplicable in this variation of our feelings; but it is what we have experience of with regard to all our passions and sentiments.

SECTION VI

CONCLUSION OF THIS BOOK

Thus, upon the whole, I am hopeful that nothing is wanting to an accurate proof of this system of ethics. We are certain that sympathy is a very powerful principle in human nature. We are also certain that it has a great influence on our sense of beauty when we regard external objects as well as when we judge of morals. We find that it has force sufficient to give us the strongest sentiments of approbation when it operates alone, without the concurrence of any other principle, as in the cases of justice, allegiance, chastity, and good manners. We may observe that all the circumstances requisite for its operation are found in most of the virtues which have, for the most part, a tendency to the good of society, or to that of the person possessed of them. If we compare all these circumstances, we shall not doubt that sympathy is the chief source of moral distinctions, especially when we reflect that no objection can be raised against this hypothesis in one case which will not extend to all cases. Justice is certainly approved of, for no other reason than because it has a tendency to the public good; and the public good is indifferent to us, except so far as sympathy interests us in it. We may presume the like with regard to all the other virtues which have a like tendency to the public good. They must derive all their merit from our sympathy with those who reap any advantage from them, as the virtues which have a tendency to the good of the person possessed of them derive their merit from our sympathy with him.

Most people will readily allow that the useful qualities of the mind are virtuous because of their utility. This way of thinking is so natural and occurs on so many occasions that few will make any scruple of admitting it. Now this being once admitted, the force of sympathy must necessarily be acknowledged. Virtue is considered as means to an end. Means to an end are only valued so far as the end is valued. But the happiness of strangers affects us by sympathy alone. To that principle, therefore, we are to ascribe the sentiment of approbàtion which arises from the survey of all those virtues that are useful to society or to the person possessed of them. These form the most considerable part of morality.

Were it proper, in such a subject, to bribe the reader's assent, or employ anything but solid argument, we are here abundantly supplied with topics to engage the affections. All lovers of virtue — and such we all are in speculation, however we may degenerate in practice — must certainly be pleased to see moral distinctions derived from so noble a source, which gives us a just notion both of the *generosity* and *capacity* of human nature. It requires but very little knowledge of human affairs to perceive that a sense of morals is a principle inherent in the soul, and one of the most powerful that enters into the composition. But this sense must certainly acquire new force when, reflecting on itself, it approves of those principles from whence it is derived, and finds nothing but what is great and good in its rise and origin. Those who resolve the sense of morals into original instincts of the human mind may defend the cause of virtue with sufficient authority, but want the advantage which those possess who account for that sense by an extensive sympathy with mankind. According to their system, not only virtue must be approved of, but also the sense of virtue: and not only that sense, but also the principles from whence it is derived. So that nothing is presented on any side but what is laudable and good.

This observation may be extended to justice and the other virtues of that kind. Though justice be artificial, the sense of its morality is natural. It is the combination of men in a system of conduct which renders any act of justice beneficial to society. But when once it has that tendency, we *naturally* approve of it; and if we did not so, it is impossible any combination or convention could ever produce that sentiment.

Most of the inventions of men are subject to change. They depend upon humour and caprice. They have a vogue for a time, and then

CONCLUSION OF THIS BOOK

sink into oblivion. It may perhaps be apprehended that, if justice were allowed to be of human invention, it must be placed on the same footing. But the cases are widely different. The interest on which justice is founded is the greatest imaginable and extends to all times and places. It cannot possibly be served by any other invention. It is obvious and discovers itself on the very first formation of society. All these causes render the rules of justice steadfast and immutable; at least, as immutable as human nature. And if they were founded on original instincts, could they have any greater stability?

The same system may help us to form a just notion of the *happiness* as well as of the *dignity* of virtue, and may interest every principle of our nature in the embracing and cherishing that noble quality. Who indeed does not feel an accession of alacrity in his pursuits of knowledge and ability of every kind, when he considers that, besides the advantages which immediately result from these acquisitions, they also give him a new lustre in the eyes of mankind, and are universally attended with esteem and approbation? And who can think any advantage of fortune a sufficient compensation for the least breach of the *social* virtues, when he considers that not only his character with regard to others, but also his peace and inward satisfaction entirely depend upon his strict observance of them; and that a mind will never be able to bear its own survey that has been wanting in its parts to mankind and society? But I forbear insisting on this subject. Such reflections require a work apart, very different from the genius of the present. The anatomist ought never to emulate the painter; nor in his accurate dissections and portraitures of the smaller parts of the human body pretend to give his figures any graceful and engaging attitude or expression. There is even something hideous or at least minute in the views of things which he presents; and it is necessary the objects should be set more at a distance, and be more covered up from sight, to make them engaging to the eye and imagination. An anatomist, however, is admirably fitted to give advice to a painter and it is even impracticable to excel in the latter art without the assistance of the former. We must have an exact knowledge of the parts, their situation and connection, before we can design with any elegance or correctness. And thus the most abstract speculations concerning human nature, however cold and unentertaining, become subservient to *practical morality*, and may render this latter science more correct in its precepts and more persuasive in its exhortations.

II

AN ENQUIRY CONCERNING THE PRINCIPLES OF MORALS

AUTHOR'S ADVERTISEMENT

Most of the principles and reasonings contained in this volume[1] were published in a work in three volumes, called *A Treatise of Human Nature*, a work which the Author had projected before he left College, and which he wrote and published not long after. But not finding it successful, he was sensible of his error in going to the press too early, and he cast the whole anew in the following pieces, where some negligences in his former reasoning and more in the expression are, he hopes, corrected. Yet several writers who have honoured the Author's philosophy with answers have taken care to direct all their batteries against that juvenile work which the author never acknowledged, and have affected to triumph in any advantages which, they imagined, they had obtained over it: A practice very contrary to all rules of candour and fair-dealing, and a strong instance of those polemical artifices which a bigoted zeal thinks itself authorized to employ. Henceforth, the Author desires that the following Pieces may alone be regarded as containing his philosophical sentiments and principles.

[1] This note refers to Volume II of the posthumous edition, published 1777, which contains, besides the *Enquiry Concerning the Principles of Morals*, *An Enquiry Concerning Human Understanding* and *A Dissertation on the Passions*.

SECTION I

DISPUTES with men pertinaciously obstinate in their principles are of all others the most irksome; except, perhaps, those with persons entirely disingenuous, who really do not believe the opinions they defend, but engage in the controversy from affectation, from a spirit of opposition, or from a desire of showing wit and ingenuity superior to the rest of mankind. The same blind adherence to their own arguments is to be expected in both, the same contempt of their antagonists, and the same passionate vehemence in enforcing sophistry and falsehood. And as reasoning is not the source whence either disputant derives his tenets, it is in vain to expect that any logic, which speaks not to the affections, will ever engage him to embrace sounder principles.

Those who have denied the reality of moral distinctions may be ranked among the disingenuous disputants; nor is it conceivable that any human creature could ever seriously believe that all characters and actions were alike entitled to the affection and regard of everyone. The difference which nature has placed between one man and another is so wide, and this difference is still so much farther widened by education, example, and habit, that, where the opposite extremes come at once under our apprehension, there is no scepticism so scrupulous and scarce any assurance so determined, as absolutely to deny all distinction between them. Let a man's insensibility be ever so great, he must often be touched with the images of Right and Wrong; and let his prejudices be ever so obstinate, he must observe that others are susceptible of like impressions. The only way, therefore, of converting an antagonist of this kind is to leave him to himself. For, finding that nobody keeps up the controversy with him, it is probable he will at last, of himself, from mere weariness come over to the side of common sense and reason.

There has been a controversy started of late, much better worth examination, concerning the general foundation of Morals; whether they be derived from Reason or from Sentiment; whether we attain the knowledge of them by a chain of argument and induction or by an immediate feeling and finer internal sense; whether, like all sound judgment of truth and falsehood, they should be the same to every rational intelligent being; or whether, like the perception of beauty and deformity, they be founded entirely on the particular fabric and constitution of the human species.

The ancient philosophers, though they often affirm that virtue is nothing but conformity to reason, yet in general seem to consider morals as deriving their existence from taste and sentiment. On the other hand, our modern enquirers, though they also talk much of the beauty of virtue and deformity of vice, yet have commonly endeavoured to account for these distinctions by metaphysical reasonings, and by deductions from the most abstract principles of the understanding. Such confusion reigned in these subjects that an opposition of the greatest consequence could prevail between one system and another, and even in the parts of almost each individual system; and yet nobody, till very lately, was ever sensible of it. The elegant Lord Shaftesbury, who first gave occasion to remark this distinction, and who in general adhered to the principles of the ancients, is not himself entirely free from the same confusion.

It must be acknowledged that both sides of the question are susceptible of specious arguments. Moral distinctions, it may be said, are discernible by pure *reason;* else, whence the many disputes that reign in common life, as well as in philosophy, with regard to this subject: the long chain of proofs often produced on both sides, the examples cited, the authorities appealed to, the analogies employed, the fallacies detected, the inferences drawn, and the several conclusions adjusted to their proper principles. Truth is disputable, not taste; what exists in the nature of things is the standard of our judgment; what each man feels within himself is the standard of sentiment. Propositions in geometry may be proved, systems in physics may be controverted; but the harmony of verse, the tenderness of passion, the brilliancy of wit, must give immediate pleasure. No man reasons concerning another's beauty, but frequently concerning the justice or injustice of his actions. In every criminal trial the first object of the prisoner is to disprove the facts alleged and deny the actions imputed to him; the second, to prove that, even if these actions were real, they might be justified as innocent and lawful. It is confessedly by deductions of the understanding that the first point is ascertained: how can we suppose that a different faculty of the mind is employed in fixing the other?

On the other hand, those who would resolve all moral determinations into *sentiment* may endeavour to show that it is impossible for reason ever to draw conclusions of this nature. To virtue, say they, it belongs to be *amiable*, and vice *odious*. This forms their very nature or essence. But can reason or argumentation distribute these different epithets to any subjects, and pronounce beforehand that this must produce love, and that hatred? Or what other reason can we ever assign for these affections but the original fabric and formation of the human mind, which is naturally adapted to receive them?

The end of all moral speculations is to teach us our duty; and by proper representations of the deformity of vice and beauty of virtue, beget correspondent habits, and engage us to avoid the one and embrace the other. But is this ever to be expected from inferences and conclusions of the understanding, which of themselves have no hold of the affections or set in motion the active powers of men? They discover truths; but where the truths which they discover are indifferent and beget no desire or aversion, they can have no influence on conduct and behaviour. What is honourable, what is fair, what is becoming, what is noble, what is generous, takes possession of the heart and animates us to embrace and maintain it. What is intelligible, what is evident, what is probable, what is true, procures only the cool assent of the understanding and, gratifying a speculative curiosity, puts an end to our researches.

Extinguish all the warm feelings and prepossessions in favour of virtue, and all disgust or aversion to vice; render men totally indifferent towards these distinctions, and morality is no longer a practical study, nor has any tendency to regulate our lives and actions.

These arguments on each side — and many more might be produced — are so plausible that I am apt to suspect they may, the one as well as the other, be solid and satisfactory, and that *reason* and *sentiment* concur in almost all moral determinations and conclusions. The final sentence, it is probable, which pronounces characters and actions amiable or odious, praiseworthy or blamable; that which stamps on them the mark of honour or infamy, approbation or censure; that which renders morality an active principle and constitutes virtue our happiness, and vice our misery — it is probable, I say, that this final sentence depends on some internal sense or feeling which nature has made universal in the whole species. For what else can have an influence of this nature? But in order to pave the way for such a sentiment, and give a proper discernment of its object, it is often necessary, we find, that much reasoning should precede, that nice distinctions be made, just conclusions drawn, distant comparisons formed, complicated relations examined, and general facts fixed and ascertained. Some species of beauty, especially the natural kinds, on their first appearance command our affection and approbation; and where they fail of this effect, it is impossible for any reasoning to redress their influence, or adapt them better to our taste and sentiment. But in many orders of beauty, particularly those of the finer arts, it is requisite to employ much reasoning in order to feel the proper sentiment; and a false relish may frequently be corrected by argument and reflection. There are just grounds to conclude that moral beauty partakes much of this latter species, and demands the assistance of our intellectual faculties in order to give it a suitable influence on the human mind.

But though this question concerning the general principles of morals be curious and important, it is needless for us, at present, to employ further care in our researches concerning it. For if we can be so happy, in the course of this enquiry, as to discover the true origin of morals, it will then easily appear how far either sentiment or reason enters into all determinations of this nature.[1] In order to attain this purpose, we shall endeavour to follow a very simple method: we shall analyze that complication of mental qualities which form what, in common life, we call "personal merit"; we shall consider every attribute of the mind which renders a man an object either of esteem and affection, or of hatred and contempt; every habit or sentiment or faculty which, if ascribed to any person, implies either praise or blame, and may enter into any panegyric or satire of his character and manners. The quick sensibility, which, on this head, is so universal among mankind, gives a philosopher sufficient assurance that he can never be considerably mistaken in framing the catalogue, or incur any danger of misplacing the objects of his contemplation: he

[1] See Appendix I.

needs only enter into his own breast for a moment, and consider whether or not he should desire to have this or that quality ascribed to him, and whether such or such an imputation would proceed from a friend or an enemy. The very nature of language guides us almost infallibly in forming a judgment of this nature; and as every tongue possesses one set of words which are taken in a good sense, and another in the opposite, the least acquaintance with the idiom suffices, without any reasoning, to direct us in collecting and arranging the estimable or blamable qualities of men. The only object of reasoning is to discover the circumstances on both sides which are common to these qualities; to observe that particular in which the estimable qualities agree on the one hand, and the blamable on the other; and thence to reach the foundation of ethics, and find those universal principles from which all censure or approbation is ultimately derived. As this is a question of fact, not of abstract science, we can only expect success by following the experimental method and deducing general maxims from a comparison of particular instances. The other scientific method, where a general abstract principle is first established, and is afterwards branched out into a variety of inferences and conclusions, may be more perfect in itself, but suits less the imperfection of human nature, and is a common source of illusion and mistake in this as well as in other subjects. Men are now cured of their passion for hypotheses and systems in natural philosophy, and will hearken to no arguments but those which are derived from experience. It is full time they should attempt a like reformation in all moral disquisitions and reject every system of ethics, however subtle or ingenious, which is not founded on fact and observation.

We shall begin our enquiry on this head by the consideration of the social virtues, Benevolence and Justice. The explication of them will probably give us an opening by which the others may be accounted for.

SECTION II

OF BENEVOLENCE

Part I

IT MAY BE ESTEEMED, perhaps, a superfluous task to prove that the benevolent or softer affections are estimable; and wherever they appear, engage the approbation and good-will of mankind. The epithets *sociable, good-natured, humane, merciful, grateful, friendly, generous, beneficent,* or their equivalents, are known in all languages, and universally express the highest merit which *human nature* is capable of attaining. Where these amiable qualities are attended with birth and power and eminent abilities, and display themselves in the good government or useful instruction of mankind, they seem even to raise the possessors of them above the rank of *human nature,* and make them approach in some measure to the divine. Exalted capacity, undaunted courage, prosperous success; these may only expose a hero or politician to the envy and ill-will of the public: but as soon as the praises are added of humane and beneficent, when instances are displayed of lenity, tenderness or friendship, envy itself is silent, or joins the general voice of approbation and applause.

When Pericles, the great Athenian statesman and general, was on his death-bed, his surrounding friends, deeming him now insensible, began to indulge their sorrow for their expiring patron by enumerating his great qualities and successes, his conquests and victories, the unusual length of his administration, and his nine trophies erected over the enemies of the republic. *You forget,* cries the dying hero, who had heard all, *you forget the most eminent of my praises, while you dwell so much on those vulgar advantages in which fortune had a principal share. You have not observed that no citizen has ever yet worn mourning on my account.*[1]

In men of more ordinary talents and capacity the social virtues become, if possible, still more essentially requisite; there being nothing eminent, in that case, to compensate for the want of them, or preserve the person from our severest hatred as well as contempt. A high ambition, an elevated courage, is apt, says Cicero, in less perfect

[1] Plut. in *Pericle.*

characters, to degenerate into a turbulent ferocity. The more social and softer virtues are there chiefly to be regarded. These are always good and amiable.[2]

The principal advantage which Juvenal discovers in the extensive capacity of the human species is that it renders our benevolence also more extensive, and gives us larger opportunities of spreading our kindly influence than what are indulged to the inferior creation.[3] It must, indeed, be confessed that by doing good only can a man truly enjoy the advantages of being eminent. His exalted station of itself but the more exposes him to danger and tempest. His sole prerogative is to afford shelter to inferiors who repose themselves under his cover and protection.

But I forget that it is not my present business to recommend generosity and benevolence, or to paint in their true colours all the genuine charms of the social virtues. These, indeed, sufficiently engage every heart on the first apprehension of them; and it is difficult to abstain from some sally of panegyric as often as they occur in discourse or reasoning. But our object here being more the speculative than the practical part of morals, it will suffice to remark (what will readily, I believe, be allowed) that no qualities are more entitled to the general good-will and approbation of mankind than beneficence and humanity, friendship and gratitude, natural affection and public spirit, or whatever proceeds from a tender sympathy with others and a generous concern for our kind and species. These wherever they appear seem to transfuse themselves, in a manner, into each beholder, and to call forth, in their own behalf, the same favourable and affectionate sentiments which they exert on all around.

Part II

We may observe that, in displaying the praises of any humane, beneficent man, there is one circumstance which never fails to be amply insisted on, namely, the happiness and satisfaction derived to society from his intercourse and good offices. To his parents, we are apt to say, he endears himself by his pious attachment and duteous care still more than by the connexions of nature. His children never

[2] Cic. *De Officiis*, lib. I.
[3] Satire xv. 139 and seq.

feel his authority but when employed for their advantage. With him, the ties of love are consolidated by beneficence and friendship. The ties of friendship approach, in a fond observance of each obliging office, to those of love and inclination. His domestics and dependents have in him a sure resource, and no longer dread the power of fortune but so far as she exercises it over him. From him the hungry receive food, the naked clothing, the ignorant and slothful skill and industry. Like the sun, an inferior minister of providence he cheers, invigorates, and sustains the surrounding world.

If confined to private life, the sphere of his activity is narrower; but his influence is all benign and gentle. If exalted into a higher station, mankind and posterity reap the fruit of his labours.

As these topics of praise never fail to be employed, and with success, where we would inspire esteem for any one, may it not thence be concluded that the utility resulting from the social virtues forms at least a *part* of their merit, and is one source of that approbation and regard so universally paid to them?

When we recommend even an animal or a plant as *useful* and *beneficial*, we give it an applause and recommendation suited to its nature. As, on the other hand, reflection on the baneful influence of any of these inferior beings always inspires us with the sentiment of aversion. The eye is pleased with the prospect of corn-fields and loaded vineyards, horses grazing, and flocks pasturing; but flies the view of briars and brambles, affording shelter to wolves and serpents.

A machine, a piece of furniture, a vestment, a house well contrived for use and convenience, is so far beautiful, and is contemplated with pleasure and approbation. An experienced eye is here sensible to many excellences which escape persons ignorant and uninstructed.

Can anything stronger be said in praise of a profession, such as merchandise or manufacture, than to observe the advantages which it procures to society; and is not a monk and inquisitor enraged when we treat his order as useless or pernicious to mankind?

The historian exults in displaying the benefit arising from his labours. The writer of romance alleviates or denies the bad consequences ascribed to his manner of composition.

In general, what praise is implied in the simple epithet *useful!* What reproach in the contrary!

Your gods, says Cicero [4] in opposition to the Epicureans, cannot justly claim any worship or adoration, with whatever imaginary perfections you may suppose them endowed. They are totally useless and inactive. Even the Egyptians, whom you so much ridicule, never consecrated any animal but on account of its utility.

The sceptics assert,[5] though absurdly, that the origin of all religious worship was derived from the utility of inanimate objects, as the sun and moon, to the support and well-being of mankind. This is also the common reason assigned by historians for the deification of eminent heroes and legislators.[6]

To plant a tree, to cultivate a field, to beget children: meritorious acts, according to the religion of Zoroaster.

In all determinations of morality this circumstance of public utility is ever principally in view; and wherever disputes arise, either in philosophy or common life, concerning the bounds of duty, the question cannot by any means be decided with greater certainty than by ascertaining, on any side, the true interests of mankind. If any false opinion, embraced from appearances, has been found to prevail, as soon as farther experience and sounder reasoning have given us juster notions of human affairs, we retract our first sentiment and adjust anew the boundaries of moral good and evil.

Giving alms to common beggars is naturally praised, because it seems to carry relief to the distressed and indigent; but when we observe the encouragement thence arising to idleness and debauchery, we regard that species of charity rather as a weakness than a virtue.

Tyrannicide, or the assassination of usurpers and oppressive princes, was highly extolled in ancient times, because it both freed mankind from many of these monsters, and seemed to keep the others in awe, whom the sword or poniard could not reach. But history and experience having since convinced us that this practice increases the jealousy and cruelty of princes, a Timoleon and a Brutus, though treated with indulgence on account of the prejudices of their times, are now considered as very improper models for imitation.

Liberality in princes is regarded as a mark of beneficence, but when it occurs that the homely bread of the honest and industrious is often

[4] De Nat. Deor. lib. i.
[5] Sext. Emp. adversus Math. lib. viii.
[6] Diod. Sic. passim.

thereby converted into delicious cates for the idle and the prodigal, we soon retract our heedless praises. The regrets of a prince for having lost a day were noble and generous; but had he intended to have spent it in acts of generosity to his greedy courtiers, it was better lost than misemployed after that manner.

Luxury, or a refinement on the pleasures and conveniences of life, had not long been supposed the source of every corruption in government, and the immediate cause of faction, sedition, civil wars, and the total loss of liberty. It was, therefore, universally regarded as a vice, and was an object of declamation to all satirists and severe moralists. Those who prove or attempt to prove that such refinements rather tend to the increase of industry, civility, and arts, regulate anew our *moral* as well as *political* sentiments, and represent as laudable or innocent what had formerly been regarded as pernicious and blamable.

Upon the whole, then, it seems undeniable *that* nothing can bestow more merit on any human creature than the sentiment of benevolence in an eminent degree; and *that* a *part*, at least, of its merit arises from its tendency to promote the interests of our species, and bestow happiness on human society. We carry our view into the salutary consequences of such a character and disposition; and whatever has so benign an influence, and forwards so desirable an end, is beheld with complacency and pleasure. The social virtues are never regarded without their beneficial tendencies, nor viewed as barren and unfruitful. The happiness of mankind, the order of society, the harmony of families, the mutual support of friends, are always considered as the result of their gentle dominion over the breasts of men.

How considerable a *part* of their merit we ought to ascribe to their utility will better appear from future disquisitions;[7] as well as the reason why this circumstance has such a command over our esteem and approbation.[8]

[7] Sect. III. and IV.
[8] Sect. V.

SECTION III

OF JUSTICE

Part I

THAT JUSTICE is useful to society, and consequently that *part* of its merit, at least, must arise from that consideration, it would be a superfluous undertaking to prove. That public utility is the *sole* origin of justice, and that reflections on the beneficial consequences of this virtue are the *sole* foundation of its merit; this proposition, being more curious and important, will better deserve our examination and enquiry.

Let us suppose that nature has bestowed on the human race such profuse *abundance* of all *external* conveniences that, without any uncertainty in the event, without any care or industry on our part, every individual finds himself fully provided with whatever his most voracious appetites can want, or luxurious imagination wish or desire. His natural beauty, we shall suppose, surpasses all acquired ornaments; the perpetual clemency of the seasons renders useless all clothes or covering; the raw herbage affords him the most delicious fare; the clear fountain, the richest beverage. No laborious occupation required; no tillage; no navigation. Music, poetry, and contemplation form his sole business; conversation, mirth, and friendship his sole amusement.

It seems evident that in such a happy state every other social virtue would flourish and receive tenfold increase; but the cautious, jealous virtue of justice would never once have been dreamed of. For what purpose make a partition of goods where every one has already more than enough? Why give rise to property where there cannot possibly be any injury? Why call this object *mine* when, upon the seizing of it by another, I need but stretch out my hand to possess myself to what is equally valuable? Justice in that case, being totally useless, would be an idle ceremonial, and could never possibly have place in the catalogue of virtues.

We see, even in the present necessitous condition of mankind, that, wherever any benefit is bestowed by nature in an unlimited abundance, we leave it always in common among the whole human race, and make no subdivisions of right and property. Water and air, though the most necessary of all objects, are not challenged as the property of individuals; nor can any man commit injustice by the most lavish use and enjoyment of these blessings. In fertile extensive countries, with few inhabitants, land is regarded on the same footing. And no topic is so much insisted on by those who defend the liberty of the seas as the unexhausted use of them in navigation. Were the advantages procured by navigation as inexhaustible, these reasoners had never had any adversaries to refute; nor had any claims ever been advanced of a separate, exclusive dominion over the ocean.

It may happen, in some countries, at some periods, that there be established a property in water, none in land;[1] if the latter be in greater abundance than can be used by the inhabitants, and the former be found with difficulty and in very small quantities.

Again, suppose that, though the necessities of human race continue the same as at present, yet the mind is so enlarged, and so replete with friendship and generosity, that every man has the utmost tenderness for every man and feels no more concern for his own interest than for that of his fellows; it seems evident that the use of justice would in this case be suspended by such an extensive benevolence, nor would the divisions and barriers of property and obligation have ever been thought of. Why should I bind another by a deed or promise to do me any good office, when I know that he is already prompted by the strongest inclination to seek my happiness and would of himself perform the desired service, except the hurt he thereby receives be greater than the benefit accruing to me? in which case he knows that, from my innate humanity and friendship, I should be the first to oppose myself to his imprudent generosity.   Why raise landmarks between my neighbour's field and mine, when my heart has made no division between our interests, but shares all his joys and sorrows with the same force and vivacity as if originally my own? Every man, upon this supposition, being a second self to another, would trust all his interests to the discretion of every man, without jealousy, without partition, without distinction. And the whole human race would form only one family, where all would lie in common and be used freely, without regard to property; but cautiously too, with as

[1] Genesis, chaps. xiii. and xxi.

entire regard to the necessities of each individual as if our own interests were most intimately concerned.

In the present disposition of the human heart, it would, perhaps, be difficult to find complete instances of such enlarged affections; but still we may observe that the case of families approaches towards it; and the stronger the mutual benevolence is among the individuals, the nearer it approaches; till all distinction of property be, in a great measure, lost and confounded among them. Between married persons the cement of friendship is by the laws supposed so strong as to abolish all division of possessions, and has often, in reality, the force ascribed to it. And it is observable that during the ardour of new enthusiasms, when every principle is inflamed into extravagance, the community of goods has frequently been attempted; and nothing but experience of its inconveniences, from the returning or disguised selfishness of men, could make the imprudent fanatics adopt anew the ideas of justice and of separate property. So true is it that this virtue derives its existence entirely from its necessary *use* to the intercourse and social state of mankind.

To make this truth more evident, let us reverse the foregoing suppositions and, carrying everything to the opposite extreme, consider what would be the effect of these new situations. Suppose a society to fall into such want of all common necessaries that the utmost frugality and industry cannot preserve the greater number from perishing, and the whole from extreme misery; it will readily, I believe, be admitted that the strict laws of justice are suspended in such a pressing emergency, and give place to the stronger motives of necessity and self-preservation. Is it any crime, after a shipwreck, to seize whatever means or instrument of safety one can lay hold of, without regard to former limitations of property? Or if a city besieged were perishing with hunger, can we imagine that men will see any means of preservation before them, and lose their lives from a scrupulous regard to what, in other situations, would be the rules of equity and justice? The use and tendency of that virtue is to procure happiness and security by preserving order in society; but where the society is ready to perish from extreme necessity, no greater evil can be dreaded from violence and injustice; and every man may now provide for himself by all the means which prudence can dictate or humanity permit.

The public, even in less urgent necessities, opens granaries without the consent of proprietors, as justly supposing that the authority of magistracy may, consistent with equity, extend so far; but were any number of men to assemble, without the tie of laws or civil jurisdiction, would an equal partition of bread in a famine, though effected by power and even violence, be regarded as criminal or injurious?

Suppose likewise that it should be a virtuous man's fate to fall into the society of ruffians, remote from the protection of laws and government; what conduct must he embrace in that melancholy situation? He sees such a desperate rapaciousness prevail, such a disregard to equity, such contempt of order, such stupid blindness to future consequences, as must immediately have the most tragical conclusion, and must terminate in destruction to the greater number, and in a total dissolution of society to the rest. He, meanwhile, can have no other expedient than to arm himself, to whomever the sword he seizes, or the buckler, may belong: to make provision of all means of defence and security; and his particular regard to justice being no longer of use to his own safety or that of others, he must consult the dictates of self-preservation alone, without concern for those who no longer merit his care and attention.

When any man, even in political society, renders himself by his crimes obnoxious to the public, he is punished by the laws in his goods and person; that is, the ordinary rules of justice are, with regard to him, suspended for a moment, and it becomes equitable to inflict on him, for the *benefit* of society, what otherwise he could not suffer without wrong or injury.

The rage and violence of public war: what is it but a suspension of justice among the warring parties, who perceive that this virtue is now no longer of any *use* or advantage to them? The laws of war, which then succeed to those of equity and justice, are rules calculated for the *advantage* and *utility* of that particular state in which men are now placed. And were a civilized nation engaged with barbarians, who observed no rules even of war, the former must also suspend their observance of them, where they no longer serve to any purpose, and must render every action or recounter as bloody and pernicious as possible to the first aggressors.

Thus the rules of equity or justice depend entirely on the particular state and condition in which men are placed, and owe their origin and existence to that utility which results to the public from their strict and regular observance. Reverse, in any considerable circumstance, the condition of men; produce extreme abundance or extreme necessity; implant in the human breast perfect moderation and humanity, or perfect rapaciousness and malice — by rendering justice totally *useless*, you thereby totally destroy its essence and suspend its obligation upon mankind.

The common situation of society is a medium amidst all these extremes. We are naturally partial to ourselves and to our friends; but are capable of learning the advantage resulting from a more equitable conduct. Few enjoyments are given us from the open and liberal hand of nature; but by art, labour, and industry, we can extract them in great abundance. Hence the ideas of property become necessary in all civil society; hence justice derives its usefulness to the public; and hence alone arises its merit and moral obligation.

These conclusions are so natural and obvious that they have not escaped even the poets, in their descriptions of the felicity attending the golden age or the reign of Saturn. The seasons in that first period of nature were so temperate, if we credit these agreeable fictions, that there was no necessity for men to provide themselves with clothes and houses as a security against the violence of heat and cold. The rivers flowed with wine and milk; the oaks yielded honey; and nature spontaneously produced her greatest delicacies. Nor were these the chief advantages of that happy age. Tempests were not alone removed from nature; but those more furious tempests were unknown to human breasts, which now cause such uproar and engender such confusion. Avarice, ambition, cruelty, selfishness, were never heard of. Cordial affection, compassion, sympathy, were the only movements with which the mind was yet acquainted. Even the punctilious distinction of *mine* and *thine* was banished from among the happy race of mortals, and carried with it the very notion of property and obligation, justice and injustice.

This *poetical* fiction of the *golden age* is in some respects of a piece with the *philosophical* fiction of the *state of nature;* only that the former is represented as the most charming and most peaceable condition which can possibly be imagined, whereas the latter is painted out as a state of mutual war and violence attended with the most extreme necessity. On the first origin of mankind, we are told, their ignorance and savage nature were so prevalent that they could give no mutual trust, but must each depend upon himself and his own force or cunning for protection and security. No law was heard of; no rule of justice known; no distinction of property regarded. Power was the only measure of right, and a perpetual war of all against all was the result of men's untamed selfishness and barbarity.[2]

Whether such a condition of human nature could ever exist, or if it did, could continue so long as to merit the appellation of a *state*, may justly be doubted. Men are necessarily born in a family-society, at least; and are trained up by their parents to some rule of conduct and behaviour. But this must be admitted that, if such a state of mutual war and violence was ever real, the suspension of all laws of justice, from their absolute inutility, is a necessary and infallible consequence.

The more we vary our views of human life, and the newer and more unusual the lights are in which we survey it, the more shall we be convinced that the origin here assigned for the virtue of justice is real and satisfactory.

Were there a species of creatures intermingled with men, which, though rational, were possessed of such inferior strength, both of body and mind, that they were incapable of all resistance, and could never, upon the highest provocation, make us feel the effects of their resent-

---

[2] This fiction of a state of nature, as a state of war, was not first started by Mr. Hobbes, as is commonly imagined. Plato endeavours to refute an hypothesis very like it in the second, third, and fourth books *De Republica*. Cicero, on the contrary, supposes it certain and universally acknowledged in the following passage. "Quis enim vestrûm, judices, ignorat, ita naturam rerum tulisse, ut quodam tempore homines, nondum neque naturali neque civili jure descripto, fusi per agros ac dispersi vagarentur tantumque haberent quantum manu ac viribus, per caedem ac vulnera, aut eripere aut retinere potuissent? Qui igitur primi virtute & consilio praestanti exstiterunt, ii perspecto genere humanae docilitatis atque ingenii, dissipatos unum in locum congregarunt, eosque ex feritate illa ad justitiam atque mansuetudinem transduxerunt. Tum res ad communem utilitatem, quas publicas appellamus, tum conventicula hominum, quae postea civitates nominatae sunt, tum domicilia conjuncta, quas urbes dicimus, invento et divino et humano jure moenibus sepserunt. Atque inter hanc vitam perpolitam humanitate, et illam immanem, nihil tam interest quam JUS atque VIS. Horum utro uti nolimus, altero est utendum. Vim volumus extingui: jus valeat necesse est, id est, judicia, quibus omne jus continetur. Judicia displicent, aut nulla sunt: vis dominetur necesse est. Haec vident omnes." *Pro Sext.* 42.

ment, the necessary consequence, I think, is that we should be bound by the laws of humanity to give gentle usage to these creatures, but should not, properly speaking, lie under any restraint of justice with regard to them, nor could they possess any right or property, exclusive of such arbitrary lords. Our intercourse with them could not be called society — which supposes a degree of equality — but absolute command on the one side, and servile obedience on the other. Whatever we covet, they must instantly resign. Our permission is the only tenure by which they hold their possessions; our compassion and kindness the only check by which they curb our lawless will; and as no inconvenience ever results from the exercise of a power so firmly established in nature, the restraints of justice and property, being totally *useless*, would never have place in so unequal a confederacy.

This is plainly the situation of men with regard to animals; and how far these may be said to possess reason, I leave it to others to determine. The great superiority of civilized Europeans above barbarous Indians tempted us to imagine ourselves on the same footing with regard to them, and made us throw off all restraints of justice and even of humanity, in our treatment of them. In many nations the female sex are reduced to like slavery, and are rendered incapable of all property, in opposition to their lordly masters. But though the males, when united, have in all countries bodily force sufficient to maintain this severe tyranny, yet such are the insinuation, address, and charms of their fair companions that women are commonly able to break the confederacy and share with the other sex in all the rights and privileges of society.

Were the human species so framed by nature as that each individual possessed within himself every faculty requisite both for his own preservation and for the propagation of his kind, were all society and intercourse cut off between man and man by the primary intention of the supreme Creator, it seems evident that so solitary a being would be as much incapable of justice as of social discourse and conversation. Where mutual regards and forbearance serve to no manner of purpose, they would never direct the conduct of any reasonable man. The headlong course of the passions would be checked by no reflection on future consequences. And as each man is here supposed to love himself alone, and to depend only on himself and his own activity for safety and happiness, he would, on every occasion, to the utmost of his power, challenge the preference above every other being, to none of which he is bound by any ties, either of nature or of interest.

But suppose the conjunction of the sexes to be established in nature, a family immediately arises; and particular rules being found requisite for its subsistence, these are immediately embraced, though without comprehending the rest of mankind within their prescriptions. Suppose that several families unite together into one society which is totally disjoined from all others, the rules which preserve peace and order enlarge themselves to the utmost extent of that society; but becoming then entirely useless, lose their force when carried one step farther. But again suppose that several distinct societies maintain a kind of intercourse for mutual convenience and advantage; the boundaries of justice still grow larger, in proportion to the largeness of men's views and the force of their mutual connexions. History, experience, reason sufficiently instruct us in this natural progress of human sentiments and in the gradual enlargement of our regards to justice, in proportion as we become acquainted with the extensive utility of that virtue.

Part II

If we examine the *particular* laws by which justice is directed and property determined, we shall still be presented with the same conclusion. The good of mankind is the only object of all these laws and regulations. Not only is it requisite for the peace and interest of society that men's possessions should be separated, but the rules which we follow in making the separation are such as can best be contrived to serve further the interests of society.

We shall suppose that a creature, possessed of reason, but unacquainted with human nature, deliberates with himself what rules of justice or property would best promote public interest and establish peace and security among mankind. His most obvious thought would be to assign the largest possessions to the most extensive virtue, and give every one the power of doing good, proportioned to his inclination. In a perfect theocracy, where a being, infinitely intelligent, governs by particular volitions, this rule would certainly have place and might serve to the wisest purposes. But were mankind to execute such a law, so great is the uncertainty of merit, both from its natural obscurity and from the self-conceit of each individual, that no determinate rule of conduct would ever result from it; and the total dissolution of society must be the immediate consequence. Fanatics may suppose *that dominion is founded on grace*, and *that saints alone inherit the earth;* but the civil magistrate very justly puts these sublime theorists on the same footing with common robbers, and teaches them by the severest discipline that a rule, which in speculation may seem the most advantageous to society, may yet be found, in practice, totally pernicious and destructive.

That there were *religious* fanatics of this kind in England, during the civil wars, we learn from history; though it is probable that the obvious *tendency* of these principles excited such horror in mankind, as soon obliged the dangerous enthusiasts to renounce or at least conceal their tenets. Perhaps the *levellers*, who claimed an equal distribution of property, were a kind of *political* fanatics which arose from the religious species and more openly avowed their pretensions, as carrying a more plausible appearance of being practicable in themselves as well as useful to human society.

It must, indeed, be confessed that nature is so liberal to mankind that, were all her presents equally divided among the species and improved by art and industry, every individual would enjoy all the necessaries and even most of the comforts of life, nor would ever be liable to any ills but such as might accidentally arise from the sickly frame and constitution of his body. It must also be confessed that, wherever we depart from this equality, we rob the poor of more satisfaction than we add to the rich, and that the slight gratification of a frivolous vanity in one individual frequently costs more than bread to many families and even provinces. It may appear withal that the rule of equality, as it would be highly *useful*, is not altogether *impracticable*, but has taken place, at least in an imperfect degree, in some republics, particularly that of Sparta, where it was attended, it is said, with the most beneficial consequences. Not to mention that the Agrarian laws, so frequently claimed in Rome, and carried into execution in many Greek cities, proceeded, all of them, from a general idea of the utility of this principle.

But historians, and even common sense, may inform us that, however specious these ideas of *perfect* equality may seem, they are really at bottom *impracticable;* and were they not so, would be extremely *pernicious* to human society. Render possessions ever so equal, men's different degrees of art, care, and industry will immediately break that equality. Or if you check these virtues, you reduce society to the most extreme indigence; and instead of preventing want and beggary in a few, render it unavoidable to the whole community. The most rigorous inquisition too is requisite to watch every inequality on its first appearance; and the most severe jurisdiction, to punish and redress it. But besides that so much authority must soon degenerate into tyranny and be exerted with great partialities, who can possibly be possessed of it in such a situation as is here supposed? Perfect equality of possessions, destroying all subordination, weakens extremely the authority of magistracy, and must reduce all power nearly to a level, as well as property.

We may conclude, therefore, that, in order to establish laws for the regulation of property, we must be acquainted with the nature and situation of man, must reject appearances which may be false though specious, and must search for those rules which are on the whole most *useful* and *beneficial*. Vulgar sense and slight experience are sufficient for this purpose, where men give not way to too selfish avidity or too extensive enthusiasm.

Who sees not, for instance, that whatever is produced or improved by a man's art or industry ought, for ever, to be secured to him, in order to give encouragement to such *useful* habits and accomplishments? That the property ought also to descend to children and relations for the same *useful* purpose? That it may be alienated by consent in order to beget that commerce and intercourse which is so *beneficial* to human society? And that all contracts and promises ought carefully to be fulfilled in order to secure mutual trust and confidence by which the general *interest* of mankind is so much promoted?

Examine the writers on the laws of nature, and you will always find that, whatever principles they set out with, they are sure to terminate here at last, and to assign as the ultimate reason for every rule which they establish, the convenience and necessities of mankind. A concession thus extorted in opposition to systems has more authority than if it had been made in prosecution of them.

What other reason, indeed, could writers ever give why this must be *mine* and that *yours,* since uninstructed nature surely never made any such distinction? The objects which receive those appellations are of themselves foreign to us; they are totally disjoined and separated from us, and nothing but the general interests of society can form the connexion.

Sometimes the interests of society may require a rule of justice in a particular case, but may not determine any particular rule among several, which are all equally beneficial. In that case the slightest *analogies* are laid hold of, in order to prevent that indifference and ambiguity, which would be the source of perpetual dissension. Thus possession alone, and first possession, is supposed to convey property, where nobody else has any preceding claim and pretension. Many of the reasonings of lawyers are of this analogical nature, and depend on very slight connexions of the imagination.

Does any one scruple, in extraordinary cases, to violate all regard to the private property of individuals, and sacrifice to public interest a distinction which had been established for the sake of that interest? The safety of the people is the supreme law. All other particular laws are subordinate to it and dependent on it. And if, in the *common* course of things, they be followed and regarded, it is only because the public safety and interest *commonly* demand so equal and impartial an administration.

Sometimes both *utility* and *analogy* fail and leave the laws of justice in total uncertainty. Thus it is highly requisite that prescription or long possession should convey property; but what number of days or months or years should be sufficient for that purpose, it is impossible for reason alone to determine. *Civil laws* here supply the place of the natural *code*, and assign different terms for prescription, according to the different *utilities* proposed by the legislator. Bills of exchange and promissory notes, by the laws of most countries, prescribe sooner than bonds, and mortgages, and contracts of a more formal nature.

In general we may observe that all questions of property are subordinate to the authority of civil laws, which extend, restrain, modify, and alter the rules of natural justice, according to the particular *convenience* of each community. The laws have or ought to have a constant reference to the constitution of government, the manners, the climate, the religion, the commerce, the situation of each society. A late author of genius as well as learning has prosecuted this subject at large, and has established from these principles a system of political knowledge which abounds in ingenious and brilliant thoughts and is not wanting in solidity.[3]

What is a man's property? Anything which it is lawful for him, and for him alone, to use. *But what rule have we by which we can distinguish these objects?* Here we must have recourse to statutes, customs, precedents, analogies, and a hundred other circumstances, some of which are constant and inflexible, some variable and arbitrary. But the ultimate point, in which they all professedly terminate, is the interest and happiness of human society. Where this enters not into consideration, nothing can appear more whimsical, unnatural, and even superstitious, than all or most of the laws of justice and of property.

Those who ridicule vulgar superstitions and expose the folly of

---

[3] The author of *L'Esprit des Loix.* This illustrious writer, however, sets out with a different theory, and supposes all right to be founded on certain *rapports* or relations; which is a system that, in my opinion, never will be reconciled with true philosophy. Father Malebranche, as far as I can learn, was the first that started this abstract theory of morals which was afterwards adopted by Cudworth, Clarke, and others; and as it excludes all sentiment and pretends to found everything on reason, it has not wanted followers in this philosophic age. See Section I, Appendix I. With regard to justice, the virtue here treated of, the inference against this theory seems short and conclusive. Property is allowed to be dependent on civil laws; civil laws are allowed to have no other object but the interest of society: this therefore must be allowed to be the sole foundation of property and justice. Not to mention that our obligation itself to obey the magistrate and his laws is founded on nothing but the interests of society.

If the ideas of justice, sometimes, do not follow the dispositions of civil law, we shall find that these cases, instead of objections, are confirmations of the theory delivered above. Where a civil law is so perverse as to cross all the interests of society, it loses all its authority, and men judge by the ideas of natural justice, which are conformable to those interests. Sometimes also civil laws, for useful purposes, require a ceremony or form to any deed; and where that is wanting, their decrees run contrary to the usual tenor of justice; but one who takes advantage of such chicanes is not commonly regarded as an honest man. Thus, the interests of society require that contracts be fulfilled; and there is not a more material article either of natural or civil justice; but the omission of a trifling circumstance will often, by law, invalidate a contract, *in foro humano,* but not *in foro conscientiae,* as divines express themselves. In these cases, the magistrate is supposed only to withdraw his power of enforcing the right, not to have altered the right. Where his intention extends to the right, and is conformable to the interests of society, it never fails to alter the right — a clear proof of the origin of justice and of property, as assigned above.

particular regards to meats, days, places, postures, apparel, have an easy task, while they consider all the qualities and relations of the objects and discover no adequate cause for that affection or antipathy, veneration or horror, which have so mighty an influence over a considerable part of mankind. A Syrian would have starved rather than taste pigeon; an Egyptian would not have approached bacon. But if these species of food be examined by the senses of sight, smell, or taste, or scrutinized by the sciences of chemistry, medicine, or physics, no difference is ever found between them and any other species, nor can that precise circumstance be pitched on which may afford a just foundation for the religious passion. A fowl on Thursday is lawful food; on Friday abominable; eggs in this house and in this diocese are permitted during Lent; a hundred paces farther, to eat them is a damnable sin. This earth or building yesterday was profane; today, by the muttering of certain words, it has become holy and sacred. Such reflections as these in the mouth of a philosopher, one may safely say, are too obvious to have any influence, because they must always to every man occur at first sight; and where they prevail not of themselves, they are surely obstructed by education, prejudice, and passion, not by ignorance or mistake.

It may appear to a careless view, or rather a too abstracted reflection, that there enters a like superstition into all the sentiments of justice; and that if a man expose its object or what we call "property" to the same scrutiny of sense and science, he will not, by the most accurate enquiry, find any foundation for the difference made by moral sentiment. I may lawfully nourish myself from this tree; but the fruit of another of the same species, ten places off, it is criminal for me to touch. Had I worn this apparel an hour ago, I had merited the severest punishment; but a man, by pronouncing a few magical syllables, has now rendered it fit for my use and service. Were this house placed in the neighbouring territory, it had been immoral for me to dwell in it; but being built on this side the river, it is subject to a different municipal law, and by its becoming mine I incur no blame or censure. The same species of reasoning, it may be thought, which so successfully exposes superstition, is also applicable to justice; nor is it possible, in the one case more than in the other, to point out in the object that precise quality or circumstance which is the foundation of the sentiment.

But there is this material difference between *superstition* and *justice*, that the former is frivolous, useless, and burdensome; the latter is absolutely requisite to the well-being of mankind and existence of society. When we abstract from this circumstance — for it is too apparent ever to be overlooked — it must be confessed that all regards to right and property seem entirely without foundation, as much as the grossest and most vulgar superstition. Were the interests of society nowise concerned, it is as unintelligible why another's articulating certain sounds implying consent should change the nature of my actions with regard to a particular object, as why the reciting of a liturgy by a priest in a certain habit and posture should dedicate a heap of brick and timber, and render it thenceforth and for ever sacred.[4]

These reflections are far from weakening the obligations of justice, or diminishing anything from the most sacred attention to property. On the contrary, such sentiments must acquire new force from the present reasoning. For what stronger foundation can be desired or conceived for any duty than to observe that human society, or even

[4] It is evident that the will or consent alone never transfers property, nor causes the obligation of a promise (for the same reasoning extends to both), but the will must be expressed by words or signs, in order to impose a tie upon any man. The expression, being once brought in as subservient to the will, soon becomes the principal part of the promise; nor will a man be less bound by his word, though he secretly give a different direction to his intention and withhold the assent of his mind. But though the expression makes, on most occasions, the whole of the promise, yet it does not always so; and one who should make use of any expression of which he knows not the meaning, and which he uses without any sense of the consequences, would not certainly be bound by it. Nay, though he know its meaning, yet if he use it in jest only, and with such signs as evidently show that he has no serious intention of binding himself, he would not lie under any obligation of performance; but it is necessary that the words be a perfect expression of the will, without any contrary signs. Nay, even this we must not carry so far as to imagine that one, whom by our quickness of understanding we conjecture from certain signs to have an intention of deceiving us, is not bound by his expression or verbal promise, if we accept of it; but must limit this conclusion to those cases where the signs are of a different nature from those of deceit. All these contradictions are easily accounted for if justice arise entirely from its usefulness to society, but will never be explained on any other hypothesis.

It is remarkable that the moral decisions of the *Jesuits* and other relaxed casuists were commonly formed in prosecution of some such subtilties of reasoning as are here pointed out, and proceed as much from the habit of scholastic refinement as from any corruption of the heart, if we may follow the authority of Mons. Bayle.

human nature, could not subsist without the establishment of it; and will still arrive at greater degrees of happiness and perfection, the more inviolable the regard is which is paid to that duty?

The dilemma seems obvious: as justice evidently tends to promote public utility and to support civil society, the sentiment of justice is either derived from our reflecting on that tendency, or like hunger, thirst, and other appetites, resentment, love of life, attachment to offspring, and other passions, arises from a simple original instinct in the human breast, which nature has implanted for like salutary purposes. If the latter be the case, it follows that property, which is the object of justice, is also distinguished by a simple original instinct and is not ascertained by any argument or reflection. But who is there that ever heard of such an instinct? Or is this a subject in which new discoveries can be made? We may as well expect to discover in the body new senses which had before escaped the observation of all mankind.

But further, though it seems a very simple proposition to say that nature by an instinctive sentiment distinguishes property, yet in reality

See his *Dictionary*, article "Loyola." And why has the indignation of mankind risen so high against these casuists; but because every one perceived that human society could not subsist, were such practices authorized, and that morals must always be handled with a view to public interest more than philosophical regularity? If the secret direction of the intention, said every man of sense, could invalidate a contract, where is our security? And yet a metaphysical schoolman might think that, where an intention was supposed to be requisite, if that intention really had not place, no consequence ought to follow and no obligation be imposed. The casuistical subtilties may not be greater than the subtilties of lawyers hinted at above; but as the former are *pernicious* and the latter *innocent* and even *necessary*, this is the reason of the very different reception they meet with from the world.

It is a doctrine of the Church of Rome that the priest by a secret direction of his intention can invalidate any sacrament. This position is derived from a strict and regular prosecution of the obvious truth that empty words alone, without any meaning or intention in the speaker, can never be attended with any effect. If the same conclusion be not admitted in reasonings concerning civil contracts, where the affair is allowed to be of so much less consequence than the eternal salvation of thousands, it proceeds entirely from men's sense of the danger and inconvenience of the doctrine in the former case. And we may thence observe that, however positive, arrogant, and dogmatical any superstition may appear, it never can convey any thorough persuasion of the reality of its objects, or put them in any degree on a balance with the common incidents of life which we learn from daily observation and experimental reasoning.

we shall find that there are required for that purpose ten thousand different instincts, and these employed about objects of the greatest intricacy and nicest discernment. For when a definition of *property* is required, that relation is found to resolve itself into any possession acquired by occupation, by industry, by prescription, by inheritance, by contract, etc. Can we think that nature, by an original instinct, instructs us in all these methods of acquisition?

These words, too, "inheritance" and "contract," stand for ideas infinitely complicated; and to define them exactly, a hundred volumes of laws and a thousand volumes of commentators have not been found sufficient. Does nature, whose instincts in men are all simple, embrace such complicated and artificial objects, and create a rational creature without trusting anything to the operation of his reason?

But even though all this were admitted, it would not be satisfactory. Positive laws can certainly transfer property. It is by another original instinct that we recognize the authority of kings and senates, and mark all the boundaries of their jurisdiction? Judges, too, even though their sentence be erroneous and illegal, must be allowed for the sake of peace and order to have decisive authority and ultimately to determine property. Have we original innate ideas of praetors and chancellors and juries? Who sees not that all these institutions arise merely from the necessities of human society?

All birds of the same species in every age and country built their nests alike: in this we see the force of instinct. Men in different times and places frame their houses differently: here we perceive the influence of reason and custom. A like inference may be drawn from comparing the instinct of generation and the institution of property.

How great soever the variety of municipal laws, it must be confessed that their chief outlines pretty regularly concur, because the purposes to which they tend are everywhere exactly similar. In like manner, all houses have a roof and walls, windows and chimneys, though diversified in their shape, figure, and materials. The purposes of the latter, directed to the conveniences of human life, discover not more plainly their origin from reason and reflection than do those of the former, which point all to a like end.

I need not mention the variations which all the rules of property receive from the finer turns and connexions of the imagination, and from the subtilties and abstractions of law-topics and reasonings. There is no possibility of reconciling this observation to the notion of original instincts.

What alone will beget a doubt concerning the theory on which I insist is the influence of education and acquired habits, by which we are so accustomed to blame injustice that we are not in every instance conscious of any immediate reflection on the pernicious consequences of it. The views the most familiar to us are apt, for that very reason, to escape us; and what we have very frequently performed from certain motives, we are apt likewise to continue mechanically without recalling on every occasion the reflections which first determined us. The convenience or rather necessity which leads to justice is so universal and everywhere points so much to the same rules that the habit takes place in all societies; and it is not without some scrutiny that we are able to ascertain its true origin. The matter, however, is not so obscure, but that even in common life we have every moment recourse to the principle of public utility, and ask, *What must become of the world, if such practices prevail? How could society subsist under such disorders?* Were the distinction or separation of possessions entirely useless, can any one conceive that it ever should have obtained in society?

Thus we seem, upon the whole, to have attained a knowledge of the force of that principle here insisted on, and can determine what degree of esteem or moral approbation may result from reflections on public interest and utility. The necessity of justice to the support of society is the sole foundation of that virtue; and since no moral excellence is more highly esteemed, we may conclude that this circumstance of usefulness has, in general, the strongest energy and most entire command over our sentiments. It must, therefore, be the source of a considerable part of the merit ascribed to humanity, benevolence, friendship, public spirit, and other social virtues of that stamp; as it is the sole source of the moral approbation paid to fidelity, justice, veracity, integrity, and those other estimable and useful qualities and principles. It is entirely agreeable to the rules of philosophy and even of common reason, where any principle has been found to have a great force and energy in one instance, to ascribe to it a like energy in all similar instances. This indeed is Newton's chief rule of philosophizing.[5]

[5] *Principia*, Lib. iii.

SECTION IV

OF POLITICAL SOCIETY

HAD EVERY MAN sufficient *sagacity* to perceive at all times the strong interest which binds him to the observance of justice and equity, and *strength of mind* sufficient to persevere in a steady adherence to a general and a distant interest, in opposition to the allurements of present pleasure and advantage; there had never, in that case, been any such thing as government or political society, but each man, following his natural liberty, had lived in entire peace and harmony with all others. What need of positive law where natural justice is of itself a sufficient restraint? Why create magistrates, where there never arises any disorder or iniquity? Why abridge our native freedom, when in every instance the utmost exertion of it is found innocent and beneficial? It is evident that, if government were totally useless, it never could have place, and that the sole foundation of the duty of allegiance is the *advantage* which it procures to society by preserving peace and order among mankind.

When a number of political societies are erected, and maintain a great intercourse together, a new set of rules are immediately discovered to be *useful* in that particular situation; and accordingly take place under the title of Laws of Nations. Of this kind are the sacredness of the person of ambassadors, abstaining from poisoned arms, quarter in war, with others of that kind which are plainly calculated for the *advantage* of states and kingdoms in their intercourse with each other.

The rules of justice, such as prevail among individuals, are not entirely suspended among political societies. All princes pretend a regard to the rights of other princes; and some, no doubt, without hypocrisy. Alliances and treaties are every day made between independent states, which would only be so much waste of parchment if they were not found by experience to have *some* influence and authority. But here is the difference between kingdoms and individuals. Human nature cannot by any means subsist without the association of individuals; and that association never could have place, were no regard paid to the laws of equity and justice. Disorder, confusion, the war of all against all, are the necessary consequences of such a licentious conduct. But nations can subsist without intercourse. They may even subsist in some degree under a general war. The observance of justice, though useful among them, is not guarded by so strong a necessity as among individuals; and the *moral obligation* holds proportion with the *usefulness*. All politicians will allow, and most philosophers, that reasons of state may in particular emergencies dispense with the rules of justice, and invalidate any treaty or alliance where the strict observance of it would be prejudicial in a considerable degree to either of the contracting parties. But nothing less than the most extreme necessity, it is confessed, can justify individuals in a breach of promise, or an invasion of the properties of others.

In a confederated commonwealth, such as the Achaean republic of old, or the Swiss Cantons and United Provinces in modern times; as the league has here a peculiar *utility*, the conditions of union have a peculiar sacredness and authority, and a violation of them would be regarded as no less, or even as more, criminal than any private injury or injustice.

The long and helpless infancy of man requires the combination of parents for the subsistence of their young; and that combination requires the virtue of chastity or fidelity to the marriage bed. Without such a *utility*, it will readily be owned that such a virtue would never have been thought of.[1]

---

[1] The only solution which Plato gives to all the objections that might be raised against the community of women established in his imaginary commonwealth is Κάλλιστα γὰρ δή τοῦτο καὶ λέγεται καὶ λελέξεται, ὅτι τὸ μὲν ὠφέλιμον καλόν, τὸ δὲ βλαβερὸν αἰσχρόν [For it is an excellent statement and will always be an excellent statement, that whatever is useful is good, and what is harmful is bad]. *Scite enim instud et dicitur et dicetur, Id quod utile sit honestum esse, quod autem inutile sit turpe esse.* De Rep. lib. v. p. 457. ex. edit. Serrani. And this maxim will admit of no doubt where public utility is concerned, which is Plato's meaning. And indeed, to what other purpose do all the ideas of chastity and modesty serve? *Nisi utile est quod facimus, frustra est gloria,* says Phædrus. Καλὸν τῶν βλαβερῶν οὐδέν [nothing that is harmful is good], says Plutarch, De vitioso pudore. *Nihil eorum quæ damnosa sunt, pulchrum est.* The same was the opinion of the Stoics. Φασὶν οὖν οἱ Στωικοὶ ἀγαθὸν εἶναι ὠφέλειαν ἢ οὐχ ἕτερον ὠφελείας, ὠφέλειαν μὲν λέγοντες τὴν ἀρετὴν καὶ τὴν σπουδαίαν πρᾶξιν [The Stoics, then, assert that good is "utility and nothing other than utility," meaning by "utility" virtue and right action]. Sext. Emp. lib. iii. cap. 20.

An infidelity of this nature is much more *pernicious* in *women* than in *men*. Hence the laws of chastity are much stricter over the one sex than over the other.

These rules have all a reference to generation; and yet women past child-bearing are no more supposed to be exempted from them than those in the flower of their youth and beauty. *General rules* are often extended beyond the principle whence they first arise; and this in all matters of taste and sentiment. It is a vulgar story at Paris that during the rage of the Mississippi a hump-backed fellow went every day into the Rue de Quincempoix, where the stock-jobbers met in great crowds, and was well paid for allowing them to make use of his hump as a desk in order to sign their contracts upon it. Would the fortune which he raised by this expedient make him a handsome fellow, though it be confessed that personal beauty arises very much from ideas of utility? The imagination is influenced by associations of ideas which, though they arise at first from the judgment, are not easily altered by every particular exception that occurs to us. To which we may add, in the present case of chastity, that the example of the old would be pernicious to the young, and that women, continually foreseeing that a certain time would bring them the liberty of indulgence, would naturally advance that period and think more lightly of this whole duty, so requisite to society.

Those who live in the same family have such frequent opportunities of licence of this kind that nothing could prevent purity of manners were marriage allowed among the nearest relations or any intercourse of love between them ratified by law and custom. Incest, therefore, being *pernicious* in a superior degree, has also a superior turpitude and moral deformity annexed to it.

What is the reason why, by the Athenian laws, one might marry a half-sister by the father but not by the mother? Plainly this: the manners of the Athenians were so reserved that a man was never permitted to approach the women's apartment, even in the same family, unless where he visited his own mother. His step-mother and her children were as much shut up from him as the woman of any other family, and there was as little danger of any criminal correspondence between them. Uncles and nieces, for a like reason, might marry at Athens; but neither these, nor half-brothers and sisters, could contract that alliance at Rome, where the intercourse was more open between the sexes. Public utility is the cause of all these variations.

To repeat, to a man's prejudice, anything that escaped him in private conversation, or to make any such use of his private letters, is highly blamed. The free and social intercourse of minds must be extremely checked, where no such rules of fidelity are established.

Even in repeating stories whence we can foresee no ill consequences to result, the giving of one's author is regarded as a piece of indiscretion, if not of immorality. These stories, in passing from hand to hand and receiving all the usual variations, frequently come about to the persons concerned and produce animosities and quarrels among people whose intentions are the most innocent and inoffensive.

To pry into secrets, to open or even read the letters of others, to play the spy upon their words and looks and actions; what habits more inconvenient in society? What habits, of consequence, more blamable?

This principle is also the foundation of most of the laws of good manners; a kind of lesser morality, calculated for the ease of company and conversation. Too much or too little ceremony are both blamed, and everything which promotes ease without an indecent familiarity is useful and laudable.

Constancy in friendships, attachments, and familiarities, is commendable and is requisite to support trust and good correspondence in society. But in places of general, though casual, concourse, where the pursuit of health and pleasure brings people promiscuously together, public convenience has dispensed with this maxim; and custom there promotes an unreserved conversation for the time, by indulging the privilege of dropping afterwards every indifferent acquaintance without breach of civility or good manners.

Even in societies which are established on principles the most immoral and the most destructive to the interests of the general society, there are required certain rules, which a species of false honour, as well as private interest, engages the members to observe. Robbers and pirates, it has often been remarked, could not maintain their pernicious confederacy, did they not establish a new distributive justice among themselves, and recall those laws of equity which they have violated with the rest of mankind.

I hate a drinking companion, says the Greek proverb, who never forgets. The follies of the last debauch should be buried in eternal oblivion in order to give full scope to the follies of the next.

Among nations where an immoral gallantry, if covered with a thin veil of mystery, is in some degree authorized by custom, there immediately arise a set of rules calculated for the convenience of that attachment. The famous court or parliament of love in Provence formerly decided all difficult cases of this nature.

In societies for play there are laws required for the conduct of the game; and these laws are different in each game. The foundation, I own, of such societies is frivolous; and the laws are in a great measure, though not altogether, capricious and arbitrary. So far is there a material difference between them and the rules of justice, fidelity, and loyalty. The general societies of men are absolutely requisite for the subsistence of the species; and the public convenience, which regulates morals, is inviolably established in the nature of man and of the world in which he lives. The comparison, therefore, in these respects, is very imperfect. We may only learn from it the necessity of rules wherever men have any intercourse with each other.

They cannot even pass each other on the road without rules. Waggoners, coachmen, and postilions have principles by which they give the way; and these are chiefly founded on mutual ease and convenience. Sometimes also they are arbitrary, at least dependent on a kind of capricious analogy like many of the reasonings of lawyers.[2]

To carry the matter farther, we may observe that it is impossible for men so much as to murder each other without statutes, and maxims, and an idea of justice and honour. War has its laws as well as peace; and even that sportive kind of war carried on among wrestlers, boxers, cudgel-players, gladiators, is regulated by fixed principles. Common interest and utility beget infallibly a standard of right and wrong among the parties concerned.

[2] That the lighter machine yield to the heavier, and, in machines of the same kind, that the empty yield to the loaded; this rule is founded on convenience. That those who are going to the capital take place of those who are coming from it; this seems to be founded on some idea of the dignity of the great city, and of the preference of the future to the past. From like reasons, among foot-walkers, the right-hand entitles a man to the wall, and prevents jostling, which peaceable people find very disagreeable and inconvenient.

SECTION V

WHY UTILITY PLEASES

Part I

IT SEEMS so natural a thought to ascribe to their utility the praise which we bestow on the social virtues that one would expect to meet with this principle everywhere in moral writers as the chief foundation of their reasoning and enquiry. In common life, we may observe that the circumstance of utility is always appealed to; nor is it supposed that a greater eulogy can be given to any man than to display his usefulness to the public and enumerate the services which he has performed to mankind and society. What praise, even of an inanimate form, if the regularity and elegance of its parts destroy not its fitness for any useful purpose! And how satisfactory an apology for any disproportion or seeming deformity, if we can show the necessity of that particular construction for the use intended! A ship appears more beautiful to an artist or one moderately skilled in navigation where its prow is wide and swelling beyond its poop than if it were framed with a precise geometrical regularity, in contradiction to all the laws of mechanics. A building whose doors and windows were exact squares would hurt the eye by that very proportion, as ill adapted to the figure of a human creature for whose service the fabric was intended. What wonder, then, that a man whose habits and conduct are hurtful to society and dangerous or pernicious to every one who has an intercourse with him, should on that account be an object of disapprobation, and communicate to every spectator the strongest sentiment of disgust and hatred.[1]

But perhaps the difficulty of accounting for these effects of useful-

---

[1] We ought not to imagine, because an inanimate object may be useful as well as a man, that therefore it ought also, according to this system, to merit the appellation of *virtuous*. The sentiments, excited by utility, are in the two cases very different; and the one is mixed with affection, esteem, approbation, etc., and not the other. In like manner, an inanimate object may have good colour and proportions as well as a human figure. But can we ever be in love with the former? There are a numerous set of passions and sentiments, of which thinking rational beings are, by the original constitution of nature, the only proper objects; and though the very same qualities be transferred to an insensible, inanimate being, they will not excite the

ness, or its contrary, has kept philosophers from admitting them into their systems of ethics, and has induced them rather to employ any other principle in explaining the origin of moral good and evil. But it is no just reason for rejecting any principle, confirmed by experience, that we cannot give a satisfactory account of its origin, nor are able to resolve it into other more general principles. And if we would employ a little thought on the present subject, we need be at no loss to account for the influence of utility, and to deduce it from principles the most known and avowed in human nature.

From the apparent usefulness of the social virtues it has readily been inferred by sceptics, both ancient and modern, that all moral distinctions arise from education, and were at first invented and afterwards encouraged by the art of politicians, in order to render men tractable and subdue their natural ferocity and selfishness, which incapacitated them for society. This principle, indeed, of precept and education must so far be owned to have a powerful influence that it may frequently increase or diminish beyond their natural standard the sentiments of approbation or dislike, and may even in particular instances create, without any natural principle, a new sentiment of this kind, as is evident in all superstitious practices and observances; but that *all* moral affection or dislike arises from this origin will never surely be allowed by any judicious enquirer. Had nature made no such distinction, founded on the original constitution of the mind, the words *honourable* and *shameful*, *lovely* and *odious*, *noble* and *despicable*, had never had place in any language; nor could politicians, had they invented these terms, ever have been able to render them intelligible or make them convey any idea to the audience. So that nothing can be more superficial than this paradox of the sceptics; and it were well if, in the abstruser studies of logic and metaphysics, we could as easily obviate the cavils of that sect, as in

same sentiments. The beneficial qualities of herbs and minerals are, indeed, sometimes called their *virtues;* but this is an effect of the caprice of language, which ought not to be regarded in reasoning. For though there be a species of approbation attending even inanimate objects when beneficial, yet this sentiment is so weak and so different from that which is directed to beneficent magistrates or statesmen that they ought not to be ranked under the same class or appellation.

A very small variation of the object, even where the same qualities are preserved, will destroy a sentiment. Thus the same beauty, transferred to a different sex, excites no amorous passion, where nature is not extremely perverted.

the practical and more intelligible sciences of politics and morals. The social virtues must, therefore, be allowed to have a natural beauty and amiableness, which, at first, antecedent to all precept or education, recommends them to the esteem of uninstructed mankind and engages their affections. And as the public utility of these virtues is the chief circumstance whence they derive their merit, it follows that the end, which they have a tendency to promote, must be some way agreeable to us and take hold of some natural affection. It must please either from considerations of self-interest or from more generous motives and regards.

It has often been asserted that, as every man has a strong connexion with society and perceives the impossibility of his solitary subsistence, he becomes on that account favourable to all those habits or principles which promote order in society and insure to him the quiet possession of so inestimable a blessing. As much as we value our own happiness and welfare, as much must we applaud the practice of justice and humanity by which alone the social confederacy can be maintained and every man reap the fruits of mutual protection and assistance.

This deduction of morals from self-love or a regard to private interest is an obvious thought, and has not arisen wholly from the wanton sallies and sportive assaults of the sceptics. To mention no others, Polybius, one of the gravest and most judicious as well as most moral writers of antiquity, has assigned this selfish origin to all our sentiments of virtue.[2] But though the solid practical sense of that author and his aversion to all vain subtilties render his authority on the present subject very considerable, yet is not this an affair to be decided by authority, and the voice of nature and experience seems plainly to oppose the selfish theory.

[2] Undutifulness to parents is disapproved of by mankind, προορωμένους τὸ μέλλον, καὶ συλλογιζομένους ὅτι τὸ παραπλήσιον ἑκάστοις αὐτῶν συγκυρήσει [anticipating (scil. they) the future, and reflecting that the same will happen to each of them]. Ingratitude for a like reason (though he seems there to mix a more generous regard) συναγανακτοῦντας μὲν τῷ πέλας, ἀναφέροντας δ' ἐπ' αὐτοὺς τὸ παραπλήσιον, ἐξ ὧν ὑπογίγνεταί τις ἔννοια παρ' ἑκάστῳ τῆς τοῦ καθήκοντος δυνάμεως καὶ θεωρίας [getting irritated along with the other man (their "neighbor") and imagining themselves in his situation. Hence, in each of them there arises a notion of the meaning and of the theory of the "befitting"]. Lib. vi. cap. 4. (Ed. Gronovius.) Perhaps the historian only meant that our sympathy and humanity was more enlivened by our considering the similarity of our case with that of the person suffering, which is a just sentiment.

We frequently bestow praise on virtuous actions performed in very distant ages and remote countries, where the utmost subtilty of imagination would not discover any appearance of self-interest, or find any connexion of our present happiness and security with events so widely separated from us.

A generous, a brave, a noble deed performed by an adversary commands our approbation, while in its consequences it may be acknowledged prejudicial to our particular interest.

Where private advantage concurs with general affection for virtue, we readily perceive and avow the mixture of these distinct sentiments, which have a very different feeling and influence on the mind. We praise, perhaps, with more alacrity where the generous humane action contributes to our particular interest; but the topics of praise which we insist on are very wide of this circumstance. And we may attempt to bring over others to our sentiments, without endeavouring to convince them that they reap any advantage from the actions which we recommend to their approbation and applause.

Frame the model of a praiseworthy character consisting of all the most amiable moral virtues, give instances in which these display themselves after an eminent and extraordinary manner: you readily engage the esteem and approbation of all your audience, who never so much as enquire in what age and country the person lived who possessed these noble qualities — a circumstance, however, of all others the most material to self-love or a concern for our own individual happiness.

Once on a time, a statesman, in the shock and contest of parties, prevailed so far as to procure by his eloquence the banishment of an able adversary, whom he secretly followed, offering him money for his support during his exile, and soothing him with topics of consolation in his misfortunes. *Alas!* cries the banished statesman, *with what regret must I leave my friends in this city, where even enemies are so generous!* Virtue, though in an enemy, here pleased him. And we also give it the just tribute of praise and approbation; nor do we retract these sentiments when we hear that the action passed at Athens, about two thousand years ago, and that the persons' names were Eschines and Demosthenes.

What is that to me? There are few occasions when this question is not pertinent; and had it that universal, infallible influence supposed, it would turn into ridicule every composition and almost every conversation which contain any praise or censure of men and manners.

It is but a weak subterfuge, when pressed by these facts and arguments, to say that we transport ourselves by the force of imagination into distant ages and countries and consider the advantage which we should have reaped from these characters, had we been contemporaries and had any commerce with the persons. It is not conceivable how a *real* sentiment or passion can ever arise from a known *imaginary* interest, especially when our *real* interest is still kept in view and is often acknowledged to be entirely distinct from the imaginary, and even sometimes opposite to it.

A man, brought to the brink of a precipice, cannot look down without trembling; and the sentiment of *imaginary* danger actuates him, in opposition to the opinion and belief of *real* safety. But the imagination is here assisted by the presence of a striking object, and yet prevails not, except it be also aided by novelty and the unusual appearance of the object. Custom soon reconciles us to heights and precipices and wears off these false and delusive terrors. The reverse is observable in the estimates which we form of characters and manners; and the more we habituate ourselves to an accurate scrutiny of morals, the more delicate feeling do we acquire of the most minute distinctions between vice and virtue. Such frequent occasion, indeed, have we in common life to pronounce all kinds of moral determinations that no object of this kind can be new or unusual to us; nor could any *false* views or prepossessions maintain their ground against an experience so common and familiar. Experience being chiefly what forms the associations of ideas, it is impossible that any association could establish and support itself in direct opposition to that principle.

Usefulness is agreeable and engages our approbation. This is a matter of fact confirmed by daily observation. But *useful?* For what? For somebody's interest, surely. Whose interest then? Not our own only; for our approbation frequently extends farther. It must, therefore, be the interest of those who are served by the character or action approved of; and these, we may conclude, however remote, are not totally indifferent to us. By opening up this principle, we shall discover one great source of moral distinctions.

Part II

Self-love is a principle in human nature of such extensive energy, and the interest of each individual is, in general, so closely connected with that of the community, that those philosophers were excusable who fancied that all our concern for the public might be resolved into a concern for our own happiness and preservation. They saw every moment instances of approbation or blame, satisfaction or displeasure towards characters and actions; they denominated the objects of these sentiments *virtues* or *vices;* they observed that the former had a tendency to increase the happiness, and the latter the misery of mankind; they asked whether it were possible that we could have any general concern for society or any disinterested resentment of the welfare or injury of others; they found it simpler to consider all these sentiments as modifications of self-love; and they discovered a pretence, at least, for this unity of principle, in that close union of interest which is so observable between the public and each individual.

But notwithstanding this frequent confusion of interests, it is easy to attain what natural philosophers, after Lord Bacon, have affected to call the *experimentum crucis,* or that experiment which points out the right way in any doubt or ambiguity. We have found instances in which private interest was separate from public, in which it was even contrary; and yet we observed the moral sentiment to continue, notwithstanding this disjunction of interests. And wherever these distinct interests sensibly concurred, we always found a sensible increase of the sentiment and a more warm affection to virtue and detestation of vice, or what we properly call *gratitude* and *revenge.* Compelled by these instances, we must renounce the theory which accounts for every moral sentiment by the principle of self-love. We must adopt a more public affection and allow that the interests of society are not, even on their own account, entirely indifferent to us. Usefulness is only a tendency to a certain end; and it is a contradiction in terms that anything pleases as means to an end where the end itself no wise affects us. If usefulness, therefore, be a source of moral sentiment, and if this usefulness be not always considered with a reference to self, it follows that everything which contributes to the happiness of society recommends itself directly to our approbation and good-will. Here is a principle which accounts, in great part, for the origin of morality; and what need we seek for abstruse and remote systems, when there occurs one so obvious and natural?[3]

Have we any difficulty to comprehend the force of humanity and benevolence? Or to conceive that the very aspect of happiness, joy, prosperity, gives pleasure; that of pain, suffering, sorrow, communicates uneasiness? The human countenance, says Horace,[4] borrows smiles or tears from the human countenance. Reduce a person to solitude, and he loses all enjoyment, except either of the sensual or speculative kind; and that because the movements of his heart are not forwarded by correspondent movements in his fellow creatures. The signs of sorrow and mourning, though arbitrary, affect us with melancholy; but the natural symptoms, tears and cries and groans, never fail to infuse compassion and uneasiness. And if the effects of misery touch us in so lively a manner, can we be supposed altogether insensible or indifferent towards its causes, when a malicious or treacherous character and behaviour are presented to us?

We enter, I shall suppose, into a convenient, warm, well-contrived apartment. We necessarily receive a pleasure from its very survey, because it presents us with the pleasing ideas of ease, satisfaction, and enjoyment. The hospitable, good-humoured, humane landlord appears. This circumstance surely must embellish the whole, nor can we easily forbear reflecting with pleasure on the satisfaction which results to every one from his intercourse and good offices.

His whole family, by the freedom, ease, confidence, and calm enjoyment diffused over their countenances, sufficiently express their happiness. I have a pleasing sympathy in the prospect of so much

---

[3] It is needless to push our researches so far as to ask why we have humanity or a fellow-feeling with others. It is sufficient that this is experienced to be a principle in human nature. We must stop somewhere in our examination of causes; and there are, in every science, some general principles beyond which we cannot hope to find any principle more general. No man is absolutely indifferent to the happiness and misery of others. The first has a natural tendency to give pleasure; the second, pain. This every one may find in himself. It is not probable that these principles can be resolved into principles more simple and universal, whatever attempts may have been made to that purpose. But if it were possible, it belongs not to the present subject; and we may here safely consider these principles as original; happy, if we can render all the consequences sufficiently plain and perspicuous!

[4] *"Ut ridentibus arrident, ita flentibus adflent
Humani vultus."* — Hor.

joy and can never consider the source of it without the most agreeable emotions.

He tells me that an oppressive and powerful neighbour had attempted to dispossess him of his inheritance, and had long disturbed all his innocent and social pleasures. I feel an immediate indignation arise in me against such violence and injury.

But it is no wonder, he adds, that a private wrong should proceed from a man who had enslaved provinces, depopulated cities, and made the field and scaffold stream with human blood. I am struck with horror at the prospect of so much misery and am actuated by the strongest antipathy against its author.

In general, it is certain that, wherever we go, whatever we reflect on or converse about, everything still presents us with the view of human happiness or misery, and excites in our breast a sympathetic movement of pleasure or uneasiness. In our serious occupations, in our careless amusements, this principle still exerts its active energy.

A man who enters the theatre is immediately struck with the view of so great a multitude participating of one common amusement, and experiences, from their very aspect, a superior sensibility or disposition of being affected with every sentiment which he shares with his fellow creatures.

He observes the actors to be animated by the appearance of a full audience, and raised to a degree of enthusiasm which they cannot command in any solitary or calm moment.

Every movement of the theatre, by a skilful poet, is communicated, as it were by magic, to the spectators, who weep, tremble, resent, rejoice, and are inflamed with all the variety of passions which actuate the several personages of the drama.

Where any event crosses our wishes and interrupts the happiness of the favourite characters, we feel a sensible anxiety and concern. But where their sufferings proceed from the treachery, cruelty, or tyranny of an enemy, our breasts are affected with the liveliest resentment against the author of these calamities.

It is here esteemed contrary to the rules of art to represent anything cool and indifferent. A distant friend or a confident who has no immediate interest in the catastrophe ought, if possible, to be avoided by the poet, as communicating a like indifference to the audience and checking the progress of the passions.

Few species of poetry are more entertaining than *pastoral;* and every one is sensible that the chief source of its pleasure arises from those images of a gentle and tender tranquillity which it represents in its personages, and of which it communicates a like sentiment to the reader. Sannazarius, who transferred the scene to the sea-shore, though he presented the most magnificent object in nature, is confessed to have erred in his choice. The idea of toil, labour, and danger, suffered by the fishermen, is painful by an unavoidable sympathy, which attends every conception of human happiness or misery.

When I was twenty, says a French poet, Ovid was my favourite. Now I am forty, I declare for Horace. We enter, to be sure, more readily into sentiments which resemble those we feel every day. But no passion, when well represented, can be entirely indifferent to us, because there is none of which every man has not within him at least the seeds and first principles. It is the business of poetry to bring every affection near to us by lively imagery and representation, and make it look like truth and reality: a certain proof that, wherever that reality is found, our minds are disposed to be strongly affected by it.

Any recent event or piece of news by which the fate of states, provinces, or many individuals is affected, is extremely interesting even to those whose welfare is not immediately engaged. Such intelligence is propagated with celerity, heard with avidity, and enquired into with attention and concern. The interest of society appears, on this occasion, to be in some degree the interest of each individual. The imagination is sure to be affected, though the passions excited may not always be so strong and steady as to have great influence on the conduct and behaviour.

The perusal of a history seems a calm entertainment, but would be no entertainment at all, did not our hearts beat with correspondent movements to those which are described by the historian.

Thucydides and Guicciardin support with difficulty our attention while the former describes the trivial rencounters of the small cities of Greece, and the latter the harmless wars of Pisa. The few persons interested and the small interest fill not the imagination and engage not the affections. The deep distress of the numerous Athenian army before Syracuse, the danger which so nearly threatens Venice — these excite compassion; these move terror and anxiety.

The indifferent, uninteresting style of Suetonius, equally with the masterly pencil of Tacitus, may convince us of the cruel depravity of Nero or Tiberius; but what a difference of sentiment! While the former coldly relates the facts, and the latter sets before our eyes the venerable figures of a Soranus and a Thrasea, intrepid in their fate, and only moved by the melting sorrows of their friends and kindred. What sympathy then touches every human heart! What indignation against the tyrant, whose causeless fear or unprovoked malice gave rise to such detestable barbarity!

If we bring these subjects nearer, if we remove all suspicion of fiction and deceit, what powerful concern is excited, and how much superior, in many instances, to the narrow attachments of self-love and private interest! Popular sedition, party zeal, a devoted obedience to factious leaders — these are some of the most visible, though less laudable, effects of this social sympathy in human nature.

The frivolousness of the subject, too, we may observe, is not able to detach us entirely from what carries an image of human sentiment and affection.

When a person stutters and pronounces with difficulty, we even sympathize with this trivial uneasiness, and suffer for him. And it is a rule in criticism that every combination of syllables or letters which gives pain to the organs of speech in the recital, appears also from a species of sympathy harsh and disagreeable to the ear. Nay, when we run over a book with our eye, we are sensible of such unharmonious composition, because we still imagine that a person recites it to us and suffers from the pronunciation of these jarring sounds. So delicate is our sympathy!

Easy and unconstrained postures and motions are always beautiful. An air of health and vigour is agreeable; clothes which warm without burthening the body, which cover without imprisoning the limbs, are well-fashioned. In every judgment of beauty, the feelings of the person affected enter into consideration, and communicate to the spectator similar touches of pain or pleasure.[5] What wonder, then, if we can pronounce no judgement concerning the character and

---

[5] "Decentior equus cujus astricta sunt ilia; sed idem velocior. Pulcher aspectu sit athleta, cujus lacertos exercitatio expressit; idem certamini paratior. Nunquam enim *species* ab *utilitate* dividitur. Sed hoc quidem discernere modici judicii est." — Quintilian, *Inst.* lib. viii. cap. 3.

conduct of men, without considering the tendencies of their actions and the happiness or misery which thence arises to society? What association of ideas would ever operate, were that principle here totally unactive?[6]

If any man from a cold insensibility or narrow selfishness of temper is unaffected with the images of human happiness or misery, he must be equally indifferent to the images of vice and virtue; as, on the other hand, it is always found that a warm concern for the interests of our species is attended with a delicate feeling of all moral distinctions, a strong resentment of injury done to men, a lively approbation of their welfare. In this particular, though great superiority is observable of one man above another, yet none are so entirely indifferent to the interest of their fellow creatures as to perceive no distinctions of moral good and evil in consequence of the different tendencies of actions and principles. How, indeed, can we suppose it possible in any one who wears a human heart that, if there be subjected to his censure one character or system of conduct which is beneficial, and another which is pernicious to his species or community, he will not so much as give a cool preference to the former, or ascribe to it the smallest merit or regard? Let us suppose such a person ever so selfish, let private interest have ingrossed ever so much his attention, yet in instances where that is not concerned, he must unavoidably feel *some* propensity to the good of mankind, and make it an object of choice if everything else be equal. Would any man who is walking along tread as willingly on another's gouty toes, whom he has no quarrel with,

[6] In proportion to the station which a man possesses, according to the relations in which he is placed, we always expect from him a greater or less degree of good, and when disappointed, blame his inutility; and much more do we blame him, if any ill or prejudice arise from his conduct and behaviour. When the interests of one country interfere with those of another, we estimate the merits of a statesman by the good or ill which results to his own country from his measures and councils, without regard to the prejudice which he brings on its enemies and rivals. His fellow citizens are the objects which lie nearest the eye, while we determine his character. And as nature has implanted in every one a superior affection to his own country, we never expect any regard to distant nations, where a competition arises. Not to mention that, while every man consults the good of his own community, we are sensible that the general interest of mankind is better promoted, than by any loose indeterminate views to the good of a species, whence no beneficial action could ever result, for want of a duly limited object on which they could exert themselves.

as on the hard flint and pavement? There is here surely a difference in the case. We surely take into consideration the happiness and misery of others in weighing the several motives of action, and incline to the former where no private regards draw us to seek our own promotion or advantage by the injury of our fellow creatures. And if the principles of humanity are capable, in many instances, of influencing our actions, they must, at all times, have *some* authority over our sentiments and give us a general approbation of what is useful to society, and blame of what is dangerous or pernicious. The degrees of these sentiments may be the subject of controversy; but the reality of their existence, one should think, must be admitted in every theory or system.

A creature, absolutely malicious and spiteful, were there any such in nature, must be worse than indifferent to the images of vice and virtue. All his sentiments must be inverted and directly opposite to those which prevail in the human species. Whatever contributes to the good of mankind, as it crosses the constant bent of his wishes and desires, must produce uneasiness and disapprobation; and on the contrary, whatever is the source of disorder and misery in society must, for the same reason, be regarded with pleasure and complacency. Timon, who, probably from his affected spleen more than an inveterate malice, was denominated the manhater, embraced Alcibiades with great fondness. *Go on, my boy!* cried he, *acquire the confidence of the people: You will one day, I foresee, be the cause of great calamities to them.*[7] Could we admit the two principles of the Manicheans, it is an infallible consequence that their sentiments of human actions, as well as of everything else, must be totally opposite, and that every instance of justice and humanity, from its necessary tendency, must please the one deity and displease the other. All mankind so far resemble the good principle that, where interest or revenge or envy perverts not our disposition, we are always inclined, from our natural philanthropy, to give the preference to the happiness of society, and consequently to virtue above its opposite. Absolute, unprovoked, disinterested malice has never, perhaps, place in any human breast; or if it had, must there pervert all the sentiments of morals as well as the feelings of humanity. If the cruelty of Nero be allowed entirely voluntary, and not rather the effect of constant fear and resentment,

[7] Plutarch in *vita Alc.*

it is evident that Tigellinus, preferably to Seneca or Burrhus, must have possessed his steady and uniform approbation.

A statesman or patriot who serves our own country in our own time has always a more passionate regard paid to him than one whose beneficial influence operated on distant ages or remote nations where the good resulting from his generous humanity, being less connected with us, seems more obscure, and affects us with a less lively sympathy. We may own the merit to be equally great, though our sentiments are not raised to an equal height in both cases. The judgment here corrects the inequalities of our internal emotions and perceptions, in like manner as it preserves us from error in the several variations of images presented to our external senses. The same object, at a double distance, really throws on the eye a picture of but half the bulk, yet we imagine that it appears of the same size in both situations, because we know that on our approach to it, its image would expand on the eye, and that the difference consists not in the object itself, but in our position with regard to it. And, indeed, without such a correction of appearances, both in internal and external sentiment, men could never think or talk steadily on any subject, while their fluctuating situations produce a continual variation on objects, and throw them into such different and contrary lights and positions.[8]

The more we converse with mankind, and the greater social intercourse we maintain, the more shall we be familiarized to these general preferences and distinctions without which our conversation and discourse could scarcely be rendered intelligible to each other. Every man's interest is peculiar to himself, and the aversions and desires

[8] For a like reason, the tendencies of actions and characters, not their real accidental consequences, are alone regarded in our moral determinations or general judgments; though in our real feeling or sentiment, we cannot help paying greater regard to one whose station, joined to virtue, renders him really useful to society, than to one who exerts the social virtues only in good intentions and benevolent affections. Separating the character from the fortune, by an easy and necessary effort of thought, we pronounce these persons alike, and give them the same general praise. The judgment corrects or endeavours to correct the appearance, but is not able entirely to prevail over sentiment.

Why is this peach-tree said to be better than that other, but because it produces more or better fruit? And would not the same praise be given it, though snails or vermin had destroyed the peaches before they came to full maturity? In morals, too, is not *the tree known by the fruit?* And cannot we easily distinguish between nature and accident, in the one case as well as in the other?

which result from it cannot be supposed to affect others in a like degree. General language, therefore, being formed for general use, must be moulded on some more general views, and must affix the epithets of praise or blame, in conformity to sentiments which arise from the general interests of the community. And if these sentiments, in most men, be not so strong as those which have a reference to private good, yet still they must make some distinction, even in persons the most depraved and selfish, and must attach the notion of good to a beneficent conduct, and of evil to the contrary. Sympathy, we shall allow, is much fainter than our concern for ourselves, and sympathy with persons remote from us much fainter than that with persons near and contiguous; but for this very reason it is necessary for us, in our calm judgments and discourse concerning the characters of men, to neglect all these differences and render our sentiments more public and social. Besides that we ourselves often change our situation in this particular, we every day meet with persons who are in a situation different from us, and who could never converse with us were we to remain constantly in that position and point of view which is peculiar to ourselves. The intercourse of sentiments, therefore, in society and conversation, makes us form some general unalterable standard by which we may approve or disapprove of characters and manners. And though the heart takes not part entirely with those general notions, nor regulates all its love and hatred by the universal abstract differences of vice and virtue, without regard to self or the persons with whom we are more intimately connected, yet have these moral differences a considerable influence and, being sufficient, at least for discourse, serve all our purposes in company, in the pulpit, on the theatre, and in the schools.[9]

Thus, in whatever light we take this subject, the merit ascribed to the social virtues appears still uniform, and arises chiefly from that regard which the natural sentiment of benevolence engages us to pay to the interests of mankind and society. If we consider the principles

[9] It is wisely ordained by nature that private connexions should commonly prevail over universal views and considerations; otherwise our affections and actions would be dissipated and lost, for want of a proper limited object. Thus a small benefit done to ourselves or our near friends excites more lively sentiments of love and approbation than a great benefit done to a distant commonwealth. But still we know here, as in all the senses, to correct these inequalities by reflection, and retain a general standard of vice and virtue founded chiefly on general usefulness.

of the human make, such as they appear to daily experience and observation, we must, *a priori*, conclude it impossible for such a creature as man to be totally indifferent to the well or ill-being of his fellow creatures, and not readily, of himself, to pronounce, where nothing gives him any particular bias, that what promotes their happiness is good, what tends to their misery is evil, without any farther regard or consideration. Here then are the faint rudiments, at least, or outlines of a *general* distinction between actions; and in proportion as the humanity of the person is supposed to increase his connexion with those who are injured or benefited, and his lively conception of their misery or happiness, his consequent censure or approbation acquires proportionable vigour. There is no necessity that a generous action, barely mentioned in an old history or remote gazette, should communicate any strong feelings of applause and admiration. Virtue, placed at such a distance, is like a fixed star which, though to the eye of reason it may appear as luminous as the sun in his meridian, is so infinitely removed as to affect the senses neither with light nor heat. Bring this virtue nearer, by our acquaintance or connexion with the persons, or even by an eloquent recital of the case; our hearts are immediately caught, our sympathy enlivened, and our cool approbation converted into the warmest sentiments of friendship and regard. These seem necessary and infallible consequences of the general principles of human nature, as discovered in common life and practice.

Again, reverse these views and reasonings: consider the matter *a posteriori*, and weighing the consequences, enquire if the merit of social virtue be not, in a great measure, derived from the feelings of humanity with which it affects the spectators. It appears to be matter of fact that the circumstance of *utility*, in all subjects, is a source of praise and approbation; that it is constantly appealed to in all moral decisions concerning the merit and demerit of actions; that it is the *sole* source of that high regard paid to justice, fidelity, honour, allegiance, and chastity; that it is inseparable from all the other social virtues, humanity, generosity, charity, affability, lenity, mercy, and moderation; and, in a word, that it is a foundation of the chief part of morals, which has a reference to mankind and our fellow creatures.

It appears also that, in our general approbation of characters and manners, the useful tendency of the social virtues moves us not by any regards to self-interest, but has an influence much more universal and extensive. It appears that a tendency to public good, and to the promoting of peace, harmony, and order in society, does always, by affecting the benevolent principles of our frame, engage us on the side of the social virtues. And it appears, as an additional confirmation, that these principles of humanity and sympathy enter so deeply into all our sentiments, and have so powerful an influence as may enable them to excite the strongest censure and applause. The present theory is the simple result of all these inferences, each of which seems founded on uniform experience and observation.

Were it doubtful whether there were any such principle in our nature as humanity or a concern for others, yet when we see in numberless instances that whatever has a tendency to promote the interests of society is so highly approved of, we ought thence to learn the force of the benevolent principle, since it is impossible for anything to please as means to an end where the end is totally indifferent. On the other hand, were it doubtful whether there were implanted in our nature any general principle of moral blame and approbation, yet when we see in numberless instances the influence of humanity, we ought thence to conclude that it is impossible but that everything which promotes the interest of society must communicate pleasure, and what is pernicious give uneasiness. But when these different reflections and observations concur in establishing the same conclusion, must they not bestow an undisputed evidence upon it?

It is however hoped that the progress of this argument will bring a farther confirmation of the present theory, by showing the rise of other sentiments of esteem and regard from the same or like principles.

SECTION VI

OF QUALITIES USEFUL TO OURSELVES

Part I

IT SEEMS EVIDENT that where a quality or habit is subjected to our examination, if it appear in any respect prejudicial to the person possessed of it, or such as incapacitates him for business and action, it is instantly blamed, and ranked among his faults and imperfections.

Indolence, negligence, want of order and method, obstinacy, fickleness, rashness, credulity; these qualities were never esteemed by any one indifferent to a character, much less extolled as accomplishments or virtues. The prejudice resulting from them immediately strikes our eye and gives us the sentiment of pain and disapprobation.

No quality, it is allowed, is absolutely either blamable or praise-worthy. It is all according to its degree. A due medium, says the Peripatetics, is the characteristic of virtue. But this medium is chiefly determined by utility. A proper celerity, for instance, and dispatch in business is commendable. When defective, no progress is ever made in the execution of any purpose; when excessive, it engages us in precipitate and ill-concerted measures and enterprises. By such reasonings, we fix the proper and commendable mediocrity in all moral and prudential disquisitions, and never lose view of the advan-tages which result from any character or habit.

Now as these advantages are enjoyed by the person possessed of the character, it can never be *self-love* which renders the prospect of them agreeable to us, the spectators, and prompts our esteem and approbation. No force of imagination can convert us into another person and make us fancy that we, being that person, reap benefit from those valuable qualities which belong to him. Or if it did, no celerity of imagination could immediately transport us back into ourselves, and make us love and esteem the person as different from us. Views and sentiments, so opposite to known truth and to each other, could never have place at the same time in the same person. All suspicion, therefore, of selfish regards is here totally excluded. It is a quite different principle which actuates our bosom and interests us in the felicity of the person whom we contemplate. Where his natural talents and acquired abilities give us the prospect of elevation, advancement, a figure in life, prosperous success, a steady command over fortune, and the execution of great or advantageous undertakings, we are struck with such agreeable images and feel a complacency and regard immediately arise towards him. The ideas of happiness, joy, triumph, prosperity, are connected with every circumstance of his character, and diffuse over our minds a pleasing sentiment of sympathy and humanity.[1]

[1] One may venture to affirm that there is no human creature to whom the appear-ance of happiness (where envy or revenge has no place) does not give pleasure, that

Let us suppose a person originally framed so as to have no manner of concern for his fellow-creatures, but to regard the happiness and misery of all sensible beings with greater indifference than even two contiguous shades of the same colour. Let us suppose, if the prosperity of nations were laid on the one hand, and their ruin on the other, and he were desired to choose, that he would stand like the schoolman's ass, irresolute and undetermined between equal motives; or rather like the same ass between two pieces of wood or marble, without any inclination or propensity to either side. The consequence, I believe, must be allowed just, that such a person, being absolutely unconcerned either for the public good of a community or the private utility of others, would look on every quality, however pernicious or however beneficial to society or to its possessor, with the same indifference as on the most common and uninteresting object.

But if, instead of this fancied monster, we suppose a *man* to form a judgment or determination in the case, there is to him a plain foundation of preference, where everything else is equal; and however cool his choice may be, if his heart be selfish, or if the persons interested be remote from him, there must still be a choice or distinction between what is useful and what is pernicious. Now this distinction is the same, in all its parts, with the *moral distinction* whose foundation has been so often, and so much in vain, enquired after. The same endowments of the mind, in every circumstance, are agreeable to the sentiment of morals and to that of humanity; the same temper is susceptible of high degrees of the one sentiment and of the other; and the same alteration in the objects, by their nearer approach or by connexions, enlivens the one and the other. By all the rules of philosophy, therefore, we must conclude that these sentiments are originally of misery, uneasiness. This seems inseparable from our make and constitution. But they are only the more generous minds that are thence prompted to seek zealously the good of others, and to have a real passion for their welfare. With men of narrow and ungenerous spirits, this sympathy goes not beyond a slight feeling of the imagination, which serves only to excite sentiments of complacency or censure, and makes them apply to the object either honourable or dishonourable appellations. A griping miser, for instance, praises extremely *industry* and *frugality* even in others, and sets them, in his estimation, above all the other virtues. He knows the good that results from them, and feels that species of happiness with a more lively sympathy than any other you could represent to him; though perhaps he would not part with a shilling to make the fortune of the industrious man whom he praises so highly.

the same, since in each particular, even the most minute, they are governed by the same laws and are moved by the same objects.

Why do philosophers infer with the greatest certainty that the moon is kept in its orbit by the same force of gravity that makes bodies fall near the surface of the earth, but because these effects are, upon computation, found similar and equal? And must not this argument bring as strong conviction in moral as in natural disquisitions?

To prove by any long detail that all the qualities useful to the possessor are approved of, and the contrary censured, would be superfluous. The least reflection on what is every day experienced in life will be sufficient. We shall only mention a few instances, in order to remove, if possible, all doubt and hesitation.

The quality the most necessary for the execution of any useful enterprise is discretion, by which we carry on a safe intercourse with others, give due attention to our own and to their character, weigh each circumstance of the business which we undertake, and employ the surest and safest means for the attainment of any end or purpose. To a Cromwell, perhaps, or a De Retz, discretion may appear an alderman-like virtue, as Dr. Swift calls it; and being incompatible with those vast designs to which their courage and ambition prompted them, it might really, in them, be a fault or imperfection. But in the conduct of ordinary life, no virtue is more requisite, not only to obtain success, but to avoid the most fatal miscarriages and disappointments. The greatest parts without it, as observed by an elegant writer, may be fatal to their owner; as Polyphemus, deprived of his eye, was only the more exposed, on account of his enormous strength and stature.

The best character, indeed, were it not rather too perfect for human nature, is that which is not swayed by temper of any kind, but alternately employs enterprise and caution, as each is *useful* to the particular purpose intended. Such is the excellence which St. Evremond ascribes to Mareschal Turenne, who displayed every campaign, as he grew older, more temerity in his military enterprises; and being now, from long experience, perfectly acquainted with every incident in war, he advanced with greater firmness and security in a road so well known to him. Fabius, says Machiavel, was cautious; Scipio enterprising. And both succeeded, because the situation of the

Roman affairs, during the command of each, was peculiarly adapted to his genius; but both would have failed had these situations been reversed. He is happy whose circumstances suit his temper; but he is more excellent who can suit his temper to any circumstances.

What need is there to display the praises of industry and to extol its advantages in the acquisition of power and riches or in raising what we call a *fortune* in the world? The tortoise, according to the fable, by his perseverance gained the race of the hare, though possessed of much superior swiftness. A man's time, when well husbanded, is like a cultivated field, of which a few acres produce more of what is useful to life than extensive provinces, even of the richest soil, when over-run with weeds and brambles.

But all prospect of success in life, or even of tolerable subsistence, must fail where a reasonable frugality is wanting. The heap, instead of increasing, diminishes daily and leaves its possessor so much more unhappy as, not having been able to confine his expenses to a large revenue, he will still less be able to live contentedly on a small one. The souls of men, according to Plato,[2] inflamed with impure appetites, and losing the body which alone afforded means of satisfaction, hover about the earth and haunt the places where their bodies are deposited, possessed with a longing desire to recover the lost organs of sensation. So may we see worthless prodigals, having consumed their fortune in wild debauches, thrusting themselves into every plentiful table and every party of pleasure, hated even by the vicious and despised even by fools.

The one extreme of frugality is *avarice*, which, as it both deprives a man of all use of his riches and checks hospitality and every social enjoyment, is justly censured on a double account. *Prodigality*, the other extreme, is commonly more hurtful to a man himself; and each of these extremes is blamed above the other, according to the temper of the person who censures, and according to his greater or less sensibility to pleasure, either social or sensual.

Qualities often derive their merit from complicated sources. *Honesty, fidelity, truth* are praised for their immediate tendency to promote the interests of society; but after those virtues are once established upon this foundation, they are also considered as advantageous to the person himself, and as the source of that trust and confidence which

[2] *Phaedo.*

can alone give a man any consideration in life. One becomes contemptible, no less than odious, when he forgets the duty which, in this particular, he owes to himself as well as to society.

Perhaps this consideration is one *chief* source of the high blame which is thrown on any instance of failure among women in point of *chastity*. The greatest regard which can be acquired by that sex is derived from their fidelity; and a woman becomes cheap and vulgar, loses her rank, and is exposed to every insult, who is deficient in this particular. The smallest failure is here sufficient to blast her character. A female has so many opportunities of secretly indulging these appetites that nothing can give us security but her absolute modesty and reserve; and where a breach is once made, it can scarcely ever be fully repaired. If a man behave with cowardice on one occasion, a contrary conduct reinstates him in his character. But by what action can a woman, whose behaviour has once been dissolute, be able to assure us that she has formed better resolutions, and has self-command enough to carry them into execution?

All men, it is allowed, are equally desirous of happiness, but few are successful in the pursuit. One considerable cause is the want of strength of mind, which might enable them to resist the temptation of present ease or pleasure, and carry them forward in the search of more distant profit and enjoyment. Our affections, on a general prospect of their objects, form certain rules of conduct and certain measures of preference of one above another; and these decisions, though really the result of our calm passions and propensities — for what else can pronounce any object eligible or the contrary? — are yet said, by a natural abuse of terms, to be the determinations of pure *reason* and reflection. But when some of these objects approach nearer to us, or acquire the advantages of favourable lights and positions which catch the heart or imagination, our general resolutions are frequently confounded, a small enjoyment preferred, and lasting shame and sorrow entailed upon us. And however poets may employ their wit and eloquence in celebrating present pleasure and rejecting all distant views to fame, health, or fortune, it is obvious that this practice is the source of all dissoluteness and disorder, repentance and misery. A man of a strong and determined temper adheres tenaciously to his general resolutions, and is neither seduced by the allurements of pleasure, nor terrified by the menaces of pain; but keeps still in view those distant pursuits by which he, at once, ensures his happiness and his honour.

Self-satisfaction, at least in some degree, is an advantage which equally attends the fool and the wise man. But it is the only one; nor is there any other circumstance in the conduct of life where they are upon an equal footing. Business, books, conversation; for all of these, a fool is totally incapacitated, and except condemned by his station to the coarsest drudgery, remains a *useless* burthen upon the earth. Accordingly, it is found that men are extremely jealous of their character in this particular; and many instances are seen of profligacy and treachery, the most avowed and unreserved; none of bearing patiently the imputation of ignorance and stupidity. Dicae-archus, the Macedonian general, who, as Polybius tells us,[3] openly erected one altar to impiety, another to injustice, in order to bid defiance to mankind; even he, I am well assured, would have started at the epithet of *fool*, and have meditated revenge for so injurious an appellation. Except the affection of parents, the strongest and most indissoluble bond in nature, no connexion has strength sufficient to support the disgust arising from this character. Love itself, which can subsist under treachery, ingratitude, malice, and infidelity, is immediately extinguished by it when perceived and acknowledged; nor are deformity and old age more fatal to the dominion of that passion. So dreadful are the ideas of an utter incapacity for any purpose or undertaking, and of continued error and misconduct in life!

When it is asked, whether a quick or a slow apprehension be most valuable? Whether one that, at first view, penetrates far into a subject, but can perform nothing upon study; or a contrary character, which must work out everything by dint of application? Whether a clear head or a copious invention? Whether a profound genius or a sure judgment? In short, what character or peculiar turn of under-standing, is more excellent than another? It is evident that we can answer none of these questions without considering which of those qualities capacitates a man best for the world, and carries him farthest in any undertaking.

If refined sense and exalted sense be not so *useful* as common sense, their rarity, their novelty, and the nobleness of their objects make

[3] Lib. xvii. Cap. 35.

some compensation, and render them the admiration of mankind; as gold, though less serviceable than iron, acquires from its scarcity a value which is much superior.

The defects of judgment can be supplied by no art or invention; but those of memory frequently may, both in business and in study, by method and industry, and by diligence in committing everything to writing; and we scarcely ever hear a short memory given as a reason for a man's failure in any undertaking. But in ancient times, when no man could make a figure without the talent of speaking, and when the audience were too delicate to bear such crude, undigested harangues as our extemporary orators offer to public assemblies, the faculty of memory was then of the utmost consequence, and was accordingly much more valued than at present. Scarce any great genius is mentioned in antiquity who is not celebrated for this talent; and Cicero enumerates it among the other sublime qualities of Caesar himself.[4]

Particular customs and manners alter the usefulness of qualities; they also alter their merit. Particular situations and accidents have, in some degree, the same influence. He will always be more esteemed who possesses those talents and accomplishments which suit his station and profession than he whom fortune has misplaced in the part which she has assigned him. The private or selfish virtues are, in this respect, more arbitrary than the public and social. In other respects they are, perhaps, less liable to doubt and controversy.

In this kingdom, such continued ostentation of late years has prevailed among men in *active* life with regard to *public spirit*, and among those in *speculative* with regard to *benevolence;* and so many false pretensions to each have been, no doubt, detected, that men of the world are apt, without any bad intention, to discover a sullen incredulity on the head of those moral endowments, and even sometimes absolutely to deny their existence and reality. In like manner I find that, of old, the perpetual cant of the *Stoics* and *Cynics* concerning *virtue*, their magnificent professions and slender performances, bred a disgust in mankind; and Lucian, who, though licentious with regard to pleasure, is yet in other respects a very moral writer, cannot sometimes talk of virtue so much boasted without betraying symptoms

---

[4] *Fuit in illo ingenium, ratio, memoria, literae, cura, cogitatio, diligentia, etc.* Philip. 2.

of spleen and irony.[5] But surely this peevish delicacy, whencever it arises, can never be carried so far as to make us deny the existence of every species of merit, and all distinction of manners and behaviour. Besides *discretion, caution, enterprise, industry, assiduity, frugality, economy, good-sense, prudence, discernment;* besides these endowments, I say, whose very names force an avowal of their merit, there are many others to which the most determined scepticism cannot for a moment refuse the tribute of praise and approbation. *Temperance, sobriety, patience, constancy, perseverance, forethought, considerateness, secrecy, order, insinuation, address, presence of mind, quickness of conception, facility of expression,* these and a thousand more of the same kind no man will ever deny to be excellences and perfections. As their merit consists in their tendency to serve the person possessed of them without any magnificent claim to public and social desert, we are the less jealous of their pretensions, and readily admit them into the catalogue of laudable qualities. We are not sensible that, by this concession, we have paved the way for all the other moral excellences, and cannot consistently hesitate any longer with regard to disinterested benevolence, patriotism, and humanity.

It seems, indeed, certain that first appearances are here, as usual, extremely deceitful, and that it is more difficult, in a speculative way, to resolve into self-love the merit which we ascribe to the selfish virtues above mentioned than that even of the social virtues, justice and beneficence. For this latter purpose, we need but say that whatever conduct promotes the good of the community is loved, praised, and esteemed by the community, on account of that utility and interest of which every one partakes; and though this affection and regard be in reality gratitude, not self-love, yet a distinction even of this obvious nature may not readily be made by superficial reasoners; and there is room, at least, to support the cavil and dispute

---

[5] Ἀρετήν τινα, καὶ ἀσώματα, καὶ λήρους μεγάλῃ τῇ φωνῇ ξυνειρόντων [who hold forth about "virtue," "immaterial substances," and all kinds of nonsense]. Luc. Timon. 9. Again, Καὶ συναγαγόντες (οἱ φιλόσοφοι) εὐεξαπάτητα μειράκια τήν τε πολυθρύλητον ἀρετὴν τραγῳδοῦσι [And gathering around themselves young people who are easily deceived, they (*scil.* the philosophers) declaim about virtue so much boasted]. *Icaromenippus.* In another place, Ἡ ποῦ γάρ ἐστιν ἡ πολυθρύλητος ἀρετή, καὶ φύσις, καὶ εἱμαρμένη, καὶ τύχη, ἀνυπόστατα καὶ κενὰ πραγμάτων ὀνόματα [Or where then is the much boasted virtue, and nature, and fate, and fortune, all of them empty names without substance]; *Deor. Concil.* 1.3.

for a moment. But as qualities which tend only to the utility of their possessor, without any reference to us or to the community, are yet esteemed and valued; by what theory or system can we account for this sentiment from self-love, or deduce it from that favourite origin? There seems here a necessity for confessing that the happiness and misery of others are not spectacles entirely indifferent to us; but that the view of the former, whether in its causes or effects, like sunshine or the prospect of well-cultivated plains — to carry our pretensions no higher — communicates a secret joy and satisfaction; the appearance of the latter, like a lowering cloud or barren landscape, throws a melancholy damp over the imagination. And this concession being once made, the difficulty is over, and a natural unforced interpretation of the phenomena of human life will afterwards, we may hope, prevail among all speculative enquirers.

Part II

It may not be improper, in this place, to examine the influence of bodily endowments, and of the goods of fortune, over our sentiments of regard and esteem, and to consider whether these phenomena fortify or weaken the present theory. It will naturally be expected that the beauty of the body, as is supposed by all ancient moralists, will be similar, in some respects, to that of the mind; and that every kind of esteem which is paid to a man will have something similar in its origin, whether it arise from his mental endowments or from the situation of his exterior circumstances.

It is evident that one considerable source of *beauty* in all animals is the advantage which they reap from the particular structure of their limbs and members, suitably to the particular manner of life to which they are by nature destined. The just proportions of a horse, described by Xenophon and Virgil, are the same that are received at this day by our modern jockeys; because the foundation of them is the same, namely, experience of what is detrimental or useful in the animal.

Broad shoulders, a lank belly, firm joints, taper legs; all these are beautiful in our species, because signs of force and vigour. Ideas of utility and its contrary, though they do not entirely determine what is handsome or deformed, are evidently the source of a considerable part of approbation or dislike.

In ancient times, bodily strength and dexterity, being of greater *use* and importance in war, was also much more esteemed and valued than at present. Not to insist on Homer and the poets, we may observe that historians scruple not to mention *force of body* among the other accomplishments even of Epaminondas, whom they acknowledge to be the greatest hero, statesman, and general of all the Greeks.[6] A like praise is given to Pompey, one of the greatest of the Romans.[7] This instance is similar to what we observed above with regard to memory.

What derision and contempt, with both sexes, attend *impotence;* while the unhappy object is regarded as one deprived of so capital a pleasure in life and, at the same time, as disabled from communicating it to others. *Barrenness* in women, being also a species of *inutility*, is a reproach, but not in the same degree; of which the reason is very obvious, according to the present theory.

There is no rule in painting or statuary more indispensible than that of balancing the figures, and placing them with the greatest exactness on their proper centre of gravity. A figure which is not justly balanced is ugly, because it conveys the disagreeable ideas of fall, harm, and pain.[8]

A disposition or turn of mind which qualifies a man to rise in the

[6] Diodorus Siculus, lib. xv. It may not be improper to give the character of Epaminondas, as drawn by the historian, in order to show the ideas of perfect merit which prevailed in those ages. In other illustrious men, says he, you will observe that each possessed some one shining quality which was the foundation of his fame: In Epaminondas all the *virtues* are found united: force of body, eloquence of expression, vigour of mind, contempt of riches, gentleness of disposition, and, *what is chiefly to be regarded*, courage and conduct in war.

[7] *Cum alacribus, saltu; cum velocibus, cursu; cum validis recte certabat.* Sallust apud Veget.

[8] All men are equally liable to pain and disease and sickness; and may again recover health and ease. These circumstances, as they make no distinction between one man and another, are no source of pride or humility, regard or contempt. But comparing our own species to superior ones, it is a very mortifying consideration that we should all be so liable to diseases and infirmities; and divines accordingly employ this topic in order to depress self-conceit and vanity. They would have more success if the common bent of our thoughts were not perpetually turned to compare ourselves with others. The infirmities of old age are mortifying, because a comparison with the young may take place. The king's evil is industriously concealed because it affects others and is often transmitted to posterity. The case is nearly the same with such diseases as convey any nauseous or frightful images; the epilepsy, for instance, ulcers, sores, scabs, etc.

world and advance his fortune is entitled to esteem and regard, as has already been explained. It may, therefore, naturally be supposed that the actual possession of riches and authority will have a considerable influence over these sentiments.

Let us examine any hypothesis by which we can account for the regard paid to the rich and powerful; we shall find none satisfactory but that which derives it from the enjoyment communicated to the spectator by the images of prosperity, happiness, ease, plenty, authority, and the gratification of every appetite. Self-love, for instance, which some affect so much to consider as the source of every sentiment, is plainly insufficient for this purpose. Where no good-will or friendship appears, it is difficult to conceive on what we can found our hope of advantage from the riches of others; though we naturally respect the rich, even before they discover any such favourable disposition towards us.

We are affected with the same sentiments when we lie so much out of the sphere of their activity that they cannot even be supposed to possess the power of serving us. A prisoner of war, in all civilized nations, is treated with a regard suited to his condition; and riches, it is evident, go far towards fixing the condition of any person. If birth and quality enter for a share, this still affords us an argument to our present purpose. For what is it we call a man of birth, but one who is descended from a long succession of rich and powerful ancestors, and who acquires our esteem by his connexion with persons whom we esteem? His ancestors, therefore, though dead, are respected, in some measure, on account of their riches; and consequently, without any kind of expectation.

But not to go so far as prisoners of war or the dead, to find instances of this disinterested regard for riches; we may only observe with a little attention those phenomena which occur in common life and conversation. A man who is himself, we shall suppose, of a competent fortune and of no profession, being introduced to a company of strangers, naturally treats them with different degrees of respect, as he is informed of their different fortunes and conditions; though it is impossible that he can so suddenly propose, and perhaps he would not accept of, any pecuniary advantage from them. A traveller is always admitted into company, and meets with civility, in proportion as his train and equipage speak him a man of great or moderate fortune. In short, the different ranks of men are, in a great measure, regulated by riches; and that with regard to superiors as well as inferiors, strangers as well as acquaintance.

What remains, therefore, but to conclude that, as riches are desired for ourselves only as the means of gratifying our appetites, either at present or in some imaginary future period, they beget esteem in others merely from their having that influence. This indeed is their very nature or offence: they have a direct reference to the commodities, conveniences, and pleasures of life. The bill of a banker who is broke, or gold in a desert island, would otherwise be full as valuable. When we approach a man who is, as we say, at his ease, we are presented with the pleasing ideas of plenty, satisfaction, cleanliness, warmth; a cheerful house, elegant furniture, ready service, and whatever is desirable in meat, drink, or apparel. On the contrary, when a poor man appears, the disagreeable images of want, penury, hard labour, dirty furniture, coarse or ragged clothes, nauseous meat and distasteful liquor, immediately strike our fancy. What else do we mean by saying that one is rich, the other poor? And as regard or contempt is the natural consequence of those different situations in life, it is easily seen what additional light and evidence this throws on our preceding theory, with regard to all moral distinctions.[9]

A man who has cured himself of all ridiculous prepossessions, and is fully, sincerely, and steadily convinced, from experience as well as philosophy, that the difference of fortune makes less difference in happiness than is vulgarly imagined; such a one does not measure out degrees of esteem according to the rent-rolls of his acquaintance. He may, indeed, externally pay a superior deference to the great lord

[9] There is something extraordinary and seemingly unaccountable in the operation of our passions, when we consider the fortune and situation of others. Very often another's advancement and prosperity produces envy, which has a strong mixture of hatred, and arises chiefly from the comparison of ourselves with the person. At the very same time, or, at least in very short intervals, we may feel the passion of respect, which is a species of affection or good-will with a mixture of humility. On the other hand, the misfortunes of our fellows often cause pity, which has in it a strong mixture of good-will. This sentiment of pity is nearly allied to contempt, which is a species of dislike with a mixture of pride. I only point out these phenomena as a subject of speculation to such as are curious with regard to moral enquiries. It is sufficient for the present purpose to observe in general that power and riches commonly cause respect, poverty and meanness contempt, though particular views and incidents may sometimes raise the passions of envy and of pity.

above the vassal, because riches are the most convenient, being the most fixed and determinate, source of distinction.   But his internal sentiments are more regulated by the personal characters of men than by the accidental and capricious favours of fortune.

In most countries of Europe, family, that is, hereditary riches marked with titles and symbols from the sovereign, is the chief source of distinction.   In England, more regard is paid to present opulence and plenty.   Each practice has its advantages and disadvantages. Where birth is respected, unactive, spiritless minds remain in haughty indolence, and dream of nothing but pedigrees and genealogies; the generous and ambitious seek honour and authority and reputation and favour.   Where riches are the chief idol, corruption, venality, rapine prevail; arts, manufactures, commerce, agriculture flourish. The former prejudice, being favourable to military virtue, is more suited to monarchies.   The latter, being the chief spur to industry, agrees better with a republican government.   And we accordingly find that each of these forms of government, by varying the *utility* of those customs, has commonly a proportionable effect on the sentiments of mankind.

SECTION VII

OF QUALITIES IMMEDIATELY AGREEABLE TO OURSELVES

Whoever has passed an evening with serious melancholy people, and has observed how suddenly the conversation was animated, and what sprightliness diffused itself over the countenance, discourse, and behaviour of every one, on the accession of a good-humoured, lively companion; such a one will easily allow that cheerfulness carries great merit with it, and naturally conciliates the good-will of mankind.   No quality, indeed, more readily communicates itself to all around, because no one has a greater propensity to display itself in jovial talk and pleasant entertainment.   The flame spreads through the whole circle, and the most sullen and morose are often caught by it.   That the melancholy hate the merry, even though Horace says it, I have some difficulty to allow, because I have always observed that, where the jollity is moderate and decent, serious people are so much the more delighted, as it dissipates the gloom with which they are commonly oppressed and gives them an unusual enjoyment.

From this influence of cheerfulness both to communicate itself and to engage approbation, we may perceive that there is another set of mental qualities which, without any utility or any tendency to further good, either of the community or of the possessor, diffuse a satisfaction on the beholders and procure friendship and regard. Their immediate sensation, to the person possessed of them, is agreeable. Others enter into the same humour and catch the sentiment by a contagion or natural sympathy; and as we cannot forbear loving whatever pleases, a kindly emotion arises towards the person who communicates so much satisfaction. He is a more animating spectacle; his presence diffuses over us more serene complacency and enjoyment; our imagination, entering into his feelings and disposition, is affected in a more agreeable manner than if a melancholy, dejected, sullen, anxious temper were presented to us. Hence the affection and probation which attend the former, the aversion and disgust with which we regard the latter.[1]

Few men would envy the character which Caesar gives of Cassius:

> He loves no play,
> As thou do'st, Anthony: he hears no music:
> Seldom he smiles; and smiles in such a sort,
> As if he mock'd himself, and scorn'd his spirit
> That could be mov'd to smile at anything.

Not only such men, as Caesar adds, are commonly *dangerous*, but also, having little enjoyment within themselves, they can never become agreeable to others or contribute to social entertainment. In all polite nations and ages, a relish for pleasure, if accompanied with temperance and decency, is esteemed a considerable merit, even in the greatest men, and becomes still more requisite in those of inferior rank and character. It is an agreeable representation which a French

[1] There is no man who, on particular occasions, is not affected with all the disagreeable passions, fear, anger, dejection, grief, melancholy, anxiety, etc. But these, so far as they are natural and universal, make no difference between one man and another, and can never be the object of blame. It is only when the disposition gives a *propensity* to any of these disagreeable passions, that they disfigure the character and, by giving uneasiness, convey the sentiment of disapprobation to the spectator.

writer gives of the situation of his own mind in this particular: *Virtue I love*, says he, *without austerity; Pleasure, without effeminacy; And life, without fearing its end.*[2]

Who is not struck with any signal instance of greatness of mind or dignity of character, with elevation of sentiment, disdain of slavery, and with that noble pride and spirit which arises from conscious virtue? The sublime, says Longinus, is often nothing but the echo or image of magnanimity; and where this quality appears in any one, even though a syllable be not uttered, it excites our applause and admiration, as may be observed of the famous silence of Ajax in the Odyssey, which expresses more noble disdain and resolute indignation than any language can convey.[3]

Were I Alexander, said Parmenio, *I would accept of these offers made by Darius. So would I too*, replied Alexander, *were I Parmenio.* This saying is admirable, says Longinus, from a like principle.[4]

Go! cries the same hero to his soldiers, when they refused to follow him to the Indies, *go tell your countrymen that you left Alexander completing the conquest of the world.* "Alexander," said the Prince of Condé, who always admired this passage, "abandoned by his soldiers, among barbarians, not yet fully subdued, felt in himself such a dignity and right of empire that he could not believe it possible that any one would refuse to obey him. Whether in Europe or in Asia, among Greeks or Persians, all was indifferent to him: wherever he found men, he fancied he should find subjects."

The confidant of Medea in the tragedy recommends caution and submission; and enumerating all the distresses of that unfortunate heroine, asks her what she has to support her against her numerous and implacable enemies. *Myself*, replies she; *Myself, I say, and it is enough.* Boileau justly recommends this passage as an instance of true sublime.[5]

When Phocion, the modest, the gentle Phocion, was led to execution, he turned to one of his fellow sufferers, who was lamenting his own

---

[2] *J'aime la vertu, sans rudesse;*
J'aime le plaisir, sans molesse;
J'aime la vie, et n'en crains point la fin. — St. Evremond.

[3] Cap. 9.

[4] *Idem.*

[5] *Réflexion 10 sur Longin.*

hard fate, *Is it not glory enough for you, says he, that you die with Phocion?* [6]

Place in opposition the picture which Tacitus draws of Vitellius, fallen from empire, prolonging his ignominy from a wretched love of life, delivered over to the merciless rabble, tossed, buffeted, and kicked about, constrained by their holding a poniard under his chin to raise his head, and expose himself to every contumely. What abject infamy! What low humiliation! Yet even here, says the historian, he discovered some symptoms of a mind not wholly degenerate. To a tribune, who insulted him, he replied, *I am still your emperor.*[7]

We never excuse the absolute want of spirit and dignity of character, or a proper sense of what is due to one's self, in society and the common intercourse of life. This vice constitutes what we properly call *meanness;* when a man can submit to the basest slavery in order to gain his ends, fawn upon those who abuse him, and degrade himself by intimacies and familiarities with undeserving inferiors. A certain degree of generous pride or self-value is so requisite that the absence of it in the mind displeases, after the same manner as the want of a nose, eye, or any of the most material feature of the face or member of the body.[8]

The utility of courage, both to the public and to the person possessed of it, is an obvious foundation of merit. But to any one who duly considers of the matter, it will appear that this quality has a peculiar lustre which it derives wholly from itself and from that noble eleva-

---

[6] Plutarch in Phoc.

[7] Tacit. *Hist.* lib. iii. The author, entering upon the narration, says, *Laniata veste, foedum spectaculum ducebatur, multis increpantibus, nullo inlacrimante: deformitas exitus misericordiam abstulerat.* To enter thoroughly into this method of thinking, we must make allowance for the ancient maxims, that no one ought to prolong his life after it became dishonourable; but, as he had always a right to dispose of it, it then became a duty to part with it.

[8] The absence of virtue may often be a vice, and that of the highest kind, as in the instance of ingratitude, as well as meanness. Where we expect a beauty, the disappointment gives an uneasy sensation and produces a real deformity. An abjectness of character, likewise, is disgustful and contemptible in another view. Where a man has no sense of value in himself, we are not likely to have any higher esteem of him. And if the same person who crouches to his superiors is insolent to his inferiors (as often happens), this contrariety of behaviour, instead of correcting the former vice, aggravates it extremely by the addition of a vice still more odious. See Sect. VIII.

tion inseparable from it. Its figure, drawn by painters and by poets, displays in each feature a sublimity and daring confidence which catches the eye, engages the affections, and diffuses, by sympathy, a like sublimity of sentiment over every spectator.

Under what shining colours does Demosthenes [9] represent Philip, where the orator apologizes for his own administration and justifies that pertinacious love of liberty with which he had inspired the Athenians. "I beheld Philip," says he, "he with whom was your contest, resolutely, while in pursuit of empire and dominion, exposing himself to every wound; his eye gored, his neck wrested, his arm, his thigh pierced, whatever part of his body fortune should seize on, that cheerfully relinquishing, provided that, with what remained, he might live in honour and renown. And shall it be said that he, born in Pella, a place heretofore mean and ignoble, should be inspired with so high an ambition and thirst of fame, while you, Athenians, etc." These praises excite the most lively admiration; but the views presented by the orator carry us not, we see, beyond the hero himself, nor ever regard the future advantageous consequences of his valour.

The material temper of the Romans, inflamed by continual wars, had raised their esteem of courage so high that, in their language, it was called *virtue*, by way of excellence and of distinction from all other moral qualities. *The Suevi*, in the opinion of Tacitus,[10] *dressed their hair with a laudable intent: not for the purpose of loving or being loved; they adorned themselves only for their enemies, and in order to appear more terrible.* A sentiment of the historian, which would sound a little oddly in other nations and other ages.

The Scythians, according to Herodotus,[11] after scalping their enemies, dressed the skin like leather, and used it as a towel; and whoever had the most of those towels was most esteemed among them. So much had martial bravery, in that nation as well as in many others, destroyed the sentiments of humanity — a virtue surely much more useful and engaging.

It is indeed observable that among all uncultivated nations who have not as yet had full experience of the advantages attending beneficence, justice, and the social virtues, courage is the predominant

[9] *De Corona.*
[10] *De moribus Germ.*
[11] Lib. iv.

excellence: what is most celebrated by poets, recommended by parents and instructors, and admired by the public in general. The ethics of Homer are, in this particular, very different from those of Fénélon, his elegant imitator; and such as were well suited to an age when one hero, as remarked by Thucydides,[12] could ask another without offence whether he were a robber or not. Such also very lately was the system of ethics which prevailed in many barbarous parts of Ireland, if we may credit Spencer in his judicious account of the state of that kingdom.[13]

Of the same class of virtues with courage is that undisturbed philosophical tranquillity, superior to pain, sorrow, anxiety, and each assault of adverse fortune. Conscious of his own virtue, say the philosophers, the sage elevates himself above every accident of life and, securely placed in the temple of wisdom, looks down on inferior mortals engaged in pursuit of honours, riches, reputation, and every frivolous enjoyment. These pretentions, no doubt, when stretched to the utmost, are by far too magnificent for human nature. They carry, however, a grandeur with them, which seizes the spectator and strikes him with admiration. And the nearer we can approach in practice to this sublime tranquillity and indifference — for we must distinguish it from a stupid insensibility — the more secure enjoyment shall we attain within ourselves, and the more greatness of mind shall we discover to the world. The philosophical tranquillity may, indeed, be considered only as a branch of magnanimity.

Who admires not Socrates, his perpetual serenity and contentment amidst the greatest poverty and domestic vexations, his resolute contempt of riches and his magnanimous care of preserving liberty, while he refused all assistance from his friends and disciples, and avoided even the dependence of an obligation? Epictetus had not so much as a door to his little house or hovel, and therefore soon lost his iron lamp, the only furniture which he had worth taking. But resolving to disappoint all robbers for the future, he supplied its place with an

[12] Lib. i.

[13] It is a common use, says he, amongst their gentlemen's sons, that, as soon as they are able to use their weapons, they straight gather to themselves three or four stragglers or kern, with whom wandering a while up and down idly the country, taking only meat, he at last falleth into some bad occasion that shall be offered; which being once made known, he is thenceforth counted a man of worth, in whom there is courage.

earthen lamp, of which he very peacefully kept possession ever after.

Among the ancients, the heroes in philosophy, as well as those in war and patriotism, have a grandeur and force of sentiment which astonishes our narrow souls and is rashly rejected as extravagant and supernatural. They, in their turn, I allow, would have had equal reason to consider as romantic and incredible the degree of humanity, clemency, order, tranquillity, and other social virtues to which, in the administration of government, we have attained in modern times, had any one been then able to have made a fair representation of them. Such is the compensation which nature, or rather education, has made in the distribution of excellences and virtues in those different ages.

The merit of benevolence, arising from its utility and its tendency to promote the good of mankind, has been already explained, and is, no doubt, the source of a *considerable* part of that esteem which is so universally paid to it. But it will also be allowed that the very softness and tenderness of the sentiment, its engaging endearments, its fond expressions, its delicate attentions, and all that flow of mutual confidence and regard which enters into a warm attachment of love and friendship — it will be allowed, I say, that these feelings, being delightful in themselves, are necessarily communicated to the spectators and melt them into the same fondness and delicacy. The tear naturally starts in our eye on the apprehension of a warm sentiment of this nature; our breast heaves, our heart is agitated, and every humane tender principle of our frame is set in motion, and gives us the purest and most satisfactory enjoyment.

When poets form descriptions of Elysian fields, where the blessed inhabitants stand in no need of each other's assistance, they yet represent them as maintaining a constant intercourse of love and friendship, and sooth our fancy with the pleasing image of these soft and gentle passions. The idea of tender tranquillity in a pastoral Arcadia is agreeable from a like principle, as has been observed above.[14]

Who would live amidst perpetual wrangling, and scolding, and mutual reproaches? The roughness and harshness of these emotions disturb and displease us; we suffer by contagion and sympathy, nor can we remain indifferent spectators, even though certain that no pernicious consequences would ever follow from such angry passions.

[14] Sect. v. Part 2.

As a certain proof that the whole merit of benevolence is not derived from its usefulness, we may observe that in a kind way of blame we say a person is *too good* when he exceeds his part in society and carries his attention for others beyond the proper bounds. In like manner we say a man *is too high-spirited, too intrepid, too indifferent about fortune* — reproaches which really, at bottom, imply more esteem than many panegyrics. Being accustomed to rate the merit and demerit of characters chiefly by their useful or pernicious tendencies, we cannot forbear applying the epithet of blame when we discover a sentiment which rises to a degree that is hurtful; but it may happen, at the same time, that its noble elevation or its engaging tenderness so seizes the heart as rather to increase our friendship and concern for the person.[15]

The amours and attachments of Harry the IVth of France, during the civil wars of the league, frequently hurt his interest and his cause; but all the young, at least, and amorous, who can sympathize with the tender passions, will allow that this very weakness, for they will readily call it such, chiefly endears that hero and interests them in his fortunes.

The excessive bravery and resolute inflexibility of Charles the XIIth ruined his own country and infested all his neighbours, but have such splendour and greatness in their appearance as strikes us with admiration; and they might, in some degree, be even approved of, if they betrayed not sometimes too evident symptoms of madness and disorder.

The Athenians pretended to the first invention of agriculture and of laws, and always valued themselves extremely on the benefit thereby procured to the whole race of mankind. They also boasted, and with reason, of their warlike enterprises, particularly against those innumerable fleets and armies of Persians which invaded Greece during the reigns of Darius and Xerxes. But though there be no comparison in point of utility between these peaceful and military honours, yet we find that the orators who have writ such elaborate panegyrics on that famous city have chiefly triumphed in displaying the warlike achievements. Lysias, Thucydides, Plato, and Isocrates discover, all

[15] Cheerfulness could scarce admit of blame from its excess, were it not that dissolute mirth, without a proper cause or subject, is a sure symptom and characteristic of folly, and on that account disgustful.

of them, the same partiality; which, though condemned by calm reason and reflection, appears so natural in the mind of man.

It is observable that the great charm of poetry consists in lively pictures of the sublime passions, magnanimity, courage, disdain of fortune; or those of the tender affections, love and friendship, which warm the heart and diffuse over it similar sentiments and emotions. And though all kinds of passion, even the most disagreeable, such as grief and anger, are observed, when excited by poetry, to convey a satisfaction from a mechanism of nature not easy to be explained; yet those more elevated or softer affections have a peculiar influence, and please from more than one cause or principle. Not to mention that they alone interest us in the fortune of the persons represented, or communicate any esteem and affection for their character.

And can it possibly be doubted that this talent itself of poets to move the passions, this pathetic and sublime of sentiment, is a very considerable merit and, being enhanced by its extreme rarity, may exalt the person possessed of it above every character of the age in which he lives? The prudence, address, steadiness, and benign government of Augustus, adorned with all the splendour of his noble birth and imperial crown, render him but an unequal competitor for fame with Virgil, who lays nothing into the opposite scale but the divine beauties of his poetical genius.

The very sensibility to these beauties, or a delicacy of taste, is itself a beauty in any character, as conveying the purest, the most durable, and most innocent of all enjoyments.

These are some instances of the several species of merit that are valued for the immediate pleasure which they communicate to the person possessed of them. No views of utility or of future beneficial consequences enter into this sentiment of approbation; yet is it of a kind similar to that other sentiment which arises from views of a public or private utility. The same social sympathy, we may observe, or fellow feeling with human happiness or misery, gives rise to both; and this analogy, in all the parts of the present theory, may justly be regarded as a confirmation of it.

SECTION VIII

OF QUALITIES IMMEDIATELY AGREEABLE TO OTHERS [1]

As THE MUTUAL SHOCKS in *society*, and the oppositions of interest and self-love, have constrained mankind to establish the laws of *justice* in order to preserve the advantages of mutual assistance and protection, in like manner the eternal contrarieties in *company*, of men's pride and self-conceit, have introduced the rules of "good manners" or "politeness" in order to facilitate the intercourse of minds and an undisturbed commerce and conversation. Among well-bred people a mutual deference is affected; contempt of others disguised, authority concealed, attention given to each in his turn; and an easy stream of conversation maintained, without vehemence, without interruption, without eagerness for victory, and without any airs of superiority. These attentions and regards are immediately *agreeable* to others, abstracted from any consideration of utility or beneficial tendencies. They conciliate affection, promote esteem, and extremely enhance the merit of the person who regulates his behaviour by them.

Many of the forms of breeding are arbitrary and casual, but the thing expressed by them is still the same. A Spaniard goes out of his own house before his guest, to signify that he leaves him master of all. In other countries, the landlord walks out last, as a common mark of deference and regard.

But, in order to render a man perfect *good company*, he must have Wit and Ingenuity as well as good manners. What wit is, it may not be easy to define; but it is easy surely to determine that it is a quality immediately *agreeable* to others and communicating, on its first appearance, a lively joy and satisfaction to every one who has any comprehension of it. The most profound metaphysics, indeed, might be employed in explaining the various kinds and species of wit; and many classes of it, which are now received on the sole testimony of taste and sentiment, might, perhaps, be resolved into more general principles.

---

[1] It is the nature and, indeed, the definition of virtue that it is *a quality of the mind agreeable to or approved of by every one who considers or contemplates it*. But some qualities produce pleasure because they are useful to society or useful or agreeable to the person himself; others produce it more immediately, which is the case with the class of virtues here considered.

But this is sufficient for our present purpose, that it does affect taste and sentiment and, bestowing an immediate enjoyment, is a sure source of approbation and affection.

In countries where men pass most of their time in conversation and visits and assemblies, these *companionable* qualities, so to speak, are of high estimation and form a chief part of personal merit. In countries where men live a more domestic life, and either are employed in business or amuse themselves in a narrower circle of acquaintance, the more solid qualities are chiefly regarded. Thus I have often observed that among the French the first questions with regard to a stranger are, *Is he polite? Has he wit?* In our own country the chief praise bestowed is always that of a *good-natured, sensible fellow.*

In conversation the lively spirit of dialogue is *agreeable*, even to those who desire not to have any share in the discourse; hence the teller of long stories or the pompous declaimer is very little approved of. But most men desire likewise their turn in the conversation and regard with a very evil eye that *loquacity* which deprives them of a right they are naturally so jealous of.

There is a sort of harmless *liars*, frequently to be met with in company, who deal much in the marvelous. Their usual intention is to please and entertain; but as men are most delighted with what they conceive to be truth, these people mistake extremely the means of pleasing, and incur universal blame. Some indulgence, however, to lying or fiction is given in *humorous* stories, because it is there really agreeable and entertaining, and truth is not of any importance.

Eloquence, genius of all kinds, even good sense, and sound reasoning, when it rises to an eminent degree and is employed upon subjects of any considerable dignity and nice discernment — all these endowments seem immediately agreeable and have a merit distinct from their usefulness. Rarity, likewise, which so much enhances the price of every thing, must set an additional value on these noble talents of the human mind.

Modesty may be understood in different senses, even abstracted from chastity, which has been already treated of. It sometimes means that tenderness and nicety of honour, that apprehension of blame, that dread of intrusion or injury towards others, that *pudor* which is the proper guardian of every kind of virtue and a sure preservative against vice and corruption. But its most usual meaning is when it is opposed to *impudence* and *arrogance*, and expresses a diffidence of our own judgment and a due attention and regard for others. In young men chiefly, this quality is a sure sign of good sense and is also the certain means of augmenting that endowment, by preserving their ears open to instruction, and making them still grasp after new attainments. But it has a further charm to every spectator, by flattering every man's vanity and presenting the appearance of a docile pupil who receives with proper attention and respect every word they utter.

Men have, in general, a much greater propensity to overvalue than undervalue themselves, notwithstanding the opinion of Aristotle.[2] This makes us more jealous of the excess on the former side, and causes us to regard with a peculiar indulgence all tendency to modesty and self-diffidence as esteeming the danger less of falling into any vicious extreme of that nature. It is thus in countries where men's bodies are apt to exceed in corpulency, personal beauty is placed in a much greater degree of slenderness than in countries where that is the most usual defect. Being so often struck with instances of one species of deformity, men think they can never keep at too great a distance from it, and wish always to have a leaning to the opposite side. In like manner, were the door opened to self-praise, and were Montaigne's maxim observed, that one should say as frankly, *I have sense, I have learning, I have courage, beauty, or wit,* as it is sure we often think so; were this the case, I say, every one is sensible that such a flood of impertinence would break in upon us as would render society wholly intolerable. For this reason custom has established it as a rule, in common societies, that men should not indulge themselves in self-praise or even speak much of themselves; and it is only among intimate friends or people of very manly behaviour that one is allowed to do himself justice. Nobody finds fault with Maurice, Prince of Orange, for his reply to one who asked him whom he esteemed the first general of the age: *The Marquis of Spinola,* said he, *is the second;* though it is observable that the self-praise implied is here better implied than if it had been directly expressed without any cover or disguise.

He must be a very superficial thinker who imagines that all instances of mutual deference are to be understood in earnest, and that a man would be more esteemable for being ignorant of his own merits and

[2] *Ethic. ad Nicomachum.*

accomplishments. A small bias towards modesty, even in the internal sentiment, is favourably regarded, especially in young people; and a strong bias is required in the outward behaviour; but this excludes not a noble pride and spirit, which may openly display itself in its full extent when one lies under calumny or oppression of any kind. The generous contumacy of Socrates, as Cicero calls it, has been highly celebrated in all ages; and when joined to the usual modesty of his behaviour forms a shining character. Iphicrates, the Athenian, being accused of betraying the interests of his country, asked his accuser, *Would you*, says he, *have, on a like occasion, been guilty of that crime? By no means*, replied the other. *And can you then imagine*, cried the hero, *that Iphicrates would be guilty?* [3] In short, a generous spirit and self-value, well founded, decently disguised, and courageously supported under distress and calumny, is a great excellence, and seems to derive its merit from the noble elevation of its sentiment or its immediate agreeableness to its possessor. In ordinary characters, we approve of a bias towards modesty, which is a quality immediately agreeable to others. The vicious excess of the former virtue, namely, insolence or haughtiness, is immediately disagreeable to others; the excess of the latter is so to the possessor. Thus are the boundaries of these duties adjusted.

A desire of fame, reputation, or a character with others is so far from being blamable that it seems inseparable from virtue, genius, capacity, and a generous or noble disposition. An attention even to trivial matters, in order to please, is also expected and demanded by society; and no one is surprised if he find a man in company to observe a greater elegance of dress and more pleasant flow of conversation than when he passes his time at home and with his own family. Wherein, then, consists Vanity, which is so justly regarded as a fault or imperfection. It seems to consist chiefly in such an intemperate display of our advantages, honours, and accomplishments, in such an importunate and open demand of praise and admiration, as is offensive to others and encroaches too far on *their* secret vanity and ambition. It is, besides, a sure symptom of the want of true dignity and elevation of mind, which is so great an ornament in any character. For why that impatient desire of applause, as if you were not justly entitled to it, and might not reasonably expect that it would for ever attend you?

[3] Quinctil. lib. v. cap. 12.

Why so anxious to inform us of the great company which you have kept, the obliging things which were said to you, the honours, the distinctions which you met with, as if these were not things of course and what we could readily, of ourselves, have imagined without being told of them?

Decency, or a proper regard to age, sex, character, and station in the world, may be ranked among the qualities which are immediately agreeable to others, and which, by that means, acquire praise and approbation. An effeminate behaviour in a man, a rough manner in a woman; these are ugly because unsuitable to each character and different from the qualities which we expect in the sexes. It is as if a tragedy abounded in comic beauties, or a comedy in tragic. The disproportions hurt the eye and convey a disagreeable sentiment to the spectators, the source of blame and disapprobation. This is that *indecorum* which is explained so much at large by Cicero in his *Offices*.

Among the other virtues, we may also give Cleanliness a place, since it naturally renders us agreeable to others, and is no inconsiderable source of love and affection. No one will deny that a negligence in this particular is a fault; and as faults are nothing but smaller vices, and this fault can have no other origin than the uneasy sensation which it excites in others, we may in this instance, seemingly so trivial, clearly discover the origin of moral distinctions, about which the learned have involved themselves in such mazes of perplexity and error.

But besides all the *agreeable* qualities, the origin of whose beauty we can, in some degree, explain and account for, there still remains something mysterious and inexplicable which conveys an immediate satisfaction to the spectator, but how, or why, or for what reason, he cannot pretend to determine. There is a manner, a grace, an ease, a genteelness, an I-know-not-what, which some men possess above others, which is very different from external beauty and comeliness, and which, however, catches our affection almost as suddenly and powerfully. And though this *manner* be chiefly talked of in the passion between the sexes, where the concealed magic is easily explained, yet surely much of it prevails in all our estimation of characters, and forms no inconsiderable part of personal merit. This class of accomplishments, therefore, must be trusted entirely to the blind but sure testimony of taste and sentiment; and must be considered as a part of ethics, left by nature to baffle all the pride of philosophy, and make her sensible of her narrow boundaries and slender acquisitions.

We approve of another because of his wit, politeness, modesty, decency, or any agreeable quality which he possesses, although he be not of our acquaintance, nor has ever given us any entertainment by means of these accomplishments. The idea which we form of their effect on his acquaintance has an agreeable influence on our imagination, and gives us the sentiment of approbation. This principle enters into all the judgments which we form concerning manner and characters.

SECTION IX

CONCLUSION

Part I

IT MAY justly appear surprising that any man in so late an age should find it requisite to prove by elaborate reasoning that Personal Merit consists altogether in the possession of mental qualities, *useful* or *agreeable* to the *person himself* or to *others*. It might be expected that this principle would have occurred even to the first rude, unpractised enquirers concerning morals, and been received from its own evidence without any argument or disputation. Whatever is valuable in any kind, so naturally classes itself under the division of *useful* or *agreeable*, the *utile* or the *dulce*, that it is not easy to imagine why we should ever seek further or consider the question as a matter of nice research or inquiry. And as every thing useful or agreeable must possess these qualities with regard either to the *person himself* or to *others*, the complete delineation or description of merit seems to be performed as naturally as a shadow is cast by the sun or an image is reflected upon water. If the ground on which the shadow is cast be not broken and uneven, nor the surface from which the image is reflected, disturbed and confused, a just figure is immediately presented, without any art or attention. And it seems a reasonable presumption that systems and hypotheses have perverted our natural understanding, when a theory, so simple and obvious, could so long have escaped the most elaborate examination.

But however the case may have fared with philosophy, in common life these principles are still implicitly maintained; nor is any other topic of praise or blame ever recurred to when we employ any panegyric or satire, any applause or censure of human action and behaviour. If we observe men in every intercourse of business or pleasure, in every discourse and conversation, we shall find them nowhere, except in the schools, at any loss upon this subject. What so natural, for instance, as the following dialogue? You are very happy, we shall suppose one to say, addressing himself to another, that you have given your daughter to Cleanthes. He is a man of honour and humanity. Every one who has any intercourse with him is sure of *fair* and *kind* treatment.[1] I congratulate you too, says another, on the promising expectations of this son-in-law whose assiduous application to the study of the laws, whose quick penetration and early knowledge both of men aňd business, prognosticate the greatest honours and advancement.[2] You surprise me, replies a third, when you talk of Cleanthes as a man of business and application. I met him lately in a circle of the gayest company, and he was the very life and soul of our conversation: so much wit with good manners, so much gallantry without affectation, so much ingenious knowledge so genteelly delivered I have never before observed in any one.[3] You would admire him still more, says a fourth, if you knew him more familiarly. That cheerfulness which you might remark in him is not a sudden flash struck out by company; it runs through the whole tenor of his life, and preserves a perpetual serenity on his countenance and tranquillity in his soul. He has met with severe trials, misfortunes as well as dangers, and by his greatness of mind was still superior to all of them.[4] The image, gentlemen, which you have here delineated of Cleanthes, cried I, is that of accomplished merit. Each of you has given a stroke of the pencil to his figure; and you have unawares exceeded all the pictures drawn by Gratian or Castiglione. A philosopher might select this character as a model of perfect virtue.

And as every quality which is useful or agreeable to ourselves or others is, in common life, allowed to be a part of personal merit, so

[1] Qualities useful to others.
[2] Qualities useful to the person himself.
[3] Qualities immediately agreeable to others.
[4] Qualities immediately agreeable to the person himself.

no other will ever be received where men judge of things by their natural, unprejudiced reason, without the delusive glosses of superstition and false religion. Celibacy, fasting, penance, mortification, self-denial, humility, silence, solitude, and the whole train of monkish virtues — for what reason are they everywhere rejected by men of sense, but because they serve to no manner of purpose; neither advance a man's fortune in the world, nor render him a more valuable member of society; neither qualify him for the entertainment of company, nor increase his power of self-enjoyment? We observe, on the contrary, that they cross all these desirable ends, stupify the understanding and harden the heart, obscure the fancy and sour the temper. We justly, therefore, transfer them to the opposite column and place them in the catalogue of vices; nor has any superstition force sufficient among men of the world to pervert entirely these natural sentiments. A gloomy, hair-brained enthusiast, after his death, may have a place in the calendar, but will scarcely ever be admitted, when alive, into intimacy and society, except by those who are as delirious and dismal as himself.

It seems a happiness in the present theory that it enters not into that vulgar dispute concerning the *degrees* of benevolence or self-love which prevail in human nature — a dispute which is never likely to have any issue, both because men who have taken part are not easily convinced, and because the phenomena which can be produced on either side are so dispersed, so uncertain, and subject to so many interpretations, that it is scarcely possible accurately to compare them or draw from them any determinate inference or conclusion. It is sufficient for our present purpose, if it be allowed what surely without the greatest absurdity cannot be disputed, that there is some benevolence, however small, infused into our bosom, some spark of friendship for human kind, some particle of the dove kneaded into our frame, along with the elements of the wolf and serpent. Let these generous sentiments be supposed ever so weak, let them be insufficient to move even a hand or finger of our body, they must still direct the determinations of our mind and, where everything else is equal, produce a cool preference of what is useful and serviceable to mankind above what is pernicious and dangerous. A *moral distinction*, therefore, immediately arises; a general sentiment of blame and approbation; a tendency, however faint, to the objects of the one, and a proportionable aversion to those of the other. Nor will those reasoners who so earnestly maintain the predominant selfishness of human kind be any wise scandalized at hearing of the weak sentiments of virtue implanted in our nature. On the contrary, they are found as ready to maintain the one tenet as the other; and their spirit of satire — for such it appears, rather than of corruption — naturally gives rise to both opinions, which have, indeed, a great and almost an indissoluble connexion together.

Avarice, ambition, vanity, and all passions vulgarly, though improperly, comprised under the denomination of *self-love*, are here excluded from our theory concerning the origin of morals, not because they are too weak, but because they have not a proper direction for that purpose. The notion of morals implies some sentiment common to all mankind, which recommends the same object to general approbation, and makes every man, or most men, agree in the same opinion or decision concerning it. It also implies some sentiment so universal and comprehensive as to extend to all mankind and render the actions and conduct, even of the persons the most remote, an object of applause or censure, according as they agree or disagree with that rule of right which is established. These two requisite circumstances belong alone to the sentiment of humanity here insisted on. The other passions produce in every breast many strong sentiments of desire and aversion, affection and hatred; but these neither are felt so much in common nor are so comprehensive as to be the foundation of any general system and established theory of blame or approbation.

When a man denominates another his *enemy*, his *rival*, his *antagonist*, his *adversary*, he is understood to speak the language of self-love, and to express sentiments peculiar to himself and arising from his particular circumstances and situation. But when he bestows on any man the epithets of *vicious* or *odious* or *depraved*, he then speaks another language, and expresses sentiments in which he expects all his audience are to concur with him. He must here, therefore, depart from his private and particular situation and must choose a point of view common to him with others; he must move some universal principle of the human frame and touch a string to which all mankind have an accord and symphony. If he mean, therefore, to express that this man possesses qualities whose tendency is pernicious to society, he has chosen this common point of view and has touched the principle of humanity in which every man, in some degree, concurs. While the human heart is compounded of the same elements as at present, it will never be wholly indifferent to public good, nor entirely unaffected with the tendency of characters and manners. And though this affection of humanity may not generally be esteemed so strong as vanity or ambition, yet, being common to all men, it can alone be the foundation of morals or of any general system of blame or praise. One man's ambition is not another's ambition, nor will the same event or object satisfy both; but the humanity of one man is the humanity of every one, and the same object touches this passion in all human creatures.

But the sentiments which arise from humanity are not only the same in all human creatures, and produce the same approbation or censure, but they also comprehend all human creatures; nor is there any one whose conduct or character is not, by their means, an object to every one of censure or approbation. On the contrary, those other passions, commonly denominated selfish, both produce different sentiments in each individual, according to his particular situation, and also contemplate the greater part of mankind with the utmost indifference and unconcern. Whoever has a high regard and esteem for me flatters my vanity; whoever expresses contempt mortifies and displeases me; but as my name is known but to a small part of mankind, there are few who come within the sphere of this passion, or excite, on its account, either my affection or disgust. But if you represent a tyrannical, insolent, or barbarous behaviour, in any country or in any age of the world, I soon carry my eye to the pernicious tendency of such a conduct and feel the sentiment of repugnance and displeasure towards it. No character can be so remote as to be, in this light, wholly indifferent to me. What is beneficial to society or to the person himself must still be preferred. And every quality or action of every human being must, by this means, be ranked under some class or denomination expressive of general censure or applause.

What more, therefore, can we ask to distinguish the sentiments dependent on humanity from those connected with any other passion, or to satisfy us why the former are the origin of morals, not the latter? Whatever conduct gains my approbation by touching my humanity procures also the applause of all mankind, by affecting the same principle in them; but what serves my avarice or ambition pleases these passions in me alone and affects not the avarice and ambition of the rest of mankind. There is no circumstance of conduct in any man, provided it have a beneficial tendency, that is not agreeable to my humanity, however remote the person; but every man, so far removed as neither to cross nor serve my avarice and ambition, is regarded as wholly indifferent by those passions. The distinction, therefore, between these species of sentiment being so great and evident, language must soon be moulded upon it and must invent a peculiar set of terms in order to express those universal sentiments of censure or approbation which arise from humanity or from views of general usefulness and its contrary. Virtue and Vice become then known; morals are recognized; certain general ideas are framed of human conduct and behaviour; such measures are expected from men in such situations. This action is determined to be conformable to our abstract rule; that other, contrary. And by such universal principles are the particular sentiments of self-love frequently controlled and limited.[5]

From instances of popular tumults, seditions, factions, panics, and of all passions which are shared with a multitude, we may learn the influence of society in exciting and supporting any emotion; while the most ungovernable disorders are raised, we find, by that means, from the slightest and most frivolous occasions. Solon was no very cruel, though, perhaps, an unjust legislator, who punished neuters in

---

[5] It seems certain, both from reason and experience, that a rude, untaught savage regulates chiefly his love and hatred by the ideas of private utility and injury, and has but faint conceptions of a general rule or system of behaviour. The man who stands opposite to him in battle, he hates heartily, not only for the present moment, which is almost unavoidable, but for ever after; nor is he satisfied without the most extreme punishment and vengeance. But we, accustomed to society and to more enlarged reflections, consider that this man is serving his own country and community, that any man in the same situation would do the same, that we ourselves, in like circumstances, observe a like conduct; that, in general, human society is best supported on such maxims, and by these suppositions and views we correct, in some measure, our ruder and narrower passions. And though much of our friendship and enmity be still regulated by private considerations of benefit and harm, we pay, at least, this homage to general rules, which we are accustomed to respect, that we commonly pervert our adversary's conduct by imputing malice or injustice to him in order to give vent to those passions which arise from self-love and private interest. When the heart is full of rage, it never wants pretences of this nature, though sometimes as frivolous as those from which Horace, being almost crushed by the fall of a tree, affects to accuse of parricide the first planter of it.

civil wars; and few, I believe, would, in such cases, incur the penalty, were their affection and discourse allowed sufficient to absolve them. No selfishness, and scarce any philosophy, have there force sufficient to support a total coolness and indifference; and he must be more or less than man who kindles not in the common blaze. What wonder then that moral sentiments are found of such influence in life, though springing from principles which may appear, at first sight, somewhat small and delicate? But these principles, we must remark, are social and universal; they form, in a manner, the *party* of humankind against vice or disorder, its common enemy. And as the benevolent concern for others is diffused, in a greater or less degree, over all men, and is the same in all, it occurs more frequently in discourse, is cherished by society and conversation, and the blame and approbation consequent on it are thereby roused from that lethargy into which they are probably lulled in solitary and uncultivated nature. Other passions, though perhaps originally stronger, yet being selfish and private, are often overpowered by its force and yield the dominion of our breast to those social and public principles.

Another spring of our constitution that brings a great addition of force to moral sentiments is the love of fame, which rules with such uncontrolled authority in all generous minds, and is often the grand object of all their designs and undertakings. By our continual and earnest pursuit of a character, a name, a reputation in the world, we bring our own deportment and conduct frequently in review, and consider how they appear in the eyes of those who approach and regard us. This constant habit of surveying ourselves, as it were, in reflection, keeps alive all the sentiments of right and wrong, and begets in noble natures a certain reverence for themselves as well as others, which is the surest guardian of every virtue. The animal conveniences and pleasures sink gradually in their value, while every inward beauty and moral grace is studiously acquired, and the mind is accomplished in every perfection which can adorn or embellish a rational creature.

Here is the most perfect morality with which we are acquainted; here is displayed the force of many sympathies. Our moral sentiment is itself a feeling chiefly of that nature, and our regard to a character with others seems to arise only from a care of preserving a character with ourselves; and in order to attain this end, we find it necessary to prop our tottering judgment on the correspondent approbation of mankind.

But, that we may accommodate matters and remove if possible every difficulty, let us allow all these reasonings to be false. Let us allow that, when we resolve the pleasure which arises from views of utility into the sentiments of humanity and sympathy, we have embraced a wrong hypothesis. Let us confess it necessary to find some other explication of that applause which is paid to objects, whether inanimate, animate, or rational, if they have a tendency to promote the welfare and advantage of mankind. However difficult it be to conceive that an object is approved of on account of its tendency to a certain end, while the end itself is totally indifferent — let us swallow this absurdity and consider what are the consequences. The preceding delineation or definition of Personal Merit must still retain its evidence and authority: it must still be allowed that every quality of the mind which is *useful* or *agreeable* to the *person himself* or to *others* communicates a pleasure to the spectator, engages his esteem, and is admitted under the honourable denomination of virtue or merit. Are not justice, fidelity, honour, veracity, allegiance, chastity, esteemed solely on account of their tendency to promote the good of society? Is not that tendency inseparable from humanity, benevolence, lenity, generosity, gratitude, moderation, tenderness, friendship, and all the other social virtues? Can it possibly be doubted that industry, discretion, frugality, secrecy, order, perseverance, forethought, judgment, and this whole class of virtues and accomplishments of which many pages would not contain the catalogue — can it be doubted, I say, that the tendency of these qualities to promote the interest and happiness of their possessor is the sole foundation of their merit? Who can dispute that a mind which supports a perpetual serenity and cheerfulness, a noble dignity and undaunted spirit, a tender affection and good-will to all around, as it has more enjoyment within itself, is also a more animating and rejoicing spectacle than if dejected with melancholy, tormented with anxiety, irritated with rage, or sunk into the most abject baseness and degeneracy? And as to the qualities immediately *agreeable to others*, they speak sufficiently for themselves; and he must be unhappy, indeed, either in his own temper or in his situation and company, who has never perceived the

charms of a facetious wit or flowing affability, of a delicate modesty
or decent genteelness of address and manner.

I am sensible that nothing can be more unphilosophical than to be
positive or dogmatical on any subject; and that, even if *excessive*
scepticism could be maintained, it would not be more destructive to
all just reasoning and inquiry. I am convinced that, where men are
the most sure and arrogant, they are commonly the most mistaken,
and have there given reins to passion without that proper deliberation
and suspense which can alone secure them from the grossest absurdities. Yet, I must confess that this enumeration puts the matter
in so strong a light that I cannot, *at present*, be more assured of
any truth, which I learn from reasoning and argument, than
that personal merit consists entirely in the usefulness or agreeableness of qualities to the person himself possessed of them, or to others
who have any intercourse with him. But when I reflect that, though
the bulk and figure of the earth have been measured and delineated,
though the motions of the tides have been accounted for, the order
and economy of the heavenly bodies subjected to their proper laws,
and Infinite itself reduced to calculation, yet men still dispute concerning the foundation of their moral duties. When I reflect on this,
I say, I fall back into diffidence and scepticism, and suspect that an
hypothesis so obvious, had it been a true one, would long ere now
have been received by the unanimous suffrage and consent of mankind.

Part II

Having explained the moral *approbation* attending merit or virtue,
there remains nothing but briefly to consider our interested *obligation*
to it, and to inquire whether every man who has any regard to his
own happiness and welfare will not best find his account in the practice
of every moral duty. If this can be clearly ascertained from the foregoing theory, we shall have the satisfaction to reflect that we have
advanced principles which not only, it is hoped, will stand the test of
reasoning and inquiry, but may contribute to the amendment of
men's lives and their improvement in morality and social virtue.
And though the philosophical truth of any proposition by no means
depends on its tendency to promote the interests of society, yet a man

has but a bad grace who delivers a theory, however true, which, he must confess, leads to a practice dangerous and pernicious. Why rake into those corners of nature which spread a nuisance all around? Why dig up the pestilence from the pit in which it is buried? The ingenuity of your researches may be admired, but your systems will be detested; and mankind will agree, if they cannot refute them, to sink them, at least, in eternal silence and oblivion. Truths which are *pernicious* to society, if any such there be, will yield to errors which are salutary and *advantageous*.

But what philosophical truths can be more advantageous to society than those here delivered, which represent virtue in all her genuine and most engaging charms, and makes us approach her with ease, familiarity, and affection? The dismal dress falls off, with which many divines, and some philosophers, have covered her; and nothing appears but gentleness, humanity, beneficence, affability, nay, even at proper intervals, play, frolic, and gaiety. She talks not of useless austerities and rigours, suffering and self-denial. She declares that her sole purpose is to make her votaries and all mankind, during every instant of their existence, if possible, cheerful and happy; nor does she ever willingly part with any pleasure but in hopes of ample compensation in some other period of their lives. The sole trouble which she demands is that of just calculation and a steady preference of the greater happiness. And if any austere pretenders approach her, enemies to joy and pleasure, she either rejects them as hypocrites and deceivers, or, if she admit them in her train, they are ranked, however, among the least favoured of her votaries.

And, indeed, to drop all figurative expression, what hopes can we ever have of engaging mankind to a practice which we confess full of austerity and rigour? Or what theory of morals can ever serve any useful purpose unless it can show, by a particular detail, that all the duties which it recommends are also the true interest of each individual? The peculiar advantage of the foregoing system seems to be that it furnishes proper mediums for that purpose.

That the virtues which are immediately *useful* or *agreeable* to the person possessed of them are desirable in a view to self-interest, it would surely be superfluous to prove. Moralists, indeed, may spare themselves all the pains which they often take in recommending these duties. To what purpose collect arguments to evince that temperance is advantageous, and the excesses of pleasure hurtful, when it appears that these excesses are only denominated such because they are hurtful; and that, if the unlimited use of strong liquors, for instance, no more impaired health or the faculties of mind and body than the use of air or water, it would not be a whit more vicious or blamable?

It seems equally superfluous to prove that the *companionable* virtues of good manners and wit, decency and genteelness, are more desirable than the contrary qualities. Vanity alone, without any other consideration, is a sufficient motive to make us wish for the possession of these accomplishments. No man was ever willingly deficient in this particular. All our failures here proceed from bad education, want of capacity, or a perverse and unpliable disposition. Would you have your company coveted, admired, followed, rather than hated, despised, avoided? Can any one seriously deliberate in the case? As no enjoyment is sincere without some reference to company and society, so no society can be agreeable or even tolerable where a man feels his presence unwelcome and discovers all around him symptoms of disgust and aversion.

But why, in the greater society or confederacy of mankind, should not the case be the same as in particular clubs and companies? Why is it more doubtful that the enlarged virtues of humanity, generosity, beneficence, are desirable with a view of happiness and self-interest, than the limited endowments of ingenuity and politeness? Are we apprehensive lest those social affections interfere, in a greater and more immediate degree than any other pursuits, with private utility, and cannot be gratified without some important sacrifice of honour and advantage? If so, we are but ill-instructed in the nature of the human passions, and are more influenced by verbal distinctions than by real differences.

Whatever contradiction may vulgarly be supposed between the *selfish* and *social* sentiments or dispositions, they are really no more opposite than selfish and ambitious, selfish and revengeful, selfish and vain. It is requisite that there be an original propensity of some kind, in order to be a basis to self-love, by giving a relish to the objects of its pursuit; and none more fit for this purpose than benevolence or humanity. The goods of fortune are spent in one gratification or another; the miser who accumulates his annual income and lends it out at interest has really spent it in the gratification of his avarice. And it would be difficult to show why a man is more a loser by a generous action than by any other method of expense, since the utmost which he can attain by the most elaborate selfishness is the indulgence of some affection.

Now if life without passion must be altogether insipid and tiresome, let a man suppose that he has full power of modelling his own disposition, and let him deliberate what appetite or desire he would choose for the foundation of his happiness and enjoyment. Every affection, he would observe, when gratified by success, gives a satisfaction proportioned to its force and violence; but besides this advantage, common to all, the immediate feeling of benevolence and friendship, humanity and kindness, is sweet, smooth, tender, and agreeable, independent of all fortune and accidents. These virtues are, besides, attended with a pleasing consciousness or remembrance, and keep us in humour with ourselves as well as others, while we retain the agreeable reflection of having done our part towards mankind and society. And though all men show a jealousy of our success in the pursuits of avarice and ambition, yet are we almost sure of their good-will and good wishes so long as we persevere in the paths of virtue and employ ourselves in the execution of generous plans and purposes. What other passion is there where we shall find so many advantages united: an agreeable sentiment, a pleasing consciousness, a good reputation? But of these truths, we may observe, men are, of themselves, pretty much convinced; nor are they deficient in their duty to society, because they would not wish to be generous, friendly, and humane, but because they do not feel themselves such.

Treating vice with the greatest candour and making it all possible concessions, we must acknowledge that there is not, in any instance, the smallest pretext for giving it the preference above virtue, with a view of self-interest; except, perhaps, in the case of justice, where a man, taking things in a certain light, may often seem to be a loser by his integrity. And though it is allowed that without a regard to property no society could subsist; yet, according to the imperfect way in which human affairs are conducted, a sensible knave, in particular incidents, may think that an act of iniquity or infidelity will make a considerable addition to his fortune, without causing any considerable breach in the social union and confederacy. That *honesty is the best policy* may be a good general rule, but is liable to many exceptions; and he, it may perhaps be thought, conducts himself with most wisdom who observes the general rule and takes advantage of all the exceptions.

I must confess that, if a man think that this reasoning much requires an answer, it would be a little difficult to find any which will to him appear satisfactory and convincing. If his heart rebel not against such pernicious maxims, if he feel no reluctance to the thoughts of villainy or baseness, he has indeed lost a considerable motive to virtue, and we may expect that this practice will be answerable to his speculation. But in all ingenuous natures the antipathy to treachery and roguery is too strong to be counterbalanced by any views of profit or pecuniary advantage. Inward peace of mind, consciousness of integrity, a satisfactory review of our own conduct — these are circumstances very requisite to happiness, and will be cherished and cultivated by every honest man who feels the importance of them.

Such a one has, besides, the frequent satisfaction of seeing knaves, with all their pretended cunning and abilities, betrayed by their own maxims; and while they purpose to cheat with moderation and secrecy, a tempting incident occurs, nature is frail, and they give into the snare, whence they can never extricate themselves without a total loss of reputation and the forfeiture of all future trust and confidence with mankind.

But were they ever so secret and successful, the honest man, if he has any tincture of philosophy or even common observation and reflection, will discover that they themselves are, in the end, the greatest dupes, and have sacrificed the invaluable enjoyment of a character, with themselves at least, for the acquisition of worthless toys and gewgaws. How little is requisite to supply the *necessities* of nature? And in a view to *pleasure*, what comparison between the unbought satisfaction of conversation, society, study, even health and the common beauties of nature, but above all the peaceful reflection on one's own conduct— what comparison, I say, between these and the feverish, empty amusements of luxury and expense? These natural pleasures, indeed, are really without price, both because they are below all price in their attainment, and above it in their enjoyment.

APPENDIX I

IF THE FOREGOING HYPOTHESIS be received, it will now be easy for us to determine the question first started,[1] concerning the general principles of morals; and though we postponed the decision of that question, lest it should then involve us in intricate speculations which are unfit for moral discourses, we may resume it at present and examine how far either *reason* or *sentiment* enters into all decisions of praise or censure.

One principal foundation of moral praise being supposed to lie in the usefulness of any quality or action, it is evident that *reason* must enter for a considerable share in all decisions of this kind, since nothing but that faculty can instruct us in the tendency of qualities and actions, and point out their beneficial consequences to society and to their possessor. In many cases this is an affair liable to great controversy: doubts may arise, opposite interests may occur, and a preference must be given to one side from very nice views and a small overbalance of utility. This is particularly remarkable in questions with regard to justice as is, indeed, natural to suppose, from that species of utility which attends this virtue.[2] Were every single instance of justice, like that of benevolence, useful to society, this would be a more simple state of the case, and seldom liable to great controversy. But as single instances of justice are often pernicious in their first and immediate tendency, and as the advantage to society results only from the observance of the general rule and from the concurrence and combination of several persons in the same equitable conduct, the case here becomes more intricate and involved. The various circumstances of society, the various consequences of any practice, the various interests which may be proposed; these, on many occasions, are doubtful, and subject to great discussion and

[1] Sect. I.
[2] See App. III.

inquiry. The object of municipal laws is to fix all the questions with regard to justice: the debates of civilians, the reflections of politicians, the precedents of history and public records, are all directed to the same purpose. And a very accurate *reason* or *judgment* is often requisite to give the true determination amidst such intricate doubts arising from obscure or opposite utilities.

But though reason, when fully assisted and improved, be sufficient to instruct us in the pernicious or useful tendency of qualities and actions, it is not alone sufficient to produce any moral blame or approbation. Utility is only a tendency to a certain end; and were the end totally indifferent to us, we should feel the same indifference towards the means. It is requisite a *sentiment* should here display itself, in order to give a preference to the useful above the pernicious tendencies. This sentiment can be no other than a feeling for the happiness of mankind and a resentment of their misery, since these are the different ends which virtue and vice have a tendency to promote. Here therefore *reason* instructs us in the several tendencies of actions, and *humanity* makes a distinction in favour of those which are useful and beneficial.

This partition between the faculties of understanding and sentiment, in all moral decisions, seems clear from the preceding hypothesis. But I shall suppose that hypothesis false; it will then be requisite to look out for some other theory that may be satisfactory, and I dare venture to affirm that none such will ever be found so long as we suppose reason to be the sole source of morals. To prove this, it will be proper to weigh the five following considerations.

I. It is easy for a false hypothesis to maintain some appearance of truth, while it keeps wholly in generals, makes use of undefined terms, and employs comparisons instead of instances. This is particularly remarkable in that philosophy which ascribes the discernment of all moral distinctions to reason alone, without the concurrence of sentiment. It is impossible that in any particular instance this hypothesis can so much as be rendered intelligible, whatever specious figure it may make in general declamations and discourses. Examine the crime of *ingratitude*, for instance, which has place wherever we observe good-will expressed and known, together with good-offices performed, on the one side, and a return of ill-will or indifference with ill-offices or neglect on the other: anatomize all these circumstances and examine, by your reason alone, in what consists the demerit or blame. You never will come to any issue or conclusion.

Reason judges either of *matter of fact* or of *relations*. Enquire then, *first*, where is that matter of fact which we here call *crime;* point it out, determine the time of its existence, describe its essence or nature, explain the sense or faculty to which it discovers itself. It resides in the mind of the person who is ungrateful. He must, therefore, feel it and be conscious of it. But nothing is there, except the passion of ill-will or absolute indifference. You cannot say that these, of themselves, always and in all circumstances are crimes. No, they are only crimes when directed towards persons who have before expressed and displayed good-will towards us. Consequently, we may infer that the crime of ingratitude is not any particular individual *fact*, but arises from a complication of circumstances which, being presented to the spectator, excites the *sentiment* of blame by the particular structure and fabric of his mind.

This representation, you say, is false. Crime, indeed, consists not in a particular *fact*, of whose reality we are assured by *reason,* but it consists in certain *moral relations*, discovered by reason, in the same manner as we discover by reason the truths of geometry or algebra. But what are the relations, I ask, of which you here talk? In the case stated above, I see first good-will and good-offices in one person, then ill-will and ill-offices in the other. Between these, there is a relation of *contrariety*. Does the crime consist in that relation? But suppose a person bore me ill-will or did me ill-offices, and I, in return, were indifferent towards him, or did him good offices. Here is the same relation of *contrariety,* and yet my conduct is often highly laudable. Twist and turn this matter as much as you will, you can never rest the morality on relation, but must have recourse to the decisions of sentiment.

When it is affirmed that two and three are equal to the half of ten, this relation of equality I understand perfectly. I conceive that, if ten be divided into two parts, of which one has as many units as the other, and if any of these parts be compared to two added to three, it will contain as many units as that compound number. But when you draw thence a comparison to moral relations, I own that I am altogether at a loss to understand you. A moral action, a crime, such as ingratitude, is a complicated object. Does the morality consist in the relation of its parts to each other? How? After what manner? Specify the relation: be more particular and explicit in your propositions, and you will easily see their falsehood.

No, say you, the morality consists in the relation of actions to the rule of right; and they are denominated good or ill, according as they agree or disagree with it. What then is this rule of right? In what does it consist? How is it determined? By reason, you say, which examines the moral relations of actions. So that moral relations are determined by the comparison of action to a rule. And that rule is determined by considering the moral relations of objects. Is not this fine reasoning?

All this is metaphysics, you cry. That is enough; there needs nothing more to give a strong presumption of falsehood. Yes, reply I, here are metaphysics surely; but they are all on your side, who advance an abstruse hypothesis which can never be made intelligible, nor quadrate with any particular instance or illustration. The hypothesis which we embrace is plain. It maintains that morality is determined by sentiment. It defines virtue to be *whatever mental action or quality gives to a spectator the pleasing sentiment of approbation;* and vice the contrary. We then proceed to examine a plain matter of fact, to wit, what actions have this influence. We consider all the circumstances in which these actions agree, and thence endeavour to extract some general observations with regard to these sentiments. If you call this metaphysics and find anything abstruse here, you need only conclude that your turn of mind is not suited to the moral sciences.

II. When a man, at any time, deliberates concerning his own conduct — as, whether he had better, in a particular emergence, assist a brother or a benefactor — he must consider these separate relations, with all the circumstances and situations of the persons, in order to determine the superior duty and obligation; and in order to determine the proportion of lines in any triangle, it is necessary to examine the nature of that figure, and the relation which its several parts bear to each other. But notwithstanding this appearing similarity in the two cases, there is, at bottom, an extreme difference between them. A speculative reasoner concerning triangles or circles considers the several known and given relations of the parts of these figures, and thence infers some unknown relation which is dependent on the former. But in moral deliberations we must be acquainted beforehand with all the objects and all their relations to each other, and from a comparison of the whole fix our choice or approbation. No new fact to be ascertained; no new relation to be discovered. All the circumstances of the case are supposed to be laid before us, ere we can fix any sentence of blame or approbation. If any material circumstance be yet unknown or doubtful, we must first employ our inquiry or intellectual faculties to assure us of it, and must suspend for a time all moral decision or sentiment. While we are ignorant whether a man were aggressor or not, how can we determine whether the person who killed him be criminal or innocent? But after every circumstance, every relation is known, the understanding has no further room to operate, nor any object on which it could employ itself. The approbation or blame which then ensues cannot be the work of the judgment, but of the heart, and is not a speculative proposition or affirmation, but an active feeling or sentiment. In the disquisitions of the understanding, from known circumstances and relations we infer some new and unknown. In moral decisions, all the circumstances and relations must be previously known; and the mind, from the contemplation of the whole, feels some new impression of affection or disgust, esteem or contempt, approbation or blame.

Hence the great difference between a mistake of *fact* and one of *right;* and hence the reason why the one is commonly criminal and not the other. When Oedipus killed Laius, he was ignorant of the relation, and from circumstances, innocent and involuntary, formed erroneous opinions concerning the action which he committed. But when Nero killed Agrippina, all the relations between himself and the person, and all the circumstances of the fact, were previously known to him; but the motive of revenge, or fear, or interest, prevailed in his savage heart over the sentiments of duty and humanity. And when we express that detestation against him to which he himself, in a little time, became insensible, it is not that we see any relations of which he was ignorant, but that, for the rectitude of our disposition, we feel sentiments against which he was hardened from flattery and a long perseverance in the most enormous crimes. In these sentiments then, not in a discovery of relations of any kind, do all moral determinations consist. Before we can pretend to form any decision of this kind, everything must be known and ascertained on the side of the object or action. Nothing remains but to feel, on our part, some sentiment of blame or approbation, whence we pronounce the action criminal or virtuous.

III. This doctrine will become still more evident if we compare moral beauty with natural, to which in many particulars it bears so near a resemblance. It is on the proportion, relation, and position of parts, that all natural beauty depends; but it would be absurd thence to infer that the perception of beauty, like that of truth in geometrical problems, consists wholly in the perception of relations, and was performed entirely by the understanding or intellectual faculties. In all the sciences, our mind from the known relations investigates the unknown. But in all decisions of taste or external beauty, all the relations are beforehand obvious to the eye; and we thence proceed to feel a sentiment of complacency or disgust, according to the nature of the object and disposition of our organs.

Euclid has fully explained all the qualities of the circle, but has not in any proposition said a word of its beauty. The reason is evident. The beauty is not a quality of the circle. It lies not in any part of the line, whose parts are equally distant from a common centre. It is only the effect which that figure produces upon the mind, whose peculiar fabric of structure renders it susceptible of such sentiments. In vain would you look for it in the circle, or seek it, either by your senses or by mathematical reasoning, in all the properties of that figure.

Attend to Palladio and Perrault, while they explain all the parts and proportions of a pillar. They talk of the cornice, and frieze, and base, and entablature, and shaft, and architrave, and give the description and position of each of these members. But should you ask the description and position of its beauty, they would readily reply that the beauty is not in any of the parts or members of a pillar, but results from the whole, when that complicated figure is presented to an intelligent mind susceptible to those finer sensations. Till such a spectator appear, there is nothing but a figure of such particular dimensions and proportions: from his sentiments alone arise its elegance and beauty.

Again, attend to Cicero while he paints the crimes of a Verres or a Catiline. You must acknowledge that the moral turpitude results in the same manner from the contemplation of the whole, when presented to a being whose organs have such a particular structure and formation. The orator may paint rage, insolence, barbarity on the one side; meekness, suffering, sorrow, innocence on the other. But if you feel no indignation or compassion arise in you from this complication of circumstances, you would in vain ask him, in what consists the crime or villainy, which he so vehemently exclaims against? At what time or on what subject it first began to exist? And what has a few months afterwards become of it, when every disposition and thought of all the actors is totally altered or annihilated? No satisfactory answer can be given to any of these questions upon the abstract hypothesis of morals; and we must at last acknowledge that the crime or immorality is no particular fact or relation which can be the object of the understanding, but arises entirely from the sentiment of disapprobation which, by the structure of human nature, we unavoidably feel on the apprehension of barbarity or treachery.

IV. Inanimate objects may bear to each other all the same relations which we observe in moral agents, though the former can never be the object of love or hatred, nor are consequently susceptible of merit or iniquity. A young tree, which over-tops and destroys its parent, stands in all the same relations with Nero when he murdered Agrippina and, if morality consisted merely in relations, would no doubt be equally criminal.

V. It appears evident that the ultimate ends of human actions can never, in any case, be accounted for by *reason*, but recommend themselves entirely to the sentiments and affections of mankind, without any dependence on the intellectual faculties. Ask a man *why he uses exercise;* he will answer *because he desires to keep his health.* If you then enquire *why he desires health*, he will readily reply *because sickness is painful.* If you push your enquiries further and desire a reason *why he hates pain*, it is impossible he can ever give any. This is an ultimate end, and is never referred to any other object.

Perhaps to your second question, *why he desires health*, he may also reply that *it is necessary for the exercise of his calling.* If you ask *why he is anxious on that head*, he will answer *because he desires to get money.* If you demand *why? It is the instrument of pleasure*, says he. And beyond this it is an absurdity to ask for a reason. It is impossible there can be a progress *in infinitum;* and that one thing can always be a reason why another is desired. Something must be desirable on its own account, and because of its immediate accord or agreement with human sentiment and affection.

Now as virtue is an end, and is desirable on its own account without fee and reward, merely for the immediate satisfaction which it conveys, it is requisite that there should be some sentiment which it touches, some internal taste or feeling, or whatever you may please to call it, which distinguishes moral good and evil, and which embraces the one and rejects the other.

Thus the distinct boundaries and offices of *reason* and of *taste* are easily ascertained. The former conveys the knowledge of truth and falsehood; the latter gives the sentiment of beauty and deformity, vice and virtue. The one discovers objects as they really stand in nature, without addition and diminution; the other has a productive faculty and, gilding or staining all natural objects with the colours borrowed from internal sentiment, raises in a manner a new creation. Reason, being cool and disengaged, is no motive to action, and directs only the impulse received from appetite or inclination, by showing us the means of attaining happiness or avoiding misery. Taste, as it gives pleasure or pain, and thereby constitutes happiness or misery, becomes a motive to action, and is the first spring or impulse to desire and volition. From circumstances and relations, known or supposed, the former leads us to the discovery of the concealed and unknown; after all circumstances and relations are laid before us, the latter makes us feel from the whole a new sentiment of blame or approbation. The standard of the one, being founded on the nature of things, is eternal and inflexible, even by the will of the Supreme Being; the standard of the other, arising from the eternal frame and constitution of animals, is ultimately derived from that Supreme Will which bestowed on each being its peculiar nature and arranged the several classes and orders of existence.

APPENDIX II

THERE IS A PRINCIPLE, supposed to prevail among many, which is utterly incompatible with all virtue or moral sentiment; and as it can proceed from nothing but the most depraved disposition, so in its turn it tends still further to encourage that depravity. This principle is that all *benevolence* is mere hypocrisy, friendship a cheat, public spirit a farce, fidelity a snare to procure trust and confidence; and that, while all of us, at bottom, pursue only our private interest, we wear these fair disguises in order to put others off their guard and expose them the more to our wiles and machinations. What heart one must be possessed of who possesses such principles, and who feels no internal sentiment that belies so pernicious a theory, it is easy to imagine; and also what degree of affection and benevolence he can bear to a species whom he represents under such odious colours, and supposes so little susceptible of gratitude or any return of affection. Or if we should not ascribe these principles wholly to a corrupted heart, we must at least account for them from the most careless and precipitate examination. Superficial reasoners, indeed, observing many false pretences among mankind, and feeling, perhaps, no very strong restraint in their own disposition, might draw a general and a hasty conclusion that all is equally corrupted, and that men, different from all other animals, and indeed from all other species of existence, admit of no degrees of good or bad, but are, in every instance, the same creatures under different disguises and appearances.

There is another principle, somewhat resembling the former, which has been much insisted on by philosophers, and has been the foundation of many a system: that, whatever affection one may feel or imagine he feels for others, no passion is or can be disinterested; that the most generous friendship, however sincere, is a modification of self-love; and that, even unknown to ourselves, we seek only our own gratification while we appear the most deeply engaged in schemes for the liberty and happiness of mankind. By a turn of imagination, by a refinement of reflection, by an enthusiasm of passion, we seem to take part in the interests of others, and imagine ourselves divested of all selfish considerations; but, at bottom, the most generous patriot and most niggardly miser, the bravest hero and most abject coward, have, in every action, an equal regard to their own happiness and welfare.

Whoever concludes from the seeming tendency of this opinion that those who make profession of it cannot possibly feel the true sentiments of benevolence or have any regard for genuine virtue, will often find himself, in practice, very much mistaken. Probity and honour were no strangers to Epicurus and his sect. Atticus and Horace seem to have enjoyed from nature, and cultivated by reflection, as generous and friendly dispositions as any disciple of the austerer schools. And among the modern, Hobbes and Locke, who maintained the selfish system of morals, lived irreproachable lives, though the former lay not under any restraint of religion which might supply the defects of his philosophy.

An epicurean or a Hobbist readily allows that there is such a thing as a friendship in the world, without hypocrisy or disguise, though he may attempt, by a philosophical chemistry, to resolve the elements of this passion, if I may so speak, into those of another, and explain every affection to be self-love, twisted and moulded by a particular turn of imagination into a variety of appearances. But as the same turn of imagination prevails not in every man nor gives the same direction to the original passion, this is sufficient even according to the selfish system to make the widest difference in human characters, and denominate one man virtuous and humane, another vicious and meanly interested. I esteem the man whose self-love, by whatever means, is so directed as to give him a concern for others and render him serviceable to society, as I hate or despise him who has no regard to anything beyond his own gratifications and enjoyments. In vain would you suggest that these characters, though seemingly opposite, are at bottom the same, and that a very inconsiderable turn of thought forms the whole difference between them. Each character, notwithstanding these inconsiderable differences, appears to me, in practice, pretty durable and untransmutable. And I find not in this more than in other subjects that the natural sentiments arising from the general appearances of things are easily destroyed by subtile reflections concerning the minute origin of these appearances. Does not the lively, cheerful colour of a countenance inspire me with complacency and pleasure, even though I learn from philosophy that all difference of complexion arises from the most minute differences of thickness in the most minute parts of the skin, by means of which a superficies is qualified to reflect one of the original colours of light, and absorb the others?

But though the question concerning the universal or partial selfishness of man be not so material, as is usually imagined, to morality and practice, it is certainly of consequence in the speculative science of human nature, and is a proper object of curiosity and enquiry. It may not, therefore, be unsuitable in this place to bestow a few reflections upon it.[1]

The most obvious objection to the selfish hypothesis is that, as it is contrary to common feeling and our most unprejudiced notions, there is required the highest stretch of philosophy to establish so extraordinary a paradox. To the most careless observer there appear to be such dispositions as benevolence and generosity, such affections as love, friendship, compassion, gratitude. These sentiments have their causes, effects, objects, and operations, marked by common language and observation, and plainly distinguished from those of the selfish passions. And as this is the obvious appearance of things, it must be admitted, till some hypothesis be discovered which, by penetrating deeper into human nature, may prove the former affections to be nothing but modifications of the latter. All attempts of this kind have hitherto proved fruitless, and seem to have proceeded entirely from that love of *simplicity* which has been the source of much false reasoning in philosophy. I shall not here enter into any detail on the present subject. Many able philosophers have shown the insufficiency

---

[1] Benevolence naturally divides into two kinds, the *general* and the *particular*. The first is where we have no friendship or connexion or esteem for the person, but feel only a general sympathy with him or a compassion for his pains, and a congratulation with his pleasures. The other species of benevolence is founded on an opinion of virtue, on services done us, or on some particular connexions. Both these sentiments must be allowed real in human nature; but whether they will resolve into some nice considerations of self-love is a question more curious than important. The former sentiment, to wit, that of general benevolence, or humanity, or sympathy, we shall have occasion frequently to treat of in the course of this inquiry; and I assume it as real from general experience, without any other proof.

of these systems. And I shall take for granted what, I believe, the smallest reflection will make evident to every impartial enquirer.

But the nature of the subject furnishes the strongest presumption that no better system will ever, for the future, be invented, in order to account for the origin of the benevolent from the selfish affections, and reduce all the various emotions of the human mind to a perfect simplicity. The case is not the same in this species of philosophy as in physics. Many an hypothesis in nature, contrary to first appearances, has been found, on more accurate scrutiny, solid and satisfactory. Instances of this kind are so frequent that a judicious as well as witty philosopher [2] has ventured to affirm, if there be more than one way in which any phenomenon may be produced, that there is general presumption for its arising from the causes which are the least obvious and familiar. But the presumption always lies on the other side, in all enquiries concerning the origin of our passions and of the internal operations of the human mind. The simplest and most obvious cause which can there be assigned for any phenomenon is probably the true one. When a philosopher, in the explication of his system, is obliged to have recourse to some very intricate and refined reflections, and to suppose them essential to the production of any passion or emotion, we have reason to be extremely on our guard against so fallacious an hypothesis. The affections are not susceptible of any impression from the refinements of reason or imagination; and it is always found that a vigorous exertion of the latter faculties necessarily, from the narrow capacity of the human mind, destroys all activity in the former. Our predominant motive or intention is, indeed, frequently concealed from ourselves when it is mingled and confounded with other motives which the mind, from vanity or self-conceit, is desirous of supposing more prevalent; but there is no instance that a concealment of this nature has ever arisen from the abstruseness and intricacy of the motive. A man that has lost a friend and patron may flatter himself that all his grief arises from generous sentiments, without any mixture of narrow or interested considerations; but a man that grieves for a valuable friend who needed his patronage and protection, how can we suppose that his passionate tenderness arises from some metaphysical regards to a self-interest which has no foundation or reality? We may as well

[2] Mons. Fontenelle.

imagine that minute wheels and springs, like those of a watch, give motion to a loaded waggon, as account for the origin of passion from such abstruse reflections.

Animals are found susceptible of kindness, both to their own species and to ours; nor is there, in this case, the least suspicion of disguise or artifice. Shall we account for all *their* sentiments, too, from refined deductions of self-interest? Or if we admit a disinterested benevolence in the inferior species, by what rule of analogy can we refuse it in the superior?

Love between the sexes begets a complacency and good-will very distinct from the gratification of an appetite. Tenderness to their offspring, in all sensible beings, is commonly able alone to counter-balance the strongest motives of self-love, and has no manner of dependence on that affection. What interest can a fond mother have in view, who loses her health by assiduous attendance on her sick child, and afterwards languishes and dies of grief when freed by its death from the slavery of that attendance?

Is gratitude no affection of the human breast, or is that a word merely, without any meaning or reality? Have we no satisfaction in one man's company above another's, and no desire of the welfare of our friend, even though absence or death should prevent us from all participation in it? Or what is it commonly that gives us any partici-pation in it, even while alive and present, but our affection and regard to him?

These and a thousand other instances are marks of a general benevo-lence in human nature, where no *real* interest binds us to the object. And how an *imaginary* interest, known and avowed for such, can be the origin of any passion or emotion seems difficult to explain. No satisfactory hypothesis of this kind has yet been discovered, nor is there the smallest probability that the future industry of men will ever be attended with more favourable success.

But further, if we consider rightly of the matter, we shall find that the hypothesis which allows of a disinterested benevolence, distinct from self-love, has really more *simplicity* in it, and is more conformable to the analogy of nature than that which pretends to resolve all friendship and humanity into this latter principle. There are bodily wants or appetites acknowledged by every one, which necessarily precede all sensual enjoyment and carry us directly to seek possession of the object. Thus hunger and thirst have eating and drinking for their end; and from the gratification of these primary appetites arises a pleasure which may become the object of another species of desire or inclination that is secondary and interested. In the same manner there are mental passions by which we are impelled immediately to seek particular objects, such as fame, or power, or vengeance, without any regard to interest; and when these objects are attained a pleasing enjoyment ensues as the consequence of our indulged affections. Nature must, by the internal frame and constitution of the mind, give an original propensity to fame, ere we can reap any pleasure from that acquisition, or pursue it from motives of self-love and desire of happiness. If I have no vanity, I take no delight in praise; if I be void of ambition, power gives me no enjoyment; if I be not angry, the punishment of an adversary is totally indifferent to me. In all these cases there is a passion which points immediately to the object and constitutes it our good or happiness, as there are other secondary passions which afterwards arise and pursue it as a part of our happiness, when once it is constituted such by our original affections. Were there no appetite of any kind antecedent to self-love, that propensity could scarcely ever exert itself, because we should in that case have felt few and slender pains or pleasures, and have little misery or happiness to avoid or to pursue.

Now where is the difficulty in conceiving that this may likewise be the case with benevolence and friendship, and that, from the original frame of our temper, we may feel a desire of another's happiness or good, which, by means of that affection, becomes our own good, and is afterwards pursued from the combined motives of benevolence and self-enjoyments? Who sees not that vengeance, from the force alone of passion, may be so eagerly pursued as to make us knowingly neglect every consideration of ease, interest, or safety, and, like some vindictive animals, infuse our very souls into the wounds we give an enemy.[3] And what a malignant philosophy must it be that will not allow to humanity and friendship the same privileges which are undisputably granted to the darker passions of enmity and resentment. Such a philosophy is more like a satyr than a true delineation or description of human nature, and may be a good foundation for paradoxical wit and raillery, but is a very bad one for any serious argument or reasoning.

---

[3] *Animasque in vulnere ponunt*—Virg. *Dum alteri noceat, sui negligens*, says Seneca of anger.—*De Ira*, I. i.

APPENDIX III

THE INTENTION of this Appendix is to give some more particular explication of the origin and nature of Justice, and to mark some differences between it and the other virtues.

The social virtues of humanity and benevolence exert their influence immediately by a direct tendency or instinct, which chiefly keeps in view the simple object, moving the affections, and comprehends not any scheme or system nor the consequences resulting from the concurrence, imitation, or example of others. A parent flies to the relief of his child, transported by that natural sympathy which actuates him, and which affords no leisure to reflect on the sentiments or conduct of the rest of mankind in like circumstances. A generous man cheerfully embraces an opportunity of serving his friend, because he then feels himself under the dominion of the beneficent affections, nor is he concerned whether any other person in the universe were ever before actuated by such noble motives, or will ever afterwards prove their influence. In all these cases the social passions have in view a single individual object and pursue the safety or happiness alone of the person loved and esteemed. With this they are satisfied; in this they acquiesce. And as the good resulting from their benign influence is in itself complete and entire, it also excites the moral sentiment of approbation, without any reflection on further consequences, and without any more enlarged views of the concurrence or imitation of the other members of society. On the contrary, were the generous friend or disinterested patriot to stand alone in the practice of beneficence, this would rather enhance his value in our eyes and join the praise of rarity and novelty to his other more exalted merits.

The case is not the same with the social virtues of justice and fidelity. They are highly useful or indeed absolutely necessary to the well-being of mankind. But the benefit resulting from them is not the consequence of every individual single act, but arises from the whole scheme or system concurred in by the whole or the greater part of the society. General peace and order are the attendants of justice or a general abstinence from the possessions of others; but a particular regard to the particular right of one individual citizen may frequently, considered in itself, be productive of pernicious consequences. The result of the individual acts is here, in many instances, directly opposite to that of the whole system of actions; and the former may be extremely hurtful, while the latter is, to the highest degree, advantageous. Riches inherited from a parent are, in a bad man's hand, the instrument of mischief. The right of succession may, in one instance, be hurtful. Its benefit arises only from the observance of the general rule; and it is sufficient, if compensation be thereby made for all the ills and inconveniences which flow from particular characters and situations.

Cyrus, young and unexperienced, considered only the individual case before him and reflected on a limited fitness and convenience, when he assigned the long coat to the tall boy, and the short coat to the other of smaller size. His governor instructed him better, while he pointed out more enlarged views and consequences, and informed his pupil of the general, inflexible rules necessary to support general peace and order in society.

The happiness and prosperity of mankind, arising from the social virtue of benevolence and its subdivisions, may be compared to a wall built by many hands, which still rises by each stone that is heaped upon it, and receives increase proportional to the diligence and care of each workman. The same happiness raised by the social virtue of justice and its subdivisions may be compared to the building of a vault, where each individual stone would, of itself, fall to the ground; nor is the whole fabric supported but by the mutual assistance and combination of its corresponding parts.

All the laws of nature, which regulate property, as well as all civil laws, are general, and regard alone some essential circumstances of the case, without taking into consideration the characters, situations, and connexions of the person concerned, or any particular consequences which may result from the determination of these laws in any particular case which offers. They deprive, without scruple, a beneficent man of all his possessions, if acquired by mistake without a good title, in order to bestow them on a selfish miser who has already heaped up immense stores of superfluous riches. Public utility requires that property should be regulated by general inflexible rules; and though such rules are adopted as best serve the same end of public utility, it is impossible for them to prevent all particular hardships or make beneficial consequences result from every individual case. It is sufficient if the whole plan or scheme be necessary to the support of civil society, and if the balance of good, in the main, do thereby preponderate much above that of evil. Even the general laws of the universe, though planned by infinite wisdom, cannot exclude all evil or inconvenience in every particular operation.

It has been asserted by some that justice arises from human conventions and proceeds from the voluntary choice, consent, or combination of mankind. If by *convention* be here meant a *promise* — which is the most usual sense of the word — nothing can be more absurd than this position. The observance of promises is itself one of the most considerable parts of justice, and we are not surely bound to keep our word because we have given our word to keep it. But if by convention be meant a sense of common interest, which sense each man feels in his own breast, which he remarks in his fellows, and which carries him, in concurrence with others, into a general plan or system of actions which tends to public utility, it must be owned that in this sense justice arises from human conventions. For if it be allowed — what is, indeed, evident — that the particular consequences of a particular act of justice may be hurtful to the public as well as to individuals, it follows that every man, in embracing that virtue, must have an eye to the whole plan or system, and must expect the concurrence of his fellows in the same conduct and behaviour. Did all his views terminate in the consequences of each act of his own, his benevolence and humanity as well as his self-love might often prescribe to him measures of conduct very different from those which are agreeable to the strict rules of right and justice.

Thus two men pull the oars of a boat by common convention for common interest, without any promise or contract; thus gold and silver are made the measures of exchange; thus speech and words and language are fixed by human convention and agreement. Whatever is advantageous to two or more persons if all perform their part, but what loses all advantage if only one perform, can arise from no other principle. There would otherwise be no motive for any one of them to enter into that scheme of conduct.[1]

The word *natural* is commonly taken in so many senses and is of so loose a signification that it seems vain to dispute whether justice be natural or not. If self-love, if benevolence be natural to man; if reason and forethought be also natural; then may the same epithet be applied to justice, order, fidelity, property, society. Men's inclination, their necessities lead them to combine; their understanding and experience tell them that this combination is impossible where each governs himself by no rule and pays no regard to the possessions of others. And from these passions and reflections conjoined, as soon as we observe like passions and reflections in others, the sentiment of justice, throughout all ages, has infallibly and certainly had place to some degree or other in every individual of the human species. In so sagacious an animal, what necessarily arises from the exertion of his intellectual faculties may justly be esteemed natural.[2]

Among all civilized nations it has been the constant endeavour to remove everything arbitrary and partial from the decision of property,

---

[1] This theory concerning the origin of property and, consequently, of justice is in the main the same with that hinted at and adopted by Grotius, "Hinc discimus, quae fuerit causa, ob quam a primaeva communione rerum primo mobilium, deinde et immobilium discessum est: nimirum quod cum non contenti homines vesci sponte natis, antra habitare, corpore aut nudo agere, aut corticibus arborum ferarumve pellibus vestito, vitae genus exquisitius delegissent, industria opus fuit, quam singuli rebus singulis adhiberent; quo minus autem fructus in commune conferrentur, primum obstitit locorum, in quae homines discesserunt, distantia, deinde justitiae et amoris defectus, per quem fiebat, ut nec in labore, nec in consumtione fructuum, quae debebat, aequalitas servaretur. Simul discimus, quomodo res in proprietatem iverint; non animi actu solo, neque enim scire alii poterant, quid alii suum esse vellent, ut eo abstinerent, et idem velle plures poterant; sed pacto quodam aut expresso, ut per divisionem, aut tacito, ut per occupationem." *De Jure Belli et Pacis.* Lib. ii. cap. 2. § 2. art. 4 and 5.

[2] Natural may be opposed either to what is *unusual, miraculous*, or *artificial*. In the two former senses, justice and property are undoubtedly natural. But as they suppose reason, forethought, design, and a social union and confederacy among men, perhaps that epithet cannot strictly, in the last sense, be applied to them. Had men lived without society, property had never been known, and neither justice nor injustice had ever existed. But society among human creatures had been impossible without reason and forethought. Inferior animals that united are guided by instinct, which supplies the place of reason. But all these disputes are merely verbal.

and to fix the sentence of judges by such general views and considerations as may be equal to every member of society. For besides that nothing could be more dangerous than to accustom the bench, even in the smallest instance, to regard private friendship or enmity, it is certain that men, where they imagine that there was no other reason for the preference of their adversary but personal favour, are apt to entertain the strongest ill-will against the magistrates and judges. When natural reason, therefore, points out no fixed view of public utility by which a controversy of property can be decided, positive laws are often framed to supply its place and direct the procedure of all courts of judicature. Where these too fail, as often happens, precedents are called for; and a former decision, though given itself without any sufficient reason, justly becomes a sufficient reason for a new decision. If direct laws and precedents be wanting, imperfect and indirect ones are brought in aid; and the controverted case is ranged under them by analogical reasonings, and comparisons, and similitudes, and correspondences, which are often more fanciful than real. In general, it may safely be affirmed that jurisprudence is, in this respect, different from all the sciences, and that in many of its nicer questions there cannot properly be said to be truth or falsehood on either side. If one pleader bring the case under any former law or precedent, by a refined analogy or comparison, the opposite pleader is not at a loss to find an opposite analogy or comparison; and the preference given by the judge is often founded more on taste and imagination than on any solid argument. Public utility is the general object of all courts of judicature; and this utility too requires a stable rule in all controversies; but where several rules, nearly equal and indifferent, present themselves, it is a very slight turn of thought which fixes the decision in favour of either party.[3]

---

[3] That there be a separation or distinction of possessions, and that this separation be steady and constant: this is absolutely required by the interests of society, and hence the origin of justice and property. What possessions are assigned to particular persons, this is, generally speaking, pretty indifferent, and is often determined by very frivolous views and considerations. We shall mention a few particulars.

Were a society formed among several independent members, the most obvious rule which could be agreed on would be to annex property to *present* possession, and leave every one a right to what he at present enjoys. The relation of possession which takes place between the person and the object naturally draws on the relation of property.

We may just observe, before we conclude this subject, that after the laws of justice are fixed by views of general utility, the injury, the hardship, the harm, which result to any individual from a violation of them enter very much into consideration and are a great source of that universal blame which attends every wrong or iniquity. By the laws of society, this coat, this horse is mine, and *ought* to remain per-

For a like reason, occupation or first possession becomes the foundation of property.

Where a man bestows labour and industry upon any object which before belonged to nobody, as in cutting down and shaping a tree, in cultivating a field, etc., the alterations which he produces causes a relation between him and the object, and naturally engages us to annex it to him by the new relation of property. This cause here concurs with the public utility which consists in the encouragement given to industry and labour.

Perhaps, too, private humanity towards the possessor concurs in this instance with the other motives, and engages us to leave with him what he has acquired by his sweat and labour, and what he has flattered himself in the constant enjoyment of. For though private humanity can, by no means, be the origin of justice, since the latter virtue so often contradicts the former; yet when the rule of separate and constant possession is once formed by the indispensable necessities of society, private humanity and an aversion to the doing a hardship to another may, in a particular instance, give rise to a particular rule of property.

I am much inclined to think that the right succession or inheritance much depends on those connexions of the imagination, and that the relation to a former proprietor begetting a relation to the object is the cause why the property is transferred to a man after the death of his kinsman. It is true, industry is more encouraged by the transference of possession to children or near relations; but this consideration will only have place in a cultivated society, whereas the right of succession is regarded even among the greatest Barbarians.

Acquisition of property by *accession* can be explained no way but by having recourse to the relations and connexions of the imaginations.

The property of rivers, by the laws of most nations and by the natural turn of our thoughts, is attributed to the proprietors of their banks, excepting such vast rivers as the Rhine or the Danube, which seem too large to follow as an accession to the property of the neighbouring fields. Yet even these rivers are considered as the property of that nation through whose dominions they run; the idea of a nation being of a suitable bulk to correspond with them, and bear them such a relation in the fancy.

The accessions which are made to land bordering upon rivers follow the land, say the civilians, provided it be made by what they call *alluvion*, that is, insensibly and imperceptibly; which are circumstances that assist the imagination in the conjunction.

Where there is any considerable portion torn at once from one bank and added to another, it becomes not *his* property whose land it falls on till it unite with the

petually in my possession. I reckon on the secure enjoyment of it; by depriving me of it, you disappoint my expectations, and doubly displease me and offend every bystander. It is a public wrong, so far as the rules of equity are violated; it is a private harm, so far as an individual is injured. And though the second consideration could have no place, were not the former previously established — for otherwise the distinction of *mine* and *thine* would be unknown in society — yet there is no question but the regard to general good is much enforced by the respect to particular. What injures the community, without hurting any individual, is often more lightly thought of. But where the greatest public wrong is also conjoined with a considerable private one, no wonder the highest disapprobation attends so iniquitous a behaviour.

land and till the trees and plants have spread their roots into both. Before that, the thought does not sufficiently join them.

In short, we must ever distinguish between the necessity of a separation and constancy in men's possession and the rules which assign particular objects to particular persons. The first necessity is obvious, strong, and invincible; the latter may depend on a public utility more light and frivolous, on the sentiment of private humanity and aversion to private hardship, on positive laws, on precedents, analogies, and very fine connexions and turns of the imagination.

APPENDIX IV

OF SOME VERBAL DISPUTES

NOTHING IS MORE USUAL than for philosophers to encroach upon the province of grammarians and to engage in disputes of words while they imagine that they are handling controversies of the deepest importance and concern. It was in order to avoid altercations so frivolous and endless that I endeavoured to state with the utmost caution the object of our present enquiry, and proposed simply to collect, on the one hand, a list of those mental qualities which are the object of love or esteem and form a part of personal merit, and, on the other hand, a catalogue of those qualities which are the object of censure or reproach, and which detract from the character of the person possessed of them, subjoining some reflections concerning the origin of these sentiments of praise or blame. On all occasions where there might arise the least hesitation, I avoided the terms *virtue* and *vice*, because some of those qualities which I classed among the objects of praise receive, in the English language, the appellation of *talents* rather than of virtues, as some of the blamable or censurable qualities are often called *defects* rather than vices. It may now, perhaps, be expected that, before we conclude this moral enquiry, we should exactly separate the one from the other, should mark the precise boundaries of virtues and talents, vices and defects, and should explain the reason and origin of that distinction. But in order to excuse myself from this undertaking, which would, at last, prove only a grammatical enquiry, I shall subjoin the four following reflections, which shall contain all that I intend to say on the present subject.

First, I do not find that in the English or any other modern tongue the boundaries are exactly fixed between virtues and talents, vices and defects, or that a precise definition can be given of the one as contradistinguished from the other. Were we to say, for instance, that the esteemable qualities alone, which are voluntary, are entitled to the appellations of virtues, we should soon recollect the qualities of courage, equanimity, patience, self-command, with many others which almost every language classes under this appellation, though they depend little or not at all on our choice. Should we affirm that the qualities alone which prompt us to act our part in society are entitled to that honourable distinction, it must immediately occur that these are indeed the most valuable qualities and are commonly denominated the *social* virtues, but that this very epithet supposes that there are also virtues of another species. Should we lay hold of the distinction between *intellectual* and *moral* endowments, and affirm the last alone to be the real and genuine virtues because they alone lead to action, we should find that many of those qualities usually called intellectual virtues, such as prudence, penetration, discernment, discretion, had also a considerable influence on conduct. The distinction between the *heart* and the *head* may also be adopted; the qualities of the first may be defined such as in their immediate exertion are accompanied with a feeling of sentiment, and these alone may be called the genuine virtues; but industry, frugality, temperance, secrecy, perseverance, and many other laudable powers or habits generally styled virtues, are exerted without any immediate sentiment in the person possessed of them, and are only known to him by their effects. It is fortunate, amidst all this seeming perplexity, that the question, being merely verbal, cannot possibly be of any importance. A moral, philosophical discourse needs not enter into all these caprices of language, which are so variable in different dialects and in different ages of the same dialect. But on the whole, it seems to me that though it is always allowed that there are virtues of many different kinds, yet, when a man is called *virtuous* or is denominated a man of virtue, we chiefly regard his social qualities, which are, indeed, the most valuable. It is, at the same time, certain that any remarkable defect in courage, temperance, economy, industry, understanding, dignity of mind, would bereave even a very good-natured, honest man of this honourable appellation. Who did ever say, except by way of irony, that such a one was a man of great virtue, but an egregious blockhead?

But, *secondly*, it is no wonder that languages should not be very precise in marking the boundaries between virtues and talents, vices and defects, since there is so little distinction made in our internal estimation of them. It seems, indeed, certain that the *sentiment* of conscious worth, the self-satisfaction proceeding from a review of a man's own conduct and character — it seems certain, I say, that this sentiment, which, though the most common of all others, has no proper name in our language,[1] arises from the endowments of courage and capacity, industry and ingenuity, as well as from any other mental excellences. Who, on the other hand, is not deeply mortified with reflecting on his own folly and dissoluteness, and feels not a secret sting or compunction whenever his memory presents any past occurrence where he behaved with stupidity or ill-manners? Nor time can efface the cruel ideas of a man's own foolish conduct, or of affronts which cowardice or impudence has brought upon him. They still haunt his solitary hours, damp his most aspiring thoughts, and show him, even to himself, in the most contemptible and most odious colours imaginable.

What is there, too, we are more anxious to conceal from others than such blunders, infirmities, and meannesses, or more dread to have exposed by raillery and satire? And is not the chief object of vanity our bravery or learning, our wit or breeding, our eloquence or address, our taste or abilities? These we display with care, if not with ostentation; and we commonly show more ambition of excelling in them than even in the social virtues themselves, which are, in reality, of such superior excellence. Good-nature and honesty, especially the latter, are so indispensably required that, though the greatest censure attends any violation of these duties, no eminent praise follows such common instances of them, as seem essential to the support of human society. And hence the reason, in my opinion, why, though men often extol so liberally the qualities of their heart, they are shy in commending the endowments of their head, because the latter virtues, being supposed more rare and extraordinary, are observed to be the more usual objects of pride and self-conceit, and, when boasted of, beget a strong suspicion of these sentiments.

It is hard to tell whether you hurt a man's character most by calling him a knave or a coward, and whether a beastly glutton or drunkard be not as odious and contemptible as a selfish, ungenerous miser.

[1] The term "pride" is commonly taken in a bad sense; but this sentiment seems indifferent, and may be either good or bad, according as it is well- or ill-founded, and according to the other circumstances which accompany it. The French express this sentiment by the term *amour propre*, but as they also express self-love as well as vanity by the same term, there arises thence a great confusion in Rochefoucauld and many of their moral writers.

Give me my choice, and I would rather, for my own happiness and self-enjoyment, have a friendly, humane heart than possess all the other virtues of Demosthenes and Philip united; but I would rather pass with the world for one endowed with extensive genius and intrepid courage, and should thence expect stronger instances of general applause and admiration. The figure which a man makes in life, the reception which he meets with in company, the esteem paid him by his acquaintance, all these advantages depend as much upon his good sense and judgment as upon any other part of his character. Had a man the best intentions in the world, and were the farthest removed from all injustice and violence, he would never be able to make himself be much regarded without a moderate share, at least, of parts and understanding.

What is it then we can here dispute about? If sense and courage, temperance and industry, wisdom and knowledge confessedly form a considerable part of *personal merit;* if a man, possessed of these qualities, is both better satisfied with himself and better entitled to the good-will, esteem, and services of others, than one entirely destitute of them; if, in short, the *sentiments* are similar which arise from these endowments and from the social virtues; is there any reason for being so extremely scrupulous about a *word*, or disputing whether they be entitled to the denomination of virtues? It may, indeed, be pretended that the sentiment of approbation which those accomplishments produce, besides its being *inferior*, is also somewhat *different* from that which attends the virtues of justice and humanity. But this seems not a sufficient reason for ranking them entirely under different classes and appellations. The character of Cæsar and that of Cato, as drawn by Sallust, are both of them virtuous in the strictest and most limited sense of the word, but in a different way; nor are the sentiments entirely the same which arise from them. The one produces love, the other esteem; the one is amiable, the other awful; we should wish to meet the one character in a friend; the other we should be ambitious of in ourselves. In like manner the approbation which attends temperance or industry or frugality may be somewhat different from that which is paid to the social virtues, without making them entirely of a different species. And, indeed, we may observe that these endowments, more than the other virtues, produce not, all of them, the same kind of approbation. Good sense and genius beget esteem and regard; wit and humour excite love and affection.[2]

Most people, I believe, will naturally, without premeditation, assent to the definition of the elegant and judicious poet:

> Virtue (for mere good-nature is a fool)
> Is sense and spirit with humanity.[3]

What pretensions has a man to our generous assistance or good offices who has dissipated his wealth in profuse expenses, idle vanities, chimerical projects, dissolute pleasures, or extravagant gaming? These vices — for we scruple not to call them such — bring misery unpitied and contempt on every one addicted to them.

Achaeus, a wise and prudent prince, fell into a fatal snare which cost him his crown and life, after having used every reasonable precaution to guard himself against it. On that account, says the historian, he is a just object of regard and compassion; his betrayers alone of hatred and contempt.[4]

The precipitate flight and improvident negligence of Pompey, at the beginning of the civil wars, appeared such notorious blunders to Cicero, as quite palled his friendship towards that great man. *In the*

---

[2] Love and esteem are nearly the same passion and arise from similar causes. The qualities which produce both are such as communicate pleasure. But where this pleasure is severe and serious, or where its object is great and makes a strong impression, or where it produces any degree of humility and awe — in all these cases the passion which arises from the pleasure is more properly denominated esteem than love. Benevolence attends both, but is connected with love in a more eminent degree. There seems to be still a stronger mixture of pride in contempt than of humility in esteem; and the reason would not be difficult to one who studied accurately the passions. All these various mixtures and compositions and appearances of sentiment form a very curious subject of speculation, but are wide of our present purpose. Throughout this enquiry, we always consider in general what qualities are a subject of praise or of censure, without entering into all the minute differences of sentiment which they excite. It is evident that whatever is contemned is also disliked, as well as what is hated; and we here endeavour to take objects according to their most simple views and appearances. These sciences are but too apt to appear abstract to common readers, even with all the precautions which we can take to clear them from superfluous speculations and bring them down to every capacity.

[3] *The Art of preserving Health.* Book 4.

[4] Polybius, lib. iii. cap. 2.

same manner, says he, *as want of cleanliness, decency, or discretion in a mistress are found to alienate our affections.* For so he expresses himself, where he talks, not in the character of a philosopher, but in that of a statesman and man of the world, to his friend Atticus.[5]

But the same Cicero, in imitation of all the ancient moralists, when he reasons as a philosopher, enlarges very much his ideas of virtue, and comprehends every laudable quality or endowment of the mind under that honourable appellation. This leads to the *third* reflection which we proposed to make, to wit, that the ancient moralists, the best models, made no material distinction among the different species of mental endowments and defects, but treated all alike under the appellation of virtues and vices, and made them indiscriminately the object of their moral reasonings. The *prudence* explained in Cicero's *Offices* [6] is that sagacity which leads to the discovery of truth a.id preserves us from error and mistake. *Magnanimity, temperance, decency* are there also at large discoursed of. And as that eloquent moralist followed the common received division of the four cardinal virtues, our social duties form but one head in the general distribution of his subject.[7]

[5] Lib. ix. epist. 10.

[6] Lib. i. cap 6.

[7] The following passage of Cicero is worth quoting, as being the most clear and express to our purpose, that anything can be imagined, and, in a dispute which is chiefly verbal, must, on account of the author, carry an authority from which there can be no appeal.

"Virtus autem, quae est per se ipsa laudabilis, et sine qua nihil laudari potest, tamen habet plures partes, quarum alia est alia ad laudationem aptior. Sunt enim aliae virtutes, quae videntur in moribus hominum, et quadam comitate ac beneficentia positae: aliae quae in ingenii aliqua facultate, aut animi magnitudine ac robore. Nam clementia, justitia, benignitas, fides, fortitudo in periculis communibus, jucunda est auditu in laudationibus. Omnes enim hae virtutes non tam ipsis, qui eas in se habent, quam generi hominum fructuosae putantur. Sapientia et magnitudo animi, qua omnes res humanae tenues et pro nihilo putantur, et in cogitando vis quaedam ingenii, et ipsa eloquentia admirationis habet non minus, jucunditatis minus. Ipsos enim magis videntur, quos laudamus, quam illos, apud quos laudamus ornare ac tueri: sed tamen in laudando jungenda sunt etiam haec genera virtutum. Ferunt enim aures hominum, cum illa quae jucunda et grata, tum etiam illa, quae mirabilia sunt in virtute, laudari." *De orat.* lib. ii. cap. 84.

I suppose, if Cicero were now alive, it would be found difficult to fetter his moral sentiments by narrow systems, or persuade him that no qualities were to be admitted

We need only peruse the titles of chapters in Aristotle's *Ethics* to be convinced that he ranks courage, temperance, magnificence, magnanimity, modesty, prudence, and a manly openness, among the virtues, as well as justice and friendship.

To *sustain* and to *abstain*, that is, to be patient and continent, appeared to some of the ancients a summary comprehension of all morals.

Epictetus has scarcely ever mentioned the sentiment of humanity and compassion, but in order to put his disciples on their guard against it. The virtue of the *Stoics* seems to consist chiefly in a firm temper and a sound understanding. With them as with Solomon and the eastern moralists, folly and wisdom are equivalent to vice and virtue.

Men will praise thee, says David,[8] when thou dost well unto thyself. I hate a wise man, says the Greek poet, who is not wise to himself.[9]

Plutarch is no more cramped by systems in his philosophy than in his history. Where he compares the great men of Greece and Rome, he fairly sets in opposition all their blemishes and accomplishments of whatever kind, and omits nothing considerable which can either depress or exalt their characters. His moral discourses contain the same free and natural censure of men and manners.

The character of Hannibal, as drawn by Livy,[10] is esteemed partial, but allows him many eminent virtues. Never was there a genius, says the historian, more equally fitted for those opposite offices of commanding and obeying; and it were, therefore, difficult to determine whether he rendered himself *dearer* to the general or to the army. To none would Hasdrubal entrust more willingly the conduct of any dangerous enterprise; under none did the soldiers discover more courage and confidence. Great boldness in facing danger, great prudence in the midst of it. No labour could fatigue his body or subdue his mind. Cold and heat were indifferent to him; meat and drink he sought as supplies to the necessities of nature, not as gratifications of his voluptuous appetites. Waking or rest he used indis-

---

as *virtues*, or acknowledged to be a part of *personal merit*, but what were recommended by "the whole duty of man."

[8] Psalm 49th.

[9] Μισῶ σοφιστὴν ὅστις οὐχ αὑτῷ σοφός. Euripides

[10] Lib. xxi. cap. 4.

criminately, by night or by day.   These great virtues were balanced
by great vices: inhuman cruelty, perfidy more than *punic*, no truth,
no faith, no regard to oaths, promises, or religion.

The character of Alexander the Sixth, to be found in Guicciardin,[11]
is pretty similar but juster; and is a proof that even the moderns,
where they speak naturally, hold the same language with the ancients.
In this pope, says he, there was a singular capacity and judgment:
admirable prudence, a wonderful talent of persuasion, and in all
momentous enterprises a diligence and dexterity incredible.   But these
virtues were infinitely overbalanced by his *vices:* no faith, no religion,
insatiable avarice, exorbitant ambition, and a more than barbarous
cruelty.

Polybius,[12] reprehending Timaeus for his partiality against Agatho-
cles, whom he himself allows to be the most cruel and impious of all
tyrants, says: if he took refuge in Syracuse, as asserted by that historian, flying the dirt and smoke and toil of his former profession of a
potter and, if proceeding from such slender beginnings, he became
master, in a little time, of all Sicily, brought the Carthaginian state
into the utmost danger, and at last died in old age and in possession
of sovereign dignity — must he not be allowed something prodigious
and extraordinary, and to have possessed great talents and capacity
for business and action?   His historian, therefore, ought not to have
alone related what tended to his reproach and infamy, but also what
might redound to his praise and honour.

In general, we may observe that the distinction of voluntary or
involuntary was little regarded by the ancients in their moral reasonings, where they frequently treated the question as very doubtful
whether virtue could be taught or not?[13]   They justly considered that
cowardice, meanness, levity, anxiety, impatience, folly, and many
other qualities of the mind, might appear ridiculous and deformed,
contemptible and odious, though independent of the will.   Nor could
it be supposed, at all times, in every man's power to attain every kind
of mental more than of exterior beauty.

And here there occurs the *fourth* reflection which I purposed to

---

[11] Lib. i.
[12] Lib. xii.
[13] Vid. Plato in *Menone*; Seneca, *de otio.sap.* cap. 31.   So also Horace, *Virtutem
doctrina paret, naturane donet.*   Epist. lib. i. ep. 18.   Æschines Socraticus, Dial. I.

make in suggesting the reason why modern philosophers have often followed a course in their moral enquiries so different from that of the ancients. In later times, philosophy of all kinds, especially ethics, have been more closely united with theology than ever they were observed to be among the heathens; and as this latter science admits of no terms of composition, but bends every branch of knowledge to its own purpose, without much regard to the phenomena of nature or to the unbiased sentiments of the mind, hence reasoning and even language have been warped from their natural course, and distinctions have been endeavoured to be established where the difference of the objects was, in a manner, imperceptible. Philosophers, or rather divines under that disguise, treating all morals as on a like footing with civil laws, guarded by the sanctions of reward and punishment, were necessarily led to render this circumstance of *voluntary* or *involuntary* the foundation of their whole theory. Every one may employ *terms* in what sense he pleases; but this, in the meantime, must be allowed, that *sentiments* are every day experienced of blame and praise, which have objects beyond the dominion of the will or choice, and of which it behoves us, if not as moralists, as speculative philosophers at least, to give some satisfactory theory and explication.

A blemish, a fault, a vice, a crime — these expressions seem to denote different degrees of censure and disapprobation, which are, however, all of them, at the bottom, pretty nearly all the same kind of species. The explication of one will easily lead us into a just conception of the others, and it is of greater consequence to attend to things than to verbal appellations. That we owe a duty to ourselves is confessed even in the most vulgar system of morals, and it must be of consequence to examine that duty in order to see whether it bears any affinity to that which we owe to society. It is probable that the approbation attending the observance of both is of a similar nature and arises from similar principles, whatever appellation we may give to either of these excellences.

III

ESSAYS,
MORAL AND POLITICAL

Selections

ESSAY I[1]

THAT POLITICS MAY BE REDUCED TO A SCIENCE

IT IS a question with several whether there be any essential difference between one form of government and another, and whether every form may not become good or bad, according as it is well or ill administered?[2] Were it once admitted that all governments are alike and that the only difference consists in the character and conduct of the governors, most political disputes would be at an end, and all *zeal* for one constitution above another must be esteemed mere bigotry and folly. But, though a friend to moderation, I cannot forbear condemning this sentiment and should be sorry to think that human affairs admit of no greater stability than what they receive from the casual humours and characters of particular men.

It is true, those who maintain that the goodness of all government consists in the goodness of the administration may cite many particular instances in history, where the very same government, in different hands, has varied suddenly into the two opposite extremes of good and bad. Compare the French government under Henry III and under Henry IV. Oppression, levity, artifice on the part of the rulers, faction, sedition, treachery, rebellion, disloyalty on the part of the subjects — these compose the character of the former miserable era. But when the patriot and heroic prince who succeeded was once firmly seated on the throne, the government, the people, everything, seemed to be totally changed; and all from the difference of the temper and conduct of these two sovereigns.[3] Instances of this kind may be multiplied almost without number, from ancient as well as modern history, foreign as well as domestic.

But here it may be proper to make a distinction. All absolute

[1] [Ed. 1777, Part I. Essay III.]

[2] For forms of government let fools contest,
   Whate'er is best administered is best — *Essay on Man*, Book 3.

[3] An equal difference of a contrary kind may be found in comparing the reigns of Elizabeth and James, at least with regard to foreign affairs.

governments must very much depend on the administration; and this is one of the great inconveniences attending that form of government. But a republican and free government would be an obvious absurdity if the particular checks and controls provided by the constitution had really no influence and made it not the interest, even of bad men, to act for the public good. Such is the intention of these forms of government, and such is their real effect, where they are wisely constituted; as, on the other hand, they are the source of all disorder and of the blackest crimes where either skill or honesty has been wanting in their original frame and institution.

So great is the force of laws and of particular forms of government, and so little dependence have they on the humours and tempers of men, that consequences almost as general and certain may sometimes be deduced from them as any which the mathematical sciences afford us.

The constitution of the Roman republic gave the whole legislative power to the people, without allowing a negative voice either to the nobility or consuls. This unbounded power they possessed in a collective, not in a representative body. The consequences were: when the people, by success and conquest, had become very numerous and had spread themselves to a great distance from the capital, the city tribes, though the most contemptible, carried almost every vote; they were, therefore, most cajoled by every one that affected popularity; they were supported in idleness by the general distribution of corn and by particular bribes which they received from almost every candidate. By this means they became every day more licentious, and the Campus Martius was a perpetual scene of tumult and sedition; armed slaves were introduced among these rascally citizens, so that the whole government fell into anarchy; and the greatest happiness which the Romans could look for was the despotic power of the Cæsars. Such are the effects of democracy without a representative.

A nobility may possess the whole or any part of the legislative power of a state in two different ways. Either every nobleman shares the power as a part of the whole body or the whole body enjoys the power as composed of parts which have each a distinct power and authority. The Venetian aristocracy is an instance of the first kind of government; the Polish, of the second. In the Venetian government the whole body of nobility possesses the whole power, and no nobleman has any authority which he receives not from the whole. In the Polish government every nobleman, by means of his fiefs, has a distinct hereditary authority over his vassals, and the whole body has no authority but what it receives from the concurrence of its parts. The different operations and tendencies of these two species of government might be made apparent even a priori. A Venetian nobility is preferable to a Polish, let the humours and education of men be ever so much varied. A nobility who possess their power in common will preserve peace and order both among themselves and their subjects; and no member can have authority enough to control the laws for a moment. The nobles will preserve their authority over the people, but without any grievous tyranny or any breach of private property, because such a tyrannical government promotes not the interests of the whole body, however it may that of some individuals. There will be a distinction of rank between the nobility and people, but this will be the only distinction in the state. The whole nobility will form one body and the whole people another, without any of those private feuds and animosities which spread ruin and desolation everywhere. It is easy to see the disadvantages of a Polish nobility in every one of these particulars.

It is possible so to constitute a free government as that a single person, call him a doge, prince, or king, shall possess a large share of power and shall form a proper balance or counterpoise to the other parts of the legislature. This chief magistrate may be either *elective* or *hereditary;* and though the former institution may to a superficial view appear the most advantageous, yet a more accurate inspection will discover in it greater inconveniences than in the latter, and such as are founded on causes and principles eternal and immutable. The filling of the throne in such a government is a point of too great and too general interest not to divide the whole people into factions. Whence a civil war, the greatest of ills, may be apprehended almost with certainty upon every vacancy. The prince elected must be either a *foreigner* or a *native.* The former will be ignorant of the people whom he is to govern, suspicious of his new subjects and suspected by them, giving his confidence entirely to strangers who will have no other care but of enriching themselves in the quickest manner, while their master's favour and authority are able to support them. A native will carry into the throne all his private animosities and friendships, and will never be viewed in his elevation without exciting the sentiment of envy in those who formerly considered him as their equal. Not to mention that a crown is too high a reward ever to be given to merit alone, and will always induce the candidates to employ force, or money, or intrigue, to procure the votes of the electors, so that such an election will give no better chance for superior merit in the prince than if the state had trusted to birth alone for determining the sovereign.

It may, therefore, be pronounced as an universal axiom in politics *that an hereditary prince, a nobility without vassals, and a people voting by their representatives, form the best monarchy, aristocracy and democracy.* But in order to prove more fully that politics admit of general truths which are invariable by the humour or education either of subject or sovereign, it may not be amiss to observe some other principles of this science which may seem to deserve that character.

It may easily be observed that though free governments have been commonly the most happy for those who partake of their freedom, yet are they the most ruinous and oppressive to their provinces. And this observation may, I believe, be fixed as a maxim of the kind we are here speaking of. When a monarch extends his dominions by conquest, he soon learns to consider his old and his new subjects as on the same footing, because, in reality, all his subjects are to him the same, except the few friends and favourites with whom he is personally acquainted. He does not, therefore, make any distinction between them in his *general* laws, and at the same time is careful to prevent all *particular* acts of oppression on the one as well as the other. But a free state necessarily makes a great distinction, and must always do so, till men learn to love their neighbours as well as themselves. The conquerors in such a government are all legislators and will be sure to contrive matters by restrictions on trade and by taxes so as to draw some private as well as public advantage from their conquests. Provincial governors have also a better chance in a republic to escape with their plunder by means of bribery or intrigue, and their fellow citizens, who find their own state to be enriched by the spoils of the subject provinces, will be the more inclined to tolerate such abuses. Not to mention that it is a necessary precaution in a free state to change the governors frequently, which obliges these temporary tyrants to be more expeditious and rapacious, that they may accumulate sufficient wealth before they give place to their successors. What cruel tyrants were the Romans over the world during the time of their commonwealth! It is true, they had laws to prevent oppression in their provincial magistrates, but Cicero informs us that the Romans could not better consult the interests of the provinces than by repealing these very laws. For in that case, says he, our magistrates, having entire impunity, would plunder no more than would satisfy their own rapaciousness, whereas at present they must also satisfy that of their judges and of all the great men in Rome of whose protection they stand in need. Who can read of the cruelties and oppressions of Verres without horror and astonishment? And who is not touched with indignation to hear that, after Cicero had exhausted on that abandoned criminal all the thunders of his eloquence and had prevailed so far as to get him condemned to the utmost extent of the laws, yet that cruel tyrant lived peaceably to old age, in opulence and ease, and, thirty years afterwards, was put into the proscription by Mark Antony on account of his exorbitant wealth, where he fell with Cicero himself and all the most virtuous men of Rome? After the dissolution of the commonwealth, the Roman yoke became easier upon the provinces, as Tacitus informs us;[4] and it may be observed that many of the worst emperors, Domitian,[5] for instance, were careful to prevent all oppression on the provinces. In Tiberius'[6] time Gaul was esteemed richer than Italy itself, nor do I find during the whole time of the Roman monarchy that the empire became less rich or populous in any of its provinces, though indeed its valour and military discipline were always upon the decline. The oppression and tyranny of the Carthaginians over their subject states in Africa went so far, as we learn from Polybius,[7] that, not content with exacting the half of all the produce of the land, which of itself was a very high rent, they also loaded them with many other taxes. If we pass from ancient to modern times, we shall still find the observation to hold. The provinces of absolute monarchies are always better treated than those of free states. Compare the *Païs conquis* of France with Ireland, and

[4] *Ann.* lib. i. cap. 2.

[5] Suet. in *vita Domit.*

[6] Egregium resumendae libertati tempus, si ipsi florentes, quam inops Italia, quam imbellis urbana plebs, nihil validum in exercitibus, nisi quod externum cogitarent. — Tacit. *Ann.* lib. iii.

[7] Lib. i. cap. 72.

you will be convinced of this truth; though this latter kingdom, being in a good measure peopled from England, possesses so many rights and privileges as should naturally make it challenge better treatment than that of a conquered province. Corsica is also an obvious instance to the same purpose.

There is an observation of Machiavel with regard to the conquests of Alexander the Great which, I think, may be regarded as one of those eternal political truths which no time nor accidents can vary. It may seem strange, says that politician, that such sudden conquests as those of Alexander should be possessed so peaceably by his successors, and that the Persians during all the confusions and civil wars among the Greeks never made the smallest effort towards the recovery of their former independent government. To satisfy us concerning the cause of this remarkable event, we may consider that a monarch may govern his subjects in two different ways. He may either follow the maxims of the Eastern princes and stretch his authority so far as to leave no distinction of rank among his subjects but what proceeds immediately from himself; no advantages of birth, no hereditary honours and possessions, and, in a word, no credit among the people, except from his commission alone. Or a monarch may exert his power after a milder manner, like other European princes, and leave other sources of honour beside his smile and favour: birth, titles, possessions, valour, integrity, knowledge, or great and fortunate achievements. In the former species of government, after a conquest, it is impossible ever to shake off the yoke, since no one possesses among the people so much personal credit and authority as to begin such an enterprise; whereas, in the latter, the least misfortune or discord among the victors will encourage the vanquished to take arms, who have leaders ready to prompt and conduct them in every undertaking.[8]

[8] I have taken it for granted, according to the supposition of Machiavel, that the ancient Persians had no nobility, though there is reason to suspect that the Florentine secretary, who seems to have been better acquainted with the Roman than the Greek authors, was mistaken in this particular. The more ancient Persians, whose manners are described by Xenophon, were a free people, and had nobility. Their ὁμότιμοι were preserved even after the extending of their conquests and the consequent change of their government. Arrian mentions them in Darius' time, *De exped. Alex.* lib. ii. Historians also speak often of the persons in command as men of family. Tygranes, who was general of the Medes under Xerxes, was of the race of Achaemenes. Herod. lib. vii. cap. 62. Artachæus, who directed the cutting

Such is the reasoning of Machiavel, which seems solid and conclusive, though I wish he had not mixed falsehood with truth in asserting that monarchies governed according to Eastern policy, though more easily kept when once subdued, yet are the most difficult to subdue, since they cannot contain any powerful subject whose discontent and faction may facilitate the enterprises of an enemy. For, besides that such a tyrannical government enervates the courage of men and renders them indifferent towards the fortunes of their sovereign — besides this, I say, we find by experience that even the temporary and delegated authority of the generals and magistrates, being always in such governments as absolute within its sphere as that of the prince himself, is able with barbarians accustomed to a blind submission to produce the most dangerous and fatal revolutions. So that in every respect a gentle government is preferable and gives the greatest security to the sovereign as well as to the subject.

of the canal about Mount Athos, was of the same family. *Id.* cap. 117. Megabyzus was one of the seven eminent Persians who conspired against the Magi. His son, Zopyrus, was in the highest command under Darius, and delivered Babylon to him. His grandson, Megabyzus, commanded the army defeated at Marathon. His great-grandson, Zopyrus, was also eminent and was banished from Persia. Herod. lib. iii. Thuc. lib. i. Rosaces, who commanded an army in Egypt under Artaxerxes, was also descended from one of the seven conspirators, Diod. Sic. lib. xvi. Agesilaus, in Xenophon, *Hist. Græc.* lib. iv., being desirous of making a marriage betwixt king Cotys, his ally, and the daughter of Spithridates, a Persian of rank who had deserted to him, first asks Cotys what family Spithridates is of. One of the most considerable in Persia, says Cotys. Ariæus, when offered the sovereignty by Clearchus and the ten thousand Greeks, refused it as of too low a rank, and said that so many eminent Persians would never endure his rule. *Id. De exped.* lib. ii. Some of the families descended from the seven Persians above mentioned remained during Alexander's successors; and Mithridates, in Antiochus's time, is said by Polybius to be descended from one of them, lib. v. cap. 43. Artabazus was esteemed as Arrian says, ἐν τοῖς πρώτοις Περσῶν, lib. iii. And when Alexander married in one day 80 of his captains to Persian women, his intention plainly was to ally the Macedonians with the most eminent Persian families. *Id.* lib. vii. Diodorus Siculus says they were of the most noble birth in Persia, lib. xvii. The government of Persia was despotic and conducted in many respects after the Eastern manner, but was not carried so far as to extirpate all nobility and confound all ranks and orders. It left men who were still great, by themselves and their family, independent of their office and commission. And the reason why the Macedonians kept so easily dominion over them was owing to other causes easy to be found in the historians, though it must be owned that Machiavel's reasoning is in itself just, however doubtful its application to the present case.

Legislators, therefore, ought not to trust the future government of a state entirely to chance, but ought to provide a system of laws to regulate the administration of public affairs to the latest posterity. Effects will always correspond to causes, and wise regulations in any commonwealth are the most valuable legacy that can be left to future ages. In the smallest court or office, the stated forms and methods by which business must be conducted are found to be a considerable check on the natural depravity of mankind. Why should not the case be the same in public affairs? Can we ascribe the stability and wisdom of the Venetian government, through so many ages, to anything but the form of government? And is it not easy to point out those defects in the original constitution which produced the tumultuous governments of Athens and Rome, and ended at last in the ruin of these two famous republics? And so little dependence has this affair on the humours and education of particular men that one part of the same republic may be wisely conducted and another weakly by the very same men, merely on account of the differences of the forms and institutions by which these parts are regulated. Historians inform us that this was actually the case with Genoa. For while the state was always full of sedition and tumult and disorder, the bank of St. George, which had become a considerable part of the people, was conducted for several ages with the utmost integrity and wisdom.[9]

The ages of greatest public spirit are not always most eminent for private virtue. Good laws may beget order and moderation in the government where the manners and customs have instilled little humanity or justice into the tempers of men. The most illustrious period of the Roman history, considered in a political view, is that between the beginning of the first and end of the last Punic war; the due balance between the nobility and people being then fixed by the contests of the tribunes, and not being yet lost by the extent of conquests. Yet at this very time the horrid practice of poisoning was so common that during part of the season a *prætor* punished capitally

[9] Esempio veramente raro, et da' filosofi in tante loro immaginate e vedute Repubbliche mai non trovato, vedere dentro ad un medesimo cerchio, fra medesimi cittadini, la libertà e la tirannide, la vita civile e la corrotta, la giustizia e la licenza; perche quello ordine solo mantiene quella città piena di costumi antichi e venerabili. E s'egli avvenisse, che col tempo in ogni modo avverrà, che San Giorgio tutta quella città occupasse, sarebbe quella una Repubblica più che la Veneziana memorabile. — *Delle Istorie Fiorentine*, lib. viii. 437. — Florent. 1782.

for this crime above three thousand[10] persons in a part of Italy, and found informations of this nature still multiplying upon him. There is a similar or rather a worse instance[11] in the more early times of the commonwealth, so depraved in private life were that people whom in their histories we so much admire. I doubt not but they were really more virtuous during the time of the two *Triumvirates*, when they were tearing their common country to pieces, and spreading slaughter and desolation over the face of the earth, merely for the choice of tyrants.[12]

Here, then, is a sufficient inducement to maintain with the utmost zeal in every free state those forms and institutions by which liberty is secured, the public good consulted, and the avarice or ambition of particular men restrained and punished. Nothing does more honour to human nature than to see it susceptible of so noble a passion, as nothing can be a greater indication of meanness of heart in any man than to see him destitute of it. A man who loves only himself, without regard to friendship and desert, merits the severest blame; and a man who is only susceptible of friendship, without public spirit or a regard to the community, is deficient in the most material part of virtue.

But this is a subject which needs not be longer insisted on at present. There are enough of zealots on both sides, who kindle up the passions of their partisans and, under pretence of public good, pursue the interests and ends of their particular faction. For my part, I shall always be more fond of promoting moderation than zeal, though perhaps the surest way of producing moderation in every party is to increase our zeal for the public. Let us therefore try, if it be possible from the foregoing doctrine, to draw a lesson of moderation with regard to the parties into which our country is at present divided; at the same time that we allow not this moderation to abate the industry and passion with which every individual is bound to pursue the good of his country.

Those who either attack or defend a minister in such a government as ours, where the utmost liberty is allowed, always carry matters to

---

[10] T. Livii, lib. xl. cap. 43.
[11] T. Livii, lib. viii. cap. 18.
[12] *L'Aigle contre l'Aigle, Romains contre Romains,*
    Combatans seulement pour le choix de tyrans.
                                                    CORNEILLE.

an extreme and exaggerate his merit or demerit with regard to the public. His enemies are sure to charge him with the greatest enormities, both in domestic and foreign management; and there is no meanness or crime of which, in their account, he is not capable. Unnecessary wars, scandalous treaties, profusion of public treasure, oppressive taxes, every kind of mal-administration is ascribed to him. To aggravate the charge, his pernicious conduct, it is said, will extend its baneful influence even to posterity, by undermining the best constitution in the world and disordering that wise system of laws, institutions, and customs by which our ancestors during so many centuries have been so happily governed. He is not only a wicked minister in himself, but has removed every security provided against wicked ministers for the future.

On the other hand, the partisans of the minister make his panegyric run as high as the accusation against him, and celebrate his wise, steady, and moderate conduct in every part of his administration. The honour and interest of the nation supported abroad, public credit maintained at home, persecution restrained, faction subdued — the merit of all these blessings is ascribed solely to the minister. At the same time he crowns all his other merits by a religious care of the best constitution in the world, which he has preserved in all its parts and has transmitted entire to be the happiness and security of the latest posterity.

When this accusation and panegyric are received by the partisans of each party, no wonder they beget an extraordinary ferment on both sides, and fill the nation with violent animosities. But I would fain persuade these party zealots that there is a flat contradiction both in the accusation and panegyric, and that it were impossible for either of them to run so high, were it not for this contradiction. If our constitution be really *that noble fabric, the pride of Britain, the envy of our neighbours, raised by the labour of so many centuries, repaired at the expense of so many millions, and cemented by such a profusion of blood* [13] — I say, if our constitution does in any degree deserve these eulogies, it would never have suffered a wicked and weak minister to govern triumphantly for a course of twenty years, when opposed by the greatest geniuses in the nation, who exercised the utmost liberty of tongue and pen in parliament and in their frequent appeals to the

[13] "Dissertations on Parties," Letter X.

people. But, if the minister be wicked and weak to the degree so strenuously insisted on, the constitution must be faulty in its original principles, and he cannot consistently be charged with undermining the best form of government in the world. A constitution is only so far good as it provides a remedy against mal-administration, and if the British, when in its greatest vigour, and repaired by two such remarkable events as the *Revolution* and *Accession*, by which our ancient royal family was sacrificed to it — if our constitution, I say, with so great advantages does not, in fact, provide any such remedy, we are rather beholden to any minister who undermines it and affords us an opportunity of erecting a better in its place.

I would employ the same topics to moderate the zeal of those who defend the minister. *Is our constitution so excellent?* Then a change of ministry can be no such dreadful event, since it is essential to such a constitution in every ministry, both to preserve itself from violation and to prevent all enormities in the administration. *Is our constitution very bad?* Then so extraordinary a jealousy and apprehension on account of changes is ill placed, and a man should no more be anxious in this case than a husband who had married a woman from the stews should be watchful to prevent her infidelity. Public affairs in such a government must necessarily go to confusion, by whatever hands they are conducted; and the zeal of *patriots* is in that case much less requisite than the patience and submission of *philosophers*. The virtue and good intention of Cato and Brutus are highly laudable; but to what purpose did their zeal serve? Only to hasten the fatal period of the Roman government and render its convulsions and dying agonies more violent and painful.

I would not be understood to mean that public affairs deserve no care and attention at all. Would men be moderate and consistent, their claims might be admitted, at least might be examined. The *country party* might still assert that our constitution, though excellent, will admit of mal-administration to a certain degree; and therefore, if the minister be bad, it is proper to oppose him with a *suitable* degree of zeal. And, on the other hand, the *court party* may be allowed, upon the supposition that the minister were good, to defend, and with *some* zeal too, his administration. I would only persuade men not to contend as if they were fighting *pro aris et focis*, and change a good constitution into a bad one by the violence of their factions.

I have not here considered anything that is personal in the present controversy. In the best civil constitution, where every man is restrained by the most rigid laws, it is easy to discover either the good or bad intentions of a minister, and to judge whether his personal character deserve love or hatred. But such questions are of little importance to the public, and lay those who employ their pens upon them under a just suspicion either of malevolence or of flattery.

ESSAY II[1]

OF THE FIRST PRINCIPLES OF GOVERNMENT

NOTHING APPEARS more surprising to those who consider human affairs with a philosophical eye than the easiness with which the many are governed by the few, and the implicit submission with which men resign their own sentiments and passions to those of their rulers. When we inquire by what means this wonder is effected, we shall find that, as force is always on the side of the governed, the governors have nothing to support them but opinion. It is, therefore, on opinion only that government is founded, and this maxim extends to the most despotic and most military governments as well as to the most free and most popular. The soldan of Egypt or the emperor of Rome might drive his harmless subjects like brute beasts against their sentiments and inclination. But he must, at least, have led his *mamalukes* or *prætorian bands*, like men, by their opinion.

Opinion is of two kinds, to wit, opinion of *interest*, and opinion of *right*. By opinion of interest, I chiefly understand the sense of the general advantage which is reaped from government, together with the persuasion that the particular government which is established is equally advantageous with any other that could easily be settled. When this opinion prevails among the generality of a state or among those who have the force in their hands, it gives great security to any government.

Right is of two kinds; right to *power* and right to *property*. What prevalence opinion of the first kind has over mankind may easily be understood by observing the attachment which all nations have to their ancient government and even to those names which have had the sanction of antiquity. Antiquity always begets the opinion of right; and whatever disadvantageous sentiments we may entertain of mankind, they are always found to be prodigal both of blood and

[1] [Ed. 1777, Part I. Essay IV.]

307

treasure in the maintenance of public justice.[2] There is, indeed, no particular in which, at first sight, there may appear a greater contradiction in the frame of the human mind than the present. When men act in a faction, they are apt, without shame or remorse, to neglect all the ties of honour and morality in order to serve their party; and yet, when a faction is formed upon a point of right or principle, there is no occasion where men discover a greater obstinacy and a more determined sense of justice and equity. The same social disposition of mankind is the cause of these contradictory appearances.

It is sufficiently understood that the opinion of right to property is of moment in all matters of government. A noted author has made property the foundation of all government, and most of our political writers seem inclined to follow him in that particular. This is carrying the matter too far, but still it must be owned that the opinion of right to property has a great influence in this subject.

Upon these three opinions, therefore, of public *interest*, of *right to power*, and of *right to property*, are all governments founded, and all authority of the few over the many. There are, indeed, other principles which add force to these, and determine, limit, or alter their operation, such as *self-interest*, *fear*, and *affection*. But still we may assert that these other principles can have no influence alone, but suppose the antecedent influence of those opinions above mentioned. They are, therefore, to be esteemed the secondary, not the original, principles of government.

For, *first*, as to *self-interest*, by which I mean the expectation of particular rewards distinct from the general protection which we receive from government, it is evident that the magistrate's authority must be antecedently established, at least be hoped for, in order to produce this expectation. The prospect of reward may augment his authority with regard to some particular persons, but can never give birth to it with regard to the public. Men naturally look for the greatest favours from their friends and acquaintance, and, therefore, the hopes of any considerable number of the state would never centre in any particular set of men if these men had no other title to magistracy and had no separate influence over the opinions of mankind.

[2] This passion we may denominate "enthusiasm," or we may give it what appellation we please; but a politician who should overlook its influence on human affairs would prove himself to have but a very limited understanding.

The same observation may be extended to the other two principles of *fear* and *affection*. No man would have any reason to *fear* the fury of a tyrant if he had no authority over any but from fear, since, as a single man, his bodily force can reach but a small way, and all the farther power he possesses must be founded either on our own opinion or on the presumed opinion of others. And though *affection* to wisdom and virtue in a *sovereign* extends very far and has great influence, yet he must antecedently be supposed invested with a public character; otherwise the public esteem will serve him in no stead, nor will his virtue have any influence beyond a narrow sphere.

A government may endure for several ages, though the balance of power and the balance of property do not coincide. This chiefly happens where any rank or order of the state has acquired a large share in the property, but, from the original constitution of the government, has no share in the power. Under what pretence would any individual of that order assume authority in public affairs? As men are commonly much attached to their ancient government, it is not to be expected that the public would ever favour such usurpations. But where the original constitution allows any share of power, though small, to an order of men who possess a large share of property, it is easy for them gradually to stretch their authority and bring the balance of power to coincide with that of property. This has been the case with the House of Commons in England.

Most writers that have treated of the British government have supposed that, as the Lower House represents all the Commons of Great Britain, its weight in the scale is proportioned to the property and power of all whom it represents. But this principle must not be received as absolutely true. For though the people are apt to attach themselves more to the House of Commons than to any other member of the constitution, that House being chosen by them as their representatives and as the public guardians of their liberty, yet are there instances where the House, even when in opposition to the crown, has not been followed by the people, as we may particularly observe of the *Tory* House of Commons in the reign of King William. Were the members obliged to receive instructions from their constituents, like the Dutch deputies, this would entirely alter the case; and if such immense power and riches as those of all the Commons of Great Britain were brought into the scale, it is not easy to conceive that the crown could either influence that multitude of people or withstand that balance of property. It is true, the crown has great influence over the collective body in the elections of members; but were this influence, which at present is only exerted once in seven years, to be employed in bringing over the people to every vote, it would soon be wasted, and no skill, popularity, or revenue could support it. I must, therefore, be of opinion that an alteration in this particular would introduce a total alteration in our government, and would soon reduce it to a pure republic and, perhaps, to a republic of no inconvenient form. For, though the people, collected in a body like the Roman tribes, be quite unfit for government, yet, when dispersed in small bodies, they are more susceptible both of reason and order; the force of popular currents and tides is in a great measure broken, and the public interest may be pursued with some method and constancy. But it is needless to reason any farther concerning a form of government which is never likely to have place in Great Britain, and which seems not to be the aim of any party amongst us. Let us cherish and improve our ancient government as much as possible, without encouraging a passion for such dangerous novelties.[3]

[3] I shall conclude this subject with observing that the present political controversy with regard to *instructions* is a very frivolous one and can never be brought to any decision, as it is managed by both parties. The country party do not pretend that a member is absolutely bound to follow instructions as an ambassador or general is confined by his orders, and that his vote is not to be received in the House but so far as it is conformable to them. The court party, again, do not pretend that the sentiments of the people ought to have no weight with every member, much less that he ought to despise the sentiments of those whom he represents, and with whom he is more particularly connected. And if their sentiments be of weight, why ought they not to express these sentiments? The question then is only concerning the degrees of weight which ought to be placed on instructions. But such is the nature of language that it is impossible for it to express distinctly these different degrees; and if men will carry on a controversy on this head, it may well happen that they differ in the language, and yet agree in their sentiments, or differ in their sentiments, and yet agree in their language. Besides, how is it possible to fix these degrees, considering the variety of affairs that come before the House, and the variety of places which members represent? Ought the instructions of *Totness* to have the same weight as those of London? or instructions with regard to the *Convention* which respected foreign politics, to have the same weight as those with regard to the *Excise* which respected only our domestic affairs?

ESSAY III[1]

OF THE ORIGIN OF GOVERNMENT

MAN, born in a family, is compelled to maintain society from necessity, from natural inclination, and from habit. The same creature, in his farther progress, is engaged to establish political society in order to administer justice, without which there can be no peace among them, nor safety, nor mutual intercourse. We are, therefore, to look upon all the vast apparatus of our government as having ultimately no other object or purpose but the distribution of justice, or, in other words, the support of the twelve judges. Kings and parliaments, fleets and armies, officers of the court and revenue, ambassadors, ministers and privy-councillors, are all subordinate in their end to this part of administration. Even the clergy, as their duty leads them to inculcate morality, may justly be thought, so far as regards this world, to have no other useful object of their institution.

All men are sensible of the necessity of justice to maintain peace and order, and all men are sensible of the necessity of peace and order for the maintenance of society. Yet, notwithstanding this strong and obvious necessity, such is the frailty or perverseness of our nature! it is impossible to keep men faithfully and unerringly in the paths of justice. Some extraordinary circumstances may happen in which a man finds his interests to be more promoted by fraud or rapine than hurt by the breach which his injustice makes in the social union. But much more frequently he is seduced from his great and important, but distant, interests, by the allurement of present, though often very frivolous, temptations. This great weakness is incurable in human nature.

Men must, therefore, endeavour to palliate what they cannot cure. They must institute some persons under the appellation of magistrates whose peculiar office it is to point out the decrees of equity, to punish transgressors, to correct fraud and violence, and to oblige men, however reluctant, to consult their own real and permanent interests. In

[1] [Ed. 1777, Part I. Essay V.]

a word, obedience is a new duty which must be invented to support that of justice, and the ties of equity must be corroborated by those of allegiance.

But still, viewing matters in an abstract light, it may be thought that nothing is gained by this alliance, and that the factitious duty of obedience, from its very nature, lays as feeble a hold of the human mind as the primitive and natural duty of justice. Peculiar interests and present temptations may overcome the one as well as the other. They are equally exposed to the same inconvenience, and the man who is inclined to be a bad neighbour must be led by the same motives, well or ill understood, to be a bad citizen or subject. Not to mention that the magistrate himself may often be negligent, or partial, or unjust, in his administration.

Experience, however, proves that there is a great difference between the cases. Order in society, we find, is much better maintained by means of government, and our duty to the magistrate is more strictly guarded by the principles of human nature than our duty to our fellow citizens. The love of dominion is so strong in the breast of man that many not only submit to, but court, all the dangers, and fatigues, and cares of government; and men, once raised to that station, though often led astray by private passions, find in ordinary cases a visible interest in the impartial administration of justice. The persons who first attain this distinction by the consent, tacit or express, of the people must be endowed with superior personal qualities of valour, force, integrity, or prudence, which command respect and confidence; and, after government is established, a regard to birth, rank, and station has a mighty influence over men and enforces the decrees of the magistrate. The prince or leader exclaims against every disorder which disturbs his society. He summons all his partisans and all men of probity to aid him in correcting and redressing it; and he is readily followed by all indifferent persons in the execution of his office. He soon acquires the power of rewarding these services, and, in the progress of society, he establishes subordinate ministers, and often a military force, who find an immediate and a visible interest in supporting his authority. Habit soon consolidates what other principles of human nature had imperfectly founded, and men, once accustomed to obedience, never think of departing from that path in which they and their ancestors have constantly trod, and to which they are confined by so many urgent and visible motives.

But though this progress of human affairs may appear certain and inevitable, and though the support which allegiance brings to justice be founded on obvious principles of human nature, it cannot be expected that men should beforehand be able to discover them or foresee their operation. Government commences more casually and more imperfectly. It is probable that the first ascendant of one man over multitudes begun during a state of war, where the superiority of courage and of genius discovers itself most visibly, where unanimity and concert are most requisite, and where the pernicious effects of disorder are most sensibly felt. The long continuance of that state, an incident common among savage tribes, inured the people to submission; and if the chieftain possessed as much equity as prudence and valour, he became, even during peace, the arbiter of all differences, and could gradually, by a mixture of force and consent, establish his authority. The benefit sensibly felt from his influence made it be cherished by the people, at least by the peaceable and well-disposed among them; and if his son enjoyed the same good qualities, government advanced the sooner to maturity and perfection, but was still in a feeble state, till the farther progress of improvement procured the magistrate a revenue, and enabled him to bestow rewards on the several instruments of his administration, and to inflict punishments on the refractory and disobedient. Before that period, each exertion of his influence must have been particular and founded on the peculiar circumstances of the case. After it, submission was no longer a matter of choice in the bulk of the community, but was rigorously exacted by the authority of the supreme magistrate.

In all governments there is a perpetual intestine struggle, open or secret, between Authority and Liberty, and neither of them can ever absolutely prevail in the contest. A great sacrifice of liberty must necessarily be made in every government, yet even the authority which confines liberty can never and perhaps ought never in any constitution to become quite entire and uncontrollable. The sultan is master of the life and fortune of any individual, but will not be permitted to impose new taxes on his subjects; a French monarch can impose taxes at pleasure, but would find it dangerous to attempt the lives and fortunes of individuals. Religion also, in most countries, is commonly found to be a very intractable principle; and other principles or prejudices frequently resist all the authority of the civil magistrate, whose power, being founded on opinion, can never subvert other opinions equally rooted with that of his title to dominion. The government which, in common appellation, receives the appellation of "free," is that which admits of a partition of power among several members whose united authority is no less, or is commonly greater, than that of any monarch, but who, in the usual course of administration, must act by general and equal laws that are previously known to all the members and to all their subjects. In this sense it must be owned that liberty is the perfection of civil society, but still authority must be acknowledged essential to its very existence. And in those contests which so often take place between the one and the other, the latter may, on that account, challenge the preference. Unless perhaps one may say — and it may be said with some reason — that a circumstance which is essential to the existence of civil society must always support itself, and needs be guarded with less jealousy than one that contributes only to its perfection, which the indolence of men is so apt to neglect or their ignorance to overlook.

ESSAY IV [1]

OF CIVIL LIBERTY

THOSE WHO EMPLOY their pens on political subjects, free from party rage and party prejudices, cultivate a science which, of all others, contributes most to public utility, and even to the private satisfaction of those who addict themselves to the study of it. I am apt, however, to entertain a suspicion that the world is still too young to fix many general truths in politics which will remain true to the latest posterity. We have not as yet had experience of three thousand years, so that not only the art of reasoning is still imperfect in this science, as in all others, but we even want sufficient materials upon which we can reason. It is not fully known what degree of refinement, either in virtue or vice, human nature is susceptible of, nor what may be expected of mankind from any great revolution in their education, customs, or principles. Machiavel was certainly a great genius, but, having confined his study to the furious and tyrannical governments of ancient times or to the little disorderly principalities of Italy, his reasonings, especially upon monarchical government, have been found extremely defective; and there scarcely is any maxim in his *Prince* which subsequent experience has not entirely refuted.

> A weak prince (says he) is incapable of receiving good counsel, for, if he consult with several, he will not be able to choose among their different counsels. If he abandon himself to one, that minister may perhaps have capacity, but he will not long be a minister; he will be sure to dispossess his master and place himself and his family upon the throne.

I mention this, among many instances of the errors of that politician, proceeding, in a great measure, from his having lived in too early an age of the world to be a good judge of political truth. Almost all the princes of Europe are at present governed by their ministers, and have been so for near two centuries, and yet no such event has ever

---

[1] [Ed. 1777, Part I. Essay XII.]

happened or can possibly happen. Sejanus might project dethroning the Cæsars, but Fleury, though ever so vicious, could not, while in his senses, entertain the least hopes of dispossessing the Bourbons.

Trade was never esteemed an affair of state till the last century, and there scarcely is any ancient writer on politics who has made mention of it.[2] Even the Italians have kept a profound silence with regard to it, though it has now engaged the chief attention as well of ministers of state as of speculative reasoners. The great opulence, grandeur, and military achievements of the two maritime powers seem first to have instructed mankind in the importance of an extensive commerce.

Having, therefore, intended in this Essay to make a full comparison of civil liberty and absolute government and to show the great advantages of the former above the latter, I began to entertain a suspicion that no man in this age was sufficiently qualified for such an undertaking, and that, whatever any one should advance on that head, would in all probability be refuted by further experience and be rejected by posterity. Such mighty revolutions have happened in human affairs, and so many events have arisen contrary to the expectation of the ancients, that they are sufficient to beget the suspicion of still further changes.

It had been observed by the ancients that all the arts and sciences arose among free nations, and that the Persians and Egyptians, notwithstanding their ease, opulence, and luxury, made but faint efforts towards a relish in those finer pleasures which were carried to such perfection by the Greeks amidst continual wars, attended with poverty and the greatest simplicity of life and manners. It had also been observed that, when the Greeks lost their liberty, though they increased mightily in riches by means of the conquests of Alexander, yet the arts from that moment declined among them, and have never since been able to raise their head in that climate. Learning was transplanted to Rome, the only free nation at that time in the universe, and, having met with so favourable a soil, it made prodigious shoots for above a century, till the decay of liberty produced also the decay of letters and spread a total barbarism over the world. From these

---

[2] Xenophon mentions it, but with a doubt if it be of any advantage to a state. Εἰ δὲ καὶ ἐμπορία ὠφελεῖ τι πόλιν, etc. [but if trade is also of any advantage to the state] XEN. HIERO — Plato totally excludes it from his imaginary republic. *De Legibus*, lib. iv.

two experiments of which each was double in its kind and showed the fall of learning in absolute governments as well as its rise in popular ones, Longinus thought himself sufficiently justified in asserting that the arts and sciences could never flourish but in a free government. And in this opinion he has been followed by several eminent writers [3] in our own country who either confined their view merely to ancient facts or entertained too great a partiality in favour of that form of government established among us.

But what would these writers have said to the instances of modern Rome and Florence? Of which the former carried to perfection all the finer arts of sculpture, painting, and music, as well as poetry, though it groaned under tyranny, and under the tyranny of priests, while the latter made its chief progress in the arts and sciences after it began to lose its liberty by the usurpation of the family of Medici. Ariosto, Tasso, Galileo, no more than Raphael or Michael Angelo, were not born in republics. And though the Lombard school was famous as well as the Roman, yet the Venetians have had the smallest share in its honours and seem rather inferior to the other Italians in their genius for the arts and sciences. Rubens established his school at Antwerp, not at Amsterdam. Dresden, not Hamburg, is the centre of politeness in Germany.

But the most eminent instance of the flourishing of learning in absolute governments is that of France, which scarcely ever enjoyed any established liberty, and yet has carried the arts and sciences as near perfection as any other nation. The English are, perhaps, greater philosophers, the Italians better painters and musicians, the Romans were greater orators, but the French are the only people, except the Greeks, who have been at once philosophers, poets, orators, historians, painters, architects, sculptors, and musicians. With regard to the stage, they have excelled even the Greeks, who far excelled the English. And, in common life, they have, in a great measure, perfected that art, the most useful and agreeable of any, *l'art de vivre*, the art of society and conversation.

If we consider the state of the sciences and polite arts in our own country, Horace's observation, with regard to the Romans, may in a great measure be applied to the British.

> Sed in longum tamen ævum
> Manserunt, hodieque manent *vestigia ruris.*

[3] Mr. Addison and Lord Shaftesbury.

The elegance and propriety of style have been very much neglected among us. We have no dictionary of our language, and scarcely a tolerable grammar. The first polite prose we have was writ by a man who is still alive.[4] As to Sprat, Locke, and even Temple, they knew too little of the rules of art to be esteemed elegant writers. The prose of Bacon, Harrington, and Milton is altogether stiff and pedantic, though their sense be excellent. Men in this country have been so much occupied in the great disputes of *religion, politics,* and *philosophy,* that they had no relish for the seemingly minute observations of grammar and criticism. And, though this turn of thinking must have considerably improved our sense and our talent of reasoning, it must be confessed that even in those sciences above mentioned, we have not any standard book which we can transmit to posterity. And the utmost we have to boast of are a few essays towards a more just philosophy, which indeed promise well, but have not as yet reached any degree of perfection.

It has become an established opinion that commerce can never flourish but in a free government, and this opinion seems to be founded on a longer and larger experience than the foregoing, with regard to the arts and sciences. If we trace commerce in its progress through Tyre, Athens, Syracuse, Carthage, Venice, Florence, Genoa, Antwerp, Holland, England, etc., we shall always find it to have fixed its seat in free governments. The three greatest trading towns now in Europe are London, Amsterdam, and Hamburg — all free cities and Protestant cities, that is, enjoying a double liberty. It must, however, be observed that the great jealousy entertained of late with regard to the commerce of France seems to prove that this maxim is no more certain and infallible than the foregoing, and that the subjects of an absolute prince may become our rivals in commerce as well as in learning.

Durst I deliver my opinion in an affair of so much uncertainty, I would assert that, notwithstanding the efforts of the French, there is something hurtful to commerce inherent in the very nature of absolute government and inseparable from it, though the reason I should assign for this opinion is somewhat different from that which is commonly insisted on. Private property seems to me almost as secure in a civilized European monarchy as in a republic, nor is danger much apprehended in such a government from the violence of the sovereign

[4] Dr. Swift.

more than we commonly dread harm from thunder, or earthquakes, or any accident the most unusual and extraordinary. Avarice, the spur of industry, is so obstinate a passion, and works its way through so many real dangers and difficulties, that it is not likely to be scared by an imaginary danger which is so small that it scarcely admits of calculation. Commerce, therefore, in my opinion, is apt to decay in absolute governments, not because it is there less *secure*, but because it is less *honourable*. A subordination of rank is absolutely necessary to the support of monarchy. Birth, titles, and place must be honoured above industry and riches, and, while these notions prevail, all the considerable traders will be tempted to throw up their commerce in order to purchase some of those employments to which privileges and honours are annexed.

Since I am upon this head, of the alterations which time has produced or may produce in politics, I must observe that all kinds of government, free and absolute, seem to have undergone in modern times a great change for the better, with regard both to foreign and domestic management. The *balance* of power is a secret in politics, fully known only to the present age, and I must add that the internal police of states has also received great improvements within the last century. We are informed by Sallust that Catiline's army was much augmented by the accession of the highwaymen about Rome, though I believe that all of that profession who are at present dispersed over Europe would not amount to a regiment. In Cicero's pleadings for Milo I find this argument, among others, made use of to prove that his client had not assassinated Clodius. Had Milo, said he, intended to have killed Clodius, he had not attacked him in the day-time and at such a distance from the city; he had waylaid him at night near the suburbs, where it might have been pretended that he was killed by robbers, and the frequency of the accident would have favoured the deceit. This is a surprising proof of the loose policy of Rome and of the number and force of these robbers, since Clodius[5] was at that time attended by thirty slaves, who were completely armed and sufficiently accustomed to blood and danger in the frequent tumults excited by that seditious tribune.

But though all kinds of government be improved in modern times, yet monarchical government seems to have made the greatest advances

[5] *Vide* Asc. Ped. in *Orat. pro Milone.*

towards perfection. It may now be affirmed of civilized monarchies, what was formerly said in praise of republics alone, *that they are a government of Laws, not of Men*. They are found susceptible of order, method, and constancy, to a surprising degree. Property is there secure, industry encouraged, the arts flourish, and the prince lives secure among his subjects, like a father among his children. There are, perhaps, and have been for two centuries, near two hundred absolute princes, great and small, in Europe; and allowing twenty years to each reign, we may suppose that there have been in the whole two thousand monarchs, or tyrants, as the Greeks would have called them; yet of these, there has not been one, not even Philip II of Spain, so bad as Tiberius, Caligula, Nero, or Domitian, who were four in twelve among the Roman emperors. It must, however, be confessed that, though monarchical governments have approached nearer to popular ones in gentleness and stability, they are still inferior. Our modern education and customs instil more humanity and moderation than the ancient, but have not as yet been able to overcome entirely the disadvantages of that form of government.

But here I must beg leave to advance a conjecture which seems probable, but which posterity alone can fully judge of. I am apt to think that in monarchical governments there is a source of improvement, and in popular governments a source of degeneracy, which in time will bring these species of civil polity still nearer an equality. The greatest abuses which arise in France, the most perfect model of pure monarchy, proceed not from the number or weight of the taxes, beyond what are to be met with in free countries, but from the expensive, unequal, arbitrary, and intricate method of levying them, by which the industry of the poor, especially of the peasants and farmers, is in a great measure discouraged, and agriculture rendered a beggarly and slavish employment. But to whose advantage do these abuses tend? If to that of the nobility, they might be esteemed inherent in that form of government, since the nobility are the true supports of monarchy, and it is natural their interest should be more consulted in such a constitution than that of the people. But the nobility are, in reality, the chief losers by this oppression, since it ruins their estates and beggars their tenants. The only gainers by it are the *financiers*, a race of men rather odious to the nobility and the whole kingdom. If a prince or minister, therefore, should arise, endowed with sufficient discernment to know his own and the public interest, and with sufficient force of mind to break through ancient customs, we might expect to see these abuses remedied, in which case the difference between that absolute government and our free one would not appear so considerable as at present.

The source of degeneracy which may be remarked in free governments consists in the practice of contracting debt and mortgaging the public revenues, by which taxes may, in time, become altogether intolerable and all the property of the state be brought into the hands of the public. This practice is of modern date. The Athenians, though governed by a republic, paid near two hundred per cent for those sums of money which any emergency made it necessary for them to borrow, as we learn from Xenophon.[6] Among the moderns, the Dutch first introduced the practice of borrowing great sums at low interest, and have well nigh ruined themselves by it. Absolute princes have also contracted debt, but, as an absolute prince may make a bankruptcy when he pleases, his people can never be oppressed by his debts. In popular governments, the people, and chiefly those who have the highest offices, being commonly the public creditors, it is difficult for the state to make use of this remedy which, however it may sometimes be necessary, is always cruel and barbarous. This, therefore, seems to be an inconvenience which nearly threatens all free governments, especially our own at the present juncture of affairs. And what a strong motive is this to increase our frugality of public money, lest, for want of it, we be reduced by the multiplicity of taxes or, what is worse, by our public impotence and inability for defence, to curse our very liberty and wish ourselves in the same state of servitude with all the nations who surround us?

[6] Κτῆσιν δὲ ἀπ' οὐδενὸς ἂν οὕτω καλὴν κτήσαιντο ὥσπερ ἀφ' οὗ ἂν προτελέσωσιν εἰς τὴν ἀφορμήν... Οἱ δέ γε πλεῖστοι Ἀθηναίων πλείονα λήψονται κατ' ἐνιαυτὸν ἢ ὅσα ἂν εἰσενέγκωσιν. Οἱ γὰρ μνᾶν προτελέσαντες, ἐγγὺς δυοῖν μναῖν πρόσοδον ἕξουσιν [καὶ ταῦτα ἐν πόλει] ὃ δοκεῖ τῶν ἀνθρωπίνων ἀσφαλέστατόν τε καὶ πολυχρονιώτατον εἶναι. ΞΕΝ. ΠΟΡΟΙ. [Xenophon, Ways and Means, 3, 6 ff: the author assumes that for certain kinds of governmental enterprise the state will need capital to start with, and that the money can be raised by contributions from private citizens; then he continues: "There is nothing from which they could make such a nice profit as from the money which they would invest in that capital fund ... But most of the Athenians will, in a year, get more than their contribution had been. For those who had invested one *mina* will have an income of almost two *minae* [and their security against risk is based on the state] which, of all human institutions, is supposed to be the safest and most lasting."]

ESSAY V[1]

THE EPICUREAN[2]

IT IS a great mortification to the vanity of man that his utmost art and industry can never equal the meanest of nature's productions, either for beauty or value. Art is only the under-workman, and is employed to give a few strokes of embellishment to those pieces which come from the hand of the Master. Some of the drapery may be of his drawing, but he is not allowed to touch the principal figure. Art may make a suit of clothes, but nature must produce a man.

Even in those productions commonly denominated works of art, we find that the noblest of the kind are beholden for their chief beauty to the force and happy influence of nature. To the native enthusiasm of the poets we owe whatever is admirable in their productions. The greatest genius, where nature at any time fails him — for she is not equal — throws aside the lyre and hopes not, from the rules of art, to reach that divine harmony which must proceed from her inspiration alone. How poor are those songs where a happy flow of fancy has not furnished materials for art to embellish and refine!

But of all the fruitless attempts of art, no one is so ridiculous as that which the severe philosophers have undertaken, the producing of an *artificial happiness*, and making us be pleased by rules of reason and by reflection. Why did none of them claim the reward which Xerxes promised to him who should invent a new pleasure? Unless, perhaps, they invented so many pleasures for their own use that they despised riches and stood in no need of any enjoyments which the rewards of that monarch could procure them. I am apt, indeed, to

[1] [Ed. 1777, Part I. Essay XV.]

[2] Or, *The man of elegance and pleasure.* The intention of this and the three following Essays is not so much to explain accurately the sentiments of the ancient sects of philosophy, as to deliver the sentiments of sects that naturally form themselves in the world, and entertain different ideas of human life and happiness. I have given each of them the name of the philosophical sect to which it bears the greatest affinity.

think that they were not willing to furnish the Persian court with a new pleasure by presenting it with so new and unusual an object of ridicule. Their speculations, when confined to theory and gravely delivered in the schools of Greece, might excite admiration in their ignorant pupils, but the attempting to reduce such principles to practice would soon have betrayed their absurdity.

You pretend to make me happy by reason and by rules of art. You must then create me anew by rules of art, for on my original frame and structure does my happiness depend. But you want power to effect this, and skill too, I am afraid, nor can I entertain a less opinion of nature's wisdom than yours, and let her conduct the machine which she has so wisely framed, I find that I should only spoil it by tampering.

To what purpose should I pretend to regulate, refine, or invigorate any of those springs or principles which nature has implanted in me? Is this the road by which I must reach happiness? But happiness implies ease, contentment, repose, and pleasure, not watchfulness, care, and fatigue. The health of my body consists in the facility with which all its operations are performed. The stomach digests the aliments, the heart circulates the blood, the brain separates and refines the spirits, and all this without my concerning myself in the matter. When by my will alone I can stop the blood as it runs with impetuosity along its canals, then may I hope to change the course of my sentiments and passions. In vain should I strain my faculties, and endeavour to receive pleasure from an object which is not fitted by nature to affect my organs with delight. I may give myself pain by my fruitless endeavours, but shall never reach any pleasure.

Away then with all those vain pretences of making ourselves happy within ourselves, of feasting on our own thoughts, of being satisfied with the consciousness of well-doing, and of despising all assistance and all supplies from external objects. This is the voice of pride, not of nature. And it were well if even this pride could support itself and communicate a real *inward* pleasure, however melancholy or severe. But this impotent pride can do no more than regulate the *outside*, and, with infinite pains and attention, compose the language and countenance to a philosophical dignity in order to deceive the ignorant vulgar. The heart, meanwhile, is empty of all enjoyment, and the mind, unsupported by its proper objects, sinks into the deepest sorrow and dejection. Miserable, but vain mortal! Thy mind be happy within itself! With what resources is it endowed to fill so immense a void and supply the place of all thy bodily senses and faculties? Can thy head subsist without thy other members? In such a situation,

> What foolish figure must it make?
> Do nothing else but sleep and ake.

Into such a lethargy, or such a melancholy, must thy mind be plunged when deprived of foreign occupations and enjoyments.

Keep me, therefore, no longer in this violent constraint. Confine me not within myself, but point out to me those objects and pleasures which afford the chief enjoyment. But why do I apply to you, proud and ignorant sages, to show me the road to happiness? Let me consult my own passions and inclinations. In them must I read the dictates of nature, not in your frivolous discourses.

But see, propitious to my wishes, the divine, the amiable *pleasure*,[3] the supreme love of GODS and men, advances towards me. At her approach my heart beats with genial heat, and every sense and every faculty is dissolved in joy, while she pours around me all the embellishments of the spring, and all the treasures of the autumn. The melody of her voice charms my ears with the softest music, as she invites me to partake of those delicious fruits which, with a smile that diffuses a glory on the heavens and the earth, she presents to me. The sportive cupids who attend her, or fan me with their odoriferous wings, or pour on my head the most fragrant oils, or offer me their sparkling nectar in golden goblets, O! for ever let me spread my limbs on this bed of roses, and thus, thus feel the delicious moments with soft and downy steps glide along. But cruel chance! Whither do you fly so fast? Why do my ardent wishes and that load of pleasures under which you labour rather hasten than retard your unrelenting pace? Suffer me to enjoy this soft repose, after all my fatigues in search of happiness. Suffer me to satiate myself with these delicacies, after the pains of so long and so foolish an abstinence.

But it will not do. The roses have lost their hue, the fruit its flavour, and that delicious wine whose fumes so late intoxicated all my senses with such delight now solicits in vain the sated palate. *Pleasure* smiles at my languor. She beckons her sister, *virtue*, to come

---

[3] *Dia Voluptas.* LUCRET.

to her assistance. The gay, the frolic *virtue* observes the call and
brings along the whole troop of my jovial friends. Welcome, thrice
welcome, my ever dear companions, to these shady bowers and to
this luxurious repast. Your presence has restored to the rose its hue,
and to the fruit its flavour. The vapours of this sprightly nectar now
again ply round my heart, while you partake of my delights, and
discover in your cheerful looks the pleasure which you receive from
my happiness and satisfaction. The like do I receive from yours,
and, encouraged by your joyous presence, shall again renew the feast
with which, from too much enjoyment, my senses are well nigh sated,
while the mind kept not pace with the body, nor afforded relief to her
overburdened partner.

In our cheerful discourses, better than in the formal reasoning of
the schools, is true wisdom to be found. In our friendly endearments,
better than in the hollow debates of statesmen and pretended patriots,
does true virtue display itself. Forgetful of the past, secure of the
future, let us here enjoy the present, and while we yet possess a being,
let us fix some good beyond the power of fate or fortune. Tomorrow
will bring its own pleasures along with it; or, should it disappoint our
fond wishes, we shall at least enjoy the pleasure of reflecting on the
pleasures of today.

Fear not, my friends, that the barbarous dissonance of Bacchus and
of his revellers should break in upon this entertainment and confound
us with their turbulent and clamorous pleasures. The sprightly Muses
wait around and, with their charming symphony sufficient to soften
the wolves and tigers of the savage desert, inspire a soft joy into every
bosom. Peace, harmony, and concord reign in this retreat, nor is the
silence ever broken but by the music of our songs or the cheerful
accents of our friendly voices.

But hark! the favourite of the Muses, the gentle Damon strikes the
lyre, and, while he accompanies its harmonious notes with his more
harmonious song, he inspires us with the same happy debauch of
fancy by which he is himself transported. "Ye happy youth!" he
sings, "Ye favoured of Heaven![4] while the wanton spring pours upon

[4] An imitation of the Syren's song in Tasso:
'O Giovenetti, mentre Aprile et Maggio
V' ammantan di fiorité et verde spoglie,' etc.
Giuresalemme Liberata, Canto 14.

you all her blooming honours, let not *glory* seduce you with her delusive blaze to pass in perils and dangers this delicious season, this prime of life. Wisdom points out to you the road to pleasure. Nature, too, beckons you to follow her in that smooth and flowery path. Will you shut your ears to their commanding voice? Will you harden your heart to their soft allurements? Oh, deluded mortals! thus to lose your youth, thus to throw away so invaluable a present, to trifle with so perishing a blessing. Contemplate well your recompense. Consider that glory which so allures your proud hearts and seduces you with your own praises. It is an echo, a dream, nay, the shadow of a dream, dissipated by every wind, and lost by every contrary breath of the ignorant and ill-judging multitude. You fear not that even death itself shall ravish it from you. But behold! while you are yet alive, calumny bereaves you of it, ignorance neglects it, nature enjoys it not; fancy alone, renouncing every pleasure, receives this airy recompense, empty and unstable as herself."

Thus the hours pass unperceived along and lead in their wanton train all the pleasures of sense and all the joys of harmony and friendship. Smiling *innocence* closes the procession, and, while she presents herself to our ravished eyes, she embellishes the whole scene and renders the view of these pleasures as transporting after they have past us, as when, with laughing countenances, they were yet advancing towards us.

But the sun has sunk below the horizon, and darkness, stealing silently upon us, has now buried all nature in an universal shade. "Rejoice, my friends, continue your repast, or change it for soft repose. Though absent, your joy or your tranquillity shall still be mine." *But whither do you go? Or what new pleasures call you from our society? Is there aught agreeable without your friends? And can aught please in which we partake not?* "Yes, my friends, the joy which I now seek admits not of your participation. Here alone I wish your absence, and here alone can I find a sufficient compensation for the loss of your society."

But I have not advanced far through the shades of the thick wood which spreads a double night around me, ere, methinks, I perceive through the gloom the charming Cælia, the mistress of my wishes, who wanders impatient through the grove and, preventing the appointed hour, silently chides my tardy steps. But the joy which she receives from my presence best pleads my excuse and, dissipating every anxious and every angry thought, leaves room for nought but mutual joy and rapture. With what words, my fair one, shall I express my tenderness or describe the emotions which now warm my transported bosom! Words are too faint to describe my love, and if, alas! you feel not the same flame within you, in vain shall I endeavour to convey to you a just conception of it. But your every word and every motion suffice to remove this doubt and, while they express your passion, serve also to inflame mine. How amiable this solitude, this silence, this darkness! No objects now importune the ravished soul. The thought, the sense, all full of nothing but our mutual happiness, wholly possess the mind and convey a pleasure which deluded mortals vainly seek for in every other enjoyment.

But why does your bosom heave with these sighs, while tears bathe your glowing cheeks? Why distract your heart with such vain anxieties? Why so often ask me, *How long my love shall yet endure?* Alas! my Cælia, can I resolve this question? *Do I know how long my life shall yet endure?* But does this also disturb your tender breast? And is the image of our frail mortality forever present with you, to throw a damp on your gayest hours and poison even those joys which love inspires? Consider rather that, if life be frail, if youth be transitory, we should well employ the present moment and lose no part of so perishable an existence. Yet a little moment, and *these* shall be no more. We shall be as if we had never been. Not a memory of us be left upon earth, and even the fabulous shades below will not afford us a habitation. Our fruitless anxieties, our vain projects, our uncertain speculations shall all be swallowed up and lost. Our present doubts concerning the original cause of all things must never, alas! be resolved. This alone we may be certain of, that if any governing mind preside, he must be pleased to see us fulfil the ends of our being and enjoy that pleasure for which alone we were created. Let this reflection give ease to your anxious thoughts, but render not your joys too serious by dwelling for ever upon it. It is sufficient once to be acquainted with this philosophy in order to give an unbounded loose to love and jollity, and remove all the scruples of a vain superstition. But while youth and passion, my fair one, prompt our eager desires, we must find gayer subjects of discourse to intermix with these amorous caresses.

ESSAY VI[1]

THE STOIC[2]

THERE IS this obvious and material difference in the conduct of nature with regard to man and other animals that, having endowed the former with a sublime celestial spirit and having given him an affinity with superior beings, she allows not such noble faculties to lie lethargic or idle, but urges him by necessity to employ on every emergency his utmost *art* and *industry*. Brute creatures have many of their necessities supplied by nature, being clothed and armed by this beneficent parent of all things; and where their own *industry* is requisite on any occasion, nature, by implanting instincts, still supplies them with the *art* and guides them to their good by her unerring precepts. But man, exposed naked and indigent to the rude elements, rises slowly from that helpless state by the care and vigilance of his parents, and, having attained his utmost growth and perfection, reaches only a capacity of subsisting by his own care and vigilance. Everything is sold to skill and labour, and where nature furnishes the materials, they are still rude and unfinished till industry, ever active and intelligent, refines them from their brute state and fits them for human use and convenience.

Acknowledge, therefore, O man! the beneficence of nature, for she has given thee that intelligence which supplies all thy necessities. But let not indolence, under the false appearance of gratitude, persuade thee to rest contented with her presents. Wouldst thou return to the raw herbage for thy food, to the open sky for thy covering, and to stones and clubs for thy defence against the ravenous animals of the desert? Then return also to thy savage manners, to thy timorous superstition, to thy brutal ignorance, and sink thyself below those animals whose condition thou admirest and wouldst so fondly imitate.

Thy kind parent, Nature, having given thee art and intelligence,

[1] [Ed. 1777, Part I. Essay XVI.]
[2] Or the man of action and virtue.

328

has filled the whole globe with materials to employ these talents. Harken to her voice, which so plainly tells thee that thou thyself shouldst also be the object of thy industry, and that by art and attention alone thou canst acquire that ability which will raise thee to thy proper station in the universe. Behold this artisan who converts a rude and shapeless stone into a noble metal and, moulding that metal by his cunning hands, creates, as it were by magic, every weapon for his defence and every utensil for his convenience. He has not this skill from nature; use and practice have taught it him, and if thou wouldst emulate his success, thou must follow his laborious footsteps.

But while thou *ambitiously* aspirest to perfecting thy bodily powers and faculties, wouldst thou *meanly* neglect thy mind and, from a preposterous sloth, leave it still rude and uncultivated as it came from the hands of nature? Far be such folly and negligence from every rational being. If nature has been frugal in her gifts and endowments, there is the more need of art to supply her defects. If she has been generous and liberal, know that she still expects industry and application on our part, and revenges herself in proportion to our negligent ingratitude. The richest genius, like the most fertile soil, when uncultivated shoots up into the rankest weeds and, instead of vines and olives for the pleasure and use of man, produces to its slothful owner the most abundant crop of poisons.

The great end of all human industry is the attainment of happiness. For this were arts invented, sciences cultivated, laws ordained, and societies modelled, by the most profound wisdom of patriots and legislators. Even the lonely savage, who lies exposed to the inclemency of the elements and the fury of wild beasts, forgets not for a moment this grand object of his being. Ignorant as he is of every art of life, he still keeps in view the end of all those arts and eagerly seeks for felicity amidst that darkness with which he is environed. But as much as the wildest savage is inferior to the polished citizen, who, under the protection of laws, enjoys every convenience which industry has invented, so much is this citizen himself inferior to the man of virtue and the true philosopher who governs his appetites, subdues his passions, and has learned from reason to set a just value on every pursuit and enjoyment. For is there an art and apprenticeship necessary for every other attainment? And is there no art of life, no rule, no precepts, to direct us in this principal concern? Can no particular pleasure be attained without skill, and can the whole be regulated without reflection or intelligence by the blind guidance of appetite and instinct? Sure, then, no mistakes are ever committed in this affair, but every man, however dissolute and negligent, proceeds in the pursuit of happiness with as unerring a motion as that which the celestial bodies observe when, conducted by the hand of the Almighty, they roll along the ethereal plains. But if mistakes be often, be inevitably committed, let us register these mistakes, let us consider their causes, let us weigh their importance, let us inquire for their remedies. When from this we have fixed all the rules of conduct, we are *philosophers*. When we have reduced these rules to practice, we are *sages*.

Like many subordinate artists, employed to form the several wheels and springs of a machine, such are those who excel in all the particular arts of life. *He* is the master workman who puts those several parts together, moves them according to just harmony and proportion, and produces true felicity as the result of their conspiring order.

While thou hast such an alluring object in view, shall that labour and attention requisite to the attainment of thy end ever seem burdensome and intolerable? Know that this labour itself is the chief ingredient of the felicity to which thou aspirest, and that every enjoyment soon becomes insipid and distasteful when not acquired by fatigue and industry. See the hardy hunters rise from their downy couches, shake off the slumbers which still weigh down their heavy eyelids and, ere *aurora* has yet covered the heavens with her flaming mantle, hasten to the forest. They leave behind, in their own houses and in the neighbouring plains, animals of every kind whose flesh furnishes the most delicious fare and which offer themselves to the fatal stroke. Laborious man disdains so easy a purchase. He seeks for a prey which hides itself from his search, or flies from his pursuit, or defends itself from his violence. Having exerted in the chase every passion of the mind and every member of the body, he then finds the charms of repose, and with joy compares his pleasures to those of his engaging labours.

And can vigorous industry give pleasure to the pursuit even of the most worthless prey, which frequently escapes our toils? And cannot the same industry render the cultivating of our mind, the moderating of our passions, the enlightening of our reason, an agreeable occupation, while we are every day sensible of our progress and behold our inward features and countenance brightening incessantly with new charms? Begin by curing yourself of this lethargic indolence; the task is not difficult: you need but taste the sweets of honest labour. Proceed to learn the just value of every pursuit; long study is not requisite: compare, though but for once, the mind to the body, virtue to fortune, and glory to pleasure. You will then perceive the advantages of industry; you will then be sensible what are the proper objects of your industry.

In vain do you seek repose from beds of roses, in vain do you hope for enjoyment from the most delicious wines and fruits. Your indolence itself becomes a fatigue, your pleasure itself creates disgust. The mind, unexercised, finds every delight insipid and loathsome and, ere yet the body, full of noxious humours, feels the torment of its multiplied diseases, your nobler part is sensible of the invading poison and seeks in vain to relieve its anxiety by new pleasures which still augment the fatal malady.

I need not tell you that, by this eager pursuit of pleasure, you more and more expose yourself to fortune and accidents, and rivet your affections on external objects, which chance may in a moment ravish from you. I shall suppose that your indulgent stars favour you still with the enjoyment of your riches and possessions. I prove to you that even in the midst of your luxurious pleasures you are unhappy, and that by too much indulgence you are incapable of enjoying what prosperous fortune still allows you to possess.

But surely the instability of fortune is a consideration not to be overlooked or neglected. Happiness cannot possibly exist where there is no security, and security can have no place where fortune has any dominion. Though that unstable deity should not exert her rage against you, the dread of it would still torment you, would disturb your slumbers, haunt your dreams, and throw a damp on the jollity of your most delicious banquets.

The temple of wisdom is seated on a rock, above the rage of the fighting elements, and inaccessible to all the malice of man. The rolling thunder breaks below, and those more terrible instruments of human fury reach not to so sublime a height. The sage, while he breathes that serene air, looks down with pleasure, mixed with compassion, on the errors of mistaken mortals who blindly seek for the true path of life and pursue riches, nobility, honour, or power, for genuine felicity. The greater part he beholds disappointed of their fond wishes; some lament that, having once possessed the object of their desires, it is ravished from them by envious fortune, and all complain that even their own vows, though granted, cannot give them happiness or relieve the anxiety of their distracted minds.

But does the sage always preserve himself in this philosophical indifference and rest contented with lamenting the miseries of mankind, without ever employing himself for their relief? Does he constantly indulge this severe wisdom which, by pretending to elevate him above human accidents, does in reality harden his heart and render him careless of the interests of mankind and of society? No, he knows that in this sullen *apathy* neither true wisdom nor true happiness can be found. He feels too strongly the charm of the social affections ever to counteract so sweet, so natural, so virtuous a propensity. Even when, bathed in tears, he laments the miseries of the human race, of his country, of his friends, and, unable to give succour, can only relieve them by compassion, he yet rejoices in the generous disposition and feels a satisfaction superior to that of the most indulged sense. So engaging are the sentiments of humanity that they brighten up the very face of sorrow and operate like the sun which, shining on a dusky cloud or falling rain, paints on them the most glorious colours which are to be found in the whole circle of nature.

But it is not here alone that the social virtues display their energy. With whatever ingredient you mix them, they are still predominant. As sorrow cannot overcome them, so neither can sensual pleasure obscure them. The joys of love, however tumultuous, banish not the tender sentiments of sympathy and affection. They even derive their chief influence from that generous passion and, when presented alone, afford nothing to the unhappy mind but lassitude and disgust. Behold this sprightly debauche who professes a contempt of all other pleasures but those of wine and jollity; separate him from his companions, like a spark from a fire where before it contributed to the general blaze: his alacrity suddenly extinguishes, and, though surrounded with every other means of delight, he loathes the sumptuous banquet and prefers even the most abstracted study and speculation as more agreeable and entertaining.

But the social passions never afford such transporting pleasures or make so glorious an appearance in the eyes both of God and man as when, shaking off every earthly mixture, they associate themselves with the sentiments of virtue and prompt us to laudable and worthy actions. As harmonious colours mutually give and receive a lustre by their friendly union, so do these ennobling sentiments of the human mind. See the triumph of nature in parental affection! What selfish passion, what sensual delight is a match for it, whether a man exults in the prosperity and virtue of his offspring or flies to their succour through the most threatening and tremendous dangers?

Proceed still in purifying the generous passion, you will still the more admire its shining glories. What charms are there in the harmony of minds and in a friendship founded on mutual esteem and gratitude! What satisfaction in relieving the distressed, in comforting the afflicted, in raising the fallen, and in stopping the career of cruel fortune, or of more cruel man, in their insults over the good and virtuous! But what supreme joy in the victories over vice as well as misery when, by virtuous example or wise exhortation, our fellow creatures are taught to govern their passions, reform their vices, and subdue their worst enemies, which inhabit within their own bosoms!

But these objects are still too limited for the human mind which, being of celestial origin, swells with the divinest and most enlarged affections and, carrying its attention beyond kindred and acquaintance, extends its benevolent wishes to the most distant posterity. It views liberty and laws as the source of human happiness, and devotes itself with the utmost alacrity to their guardianship and protection. Toils, dangers, death itself, carry their charms when we brave them for the public good and ennoble that being which we generously sacrifice for the interests of our country. Happy the man whom indulgent fortune allows to pay to virtue what he owes to nature and to make a generous gift of what must otherwise be ravished from him by cruel necessity.

In the true sage and patriot are united whatever can distinguish human nature or elevate mortal man to a resemblance with the Divinity. The softest benevolence, the most undaunted resolution, the tenderest sentiments, the most sublime love of virtue — all these animate successively his transported bosom. What satisfaction, when he looks within, to find the most turbulent passions tuned to just harmony and concord, and every jarring sound banished from this enchanting music! If the contemplation even of inanimate beauty is so delightful, if it ravishes the senses even when the fair form is foreign to us, what must be the effects of moral beauty? And what influence must it have when it embellishes our own mind and is the result of our own reflection and industry?

But where is the reward of virtue? And what recompense has nature provided for such important sacrifices as those of life and fortune which we must often make to it? Oh, sons of earth! Are ye ignorant of the value of this celestial mistress? And do ye meanly inquire for her portion when ye observe her genuine charms? But know that nature has been indulgent to human weakness and has not left this favourite child naked and unendowed. She has provided virtue with the richest dowry. But being careful lest the allurements of interest should engage such suitors as were insensible of the native worth of so divine a beauty, she has wisely provided that this dowry can have no charms but in the eyes of those who are already transported with the love of virtue. Glory is the portion of virtue, the sweet reward of honourable toils, the triumphant crown which covers the thoughtful head of the disinterested patriot or the dusty brow of the victorious warrior. Elevated by so sublime a prize, the man of virtue looks down with contempt on all the allurements of pleasure, and all the menaces of danger. Death itself loses its terrors when he considers that its dominion extends only over a part of him, and that, in spite of death and time, the rage of the elements, and the endless vicissitude of human affairs, he is assured of an immortal fame among all the sons of men.

There surely is a Being who presides over the universe and who, with infinite wisdom and power, has reduced the jarring elements into just order and proportion. Let speculative reasoners dispute how far this beneficent Being extends his care, and whether he prolongs our existence beyond the grave in order to bestow on virtue its just reward and render it fully triumphant. The man of morals, without deciding anything on so dubious a subject, is satisfied with the portion marked out to him by the Supreme Disposer of all things. Gratefully he accepts of that farther reward prepared for him, but, if disappointed, he thinks not virtue an empty name, but, justly esteeming it its own reward, he gratefully acknowledges the bounty of his Creator who, by calling him into existence, has thereby afforded him an opportunity of once acquiring so invaluable a possession.

ESSAY VII[1]

THE PLATONIST[2]

To SOME PHILOSOPHERS it appears matter of surprise that all mankind, possessing the same nature and being endowed with the same
faculties, should yet differ so widely in their pursuits and inclinations,
and that one should utterly condemn what is fondly sought after by
another. To some it appears matter of still more surprise that a man
should differ so widely from himself at different times and, after
possession, reject with disdain what before was the object of all his
vows and wishes. To me this feverish uncertainty and irresolution
in human conduct seems altogether unavoidable; nor can a rational
soul, made for the contemplation of the Supreme Being and of his
works, ever enjoy tranquillity or satisfaction while detained in the
ignoble pursuits of sensual pleasure or popular applause. The Divinity
is a boundless ocean of bliss and glory; human minds are smaller
streams which, arising at first from this ocean, seek still, amid all their
wanderings, to return to it and to lose themselves in that immensity
of perfection. When checked in this natural course by vice or folly,
they become furious and enraged and, swelling to a torrent, do then
spread horror and devastation on the neighbouring plains.

In vain, by pompous phrase and passionate expression, each recommends his own pursuit and invites the credulous hearers to an imitation
of his life and manners. The heart belies the countenance and sensibly
feels, even amid the highest success, the unsatisfactory nature of all
those pleasures which detain it from its true object. I examine the
voluptuous man before enjoyment; I measure the vehemence of his
desire and the importance of his object; I find that all his happiness
proceeds only from that hurry of thought which takes him from himself
and turns his view from his guilt and misery. I consider him a moment
after; he has now enjoyed the pleasure which he fondly sought after.

---

[1] [Ed. 1777, Part I. Essay XVII.]

[2] Or the man of contemplation and *philosophical* devotion.

The sense of his guilt and misery returns upon him with double anguish, his mind tormented with fear and remorse, his body depressed with disgust and satiety.

But a more august, at least a more haughty personage, presents himself boldly to our censure and, assuming the title of a philosopher and man of morals, offers to submit to the most rigid examination. He challenges with a visible, though concealed, impatience our approbation and applause, and seems offended that we should hesitate a moment before we break out into admiration of his virtue. Seeing this impatience, I hesitate still more; I begin to examine the motives of his seeming virtue. But, behold! ere I can enter upon this inquiry, he flings himself from me, and, addressing his discourse to that crowd of heedless auditors, fondly amuses them by his magnificent pretensions.

O philosopher! thy wisdom is vain and thy virtue unprofitable. Thou seekest the ignorant applauses of men, not the solid reflections of thy own conscience, or the more solid approbation of that Being who, with one regard of his all-seeing eye, penetrates the universe. Thou surely art conscious of the hollowness of thy pretended probity; whilst calling thyself a citizen, a son, a friend, thou forgettest thy higher sovereign, thy true father, thy greatest benefactor. Where is the adoration due to infinite perfection, whence everything good and valuable is derived! Where is the gratitude owing to thy Creator, who called thee forth from nothing, who placed thee in all these relations to thy fellow creatures, and, requiring thee to fulfil the duty of each relation, forbids thee to neglect what thou owest to Himself, the most perfect Being, to whom thou art connected by the closest tie?

But thou art thyself thy own idol. Thou worshippest thy *imaginary* perfections, or rather, sensible of thy *real* imperfections, thou seekest only to deceive the world and to please thy fancy by multiplying thy ignorant admirers. Thus, not content with neglecting what is most excellent in the universe, thou desirest to substitute in his place what is most vile and contemptible.

Consider all the works of men's hands, all the inventions of human wit, in which thou affectest so nice a discernment. Thou wilt find that the most perfect production still proceeds from the most perfect thought, and that it is *mind* alone which we admire, while we bestow our applause on the graces of a well-proportioned statue or the symmetry of a noble pile. The statuary, the architect, come still in view and makes us reflect on the beauty of his art and contrivance which, from a heap of unformed matter, could extract such expressions and proportions. This superior beauty of thought and intelligence thou thyself acknowledgest, while thou invitest us to contemplate in thy conduct the harmony of affections, the dignity of sentiments, and all those graces of a mind which chiefly merit our attention. But why stoppest thou short? Seest thou nothing farther that is valuable? Amid thy rapturous applauses of beauty and order, art thou still ignorant where is to be found the most consummate beauty, the most perfect order? Compare the works of art with those of nature. The one are but imitations of the other. The nearer art approaches to nature, the more perfect is it esteemed. But still how wide are its nearest approaches, and what an immense interval may be observed between them! Art copies only the outside of nature, leaving the inward and more admirable springs and principles as exceeding her imitation, as beyond her comprehension. Art copies only the minute productions of nature, despairing to reach that grandeur and magnificence which are so astonishing in the masterly works of her original. Can we then be so blind as not to discover an intelligence and a design in the exquisite and most stupendous contrivance of the universe? Can we be so stupid as not to feel the warmest raptures of worship and adoration upon the contemplation of that intelligent Being, so infinitely good and wise?

The most perfect happiness surely must arise from the contemplation of the most perfect object. But what more perfect than beauty and virtue? And where is beauty to be found equal to that of the universe, or virtue which can be compared to the benevolence and justice of the Deity? If aught can diminish the pleasure of this contemplation, it must be either the narrowness of our faculties which conceals from us the greatest part of these beauties and perfections, or the shortness of our lives which allows not time sufficient to instruct us in them. But it is our comfort that, if we employ worthily the faculties here assigned us, they will be enlarged in another state of existence, so as to render us more suitable worshippers of our Maker, and that the task, which can never be finished in time, will be the business of an eternity.

ESSAY VIII[1]

THE SCEPTIC

I HAVE long entertained a suspicion with regard to the decisions of philosophers upon all subjects, and found in myself a greater inclination to dispute than assent to their conclusions. There is one mistake to which they seem liable almost without exception: they confine too much their principles and make no account of that vast variety which nature has so much affected in all her operations. When a philosopher has once laid hold of a favourite principle, which perhaps accounts for many natural effects, he extends the same principle over the whole creation and reduces to it every phenomenon, though by the most violent and absurd reasoning. Our own mind being narrow and contracted, we cannot extend our conception to the variety and extent of nature, but imagine that she is as much bounded in her operations as we are in our speculation.

But if ever this infirmity of philosophers is to be suspected on any occasion, it is in their reasonings concerning human life and the methods of attaining happiness. In that case they are led astray, not only by the narrowness of their understandings, but by that also of their passions. Almost every one has a predominant inclination to which his other desires and affections submit, and which governs him, though perhaps with some intervals, through the whole course of his life. It is difficult for him to apprehend that anything which appears totally indifferent to him can ever give enjoyment to any person or can possess charms which altogether escape his observation. His own pursuits are always, in his account, the most engaging, the objects of his passion the most valuable, and the road which he pursues the only one that leads to happiness.

But would these prejudiced reasoners reflect a moment, there are many obvious instances and arguments sufficient to undeceive them and make them enlarge their maxims and principles. Do they not see

---

[1] [Ed. 1777, Part I. Essay XVIII.]

the vast variety of inclinations and pursuits among our species, where each man seems fully satisfied with his own course of life and would esteem it the greatest unhappiness to be confined to that of his neighbour? Do they not feel in themselves that what pleases at one time displeases at another by the change of inclination, and that it is not in their power, by their utmost efforts, to recall that taste or appetite which formerly bestowed charms on what now appears indifferent or disagreeable? What is the meaning therefore of those general preferences of the town or country life, of a life of action or one of pleasure, of retirement or society, when, besides the different inclinations of different men, every one's experience may convince him that each of these kinds of life is agreeable in its turn, and that their variety or their judicious mixture chiefly contributes to the rendering all of them agreeable?

But shall this business be allowed to go altogether at adventures and must a man only consult his humour and inclination in order to determine his course of life, without employing his reason to inform him what road is preferable and leads most surely to happiness? Is there no difference, then, between one man's conduct and another?

I answer, there is a great difference. One man, following his inclination in choosing his course of life, may employ much surer means for succeeding than another who is led by his inclination into the same course of life and pursues the same object. *Are riches the chief object of your desires?* Acquire skill in your profession, be diligent in the exercise of it, enlarge the circle of your friends and acquaintance, avoid pleasure and expense, and never be generous but with a view of gaining more than you could save by frugality. *Would you acquire the public esteem?* Guard equally against the extremes of arrogance and fawning. Let it appear that you set a value upon yourself, but without despising others. If you fall into either of the extremes, you either provoke men's pride by your insolence or teach them to despise you by your timorous submission and by the mean opinion which you seem to entertain of yourself.

These, you say, are the maxims of common prudence and discretion; what every parent inculcates on his child, and what every man of sense pursues in the course of life which he has chosen. What is it then you desire more? Do you come to a philosopher as to a *cunning man*, to learn something by magic or witch-craft beyond what can be known by common prudence and discretion? Yes; we come to a philosopher to be instructed how we shall choose our ends, more than the means for attaining these ends. We want to know what desire we shall gratify, what passion we shall comply with, what appetite we shall indulge. As to the rest, we trust to common sense and the general maxims of the world for our instruction.

I am sorry, then, I have pretended to be a philosopher; for I find your questions very perplexing and am in danger, if my answer be too rigid and severe, of passing for a pedant and scholastic; if it be too easy and free, of being taken for a preacher of vice and immorality. However, to satisfy you I shall deliver my opinion upon the matter and shall only desire you to esteem it of as little consequence as I do myself. By that means you will neither think it worthy of your ridicule nor your anger.

If we can depend upon any principle which we learn from philosophy, this, I think, may be considered as certain and undoubted: that there is nothing in itself valuable or despicable, desirable or hateful, beautiful or deformed; but that these attributes arise from the particular constitution and fabric of human sentiment and affection. What seems the most delicious food to one animal appears loathsome to another; what affects the feeling of one with delight produces uneasiness in another. This is confessedly the case with regard to all the bodily senses. But, if we examine the matter more accurately, we shall find that the same observation holds even where the mind concurs with the body and mingles its sentiment with the exterior appetite.

Desire this passionate lover to give you a character of his mistress; he will tell you that he is at a loss for words to describe her charms and will ask you very seriously if ever you were acquainted with a goddess or an angel? If you answer that you never were, he will then say that it is impossible for you to form a conception of such divine beauties as those which his charmer possesses, so complete a shape, such well-proportioned features, so engaging an air, such sweetness of disposition, such gaiety of humour. You can infer nothing, however, from all this discourse but that the poor man is in love, and that the general appetite between the sexes which nature has infused into all animals is in him determined to a particular object by some qualities which give him pleasure. The same divine creature, not only to a different animal, but also to a different man, appears a mere mortal being and is beheld with the utmost indifference.

Nature has given all animals a like prejudice in favour of their offspring. As soon as the helpless infant sees the light, though in every other eye it appears a despicable and a miserable creature, it is regarded by its fond parent with the utmost affection and is preferred to every other object, however perfect and accomplished. The passion alone, arising from the original structure and formation of human nature, bestows a value on the most insignificant object.

We may push the same observation further and may conclude that even when the mind operates alone and, feeling the sentiment of blame or approbation, pronounces one object deformed and odious, another beautiful and amiable — I say that, even in this case, those qualities are not really in the objects, but belong entirely to the sentiment of that mind which blames or praises. I grant that it will be more difficult to make this proposition evident and, as it were, palpable to negligent thinkers, because nature is more uniform in the sentiments of the mind than in most feelings of the body, and produces a nearer resemblance in the inward than in the outward part of human kind. There is something approaching to principles in mental taste, and critics can reason and dispute more plausibly than cooks or perfumers. We may observe, however, that this uniformity among human kind hinders not, but that there is a considerable diversity in the sentiments of beauty and worth, and that education, custom, prejudice, caprice, and humour frequently vary our taste of this kind. You will never convince a man who is not accustomed to Italian music and has not an ear to follow its intricacies that a Scots tune is not preferable. You have not even any single argument beyond your own taste which you can employ in your behalf; and to your antagonist his particular taste will always appear a more convincing argument to the contrary. If you be wise, each of you will allow that the other may be in the right, and, having many other instances of this diversity of taste, you will both confess that beauty and worth are merely of a relative nature and consist in an agreeable sentiment, produced by an object in a particular mind, according to the peculiar structure and constitution of that mind.

By this diversity of sentiment observable in human kind, nature has, perhaps, intended to make us sensible of her authority and let us see what surprising changes she could produce on the passions and desires of mankind, merely by the change of their inward fabric, without any alteration on the objects. The vulgar may even be convinced by this argument. But men accustomed to thinking may draw a more convincing, at least a more general, argument from the very nature of the subject.

In the operation of reasoning, the mind does nothing but run over its objects as they are supposed to stand in reality, without adding anything to them or diminishing anything from them. If I examine the Ptolomaic and Copernican systems, I endeavour only, by my inquiries, to know the real situation of the planets; that is, in other words, I endeavour to give them, in my conception, the same relations that they bear towards each other in the heavens. To this operation of the mind, therefore, there seems to be always a real, though often an unknown, standard in the nature of things; nor is truth or falsehood variable by the various apprehensions of mankind. Though all human race should for ever conclude that the sun moves and the earth remains at rest, the sun stirs not an inch from his place for all these reasonings, and such conclusions are eternally false and erroneous.

But the case is not the same with the qualities of *beautiful* and *deformed*, *desirable* and *odious* as with truth and falsehood. In the former case, the mind is not content with merely surveying its objects, as they stand in themselves. It also feels a sentiment of delight or uneasiness, approbation or blame, consequent to that survey; and this sentiment determines it to affix the epithet *beautiful* or *deformed*, *desirable* or *odious*. Now it is evident that this sentiment must depend upon the particular fabric or structure of the mind, which enables such particular forms to operate in such a particular manner, and produces a sympathy or conformity between the mind and its objects. Vary the structure of the mind or inward organs, the sentiment no longer follows, though the form remains the same. The sentiment being different from the object, and arising from its operation upon the organs of the mind, an alteration upon the latter must vary the effect; nor can the same object, presented to a mind totally different, produce the same sentiment.

This conclusion every one is apt to draw of himself, without much philosophy, where the sentiment is evidently distinguishable from the object. Who is not sensible that power and glory and vengeance are not desirable of themselves, but derive all their value from the structure of human passions, which begets a desire towards such particular pursuits? But with regard to beauty, either natural or moral, the case is commonly supposed to be different. The agreeable quality is thought to lie in the object, not in the sentiment; and that merely because the sentiment is not so turbulent and violent as to distinguish itself in an evident manner from the perception of the object.

But a little reflection suffices to distinguish them. A man may know exactly all the circles and ellipses of the Copernican system and all the irregular spirals of the Ptolomaic, without perceiving that the former is more beautiful than the latter. Euclid has fully explained every quality of the circle, but has not, in any proposition, said a word of its beauty. The reason is evident. Beauty is not a quality of the circle. It lies not in any part of the line whose parts are all equally distant from a common centre. It is only the effect which that figure produces upon a mind whose particular fabric or structure renders it susceptible of such sentiments. In vain would you look for it in the circle, or seek it, either by your senses or by mathematical reasonings, in all the properties of that figure.

The mathematician who took no other pleasure in reading Virgil but that of examining Æneas's voyage by the map might perfectly understand the meaning of every Latin word employed by that divine author and, consequently, might have a distinct idea of the whole narration. He would even have a more distinct idea of it than they could attain who had not studied so exactly the geography of the poem. He knew, therefore, every thing in the poem, but he was ignorant of its beauty, because the beauty, properly speaking, lies not in the poem, but in the sentiment or taste of the reader. And where a man has no such delicacy of temper as to make him feel this sentiment, he must be ignorant of the beauty, though possessed of the science and understanding of an angel.[2]

[2] Were I not afraid of appearing too philosophical, I should remind my reader of that famous doctrine, supposed to be fully proved in modern times, "that tastes and colours, and all other sensible qualities, lie not in the bodies but merely in the senses." The case is the same with beauty and deformity, virtue and vice. This doctrine, however, takes off no more from the reality of the latter qualities than from that of the former; nor need it give any umbrage either to critics or moralists. Though colours were allowed to lie only in the eye, would dyers or painters ever

The inference upon the whole is that it is not from the value or worth of the object which any person pursues that we can determine his enjoyment, but merely from the passion with which he pursues it and the success which he meets with in his pursuit. Objects have absolutely no worth or value in themselves. They derive their worth merely from the passion. If that be strong and steady, and successful, the person is happy. It cannot reasonably be doubted but a little miss, dressed in a new gown for a dancing-school ball, receives as complete enjoyment as the greatest orator who triumphs in the splendour of his eloquence, while he governs the passions and resolutions of a numerous assembly.

All the difference, therefore, between one man and another, with regard to life, consists either in the *passion* or in the *enjoyment*. And these differences are sufficient to produce the wide extremes of happiness and misery.

To be happy, the *passion* must neither be too violent nor too remiss. In the first case, the mind is in a perpetual hurry and tumult; in the second, it sinks into a disagreeable indolence and lethargy.

To be happy, the passion must be benign and social, not rough or fierce. The affections of the latter kind are not near so agreeable to the feeling as those of the former. Who will compare rancour and animosity, envy and revenge, to friendship, benignity, clemency, and gratitude?

To be happy, the passion must be cheerful and gay, not gloomy and melancholy. A propensity to hope and joy is real riches; one to fear and sorrow, real poverty.

Some passions or inclinations in the *enjoyment* of their object are not so steady or constant as others, nor convey such durable pleasure and satisfaction. *Philosophical devotion*, for instance, like the enthusiasm of a poet, is the transitory effect of high spirits, great leisure, a fine genius, and a habit of study and contemplation. But notwithstanding all these circumstances, an abstract, invisible object, like that which *natural* religion alone presents to us, cannot long actuate

be less regarded or esteemed? There is a sufficient uniformity in the senses and feelings of mankind to make all these qualities the objects of art and reasoning, and to have the greatest influence on life and manners. And as it is certain that the discovery above mentioned in natural philosophy makes no alteration on action and conduct, why should a like discovery in moral philosophy make any alteration?

the mind or be of any moment in life. To render the passion of continuance, we must find some method of affecting the senses and imagination, and must embrace some *historical* as well as *philosophical* account of the Divinity. Popular superstitions and observances are even found to be of use in this particular.

Though the tempers of men be very different, yet we may safely pronounce in general that a life of pleasure•cannot support itself so long as one of business, but is much more subject to satiety and disgust. The amusements which are the most durable have all a mixture of application and attention in them, such as gaming and hunting. And in general, business and action fill up all the great vacancies in human life.

But where the temper is the best disposed for any *enjoyment*, the object is often wanting. And in this respect, the passions which pursue external objects contribute not so much to happiness as those which rest in ourselves, since we are neither so certain of attaining such objects, nor so secure in possessing them. A passion for learning is preferable, with regard to happiness, to one for riches.

Some men are possessed of great strength of mind and, even when they pursue *external* objects, are not much affected by a disappointment, but renew their application and industry with the greatest cheerfulness. Nothing contributes more to happiness than such a turn of mind.

According to this short and imperfect sketch of human life, the happiest disposition of mind is the *virtuous*, or, in other words, that which leads to action and employment, renders us sensible to the social passions, steels the heart against the assaults of fortune, reduces the affections to a just moderation, makes our own thoughts an entertainment to us, and inclines us rather to the pleasures of society and conversation than to those of the senses. This, in the mean time, must be obvious to the most careless reasoner, that all dispositions of mind are not alike favourable to happiness, and that one passion or humour may be extremely desirable, while another is equally disagreeable. And, indeed, all the difference between the conditions of life depends upon the mind, nor is there any one situation of affairs in itself preferable to another. Good and ill, both natural and moral, are entirely relative to human sentiment and affection. No man would ever be unhappy, could he alter his feelings. Proteus-like, he would elude all attacks by the continual alterations of his shape and form.

But of this resource nature has, in a great measure, deprived us. The fabric and constitution of our mind no more depends on our choice than that of our body. The generality of men have not even the smallest notion that any alteration in this respect can ever be desirable. As a stream necessarily follows the several inclinations of the ground on which it runs, so are the ignorant and thoughtless part of mankind actuated by their natural propensities. Such are effectually excluded from all pretensions to philosophy, and the *medicine of the mind*, so much boasted. But even upon the wise and thoughtful, nature has a prodigious influence, nor is it always in a man's power by the utmost art and industry to correct his temper and attain that virtuous character to which he aspires. The empire of philosophy extends over a few, and with regard to these, too, her authority is very weak and limited. Men may well be sensible of the value of virtue, and may desire to attain it, but it is not always certain that they will be successful in their wishes.

Whoever considers without prejudice the course of human actions will find that mankind are almost entirely guided by constitution and temper, and that general maxims have little influence but so far as they affect our taste or sentiment. If a man have a lively sense of honour and virtue, with moderate passions, his conduct will always be conformable to the rules of morality, or, if he depart from them, his return will be easy and expeditious. On the other hand, where one is born of so perverse a frame of mind, of so callous and insensible a disposition, as to have no relish for virtue and humanity, no sympathy with his fellow creatures, no desire of esteem and applause, such a one must be allowed entirely incurable, nor is there any remedy in philosophy. He reaps no satisfaction but from low and sensual objects, or from the indulgence of malignant passions. He feels no remorse to control his vicious inclinations; he has not even that sense or taste which is requisite to make him desire a better character. For my part, I know not how I should address myself to such a one, or by what arguments I should endeavour to reform him. Should I tell him of the inward satisfaction which results from laudable and humane actions, and delicate pleasure of disinterested love and friendship, the lasting enjoyments of a good name and an established character, he might still reply that these were, perhaps, pleasures to such as were susceptible of them, but that, for his part, he finds himself of a quite different turn and disposition. I must repeat it, my philosophy affords no remedy in such a case, nor could I do anything but lament this person's unhappy condition. But, then, I ask if any other philosophy can afford a remedy, or if it be possible, by any system, to render all mankind virtuous, however perverse may be their natural frame of mind? Experience will soon convince us of the contrary; and I will venture to affirm that, perhaps, the chief benefit which results from philosophy arises in an indirect manner and proceeds more from its secret insensible influence than from its immediate application.

It is certain that a serious attention to the sciences and liberal arts softens and humanizes the temper, and cherishes those fine emotions in which true virtue and honour consists. It rarely, very rarely, happens that a man of taste and learning is not at least an honest man, whatever frailties may attend him. The bent of his mind to speculative studies must mortify in him the passions of interest and ambition, and must, at the same time, give him a greater sensibility of all the decencies and duties of life. He feels more fully a moral distinction in characters and manners, nor is his sense of this kind diminished, but, on the contrary, it is much increased, by speculation.

Besides such insensible changes upon the temper and disposition, it is highly probable that others may be produced by study and application. The prodigious effects of education may convince us that the mind is not altogether stubborn and inflexible, but will admit of many alterations from its original make and structure. Let a man propose to himself the model of a character which he approves, let him be well acquainted with those particulars in which his own character deviates from this model, let him keep a constant watch over himself and bend his mind by a continual effort from the vices towards the virtues, and I doubt not but in time he will find in his temper an alteration for the better.

Habit is another powerful means of reforming the mind and implanting in it good dispositions and inclinations. A man who continues in a course of sobriety and temperance will hate riot and disorder; if he engage in business or study, indolence will seem a punishment to him; if he constrain himself to practise beneficence and affability, he will soon abhor all instances of pride and violence. Where one is thoroughly convinced that the virtuous course of life is preferable, if he have but resolution enough, for some time, to impose a violence on himself, his reformation needs not be despaired of. The misfortune is that this conviction and this resolution never can have place, unless a man be, beforehand, tolerably virtuous.

Here then is the chief triumph of art and philosophy: it insensibly refines the temper, and it points out to us those dispositions which we should endeavour to attain by a constant *bent* of mind and by repeated *habit*. Beyond this I cannot acknowledge it to have great influence, and I must entertain doubts concerning all those exhortations and consolations which are in such vogue among speculative reasoners.

We have already observed that no objects are, in themselves, desirable or odious, valuable or despicable, but that objects acquire these qualities from the particular character and constitution of the mind which surveys them. To diminish, therefore, or augment any person's value for an object, to excite or moderate his passions, there are no direct arguments or reasons which can be employed with any force or influence. The catching of flies, like Domitian, if it give more pleasure, is preferable to the hunting of wild beasts, like William Rufus, or conquering of kingdoms, like Alexander.

But though the value of every object can be determined only by the sentiment or passion of every individual, we may observe that the passion, in pronouncing its verdict, considers not the object simply as it is in itself, but surveys it with all the circumstances which attend it. A man, transported with joy on account of his possessing a diamond, confines not his view to the glittering stone before him. He also considers its rarity, and thence chiefly arises his pleasure and exultation. Here, therefore, a philosopher may step in and suggest particular views, and considerations, and circumstances, which otherwise would have escaped us, and by that means he may either moderate or excite any particular passion.

It may seem unreasonable absolutely to deny the authority of philosophy in this respect, but it must be confessed that there lies this strong presumption against it: that, if these views be natural and obvious, they would have occurred of themselves without the assistance of philosophy; if they be not natural, they never can have any influence on the affections. *These* are of a very delicate nature and cannot be forced or constrained by the utmost art or industry. A consideration which we seek for on purpose, which we enter into with difficulty, which we cannot retain without care and attention, will never produce those genuine and durable movements of passion which are the result of nature and the constitution of the mind. A man may as well pretend to cure himself of love by viewing his mistress through the *artificial* medium of a microscope or prospect and beholding there the coarseness of her skin and monstrous disproportion of her features, as hope to excite or moderate any passion by the *artificial* arguments of a Seneca or an Epictetus. The remembrance of the natural aspect and situation of the object will, in both cases, still recur upon him. The reflections of philosophy are too subtile and distant to take place in common life or eradicate any affection. The air is too fine to breathe in, where it is above the winds and clouds of the atmosphere.

Another defect of those refined reflections which philosophy suggests to us is that commonly they cannot diminish or extinguish our vicious passions without diminishing or extinguishing such as are virtuous, and rendering the mind totally indifferent and inactive. They are, for the most part, general, and are applicable to all our affections. In vain do we hope to direct their influence only to one side. If by incessant study and meditation we have rendered them intimate and present to us, they will operate throughout and spread an universal insensibility over the mind. When we destroy the nerves, we extinguish the sense of pleasure, together with that of pain, in the human body.

It will be easy, by one glance of the eye, to find one or other of these defects in most of those philosophical reflections so much celebrated both in ancient and modern times. *Let not the injuries or violence of men*, say the philosophers,[3] *ever discompose you by anger or hatred. Would you be angry at the ape for its malice, or the tiger for its ferocity?* This reflection leads us into a bad opinion of human nature and must extinguish the social affections. It tends also to prevent all remorse for a man's own crimes when he considers that vice is as natural to mankind as the particular instincts to brute creatures.

All ills arise from the order of the universe, which is absolutely perfect. Would you wish to disturb so divine an order for the sake of your own

[3] PLUT. *De Ira cohibenda.*

particular interest? What if the ills I suffer arise from malice or oppression? *But the vices and imperfections of men are also comprehended in the order of the universe.*

> If plagues and earthquakes break not heaven's design,
> Why then a BORGIA or a CATILINE?

Let this be allowed, and my own vices will also be a part of the same order.

To one who said that none were happy who were not above opinion, a Spartan replied, *Then none are happy but knaves and robbers.*[4]

Man is born to be miserable; and is he surprised at any particular misfortune? And can he give way to sorrow and lamentation upon account of any disaster? Yes, he very reasonably laments that he should be born to be miserable. Your consolation presents a hundred ills for one of which you pretend to ease him.

You should always have before your eyes death, disease, poverty, blindness, exile, calumny, and infamy, as ills which are incident to human nature. If any one of these ills fall to your lot, you will bear it the better when you have reckoned upon it. I answer, if we confine ourselves to a general and distant reflection on the ills of human life, *that* can have no effect to prepare us for them. If by close and intense meditation we render them present and intimate to us, *that* is the true secret for poisoning all our pleasures and rendering us perpetually miserable.

Your sorrow is fruitless and will not change the course of destiny. Very true, and for that very reason I am sorry.

Cicero's consolation for deafness is somewhat curious. *How many languages are there*, says he, *which you do not understand? The Punic, Spanish, Gallic, Egyptian, etc. With regard to all these, you are as if you were deaf, yet you are indifferent about the matter. Is it then so great a misfortune to be deaf to one language more?*[5]

I like better the repartee of Antipater the Cyrenaic, when some women were condoling with him for his blindness: *What!* says he, *do you think there are no pleasures in the dark?*

Nothing can be more destructive, says Fontenelle, *to ambition and the passion for conquest than the true system of astronomy. What a poor thing is even the whole globe in comparison of the infinite extent of nature!*

[4] PLUT. *Lacon. Apophtheg.*
[5] *Tusc. Quest.* lib. v.

This consideration is evidently too distant ever to have any effect, or, if it had any, would it not destroy patriotism as well as ambition? The same gallant author adds, with some reason, that the bright eyes of the ladies are the only objects which lose nothing of their lustre or value from the most extensive views of astronomy, but stand proof against every system. Would philosophers advise us to limit our affection to them?

Exile, says Plutarch to a friend in banishment, *is no evil; mathematicians tell us that the whole earth is but a point, compared to the heavens. To change one's country, then, is little more than to remove from one street to another. Man is not a plant, rooted to a certain spot of earth; all soils and all climates are alike suited to him.*[6] These topics are admirable, could they fall only into the hands of banished persons. But what if they come also to the knowledge of those who are employed in public affairs, and destroy all their attachment to their native country? Or will they operate like the quack's medicine, which is equally good for a diabetes and a dropsy?

It is certain, were a superior being thrust into a human body, that the whole of life would to him appear so mean, contemptible and puerile that he never could be induced to take part in anything, and would scarcely give attention to what passes around him. To engage him to such a condescension as to play even the part of a Philip with zeal and alacrity, would be much more difficult than to constrain the same Philip, after having been a king and a conqueror during fifty years, to mend old shoes with proper care and attention, the occupation which Lucian assigns him in the infernal regions. Now all the same topics of disdain towards human affairs which could operate on this supposed being occur also to a philosopher; but being, in some measure, disproportioned to human capacity, and not being fortified by the experience of anything better, they make not a full impression on him. He sees, but he feels not sufficiently their truth, and is always a sublime philosopher when he needs not, that is, as long as nothing disturbs him or rouses his affections. While others play, he wonders at their keenness and ardour, but he no sooner puts in his own stake than he is commonly transported with the same passions that he had so much condemned while he remained a simple spectator.

There are two considerations chiefly to be met with in books of

[6] *De Exilio.*

philosophy from which any important effect is to be expected, and that because these considerations are drawn from common life and occur upon the most superficial view of human affairs. When we reflect on the shortness and uncertainty of life, how despicable seem all our pursuits of happiness! And even if we would extend our concern beyond our own life, how frivolous appear our most enlarged and most generous projects when we consider the incessant changes and revolutions of human affairs by which laws and learning, books and governments, are hurried away by time as by a rapid stream and are lost in the immense ocean of matter! Such a reflection certainly tends to mortify all our passions, but does it not thereby counterwork the artifice of nature, who has happily deceived us into an opinion that human life is of some importance? And may not such a reflection be employed with success by voluptuous reasoners in order to lead us from the paths of action and virtue into the flowery fields of indolence and pleasure?

We are informed by Thucydides that, during the famous plague of Athens, when death seemed present to every one, a dissolute mirth and gaiety prevailed among the people, who exhorted one another to make the most of life as long as it endured. The same observation is made by Boccace with regard to the plague of Florence. A like principle makes soldiers, during war, be more addicted to riot and expense than any other race of men.[7] Present pleasure is always of importance, and whatever diminishes the importance of all other objects must bestow on it an additional influence and value.

The *second* philosophical consideration which may often have an influence on the affections is derived from a comparison of our own condition with the condition of others. This comparison we are continually making even in common life, but the misfortune is that we are rather apt to compare our situation with that of our superiors than with that of our inferiors. A philosopher corrects this natural infirmity by turning his view to the other side in order to render himself easy in the situation to which fortune has confined him. There are few people who are not susceptible of some consolation from this reflection, though, to a very good natured man, the view of human

---

[7] And it is observable in this kingdom that long peace, by producing security, has much altered them in this particular, and has quite removed our officers from the generous character of their profession.

miseries should rather produce sorrow than comfort and add to his lamentations for his own misfortunes a deep compassion for those of others. Such is the imperfection even of the best of these philosophical topics of consolation.[8]

[8] The Sceptic, perhaps, carries the matter too far, when he limits all philosophical topics and reflections to these two. There seem to be others, whose truth is undeniable, and whose natural tendency is to tranquillize and soften all the passions. Philosophy greedily seizes these; studies them, weighs them, commits them to the memory, and familiarizes them to the mind: And their influence on tempers which are thoughtful, gentle, and moderate, may be considerable. But what is their influence, you will say, if the temper be antecedently disposed after the same manner as that to which they pretend to form it? They may, at least, fortify that temper, and furnish it with views, by which it may entertain and nourish itself. Here are a few examples of such philosophical reflections.

1. Is it not certain that every condition has concealed ills? Then why envy anybody?

2. Every one has known ills; and there is a compensation throughout. Why not be contented with the present?

3. Custom deadens the sense both of the good and the ill, and levels everything.

4. Health and humour all. The rest of little consequence, except these be affected.

5. How many other good things have I? Then why be vexed for one ill?

6. How many are happy in the condition of which I complain? How many envy me?

7. Every good must be paid for: Fortune by labour, favour by flattery. Would I keep the price, yet have the commodity?

8. Expect not too great happiness in life. Human nature admits it not.

9. Propose not a happiness too complicated. But does that depend on me? Yes: The first choice does. Life is like a game: One may choose the game, and passion, by degrees, seizes the proper object.

10. Anticipate by your hopes and fancy future consolation, which time infallibly brings to every affliction.

11. I desire to be rich. Why? That I may possess many fine objects; houses, gardens, equipage, etc. How many fine objects does nature offer to every one without expense? If enjoyed, sufficient. If not: See the effect of custom or of temper, which would soon take off the relish of the riches.

12. I desire fame. Let this occur: If I act well, I shall have the esteem of all my acquaintance. And what is all the rest to me?

These reflections are so obvious that it is a wonder they occur not to every man. So convincing that it is a wonder they persuade not every man. But, perhaps, they do occur to, and persuade most men, when they consider human life by a general and calm survey; but where any real, affecting incident happens, when passion is awakened, fancy agitated, example draws, and counsel urges, the philosopher is lost in the man, and he seeks in vain for that persuasion which before seemed so firm and unshaken. What remedy for this inconvenience? Assist yourself by a

I shall conclude this subject with observing that, though virtue be undoubtedly the best choice, when it is attainable, yet such is the disorder and confusion of human affairs that no perfect or regular distribution of happiness and misery is ever in this life to be expected. Not only the goods of fortune and the endowments of the body — both of which are important — not only these advantages, I say, are unequally divided between the virtuous and vicious, but even the mind itself partakes, in some degree, of this disorder, and the most worthy character, by the very constitution of the passions, enjoys not always the highest felicity.

It is observable that though every bodily pain proceeds from some disorder in the part or organ, yet the pain is not always proportioned to the disorder, but is greater or less, according to the greater or less sensibility of the part upon which the noxious humours exert their influence. A *toothache* produces more violent convulsions of pain than a *phthisis* or a *dropsy*. In like manner, with regard to the economy of the mind, we may observe that all vice is indeed pernicious, yet the disturbance or pain is not measured out by nature with exact proportion to the degrees of vice, nor is the man of highest virtue, even abstracting from external accidents, always the most happy. A gloomy and melancholy disposition is certainly, *to our sentiments*, a vice or imperfection; but as it may be accompanied with great sense of honour and great integrity, it may be found in very worthy characters, though it is sufficient alone to embitter life and render the person affected with it completely miserable. On the other hand, a selfish villain may possess a spring and alacrity of temper, a certain *gaiety of heart*, which is indeed a good quality, but which is rewarded much beyond its merit and, when attended with good fortune, will compensate for the uneasiness and remorse arising from all the other vices.

I shall add, as an observation to the same purpose, that, if a man

frequent perusal of the entertaining moralists: Have recourse to the learning of Plutarch, the imagination of Lucian, the eloquence of Cicero, the wit of Seneca, the gaiety of Montaigne, the sublimity of Shaftesbury. Moral precepts, so couched, strike deep, and fortify the mind against the illusions of passion. But trust not altogether to external aid. By habit and study acquire that philosophical temper which both gives force to reflection and, by rendering a great part of your happiness independent, takes off the edge from all disorderly passions, and tranquillizes the mind. Despise not these helps, but confide not too much in them neither, unless nature has been favourable in the temper with which she has endowed you.

be liable to a vice or imperfection, it may often happen that a good quality, which he possesses along with it, will render him more miserable than if he were completely vicious. A person of such imbecility of temper as to be easily broken by affliction is more unhappy for being endowed with a generous and friendly disposition, which gives him a lively concern for others and exposes him the more to fortune and accidents. A sense of shame in an imperfect character is certainly a virtue, but produces great uneasiness and remorse, from which the abandoned villain is entirely free. A very amorous complexion, with a heart incapable of friendship, is happier than the same excess in love, with a generosity of temper, which transports a man beyond himself and renders him a total slave to the object of his passion.

In a word, human life is more governed by fortune than by reason, is to be regarded more as a dull pastime than a serious occupation, and is more influenced by particular humour than by general principles. Shall we engage ourselves in it with passion and anxiety? It is not worthy of so much concern. Shall we be indifferent about what happens? We lose all the pleasure of the game by our phlegm and carelessness. While we are reasoning concerning life, life is gone, and death, though *perhaps* they receive him differently, yet treats alike the fool and the philosopher. To reduce life to exact rule and method is commonly a painful, oft a fruitless, occupation. And is it not also a proof that we overvalue the prize for which we contend? Even to reason so carefully concerning it and to fix with accuracy its just idea would be overvaluing it, were it not that, to some tempers, this occupation is one of the most amusing in which life could possibly be employed.

ESSAY IX [1]

As NO PARTY, in the present age, can well support itself without a philosophical or speculative system of principles annexed to its political or practical one, we accordingly find that each of the factions into which this nation is divided has reared up a fabric of the former kind, in order to protect and cover that scheme of actions which it pursues. The people being commonly very rude builders, especially in this speculative way, and more especially still when actuated by party zeal, it is natural to imagine that their workmanship must be a little unshapely, and discover evident marks of that violence and hurry in which it was raised. The one party, by tracing up government to the Deity, endeavour to render it so sacred and inviolate that it must be little less than sacrilege, however tyrannical it may become, to touch or invade it in the smallest article. The other party, by founding government altogether on the consent of the people, suppose that there is a kind of *original contract* by which the subjects have tacitly reserved the power of resisting their sovereign, whenever they find themselves aggrieved by that authority with which they have, for certain purposes, voluntarily entrusted him. These are the speculative principles of the two parties, and these, too, are the practical consequences deduced from them.

I shall venture to affirm *that both these systems of speculative principles are just, though not in the sense intended by the parties,* and *that both the schemes of practical consequences are prudent, though not in the extremes to which each party, in opposition to the other, has commonly endeavoured to carry them.*

That the Deity is the ultimate author of all government will never be denied by any who admit a general providence and allow that all events in the universe are conducted by an uniform plan and directed to wise purposes. As it is impossible for the human race to subsist,

---

[1] [Ed. 1777, Part II. Essay IX.]

at least in any comfortable or secure state, without the protection of government, this institution must certainly have been intended by that beneficent Being who means the good of all his creatures. And as it has universally, in fact, taken place in all countries and all ages, we may conclude, with still greater certainty, that it was intended by that omniscient Being who can never be deceived by any event or operation. But since he gave rise to it, not by any particular or miraculous interposition, but by his concealed and universal efficacy, a sovereign cannot, properly speaking, be called his vicegerent in any other sense than every power or force, being derived from him, may be said to act by his commission. Whatever actually happens is comprehended in the general plan or intention of Providence; nor has the greatest and most lawful prince any more reason, upon that account, to plead a peculiar sacredness or inviolable authority than an inferior magistrate, or even an usurper, or even a robber and a pirate. The same Divine Superintendent who, for wise purposes, invested a Titus or a Trajan with authority, did also, for purposes no doubt equally wise though unknown, bestow power on a Borgia or an Angria. The same causes which gave rise to the sovereign power in every state established likewise every petty jurisdiction in it, and every limited authority. A constable, therefore, no less than a king, acts by a divine commission and possesses an indefeasible right.

When we consider how nearly equal all men are in their bodily force, and even in their mental powers and faculties, till cultivated by education, we must necessarily allow that nothing but their own consent could at first associate them together and subject them to any authority. The people, if we trace government to its first origin in the woods and deserts, are the source of all power and jurisdiction, and voluntarily, for the sake of peace and order, abandoned their native liberty and received laws from their equal and companion. The conditions upon which they were willing to submit were either expressed or were so clear and obvious that it might well be esteemed superfluous to express them. If this, then, be meant by the *original contract*, it cannot be denied that all government is, at first, founded on a contract, and that the most ancient rude combinations of mankind were formed chiefly by that principle. In vain are we asked in what records this charter of our liberties is registered. It was not written on parchment, nor yet on leaves or barks of trees. It preceded the use of writing, and all the other civilized arts of life. But we trace it plainly in the nature of man, and in the equality, or something approaching equality, which we find in all the individuals of that species. The force which now prevails, and which is founded on fleets and armies, is plainly political, and derived from authority, the effect of established government. A man's natural force consists only in the vigour of his limbs and the firmness of his courage, which could never subject multitudes to the command of one. Nothing but their own consent and their sense of the advantages resulting from peace and order could have had that influence.

Yet even this consent was long very imperfect, and could not be the basis of a regular administration. The chieftain, who had probably acquired his influence during the continuance of war, ruled more by persuasion than command; and till he could employ force to reduce the refractory and disobedient, the society could scarcely be said to have attained a state of civil government. No compact or agreement, it is evident, was expressly formed for general submission, an idea far beyond the comprehension of savages. Each exertion of authority in the chieftain must have been particular, and called forth by the present exigencies of the case. The sensible utility resulting from his interposition made these exertions become daily more frequent; and their frequency gradually produced an habitual and, if you please to call it so, a voluntary and therefore precarious acquiescence in the people.

But philosophers who have embraced a party — if that be not a contradiction in terms — are not contented with these concessions. They assert not only that government in its earliest infancy arose from consent, or rather the voluntary acquiescence of the people, but also that, even at present, when it has attained its full maturity, it rests on no other foundation. They affirm that all men are still born equal, and owe allegiance to no prince or government unless bound by the obligation and sanction of a *promise*. And as no man, without some equivalent, would forego the advantages of his native liberty and subject himself to the will of another, this promise is always understood to be conditional, and imposes on him no obligation, unless he meet with justice and protection from his sovereign. These advantages the sovereign promises him in return; and if he fail in the execution, he has broken on his part the articles of engagement, and has thereby freed his subject from all obligations to allegiance. Such, according to these philosophers, is the foundation of authority in every government, and such the right of resistance possessed by every subject.

But would these reasoners look abroad into the world, they would meet with nothing that in the least corresponds to their ideas, or can warrant so refined and philosophical a system. On the contrary, we find everywhere princes who claim their subjects as their property, and assert their independent right of sovereignty from conquest or succession. We find also everywhere subjects who acknowledge this right in their prince, and suppose themselves born under obligations of obedience to a certain sovereign, as much as under the ties of reverence and duty to certain parents. These connexions are always conceived to be equally independent of our consent, in Persia and China, in France and Spain, and even in Holland and England, wherever the doctrines above mentioned have not been carefully inculcated. Obedience or subjection becomes so familiar that most men never make any inquiry about its origin or cause, more than about the principle of gravity, resistance, or the most universal laws of nature. Or if curiosity ever move them, as soon as they learn that they themselves and their ancestors have, for several ages, or from time immemorial, been subject to such a form of government or such a family, they immediately acquiesce and acknowledge their obligation to allegiance. Were you to preach, in most parts of the world, that political connexions are founded altogether on voluntary consent or a mutual promise, the magistrate would soon imprison you as seditious for loosening the ties of obedience, if your friends did not before shut you up as delirious for advancing such absurdities. It is strange that an act of the mind, which every individual is supposed to have formed, and after he came to the use of reason too, otherwise it could have no authority — that this act, I say, should be so much unknown to all of them that over the face of the whole earth there scarcely remain any traces or memory of it.

But the contract on which government is founded is said to be the *original contract;* and consequently may be supposed too old to fall under the knowledge of the present generation. If the agreement by which savage men first associated and conjoined their force be here meant, this is acknowledged to be real; but being so ancient, and being obliterated by a thousand changes of government and princes, it cannot now be supposed to retain any authority. If we would say anything to the purpose, we must assert that every particular government which is lawful, and which imposes any duty of allegiance on the subject, was at first founded on consent and a voluntary compact. But, besides that this supposes the consent of the fathers to bind the children, even to the most remote generations — which republican writers will never allow — besides this, I say, it is not justified by history or experience in any age or country of the world.

Almost all the governments which exist at present, or of which there remains any record in story, have been founded originally either on usurpation or conquest or both, without any pretence of a fair consent or voluntary subjection of the people. When an artful and bold man is placed at the head of an army or faction, it is often easy for him, by employing sometimes violence, sometimes false pretences, to establish his dominion over a people a hundred times more numerous than his partisans. He allows no such open communication that his enemies can know with certainty their number or force. He gives them no leisure to assemble together in a body to oppose him. Even all those who are the instruments of his usurpation may wish his fall; but their ignorance of each other's intention keeps them in awe, and is the sole cause of his security. By such arts as these many governments have been established; and this is all the *original contract* which they have to boast of.

The face of the earth is continually changing, by the increase of small kingdoms into great empires, by the dissolution of great empires into smaller kingdoms, by the planting of colonies, by the migration of tribes. Is there anything discoverable in all these events but force and violence? Where is the mutual agreement or voluntary association so much talked of?

Even the smoothest way by which a nation may receive a foreign master, by marriage or a will, is not extremely honourable for the people, but supposes them to be disposed of like a dowry or a legacy, according to the pleasure or interest of their rulers.

But where no force interposes, and election takes place, what is this election so highly vaunted? It is either the combination of a few great men, who decide for the whole and will allow of no opposition; or it is the fury of a multitude that follow a seditious ringleader who is not known, perhaps, to a dozen among them, and who owes his advancement merely to his own impudence or to the momentary caprice of his fellows.

Are these disorderly elections, which are rare too, of such mighty authority as to be the only lawful foundation of all government and allegiance?

In reality there is not a more terrible event than a total dissolution of government; which gives liberty to the multitude, and makes the determination or choice of a new establishment depend upon a number which nearly approaches to that of the body of the people. For it never comes entirely to the whole body of them. Every wise man, then, wishes to see at the head of a powerful and obedient army a general who may speedily seize the prize, and give to the people a master which they are so unfit to choose for themselves — so little correspondent is fact and reality to those philosophical notions.

Let not the establishment at the Revolution deceive us, or make us so much in love with a philosophical origin to government as to imagine all others monstrous and irregular. Even that event was far from corresponding to these refined ideas. It was only the succession, and that only in the regal part of the government, which was then changed. And it was only the majority of seven hundred who determined that change for near ten millions. I doubt not, indeed, but the bulk of those ten millions acquiesced willingly in the determination. But was the matter left in the least to their choice? Was it not justly supposed to be from that moment decided, and every man punished who refused to submit to the new sovereign? How otherwise could the matter have ever been brought to any issue or conclusion?

The republic of Athens was, I believe, the most extensive democracy that we read of in history. Yet if we make the requisite allowances for the women, the slaves, and the strangers, we shall find that that establishment was not at first made, nor any law ever voted, by a tenth part of those who were bound to pay obedience to it; not to mention the islands and foreign dominions which the Athenians claimed as theirs by right of conquest. And as it is well known that popular assemblies in that city were always full of license and disorder, notwithstanding the institutions and laws by which they were checked, how much more disorderly must they prove where they form not the established constitution, but meet tumultuously on the dissolution of the ancient government in order to give rise to a new one? How chimerical must it be to talk of a choice in such circumstances?

The Achæans enjoyed the freest and most perfect democracy of all antiquity; yet they employed force to oblige some cities to enter into their league, as we learn from Polybius.[2]

Harry IV and Harry VII of England had really no title to the throne but a parliamentary election; yet they never would acknowledge it, lest they should thereby weaken their authority. Strange, if the only real foundation of all authority be consent and promise.

It is in vain to say that all governments are or should be at first founded on popular consent, as much as the necessity of human affairs will admit. This favours entirely my pretension. I maintain that human affairs will never admit of this consent, seldom of the appearance of it; but that conquest or usurpation, that is, in plain terms, force, by dissolving the ancient governments, is the origin of almost all the new ones which were ever established in the world. And that in the few cases where consent may seem to have taken place, it was commonly so irregular, so confined, or so much intermixed either with fraud or violence that it cannot have any great authority.

My intention here is not to exclude the consent of the people from being one just foundation of government. Where it has place, it is surely the best and most sacred of any. I only contend that it has very seldom had place in any degree, and never almost in its full extent; and that, therefore, some other foundation of government must also be admitted.

Were all men possessed of so inflexible a regard to justice that of themselves they would totally abstain from the properties of others, they had for ever remained in a state of absolute liberty, without subjection to any magistrate or political society. But this is a state of perfection of which human nature is justly deemed incapable. Again, were all men possessed of so perfect an understanding as always to know their own interests, no form of government had ever been submitted to but what was established on consent, and was fully canvassed by every member of the society. But this state of perfection is likewise much superior to human nature. Reason, history, and experience show us that all political societies have had an origin much less accurate and regular; and were one to choose a period of time

[2] Lib. ii. cap. 38.

when the people's consent was the least regarded in public transactions, it would be precisely on the establishment of a new government. In a settled constitution their inclinations are often consulted; but during the fury of revolutions, conquests, and public convulsions, military force or political craft usually decides the controversy.

When a new government is established, by whatever means, the people are commonly dissatisfied with it, and pay obedience more from fear and necessity than from any idea of allegiance or of moral obligation. The prince is watchful and jealous, and must carefully guard against every beginning or appearance of insurrection. Time, by degrees, removes all these difficulties, and accustoms the nation to regard as their lawful or native princes that family which at first they considered as usurpers or foreign conquerors. In order to found this opinion, they have no recourse to any notion of voluntary consent or promise which, they know, never was in this case either expected or demanded. The original establishment was formed by violence and submitted to from necessity. The subsequent administration is also supported by power, and acquiesced in by the people, not as a matter of choice, but of obligation. They imagine not that their consent gives their prince a title. But they willingly consent, because they think that, from long possession, he has acquired a title independent of their choice or inclination.

Should it be said that, by living under the dominion of a prince which one might leave, every individual has given a *tacit* consent to his authority and promised him obedience, it may be answered that such an implied consent can only have place where a man imagines that the matter depends on his choice. But where he thinks — as all mankind do who are born under established governments — that by his birth he owes allegiance to a certain prince or certain form of government, it would be absurd to infer a consent or choice, which he expressly in this case renounces and disclaims.

Can we seriously say that a poor peasant or artisan has a free choice to leave his country, when he knows no foreign language or manners, and lives from day to day by the small wages which he acquires? We may as well assert that a man, by remaining in a vessel, freely consents to the dominion of the master, though he was carried on board while asleep, and must leap into the ocean and perish the moment he leaves her.

What if the prince forbid his subjects to quit his dominions, as in Tiberius' time it was regarded as a crime in a Roman knight that he had attempted to fly to the Parthians, in order to escape the tyranny of that emperor?[3] Or as the ancient Muscovites prohibited all travelling under pain of death? And did a prince observe that many of his subjects were seized with the frenzy of migrating to foreign countries, he would, doubtless, with great reason and justice restrain them in order to prevent the depopulation of his own kingdom. Would he forfeit the allegiance of all his subjects by so wise and reasonable a law? Yet the freedom of their choice is surely, in that case, ravished from them.

A company of men, who should leave their native country in order to people some uninhabited region, might dream of recovering their native freedom, but they would soon find that their prince still laid claim to them, and called them his subjects even in their new settlement. And in this he would but act conformably to the common ideas of mankind.

The truest *tacit* consent of this kind that is ever observed is when a foreigner settles in any country, and is beforehand acquainted with the prince, and government, and laws, to which he must submit; yet is his allegiance, though more voluntary, much less expected or depended on than that of a natural-born subject. On the contrary, his native prince still asserts a claim to him. And if he punish not the renegade when he seizes him in war with his new prince's commission, this clemency is not founded on the municipal law, which in all countries condemns the prisoner, but on the consent of princes, who have agreed to this indulgence in order to prevent reprisals.

Did one generation of men go off the stage at once, and another succeed, as is the case with silk worms and butterflies, the new race, if they had sense enough to choose their government, which surely is never the case with men, might voluntarily and by general consent establish their own form of civil polity without any regard to the laws or precedents which prevailed among their ancestors. But as human society is in perpetual flux, one man every hour going out of the world, another coming into it, it is necessary in order to preserve stability in government that the new brood should conform themselves to the established constitution, and nearly follow the path which their

[3] Tacit. *Ann*. lib. vi. cap. 14.

fathers, treading in the footsteps of theirs, had marked out to them. Some innovations must necessarily have place in every human institution; and it is happy where the enlightened genius of the age give these a direction to the side of reason, liberty, and justice. But violent innovations no individual is entitled to make. They are even dangerous to be attempted by the legislature. More ill than good is ever to be expected from them. And if history affords examples to the contrary, they are not to be drawn into precedent, and are only to be regarded as proofs that the science of politics affords few rules which will not admit of some exception, and which may not sometimes be controlled by fortune and accident. The violent innovations in the reign of Henry VIII proceeded from an imperious monarch, seconded by the appearance of legislative authority; those in the reign of Charles I were derived from faction and fanaticism; and both of them have proved happy in the issue. But even the former were long the source of many disorders, and still more dangers; and if the measures of allegiance were to be taken from the latter, a total anarchy must have place in human society, and a final period at once be put to every government.

Suppose that an usurper, after having banished his lawful prince and royal family, should establish his dominion for ten or a dozen years in any country, and should preserve so exact a discipline in his troops and so regular a disposition in his garrisons that no insurrection had ever been raised or even murmur heard against his administration. Can it be asserted that the people, who in their hearts abhor his treason, have tacitly consented to his authority and promised him allegiance, merely because, from necessity, they live under his dominion? Suppose again their native prince restored by means of an army which he levies in foreign countries. They receive him with joy and exultation, and show plainly with what reluctance they had submitted to any other yoke. I may now ask upon what foundation the prince's title stands? Not on popular consent surely; for though the people willingly acquiesce in his authority, they never imagine that their consent made him sovereign. They consent because they apprehend him to be already, by birth, their lawful sovereign. And as to tacit consent, which may now be inferred from their living under his dominion, this is no more than what they formerly gave to the tyrant and usurper.

When we assert that all lawful government arises from the consent of the people, we certainly do them a great deal more honour than they deserve, or even expect and desire from us. After the Roman dominions became too unwieldy for the republic to govern them, the people over the whole known world were extremely grateful to Augustus for that authority which, by violence, he had established over them; and they showed an equal disposition to submit to the successor whom he left them by his last will and testament. It was afterwards their misfortune that there never was, in one family, any long regular succession, but that their line of princes was continually broken either by private assassinations or public rebellions. The *prætorian* bands, on the failure of every family, set up one emperor, the legions in the East a second, those in Germany, perhaps, a third; and the sword alone could decide the controversy. The condition of the people in that mighty monarchy was to be lamented, not because the choice of the emperor was never left to them, for that was impracticable, but because they never fell under any succession of masters who might regularly follow each other. As to the violence and wars and bloodshed occasioned by every new settlement, these were not blamable, because they were inevitable.

The house of Lancaster ruled in this island about sixty years; yet the partisans of the white rose seemed daily to multiply in England. The present establishment has taken place during a still longer period. Have all views of right in another family been utterly extinguished, even though scarce any man now alive had arrived at the years of discretion when it was expelled, or could have consented to its dominion, or have promised it allegiance? — a sufficient indication, surely, of the general sentiment of mankind on this head. For we blame not the partisans of the abdicated family merely on account of the long time during which they have preserved their imaginary loyalty. We blame them for adhering to a family which we affirm has been justly expelled, and which from the moment the new settlement took place had forfeited all title to authority.

But would we have a more regular, at least a more philosophical, refutation of this principle of an original contract or popular consent, perhaps the following observations may suffice.

All *moral* duties may be divided into two kinds. The *first* are those to which men are impelled by a natural instinct or immediate propensity which operates on them, independent of all ideas of obligation and of all views either to public or private utility. Of this nature are love of children, gratitude to benefactors, pity to the unfortunate. When we reflect on the advantage which results to society from such humane instincts, we pay them the just tribute of moral approbation and esteem. But the person actuated by them feels their power and influence antecedent to any such reflection.

The *second* kind of moral duties are such as are not supported by any original instinct of nature, but are performed entirely from a sense of obligation, when we consider the necessities of human society and the impossibility of supporting it if these duties were neglected. It is thus *justice*, or a regard to the property of others, *fidelity*, or the observance of promises, become obligatory and acquire an authority over mankind. For as it is evident that every man loves himself better than any other person, he is naturally impelled to extend his acquisitions as much as possible; and nothing can restrain him in this propensity but reflection and experience, by which he learns the pernicious effects of that license and the total dissolution of society which must ensue from it. His original inclination, therefore, or instinct, is here checked and restrained by a subsequent judgment or observation.

The case is precisely the same with the political or civil duty of *allegiance* as with the natural duties of justice and fidelity. Our primary instincts lead us either to indulge ourselves in unlimited freedom, or to seek dominion over others; and it is reflection only which engages us to sacrifice such strong passions to the interests of peace and public order. A small degree of experience and observation suffices to teach us that society cannot possibly be maintained without the authority of magistrates, and that this authority must soon fall into contempt where exact obedience is not paid to it. The observation of these general and obvious interests is the source of all allegiance and of that moral obligation which we attribute to it.

What necessity, therefore, is there to found the duty of *allegiance*, or obedience to magistrates, on that of *fidelity*, or a regard to promises, and to suppose that it is the consent of each individual which subjects him to government, when it appears that both allegiance and fidelity stand precisely on the same foundation and are both submitted to by mankind on account of the apparent interests and necessities of human society? We are bound to obey our sovereign, it is said, because we have given a tacit promise to that purpose. But why are we bound to observe our promise? It must here be asserted that the commerce and intercourse of mankind, which are of such mighty advantage, can have no security where men pay no regard to their engagements. In like manner may it be said that men could not live at all in society, at least in a civilized society, without laws and magistrates and judges to prevent the encroachments of the strong upon the weak, of the violent upon the just and equitable. The obligation to allegiance being of like force and authority with the obligation to fidelity, we gain nothing by resolving the one into the other. The general interests or necessities of society are sufficient to establish both.

If the reason be asked of that obedience which we are bound to pay to government, I readily answer, *because society could not otherwise subsist;* and this answer is clear and intelligible to all mankind. Your answer is, *because we should keep our word.* But besides that nobody, till trained in a philosophical system, can either comprehend or relish this answer — besides this, I say, you find yourself embarrassed when it is asked, *why we are bound to keep our word?* Nor can you give any answer but what would immediately, without any circuit, have accounted for our obligation to allegiance.

But *to whom is allegiance due, and who is our lawful sovereign?* This question is often the most difficult of any, and liable to infinite discussions. When people are so happy that they can answer, *our present sovereign, who inherits, in a direct line, from ancestors that have governed us for many ages,* this answer admits of no reply, even though historians in tracing up to the remotest antiquity the origin of that royal family may find, as commonly happens, that its first authority was derived from usurpation and violence. It is confessed that private justice, or the abstinence from the properties of others, is a most cardinal virtue. Yet reason tells us that there is no property in durable objects such as land or houses, when carefully examined in passing from hand to hand, but must in some period have been founded on fraud and injustice. The necessities of human society, neither in private nor public life, will allow of such an accurate inquiry; and there is no virtue or moral duty but what may with facility be refined away, if we indulge a false philosophy in sifting and scrutinizing it, by every captious rule of logic, in every light or position in which it may be placed.

The questions with regard to private property have filled infinite volumes of law and philosophy, if in both we add the commentators to the original text; and in the end we may safely pronounce that many of the rules there established are uncertain, ambiguous, and arbitrary. The like opinion may be formed with regard to the succession and rights of princes and forms of government. Several cases no doubt occur, especially in the infancy of any constitution, which admit of no determination from the laws of justice and equity; and our historian Rapin pretends that the controversy between Edward the Third and Philip de Valois was of this nature, and could be decided only by an appeal to heaven, that is, by war and violence.

Who shall tell me whether Germanicus or Drusus ought to have succeeded to Tiberius, had he died while they were both alive without naming any of them for his successor? Ought the right of adoption to be received as equivalent to that of blood in a nation where it had the same effect in private families, and had already, in two instances, taken place in the public? Ought Germanicus to be esteemed the elder son because he was born before Drusus, or the younger, because he was adopted after the birth of his brother? Ought the right of the elder to be regarded in a nation where he had no advantage in the succession of private families? Ought the Roman empire at that time to be deemed hereditary, because of two examples; or ought it, even so early, to be regarded as belonging to the stronger or to the present possessor, as being founded on so recent an usurpation?

Commodus mounted the throne after a pretty long succession of excellent emperors, who had acquired their title, not by birth or public election, but by the fictitious rite of adoption. The bloody debauche being murdered by a conspiracy suddenly formed between his wench and her gallant, who happened at that time to be *Prætorian Præfect*, these immediately deliberated about choosing a master to human kind, to speak in the style of those ages, and they cast their eyes on Pertinax. Before the tyrant's death was known, the *Præfect* went secretly to that senator who, on the appearance of the soldiers, imagined that his execution had been ordered by Commodus. He was immediately saluted emperor by the officer and his attendants, cheerfully proclaimed by the populace, unwillingly submitted to by the guards, formally recognized by the senate, and passively received by the provinces and armies of the empire.

The discontent of the *Prætorian* bands broke out in a sudden sedition, which occasioned the murder of that excellent prince; and the world being now without a master and without government, the guards thought proper to set the empire formally to sale. Julian, the purchaser, was proclaimed by the soldiers, recognized by the senate, and submitted to by the people; and must also have been submitted to by the provinces, had not the envy of the legions begotten opposition and resistance. Pescennius Niger in Syria elected himself emperor, gained the tumultuary consent of his army, and was attended with the secret good will of the senate and people of Rome. Albinus in Britain found an equal right to set up his claim; but Severus, who governed Pannonia, prevailed in the end above both of them. That able politician and warrior, finding his own birth and dignity too much inferior to the imperial crown, professed at first an intention only of revenging the death of Pertinax. He marched as general into Italy, defeated Julian, and, without our being able to fix any precise commencement even of the soldiers' consent, he was from necessity acknowledged emperor by the senate and people, and fully established in his violent authority by subduing Niger and Albinus.[4]

"*Inter hæc Gordianus Cæsar,*" says Capitolinus, speaking of another period, "*sublatus a militibus. Imperator est appellatus, quia non erat alius in præsenti.*" It is to be remarked that Gordian was a boy of fourteen years of age.

Frequent instances of a like nature occur in the history of the emperors, in that of Alexander's successors, and of many other countries. Nor can anything be more unhappy than a despotic government of this kind, where the succession is disjointed and irregular and must be determined on every vacancy by force or election. In a free government, the matter is often unavoidable, and is also much less dangerous. The interests of liberty may there frequently lead the people, in their own defence, to alter the succession of the crown. And the constitution, being compounded of parts, may still maintain a sufficient stability by resting on the aristocratical or democratical members, though the monarchical be altered, from time to time, in order to accommodate it to the former.

In an absolute government, when there is no legal prince who has a title to the throne, it may safely be determined to belong to the first

[4] Herodian, lib. ii.

occupant. Instances of this kind are but too frequent, especially in the eastern monarchies. When any race of princes expires, the will or destination of the last sovereign will be regarded as a title. Thus the edict of Louis XIV, who called the bastard princes to the succession in case of the failure of all the legitimate princes, would, in such an event, have some authority.[5] Thus the will of Charles the Second disposed of the whole Spanish monarchy. The cession of the ancient proprietor, especially when joined to conquest, is likewise deemed a good title. The general obligation which binds us to government is the interest and necessities of society; and this obligation is very strong. The determination of it to this or that particular prince or form of government is frequently more uncertain and dubious. Present possession has considerable authority in these cases, and greater than in private property, because of the disorders which attend all revolutions and changes of government.

We shall only observe before we conclude that though an appeal to general opinion may justly, in the speculative sciences of metaphysics, natural philosophy, or astronomy, be deemed unfair and inconclusive, yet in all questions with regard to morals, as well as criticism, there is really no other standard by which any controversy can ever be decided. And nothing is a clearer proof that a theory of this kind is erroneous than to find that it leads to paradoxes repugnant to the common sentiments of mankind, and to the practice and opinion of all nations and all ages. The doctrine which founds all lawful government on an *original contract*, or consent of the people, is plainly of this kind; nor has the most noted of its partisans, in prosecution of it, scrupled to affirm *that absolute monarchy is inconsistent with civil*

[5] It is remarkable that, in the remonstrance of the Duke of Bourbon and the legitimate princes against this destination of Louis XIV, the doctrine of the *original contract* is insisted on, even in that absolute government. The French nation, say they, choosing Hugh Capet and his posterity to rule over them and their posterity, where the former line fails, there is a tacit right reserved to choose a new royal family; and this right is invaded by calling the bastard princes to the throne, without the consent of the nation. But the Comte de Boulainvilliers, who wrote in defence of the bastard princes, ridicules this notion of an original contract, especially when applied to Hugh Capet, who mounted the throne, says he, by the same arts which have ever been employed by all conquerors and usurpers. He got his title, indeed, recognized by the states after he had put himself in possession. But is this a choice or contract? The Comte de Boulainvilliers, we may observe, was a noted republican; but being a man of learning, and very conversant in history,

society, and so can be no form of civil government at all,[6] and *that the supreme power in a state cannot take from any man by taxes and impositions any part of his property, without his own consent or that of his representatives.*[7] What authority any moral reasoning can have, which leads into opinions so wide of the general practice of mankind in every place but this single kingdom, it is easy to determine.

The only passage I meet with in antiquity where the obligation of obedience to government is ascribed to a promise is in Plato's *Crito*, where Socrates refuses to escape from prison because he had tacitly promised to obey the laws. Thus he builds a *Tory* consequence of passive obedience on a *Whig* foundation of the original contract.

New discoveries are not to be expected in these matters. If scarce any man, till very lately, ever imagined that government was founded on compact, it is certain that it cannot in general have any such foundation.

The crime of rebellion among the ancients was commonly expressed by the terms νεωτερίζειν (*novas res moliri*).

he knew that the people were almost never consulted in these revolutions and new establishments, and that time alone bestowed right and authority on what was commonly at first founded on force and violence.   See *Etat de la France*, vol. iii.

[6] See Locke *On Government*, chap. vii.§ 90.

[7] Locke *On Government*, chap. xi. § 138, 139, 140.

ESSAY X [1]

IDEA OF A PERFECT COMMONWEALTH [2]

It is not with forms of government as with other artificial contrivances, where an old engine may be rejected if we can discover another more accurate and commodious, or where trials may safely be made even though the success be doubtful. An established government has an infinite advantage by that very circumstance of its being established, the bulk of mankind being governed by authority, not reason, and never attributing authority to anything that has not the recommendation of antiquity.

To tamper, therefore, in this affair, or try experiments merely upon the credit of supposed argument and philosophy, can never be the part of a wise magistrate, who will bear a reverence to what carries the marks of age; and though he may attempt some improvements for the public good, yet will he adjust his innovations as much as possible to the ancient fabric, and preserve entire the chief pillars and supports of the constitution.

The mathematicians in Europe have been much divided concerning that figure of a ship which is the most commodious for sailing; and Huygens, who at last determined the controversy, is justly thought to have obliged the learned as well as commercial world, though Columbus had sailed to America and Sir Francis Drake made the tour of the world without any such discovery. As one form of government must be allowed more perfect than another, independent of the manners and humours of particular men, why may we not inquire what is the most perfect of all, though the common botched and inaccurate governments seem to serve the purposes of society, and though it be not so easy to establish a new system of government as to build a

[1] [Ed. 1777, Part II. Essay XVI.]

[2] "Of all mankind, there are none so pernicious as political projectors, if they have power, nor so ridiculous, if they want it: as, on the other hand, a wise politician is the most beneficial character in nature, if accompanied with authority, and the most innocent, and not altogether useless, even if deprived of it."

vessel upon a new construction? The subject is surely the most worthy of curiosity of any the wit of man can possibly devise. And who knows, if this controversy were fixed by the universal consent of the wise and learned, but, in some future age, an opportunity might be afforded of reducing the theory to practice, either by a dissolution of some old government or by the combination of men to form a new one in some distant part of the world? In all cases, it must be advantageous to know what is the most perfect in the kind, that we may be able to bring any real constitution or form of government as near it as possible by such gentle alterations and innovations as may not give too great disturbance to society.

All I pretend to in the present Essay is to revive this subject of speculation; and therefore I shall deliver my sentiments in as few words as possible. A long dissertation on that head would not, I apprehend, be very acceptable to the public, who will be apt to regard such disquisitions both as useless and chimerical.

All plans of government which suppose great reformation in the manners of mankind are plainly imaginary. Of this nature are the *Republic* of Plato and the *Utopia* of Sir Thomas More. The *Oceana* is the only valuable model of a commonwealth that has yet been offered to the public.

The chief defects of the *Oceana* seem to be these: *first*, its rotation is inconvenient, by throwing men, of whatever abilities, by intervals, out of public employment. *Secondly*, its *Agrarian* is impracticable. Men will soon learn the art which was practised in ancient Rome of concealing their possessions under other people's names, till at last the abuse will become so common that they will throw off even the appearance of restraint. *Thirdly*, the *Oceana* provides not a sufficient security for liberty or the redress of grievances. The senate must propose, and the people consent, by which means the senate have not only a negative upon the people, but, what is of much greater consequence, their negative goes before the votes of the people. Were the king's negative of the same nature in the English constitution, and could he prevent any bill from coming into parliament, he would be an absolute monarch. As his negative follows the votes of the houses, it is of little consequence, such a difference is there in the manner of placing the same thing. When a popular bill has been debated in parliament, is brought to maturity, all its conveniences and inconveniences weighed and balanced; if afterwards it be presented for the royal assent, few princes will venture to reject the unanimous desire of the people. But could the king crush a disagreeable bill in embryo — as was the case for some time in the Scottish parliament, by means of the Lords of the Articles — the British government would have no balance, nor would grievances ever be redressed; and it is certain that exorbitant power proceeds not in any government from new laws so much as from neglecting to remedy the abuses which frequently rise from the old ones. A government, says Machiavel, must often be brought back to its original principles. It appears, then, that in the *Oceana* the whole legislature may be said to rest in the senate, which Harrington would own to be an inconvenient form of government, especially after the *Agrarian* is abolished.

Here is a form of government to which I cannot, in theory, discover any considerable objection.

Let Great Britain and Ireland, or any territory of equal extent, be divided into one hundred counties, and each county into one hundred parishes, making in all ten thousand. If the country proposed to be erected into a commonwealth be of more narrow extent, we may diminish the number of counties, but never bring them below thirty. If it be of greater extent, it were better to enlarge the parishes, or throw more parishes into a county, than increase the number of counties.

Let all the freeholders of twenty pounds a year in the county, and all the householders worth five hundred pounds in the town parishes, meet annually in the parish church and choose by ballot some freeholder of the county for their member, whom we shall call the *county representative*.

Let the one hundred county representatives, two days after their election, meet in the county town and choose by ballot, from their own body, ten county *magistrates* and one senator. There are, therefore, in the whole commonwealth one hundred senators, one thousand and one hundred county magistrates, and ten thousand county representatives; for we shall bestow on all senators the authority of county magistrates, and on all county magistrates the authority of county representatives.

Let the senators meet in the capital, and be endowed with the whole executive power of the commonwealth: the power of peace and war, of giving orders to generals, admirals, and ambassadors, and, in short, all the prerogatives of a British king except his negative.

Let the county representatives meet in their particular counties and possess the whole legislative power of the commonwealth, the greater number of counties deciding the question; and where these are equal, let the senate have the casting vote.

Every new law must first be debated in the senate, and though rejected by it, if ten senators insist and protest, it must be sent down to the counties. The senate, if they please, may join to the copy of the law their reasons for receiving or rejecting it.

Because it would be troublesome to assemble all the county representatives for every trivial law that may be requisite, the senate have their choice of sending down the law either to the county magistrates or country representatives.

The magistrates, though the law be referred to them, may, if they please, call the representatives and submit the affair to their determination.

Whether the law be referred by the senate to the county magistrates or representatives, a copy of it and of the senate's reasons must be sent to every representative eight days before the day appointed for the assembling, in order to deliberate concerning it. And though the determination be, by the senate, referred to the magistrates, if five representatives of the county order the magistrates to assemble the whole court of representatives and submit the affair to their determination, they must obey.

Either the county magistrates or representatives may give to the senator of the county the copy of a law to be proposed to the senate; and if five counties concur in the same order, the law, though refused by the senate, must come either to the county magistrates or representatives, as is contained in the order of the five counties.

Any twenty counties, by a vote either of their magistrates or representatives, may throw any man out of all public offices for a year, thirty counties for three years.

The senate has a power of throwing out any member or number of members of its own body, not to be re-elected for that year. The senate cannot throw out twice in a year the senator of the same county.

The power of the old senate continues for three weeks after the annual election of the county representatives. Then all the new senators are shut up in a conclave like the cardinals, and by an intricate ballot, such as that of Venice or Malta, they choose the following magistrates: a protector, who represents the dignity of the commonwealth and presides in the senate; two secretaries of state; these six councils, a council of state, a council of religion and learning, a council of trade, a council of laws, a council of war, a council of the admiralty, each council consisting of five persons; together with six commissioners of the treasury, and a first commissioner. All these must be senators. The senate also names all the ambassadors to foreign courts, who may either be senators or not.

The senate may continue any or all of these, but must re-elect them every year.

The protector and two secretaries have session and suffrage in the council of state. The business of that council is all foreign politics. The council of state has session and suffrage in all the other councils.

The council of religion and learning inspects the universities and clergy. That of trade inspects everything that may affect commerce. That of laws inspects all the abuses of law by the inferior magistrates, and examines what improvements may be made of the municipal law. That of war inspects the militia and its discipline, magazines, stores, etc.; and when the republic is in war, examines into the proper orders for generals. The council of admiralty has the same power with regard to the navy, together with the nomination of the captains and all inferior officers.

None of these councils can give orders themselves, except where they receive such powers from the senate. In other cases, they must communicate everything to the senate.

When the senate is under adjournment, any of the councils may assemble it before the day appointed for its meeting.

Besides these councils or courts, there is another called the court of *competitors*, which is thus constituted. If any candidates for the office of senator have more votes than a third of the representatives, that candidate who has most votes, next to the senator elected, becomes incapable for one year of all public offices, even of being a magistrate or representative; but he takes his seat in the court of competitors. Here then is a court which may sometimes consist of a hundred members, sometimes have no members at all; and by that means be for a year abolished.

The court of competitors has no power in the commonwealth. It has only the inspection of public accounts, and the accusing of any man before the senate. If the senate acquit him, the court of competitors may if they please appeal to the people, either magistrates or representatives. Upon that appeal, the magistrates or representatives meet on the day appointed by the court of competitors, and choose in each county three persons, from which number every senator is excluded. These, to the number of three hundred, meet in the capital and bring the person accused to a new trial.

The court of competitors may propose any law to the senate, and if refused, may appeal to the people, that is, to the magistrates or representatives, who examine it in their counties. Every senator who is thrown out of the senate by a vote of the court takes his seat in the court of competitors.

The senate possesses all the judicative authority of the House of Lords, that is, all the appeals from the inferior courts. It likewise appoints the Lord Chancellor and all the officers of the law.

Every county is a kind of republic within itself, and the representatives may make by-laws, which have no authority till three months after they are voted. A copy of the law is sent to the senate, and to every other county. The senate, or any single county, may at any time annul any by-law of another county.

The representatives have all the authority of the British justices of the peace in trials, commitments, etc.

The magistrates have the appointment of all the officers of the revenue in each county. All causes with regard to the revenue are carried ultimately by appeal before the magistrates. They pass the accounts of all the officers; but must have their own accounts examined and passed at the end of the year by the representatives.

The magistrates name rectors or ministers to all the parishes.

The Presbyterian government is established; and the highest ecclesiastical court is an assembly or synod of all the presbyters of the county. The magistrates may take any cause from this court, and determine it themselves.

The magistrates may try, and depose or suspend any presbyter.

The militia is established in imitation of that of Switzerland, which, being well known, we shall not insist upon it. It will only be proper to make this addition, that an army of twenty thousand men be annually drawn out by rotation, paid and encamped during six weeks in summer, that the duty of a camp may not be altogether unknown.

The magistrates appoint all the colonels and downwards, the senate all upwards. During war, the general appoints the colonel and downwards, and his commission is good for a twelvemonth; but after that, it must be confirmed by the magistrates of the county to which the regiment belongs. The magistrates may break any officer in the county regiment, and the senate may do the same to any officer in the service. If the magistrates do not think proper to confirm the general's choice, they may appoint another officer in the place of him they reject.

All crimes are tried within the county by the magistrates and a jury, but the senate can stop any trial, and bring it before themselves.

Any county may indict any man before the senate for any crime.

The protector, the two secretaries, the council of state, with any five or more that the senate appoints, are possessed on extraordinary emergencies of *dictatorial* power for six months.

The protector may pardon any person condemned by the inferior courts.

In time of war, no officer of the army that is in the field can have any civil office in the commonwealth.

The capital, which we shall call London, may be allowed four members in the senate. It may therefore be divided into four counties. The representatives of each of these choose one senator and ten magistrates. There are therefore in the city four senators, forty-four magistrates, and four hundred representatives. The magistrates have the same authority as in the counties. The representatives also have the same authority, but they never meet in one general court; they give their votes in their particular county or division of hundreds.

When they enact any by-law, the greater number of counties or divisions determines the matter. And where these are equal, the magistrates have the casting vote.

The magistrates choose the mayor, sheriff, recorder, and other officers of the city.

In the commonwealth, no representative, magistrate, or senator, as such, has any salary. The protector, secretaries, councils, and ambassadors have salaries.

The first year in every century is set apart for correcting all inequalities which time may have produced in the representative. This must be done by the legislature.

The following political aphorisms may explain the reason of these orders.

The lower sort of people and small proprietors are good enough judges of one not very distant from them in rank or habitation; and therefore, in their parochial meetings, will probably choose the best, or nearly the best representative. But they are wholly unfit for county meetings, and for electing into the higher offices of the republic. Their ignorance gives the grandees an opportunity of deceiving them.

Ten thousand, even though they were not annually elected, are a basis large enough for any free government. It is true, the nobles in Poland are more than ten thousand, and yet these oppress the people. But as power always continues there in the same persons and families, this makes them in a manner a different nation from the people. Besides, the nobles are there united under a few heads of families.

All free governments must consist of two councils, a lesser and greater, or, in other words, of a senate and people. The people, as Harrington observes, would want wisdom without the senate; the senate, without the people, would want honesty.

A large assembly of one thousand, for instance, to represent the people, if allowed to debate, would fall into disorder. If not allowed to debate, the senate has a negative upon them, and the worst kind of negative, that before resolution.

Here, therefore, is an inconvenience which no government has yet fully remedied, but which is the easiest to be remedied in the world. If the people debate, all is confusion. If they do not debate, they can only resolve; and then the senate carves for them. Divide the people into many separate bodies, and then they may debate with safety and every inconvenience seems to be prevented.

Cardinal de Retz says that all numerous assemblies, however composed, are mere mob, and swayed in their debates by the least motive. This we find confirmed by daily experience. When an absurdity strikes a member, he conveys it to his neighbour, and so on till the whole be infected. Separate this great body, and though every member be only of middling sense, it is not probable that anything but reason can prevail over the whole. Influence and example being removed, good sense will always get the better of bad among a number of people.[3]

There are two things to be guarded against in every *senate:* its combination and its division. Its combination is most dangerous; and against this inconvenience we have provided the following remedies: 1. The great dependence of the senators on the people by annual elections, and that not by an undistinguished rabble, like the English electors, but by men of fortune and education. 2. The small power they are allowed. They have few offices to dispose of; almost all are given by the magistrates in the counties. 3. The court of competitors, which, being composed of men that are their rivals next to them in interest, and uneasy in their present situation, will be sure to take all advantages against them.

The division of the senate is prevented: 1. By the smallness of their number. 2. As faction supposes a combination in a separate interest, it is prevented by their dependence on the people. 3. They have a power of expelling any factious member. It is true, when another member of the same spirit comes from the county, they have no power of expelling him; nor is it fit they should, for that shows the humour to be in the people, and may possibly arise from some ill conduct in public affairs. 4. Almost any man, in a senate so regularly chosen by the people, may be supposed fit for any civil office. It would be proper, therefore, for the senate to form some *general* resolutions with regard to the disposing of offices among the members, which resolutions would not confine them in critical times, when extraordinary parts on the one hand or extraordinary stupidity on the other appears in any senator; but they would be sufficient to prevent intrigue and faction by making the disposal of the offices a thing of course. For instance, let it be a resolution that no man shall enjoy any office till he has sat four years in the senate; that, except ambassadors, no man shall be in office two years following; that no man shall attain the higher offices but through the lower; that no man shall be protector twice, etc. The senate of Venice govern themselves by such resolutions.

[3] "Good sense is one thing, but follies are numberless; and every man has a different one. The only way of making a people wise is to keep them from uniting into large assemblies."

In foreign politics the interest of the senate can scarcely ever be divided from that of the people; and therefore it is fit to make the senate absolute with regard to them, otherwise there could be no secrecy or refined policy. Besides, without money no alliance can be executed, and the senate is still sufficiently dependent. Not to mention that the legislative power, being always superior to the executive, the magistrates or representatives may interpose whenever they think proper.

The chief support of the British government is the opposition of interest, but that, though in the main serviceable, breeds endless factions. In the foregoing plan, it does all the good without any of the harm. The *competitors* have no power of controlling the senate; they have only the power of accusing, and appealing to the people.

It is necessary, likewise, to prevent both combination and division in the thousand magistrates. This is done sufficiently by the separation of places and interests.

But, lest that should not be sufficient, their dependence on the ten thousand for their elections serves to the same purpose.

Nor is that all; for the ten thousand may resume the power whenever they please, and not only when they all please, but when any five of a hundred please, which will happen upon the very first suspicion of a separate interest.

The ten thousand are too large a body either to unite or divide, except when they meet in one place and fall under the guidance of ambitious leaders. Not to mention their annual election by the whole body of the people that are of any consideration.

A small commonwealth is the happiest government in the world within itself, because everything lies under the eye of the rulers. But it may be subdued by great force from without. This scheme seems to have all the advantages both of a great and a little commonwealth.

Every county law may be annulled either by the senate or another county, because that shows an opposition of interest, in which case no part ought to decide for itself. The matter must be referred to the whole, which will best determine what agrees with general interest.

As to the clergy and militia, the reasons of these orders are obvious. Without the dependence of the clergy on the civil magistrates, and without a militia, it is in vain to think that any free government will ever have security or stability.

In many governments, the inferior magistrates have no rewards but what arise from their ambition, vanity, or public spirit. The salaries of the French judges amount not to the interest of the sums they pay for their offices. The Dutch burgomasters have little more immediate profit than the English justices of peace, or the members of the House of Commons formerly. But lest any should suspect that this would beget negligence in the administration (which is little to be feared, considering the natural ambition of mankind), let the magistrates have competent salaries. The senators have access to so many honourable and lucrative offices that their attendance needs not be bought. There is little attendance required of the representatives.

That the foregoing plan of government is practicable, no one can doubt who considers the resemblance that it bears to the commonwealth of the United Provinces, a wise and renowned government. The alterations in the present scheme seem all evidently for the better. 1. The representation is more equal. 2. The unlimited power of the burgomasters in the towns, which forms a perfect aristocracy in the Dutch commonwealth, is corrected by a well-tempered democracy, in giving to the people the annual election of the county representatives. 3. The negative, which every province and town has upon the whole body of the Dutch Republic with regard to alliances, peace and war, and the imposition of taxes, is here removed. 4. The counties, in the present plan, are not so independent of each other, nor do they form separate bodies so much as the seven provinces, where the jealousy and envy of the smaller provinces and towns against the greater, particularly Holland and Amsterdam, have frequently disturbed the government. 5. Larger powers, though of the safest kind, are intrusted to the senate than the States-General possess; by which means the former may become more expeditious and secret in their resolutions than it is possible for the latter.

The chief alterations that could be made on the British government, in order to bring it to the most perfect model of limited monarchy, seem to be the following. *First*, the plan of Cromwell's parliament ought to be restored, by making the representation equal, and by allowing none to vote in the county elections who possess not a property of two hundred pound value. *Secondly*, as such a House of Commons would be too weighty for a frail House of Lords like the present, the Bishops and Scotch Peers ought to be removed. The number of the upper house ought to be raised to three or four hundred, the seats not hereditary, but during life. They ought to have the election of their own members, and no commoner should be allowed to refuse a seat that was offered him. By this means the House of Lords would consist entirely of the men of chief credit, abilities, and interest in the nation; and every turbulent leader in the House of Commons might be taken off, and connected by interest with the House of Peers. Such an aristocracy would be an excellent barrier both to the monarchy and against it. At present, the balance of our government depends in some measure on the abilities and behaviour of the sovereign, which are variable and uncertain circumstances.

This plan of limited monarchy, however corrected, seems still liable to three great inconveniences. *First*, it removes not entirely, though it may soften, the parties of *court* and *country*. *Secondly*, the king's personal character must still have great influence on the government. *Thirdly*, the sword is in the hands of a single person, who will always neglect to discipline the militia, in order to have a pretence for keeping up a standing army.

We shall conclude this subject with observing the falsehood of the common opinion that no large state such as France or Great Britain could ever be modelled into a commonwealth, but that such a form of government can only take place in a city or small territory. The contrary seems probable. Though it is more difficult to form a republican government in an extensive country than in a city, there is more facility, when once it is formed, of preserving it steady and uniform without tumult and faction. It is not easy for the distant parts of a large state to combine in any plan of free government; but they easily conspire in the esteem and reverence for a single person who, by means of this popular favour, may seize the power, and forcing the more obstinate to submit, may establish a monarchical government. On the other hand, a city readily concurs in the same notions of government, the natural equality of property favours liberty, and the nearness of habitation enables the citizens mutually to assist each other. Even under absolute princes, the subordinate government of cities is commonly republican; while that of counties and provinces is monarchical. But these same circumstances which facilitate the erection of commonwealths in cities render their constitution more frail and uncertain. Democracies are turbulent. For, however the people may be separated or divided into small parties, either in their votes or elections, their near habitation in a city will always make the force of popular tides and currents very sensible. Aristocracies are better adapted for peace and order, and accordingly were most admired by ancient writers; but they are jealous and oppressive. In a large government, which is modelled with masterly skill, there is compass and room enough to refine the democracy, from the lower people who may be admitted into the first elections or first concoction of the commonwealth, to the higher magistrates who direct all the movements. At the same time, the parts are so distant and remote that it is very difficult, either by intrigue, prejudice, or passion, to hurry them into any measures against the public interest.

It is needless to inquire whether such a government would be immortal. I allow the justness of the poet's exclamation on the endless projects of human race, *Man and for ever!* The world itself probably is not immortal. Such consuming plagues may arise as would leave even a perfect government a weak prey to its neighbours. We know not to what length enthusiasm or other extraordinary movements of the human mind may transport men to the neglect of all order and public good. Where difference of interest is removed, whimsical unaccountable factions often arise from personal favour or enmity. Perhaps rust may grow to the springs of the most accurate political machine, and disorder its motions. Lastly, extensive conquests, when pursued, must be the ruin of every free government; and of the more perfect governments sooner than of the imperfect; because of the very advantages which the former possess above the latter. And though such a state ought to establish a fundamental law against conquests, yet republics have ambition as well as individuals, and present interest makes men forgetful of their posterity. It is a sufficient incitement to human endeavours that such a government would flourish for many ages, without pretending to bestow on any work of man that immortality which the Almighty seems to have refused to his own productions.

INDEX

Actions, and motives, 13; merit of, due to motives, 44 ff; merit of, not due to conformity to reason, 33.

Allegiance, measures of, 110; moral obligations of, 106, 111; natural obligations, 104; not due to promises, 104 ff, 368; objects of, 113 ff, 368; source of, 101.

Aristotle, 289.

Artificial, *vs.* natural, 47, 54.

Bacon, 212, 318.

Bayle, 168 n.

Beauty, 139 ff, 342; and utility, 133, 343 n.

Benevolence, merit of, 154, 180 ff; not original motive to justice, 53; not reducible to self-love, 270 ff.

Character, and action, 12 ff; and moral approbation, 138.

Chastity, 127; obligations of sexes to, compared, 129.

Cicero, 180, 183 n, 190, 247, 248, 267, 287, 288, 299.

Civil liberty, 315 ff.

Clarke, 196 n.

Consent, not basis of government, 103 ff, 360.

Contract, as basis of government, 356 ff.

Convention, 59 ff; and common interest, 59, 278.

Cudworth, 196 n.

Duty, *see* Obligation; sense of, 50.

Epictetus, 240.

Epicurean, 322 ff.

Error, relation to morality, 34.

Fame, love of, 4 ff, 255.

Golden Age, 62, 189.

Good, *see* Valuable; equals pleasure, 4, 11.

Government, limits of authority of, 111; obligation to, 101 ff; origins of, 97 ff, 307 ff; struggle between authority and liberty, 313 ff.

Greatness of mind, 146.

Grotius, 279 n.

Harrington, 374.

Hobbes, 190 n, 270.

Justice, and public interest, 65, 185; and virtue, 66; artificiality of, 54, 59, 91 ff; compared to language, 60; motives to, 49 ff; not founded on reason, 64; origins of, 55, 276 ff; relations to interest and morality, 96.

Juvenal, 181.

Laws of nations, 124 ff.

Laws of nature, founded on convention, 194; invented by men, 86, 90, 105; rules of justice may be called "laws of nature," 55.

Liberty, 11 ff; false sensation of, 18; of spontaneity and indifference, 18; reasons for prevalence of doctrine of liberty of will, 18 ff.

Locke, 271, 318, 372 n.

Longinus, 317.

Lucian, 229.

Machiavelli, 225, 300, 301, 315.

Malebranche, 196 n.

Means, value of, 168.

Merit, consists of qualities useful or agreeable to self or others, 249 ff.

Monkish virtues, 251.

Montesquieu, 196 n.

Moral approbation, 43 ff; and benevolence, 251; and pleasure, 44, 265; constancy of, 137; corrections of, 137; universality of, 253.

387